Fashion: The Industry and Its Careers

Second Edition

Michele M. Granger, EdD, ITAA
Missouri State University

Fairchild Books
New York

Executive Director & General Manager: Michael Schluter

Executive Editor: Olga T. Kontzias

Senior Associate Acquisitions Editor: Jaclyn Bergeron

Assistant Acquisitions Editor: Amanda Breccia

Development Editor: Amy Butler

Assistant Art Director: Sarah Silberg

Production Director: Ginger Hillman

Associate Production Editor: Linda Feldman

Ancillaries Editor: Amy Butler

Associate Director of Sales: Melanie Sankel

Copyeditor: Christina MacDonald

Cover Design: Carly Grafstein

Cover Art: Melanie Acevedo / trunkarchive.com

Text Design: Loretta Reilly

Text Layout: Alicia Freile, Tango Media

Photo Research: Carly Grafstein

Second Printing, 2013

Library of Congress Catalog Card Number: 2011938723

978-1-60901-225-0

GST R 133004424

Printed in the United States of America

TP09

Fashion: The Industry and Its Careers

To the women who make my world go around: Annie, Sassy, Patricia, Nancy, Marciann, Debbie, Karla, LaRaine, LeAnn, Linda, Marci, Mimi, Patty, Randee, Sarah, Kirsty

contents

extended contents

preface

Fashion: The Industry and Its Careers, second edition, is a text written for an introductory college or university course that provides an overview or survey of the global fashion industry with a focus on the career paths available within each level of the industry. The text is based on the following four broad assumptions of postsecondary education and the fashion industry:

- Students immerse themselves in studies they find personally and professionally relevant. Most students believe that a college education is the gateway to a career, one in which they could not or would not be prepared to enter without a college degree. They often view college as a means to an end, the end being a rewarding career. Lifelong learning is an encouraged outcome as well. Many students enroll in an introductory fashion course knowing that they love the world of fashion, yet wondering what careers exist in this world. They usually recognize the careers of designer and buyer, but often do not know the multitude of other career tracks that are available and where those jobs are found. Many students cannot imagine that they can spend a lifetime working in an area (fashion) they love and in which they can apply their individual talents and skills. By examining the different levels or sectors of the fashion industry and exploring the career options that exist at each level, students will have the opportunity to see themselves on career paths and, subsequently, add career goals to their educational experiences.

- Fashion is a lifestyle that permeates many industry segments, from apparel and accessories to home fashions to beauty and wellness. We see fashion in films, books, leisure activities, travel destinations, and people. It is not limited to the world of apparel and accessories. It includes all products and services that are influenced by changing trends in form, materials, theme, and color. These trends are seen on the fashion runways, in homes, on the retail sales floors, on the Internet and television, and in publications. Consumers adapt these trends in what they wear on their bodies and the environments in which they live.

- The third premise of this text is that the careers within the sectors of the fashion industry provide an ideal way to define and explain the industry and illustrate its various levels, from raw materials to ancillary services. Designers develop products for manufacturers, but retailers with private label lines also employ designers. A fashion stylist can be the person who modifies designs, sets up a fashion shoot, or selects the apparel and accessories for a client's special occasion. Manufacturers hire people to buy, yet so do retailers. Some fashion products are not tangible; they are services. A career path may be titled one way by a manufacturer and another way by a producer in the same product area. If students understand what the jobs are and where they are located in the big picture of the fashion industry, then interpreting these position titles as actual careers is simpler. Exploring the industry by highlighting the careers in each industry segment provides a framework that allows students to see how the various levels work together.

- Finally, effective career preparation for the apparel, accessories, soft goods, and home furnishings industries requires across-the-board understanding of the following concepts:

1. The apparel and textile industry operates in a global and high-tech market, making an understanding of cultural diversity, the world economy, and technological advances essential.
2. Activities of product development, manufacturing, and retailing are interrelated, from fiber and textiles to design and production to sourcing and merchandising.
3. Successful companies recognize that product decisions are consumer-driven.

Organization of the Text

Fashion: The Industry and Its Careers, second edition, is organized in three parts, beginning with the creators and providers of raw materials and the manufacturers of products, followed by the retailers who create and/or sell the products to the consumer, and, finally, the auxiliary industries that support the work done by the product creators and product retailers. The text is organized in the following sequence: Unit 1, "Careers in Raw Materials, Manufacturing, and Design in the Fashion Industry"; Unit 2, "Careers in Product Development and Sales for the Fashion Retailer"; and Unit 3, "The Ancillary Businesses."

Unit 1: Careers in Raw Materials, Manufacturing, and Design in the Fashion Industry

The primary level of the fashion industry begins with the people responsible for the inspiration and conception of the fashion product's parts and raw materials (e.g., the forecasters, designers, and sourcing personnel). Unit 1 starts at the beginning of fashion product development and production. It provides an overview of the firms that supply the information, components, production, and design of fashion products that manufacturers produce. In addition, the "back office" departments of manufacturing firms are examined, to include accounting, finance, and human resources.

Chapter 1 presents the trend forecasters who interpret, inspire, and predict shifts in fashion preferences. They have tremendous influence on both the raw materials and the actual outcomes of fashion production. In Chapter 2, textile product developers and designers use colors, textures, patterns, and finishes to create the foundation on which fashion products are built. In Chapter 3, the sourcing personnel who locate the components and manufacturers of products are explored. Chapter 4 presents production as employees work together to manufacture the final product. Promotion (Chapter 5) and sales personnel (Chapter 6) departments collaborate to generate an interest and create a desire among the retail buyers who purchase the products for the ultimate consumer.

Chapter 7 examines the resource managers in finance, accounting, and human resources—aspects of the products and career tracks that are often overlooked by prospective fashion professionals. Chapter 8, the final chapter of Unit 1, takes a look at the field of fashion design.

Unit 2: Careers in Product Development and Sales for the Fashion Retailer

The secondary level of the fashion industry represents the retailers of fashion products, from apparel to home furnishings, and those involved with creating a desire in the consumer for the retailer's fashion goods. Some retailers purchase finished fashion merchandise from manufacturers or wholesalers; others develop and manufacture products specifically for their clientele. As a result, Unit 2 begins with a discussion of product development and design by and for the fashion retailer, in Chapter 9. A number of large retail operations own a product development division that functions as a design and production source exclusively for them. Whether the fashion product is created and manufactured by the retailer or purchased from a manufacturer or wholesaler, it must be marketed to appeal to the consumer. In Chapter 10, the promotion division of a retail operation does just that through such professionals as the advertising director and art staff, visual merchandiser, special events coordinator, Web site developer, and personal shopper. Chapter 11 explores the merchandising division of the retail operation, the buying and marketing of products. Merchandise managers, buyers, allocators, and planners work on the selection, pricing, and placement of merchandise on retail sales floors. In Chapter 12, management careers in the retail sector are examined, to include those in stores (regional, store unit, associate, and assistant managers), operations managers, and customer service managers. Finally, there are the all-in-one retail specialists, the entrepreneurs who own and operate their retail organizations, whether brick-and-mortar, brick-and-click, or solely e-retailing.

Unit 3: The Ancillary Businesses

Unit 3 presents a vast number of ancillary businesses that promote, educate, and provide support to the producers, retailers, and consumers of fashion goods. Whether working as freelancers or within a company, these ancillary business professionals frequently offer services, rather than tangible products. In Chapter 13, fashion styling and visuals as ancillary businesses are examined from the career path perspectives of the fashion show and event producer, modeling and talent agency director, fashion photographer, art photographer, stylist, and fashion costumer. In Chapter 14, "Fashion Scholarship," career opportunities in museums and educational institutions are explored. Opportunities in the fashion or costume division of a museum discussed in this chapter include: museum director, museum curator, assistant curator, collections manager, museum archivist, museum conservator, and museum technician. Another career track within the fashion scholarship segment of the industry is the fashion educator, who may instruct or conduct research in historical costume or many other facets of the fashion industry from production to design and product development to merchandising and entrepreneurship.

Chapter 15 presents another segment of fashion ancillary businesses with its focus on environments—Web sites, exteriors, and interiors. All of these environments represent spaces in which fashion businesses may be located, whether in the production, retail, or ancillary levels of the industry. The primary career tracks discussed in Chapter 15 include Web site developer, architect, interior designer, visual merchandising professional, and mall manager.

An evolving part of the fashion industry and one that requires a specific type of environment is the beauty, spa, and wellness industry. Product development and marketing in cosmetics, skin care, and hair care are also growing areas of the fashion industry. Chapter 16 examines the careers of a product developer or technician working in research and development and those of the beauty merchandising and marketing professionals working in the manufacturing and retail levels of the industry. The careers of a makeup artist and hairstylist are also examined in Chapter 16 and can take place in a theater; on a film set or photo shoot; or in an individual's home, a salon, or a spa. Finally, the career of the director of a spa is explored, as growth is expected to continue in spa and aesthetics companies. These ancillary businesses are evolving into full-service facilities that include services for makeup, hair, skin, and body. As we have watched health services integrate medicine and natural homeopathic remedies, we will continue to see beauty services integrated with health and fitness in the future, resulting in new career paths for those interested in beauty, health, and longevity.

Features of the Text

Fashion: The Industry and Its Careers, second edition, provides current visuals, discussion questions, and key terms, the terminology used in the industry. These text features are included to help clarify concepts, stimulate class discussion, and encourage critical thinking with applications and illustrations. Relevant education, work experience, personal characteristics, and career challenges are examined for each career track. Boxes feature help-wanted advertisements for key positions and profiles of individuals or companies representing various aspects of the fashion industry. Tech Talk boxes have been added to introduce students to the ways that technology is affecting each level of the industry and related career tracks.

Each chapter concludes with a summary that highlights the content of each section, followed by an interview with a fashion professional whose career is featured in the chapter. Two appendices are provided at the end of the text. The first is an appendix of career tracks and salary ranges; the second is a presentation of a sample résumé, letter of application, and related materials and information needed to secure a position in the fashion industry. A glossary of key terms is also included at the end of the text. Finally, an instructor's guide and PowerPoint presentation are available to assist with course organization, class discussions, and teaching ideas.

acknowledgments

To the daughter of my dreams, Annie, my parents, Sally and John, my brother, Joe, my sister-in-law, Wendy, and my sister, Patty. Thank you for family dinners, memories that always make me smile, a life of travel, and unconditional love.

To my circle of friends:

- Nancy and Marciann, thank you for your friendship and support, and for your wonderful book, *Careers in Interior Design*.
- Debbie, Karla, LaRaine, LeAnn, Linda, Marci, Mimi, Patty, and Randee, you help my world go 'round (and we know what goes around comes around).
- Sarah, Kirsty, and Melody, friends forever!
- My students—past, present, and future. You inspire me to do and be better. Your enthusiasm energizes me and your career success stories are a great source of pride. Special acknowledgment to Katie (entrepreneur in the making), Mandy (Zappos buyer), Julie (Byrdstyle Lounge entrepreneur), Jenn (creative director for Lee), Angie (busy mom and graduate student), and Lauren (blogger and world traveler).
- Sharon Huckaby, thank you for your review of Chapters 8 and 9. Your work as a product developer and business analyst at Walmart's headquarters illustrates your expertise.
- Olga Kontzias, executive editor at Fairchild Books. Paris, fashion, museums, family, great reads and films—these passions we share. You are the model editor and *mon amie*.

To the text's interviewees and interviewers: Jessie Cacciola, Diana Martini, Mike Flanagan, Sam Lim, Joe Karban, Nicole Doherty, Juan Carlos Gaona, Gail McInnes, Ann Pickering, Louisa Peacock, Vera Wang, Bridget Foley, Oriana DiNella, Laura Moore, Morgan, 39thandbroadway.com, Michelle Chung, embody3D.com, Macala Wright, Brian Sugar, Maranda Gorr-Diaz, Aimee Pallozzi, Jenn Everett, Rachel Zoe, Ami Gan, Vaneza Pitynski, Elizabeth Laskar, Nancy Asay, Abbe Fenimore, Anne Alexander Sieder, Jeremy McCarthy. Thank you for your generous contributions.

To Jaclyn Bergeron, Amy Butler, Linda Feldman, Sarah Silberg, Carly Grafstein, and all of Fairchild Books—Great gratitude for your direction and assistance throughout the process.

To the reviewers: Your thorough and helpful recommendations made this textbook much better than it ever could have been as a solo project. The reviewers are: Jinah Oh, Academic Director, Art Institute of California, Sunnyvale; Amanda Lovell, Chair, Art Institute of New York; Jacquee Leahy, Art Institute of California, San Diego; Allison Paster, Art Institute of Philadelphia; Alexxis Avalon, Interim Chair, IADT Tampa; Michael P. Londrigan, Chair, LIM College; Dianne Erpenbach, Columbia College; Courtney Cothren, Stephens College; Erin D. Parrish, East Carolina University; Devona Dixon, Western Kentucky University; Jaehee Jung, University of Delaware; Nancy Strickler, Purdue University; Suzanne Marshall, California State University, Long Beach; Elizabeth Mukiibi, University of California Davis and Sacramento; Lauren M. Michel, Monterey Peninsula College; Jane Swinney, Oklahoma State University; Su-Jeong Hwang Shin, Texas Tech University; Claire Kapstein, University of Rhode Island; Mary Mhango, Marshall University.

1

Careers in Raw Materials, Manufacturing, and Design in the Fashion Industry

Unit 1 starts at the beginning of fashion product development and production. It provides an overview of the firms that supply the information, components, production, and design of fashion products that manufacturers produce. In addition, the "back office" departments of manufacturing firms are examined.

In Chapter 1, trend forecasters, those who interpret, inspire, and predict shifts in fashion preferences, are examined. They have tremendous influence on both the raw materials and the actual outcomes of fashion production. In Chapter 2, textile product developers and designers use colors, textures, patterns, and finishes to create the foundation on which fashion products are built. In Chapter 3, the careers of sourcing personnel who locate the components of products are explored. Sourcing involves locating value-appropriate fabrics and findings that become part of the fashion merchandise. Sourcing personnel may also find factories, particularly overseas, to produce the merchandise. In Chapter 4, production is examined as employees work together to manufacture the final product. Promotion (Chapter 5) and sales personnel (Chapter 6) departments collaborate to generate an interest and create a desire among the retail buyers who purchase the products for the ultimate consumer.

Chapter 7 presents the resource managers in finance, accounting, and human resources—aspects of the products and career tracks that are often overlooked by prospective fashion professionals. Accounting for the manufacturer begins with determining costs of goods and wholesale prices and ends with finance, analyzing the bottom line, and determining whether the company is generating a profit. Human resources focuses on the locating, hiring, training, motivating, and rewarding of employees who work within the companies that create fashion products. Chapter 8 takes a look at the field of fashion design. The move into outsourcing production, the customer's need for speed in purchasing new looks, and the proliferation of technology in design and manufacturing have come together to generate new career opportunities in fashion design. There are a number of relatively new positions in addition to those of the fashion designer, assistant fashion designer, and patternmaker. Among them are the career paths of the technical designer and specifications technician, both explored in this unit.

chapter 1

Trend Forecasting

As consumers, when we walk into apparel, accessories, or home furnishings retail stores, we are introduced to the latest trends in fashion. Who decides what the latest themes, colors, silhouettes, styling details, or fabrics will be? From where do these concepts come? How far in advance of the retail season are these trends determined? What will next season's, or next year's, fashion trends be? No company has a crystal ball to foresee the future of fashion. The person responsible for making these predictions is the **trend forecaster**, or *fashion forecaster*.

Customers are often unaware of the amount of lead time that fashion products require. **Lead time** refers to the number of days, weeks, months, or years needed for the intricate planning and production steps to be implemented before fashion products actually arrive at the retail store. Lead time includes the time fashion forecasters need to analyze and project colors, design themes, silhouettes, fabrics, patterns or prints, and styling details—often years in advance of the actual manufacturing of the products. Without that proverbial crystal ball, fashion forecasters must combine their knowledge of fashion design, current world trends, and history with consumer research and business information. If trend forecasters develop and market their visions of the fashion future effectively, designers, retailers, and manufacturers in the textiles, apparel, accessories, and home environment sectors who subscribe to the forecasters' ideas have an edge, and their lines will be on the mark for their specific target markets. They will have lower purchasing risks and greater opportunities to increase their customer following and, ultimately, their sales volume.

Many large corporations have research and development, or R&D, departments. In essence, trend forecasters are the "R" components of the R&D departments in the fashion business. They lead the research activities of the fashion industry and may also be involved in developmental functions. As researchers, trend forecasters provide new knowledge to designers, buyers, and product developers; assist in the development of new products; and look for ways

Box 1.1 Tech Talk: The Impact of Technology on Trend Forecasting

Are online trend forecasting services and real-time forecasting revolutionizing the world of the trend forecaster? Is it a battle of digital versus traditional? Most forecasters respect online technology, while they may not embrace them as the "end all." Fran Sude, owner of Design Options in Los Angeles, said, "WGSN and Stylesight have color files, but they don't have tangibility." Others indicate that technological tools, such as the iPad, have made even texture visually accessible. Digital media has positively impacted many traditional business-to-business services in the fashion industry, including trend forecasting services. As with any business, exceptional customer service is key. With that goal, technology and forecasting are forever linked.

Ruth Staiman, former fashion director for Bloomingdale's and current CEO of The Fashion Office, states, "Technology is the new fashion. Fashion trend forecasting is a process that begins with color and fabric predictions, then trend selections, and comes full circle with trade show and fashion show attendance. Add in a global view of film, art, and popular culture and you've got it. Before the Internet, fashion direction was based on instinct. We gathered all the information by hand and presented it to our buyers." Tracking fashion trends used to mean traveling abroad five times a year to check out runway, retail, and street fashion. The forecasting team would need two weeks to research, followed by another two weeks for a team of ten to pull the complete report together. The total process would take over a month before the clients received the information.

Today, trend reporters around the world send up-to-the-minute film of what is being worn on the streets, what designers are presenting, and what retailers are showcasing. Take, for example, Stylesight, a forecasting company headquartered in New York with a large office in Paris and satellite offices in the style capitals of the world. The company's experts comb the globe to analyze runway collections, the most important world trade shows, compelling retailers, and innovative textile manufacturers. The resulting information is sorted to fit clients' needs and streamed to them daily. Covering global fashion used to be a major investment, requiring the cost and time needed to send a fashion expert around the world. It was, however, considered a worthwhile investment, as it resulted in intellectual property that was closely guarded by the forecaster, manufacturer, and retailer. Now, information that was only available to the trade is accessible to the public. This has pushed trend forecasting to a new level, as the consumer can digitally see the world, spot the trends, and demand the merchandise right now. In fact, the consumer can now get involved in developing and directing the trends through Web sites and crowdsourcing.

Fashion Web sites Stylelist, MyPantone, and Polyvore are amazing tools that provide the forecaster with information and data on the consumer's desires. Polyvore allows consumers and experts to work with current fashion to create new trends. MyPantone gives the forecaster the opportunity to see the color palettes that customers are choosing. Customers are casting their votes by the thousands. Crowdsourcing is no stranger to the fashion industry. Threadless is one of the most known and successful crowdsourcing businesses. Here, you can submit a T-shirt design, have it voted on, read comments about it, and then review the winning T-shirt designs that will actually be produced. It is an excellent opportunity for the forecaster to see and hear what a large number of potential customers want. The idea of soliciting customer input is hardly new, of course, and the open-source software movement of crowdsourcing showed that it can be done with large numbers of people. Using the Internet to solicit feedback from an enthusiastic and passionate community of customers can reduce the amount of time spent collecting data through formal focus groups or trend research, while growing a demand for upcoming products.

Social media communities are also impacting the world of many trend forecasters. Walking the streets of a location, whether Antwerp, Paris, or London, gives the forecaster only part of the trend story. Once forecasters identify the trend, they want to know why it is popular and how it came to be, in order to understand its significance. After scanning social media communities, the forecaster may pinpoint where the trend originated and where it is heading. The golden days of fashionable rendezvous around the world may be replaced by online visits to blogs or social media communities.

How has technology impacted the actual business places of fashion forecasters? There are two words to describe the shifts in the workplace: streamlining and speed. The jobs of ten persons have been replaced by five who have multiple platforms of information streaming at one time. Due to the need for speed, some forecasting businesses no longer set launch dates for trend reports. Digital sketches are created and sent to clients, who can immediately download them to use in production or online trend presentations as needed. Trend analysis reports are conducted daily. After all, the consumer's buying preferences are changing daily. One thing, however, is stable, and that is the consumer's expectation of immediate gratification. After viewing the runway collections online, the consumer wants it now and is ready to get on his or her iPad to shop the collections. The result for fashion forecasters is the need to use technology to supply their clients with the most current and

forward trend information, often using real-time information to track consumer shopping habits. Real-time data, often referred to as RTD, is data that updates on its own schedule and can be used to track fashion shows, trunk show sales, manufacturing statistics, and warehouse activity, to name a few. Real-time data is used for researching the consumer's response to new trends at retail, in a specific locale or globally.

Yes, technology and forecasting are forever linked. The level to which technology will replace the forecaster's personal connection with the world is unknown. A trend forecaster could become part of the virtual fashion world, but it is unlikely that this is an "all or nothing" scenario. While technology infinitely enhances the forecasting process, being in the real world, talking to people on the street, and networking at the designer collections may still be the driving forces behind great forecasting.

Sources:
http://fashionablymarketing.me/2010/12/technologys-impact-on-trend-fashion-forecasting/

http://www.stylesight.com/about/

to improve old products. Forecasters search for facts and then analyze the findings to define the trends that will positively affect the amount and types of fashion products consumers will buy. Technology is impacting the way trend forecasters conduct research and development, particularly in the areas of designating trends and understanding the consumer. Box 1.1 provides more detail about the ever-changing world of trend forecasters and digital media.

Few career opportunities in fashion relate to all levels of the industry. Trend forecasting is one of the few. Population trends and interests, availability of raw materials, manufacturing capabilities, retail changes, merchandising and management developments, and entrepreneurial endeavors influence fashion forecasting. This chapter will introduce the career path of fashion forecasters, from those in color and textile forecasting to those in theme, style, and detail forecasting.

The Job of a Trend Forecaster

The position of trend forecaster is one of the most influential career options in the fashion industry. Many fashion consumers and most prospective fashion industry employees wonder where the latest and greatest fashion trends originate. Fashion forecasters continually monitor consumers and the industry through traveling, reading, networking, listening, and, most important, observing. Fashion forecasters attend trade shows, where they analyze the wholesale end of the business by looking at new products and fresh designs from established and new designers. They gather information from the media on population, design, manufacturing, and retail trends to determine what the new looks, silhouettes, colors, and fabrics will be for upcoming seasons.

Types of Forecasters

There are four primary types of trend forecasters. First, there is the forecaster who works for a **fiber house** or *fabric house*, a company that represents a fiber source or a fabric. Examples include Cotton Incorporated or the Mohair Council of America. Second, there is the forecaster who specializes in color trends and is employed by a firm such as The Color Association. This forecaster provides information on color preferences and palettes for a wide variety of clients, from automobile manufacturers to flooring producers to apparel designers. Next, there is the forecaster who projects population trends and explores the social, economic, geographic, and technological changes in the world, as well as shifts in the population. The population trend forecaster tracks a population's age shifts; residential and geographic preferences; changes in family sizes and structures; entertainment preferences; spending patterns; influences by celebrities, films, and art; as well as other people-related topics. Finally, there is the forecaster who is employed by a **broad-spectrum firm**, a company that provides forecasting services for a wide range of target markets and product categories or industries. Examples are Promostyl and Trend Union, which are presented later in this chapter. These companies provide information on all of the trend areas for many target markets and product categories, including color, fabrications, silhouettes, fashion influences, design themes, and population trends. In essence, they offer a one-stop-shopping trend-forecasting service.

Sources of Information

Where do forecasters go for information? It depends on the market sector in which they specialize (e.g., color, demographics, apparel, or home) or consumer segment they are investigating (e.g., contemporary women, preteens, or men). There is, however, a range of information sources that most trend forecasters find to be valuable. Following is a list of popular trend-forecasting resources.

- **Market research firms.** There are companies that, for a fee, provide specific information on consumer market segments. Population changes that can be quantified are referred to as **demographic data**, such as age, education, residence, family size, occupation, income, and expenditures. Additionally, more general government data on demographics is available on similar subjects at no cost through resources such as the U.S. Census Bureau.

- **The couture collections.** Dior, Chanel, Celine, Gucci, Armani, Prada, Issey Miyake—the list of prominent and influential designers is a long one. The introductions of their seasonal collections are important times for fashion forecasters, as these industry leaders have a great influence on future ready-to-wear and home trends (Figure 1.1).

- **New designers:** The collections of up-and-coming designers are often viewed with as much enthusiasm and interest by trend forecasters as those of the established couturiers.

Trend forecasters are often seeking new places for design talent, such as prestigious fashion schools around the world, or in countries providing government support and new opportunities for fashion entrepreneurial businesses, such as India, Canada, and Hong Kong (Figure 1.2).

- **Other fashion services.** Apparel and accessories forecasters may subscribe to other services, such as color forecasting services. Some subscribe to competitors' services to stay on top of what the competition is doing. The primary tangible product of a trend forecasting firm is referred to as a **trend book**, or *look book*, that features the recommendations and predictions of the company for the upcoming seasons. A number of trend forecasting companies review the trend books or trend Web sites of companies with target markets or merchandise categories different from their own to gain a comprehensive picture of the fashion world (Figure 1.3).

- **Trade shows.** International fiber and fabric markets, such as Interstoff in Germany and Expofil in Paris (Figure 1.4), are primary information sources for forecasters who are researching color and textile trends. There are apparel and accessories trade shows at the markets in New York City, Dallas, Los Angeles, Las Vegas, and Chicago, to name a few. High Point, North Carolina, offers markets in home textiles and furnishings.

- **Communication with peers.** Networking is a key activity for trend forecasters. Updates from designers, buyers, and manufacturers can provide significant information on what is selling and what is not. Communication with representatives of key suppliers can assist the forecaster in identifying trends. Membership in professional organizations, such as

Figure 1.3 The Doneger Group offers color forecasting services.

Figure 1.4 Expofil in Paris is among the world's premier international fabric trade shows.

the Fashion Group International, Inc., and the American Society of Interior Designers (ASID), also provides trend forecasters with the opportunity to network with others in the know in the fashion industry.

- **E-sources.** Web sites, online music programs, chat rooms, news sites, e-catalogs, and social networks are valuable resources that are easily accessible to trend forecasters. Also, forecasters may subscribe to specific online trend-forecasting resources. A number of these sites are provided at the end of this chapter.

- **Design sources.** Reference books, historical costume collections and texts, vintage clothing shops, antique dealers, museums, bookstores, and libraries are excellent resources

Figure 1.5 Vintage clothing shops and antique dealers are excellent resources for forecasters who are exploring the influence of past eras on fashion.

for forecasters who are exploring the influence of past eras on fashion, as in Figure 1.5. Videos and photographs of recent designer collections, fashion shows, and trade show exhibitions are some examples of design resources that trend forecasters use for information on current designer and trend information.

• **Publications.** Trade journals and international consumer magazines are common, obvious sources for trend information. It is less apparent, however, that many apparel and accessories forecasters subscribe to home furnishings and home accessories magazines to identify color, fabric, and theme trends in the home. New colors in automobiles are often gleaned from successful hues in home furnishings and apparel. Auto, health, and celebrity magazines are also part of the trend forecaster's reading materials. Trend forecasters often read it all.

- **The arts.** Music concerts, visual art presentations, museum exhibits, dance performances, and theater plays can influence or interrelate with fashion trends. For example, a Matisse exhibit that travels internationally, portrayed in Figure 1.6, can have an impact on textile patterns and color palettes of a particular season. In 2010, the Victoria and Albert Museum hosted the exhibition "Grace Kelly: Style Icon." As seen in Figure 1.7, the displays featured a Van Cleef & Arpels diamond tiara, a Chanel suit, an Yves Saint Laurent dress, a Balenciaga jacket, several pairs of Christian Dior sunglasses, and eyeglasses from a number of other designers. The impact? The eyewear was copied and added to accessory lines around the world. Additionally, the wardrobe and costume designers for a play, film, or television show can influence fashion trends. Costume designer Patricia Field, as featured in Box 1.2 and Figure 1.8, clearly influenced fashion through her work in *Sex and the City* and *The Devil Wears Prada*.

- **Entertainment headliners.** Celebrities greatly influence fashion trends. People in music and the news, on talk shows, on the red carpet, in videos, and on the big screen have the ability to set trends. For example, celebrity gowns are copied and made available to

Figure 1.6 Matisse's *Purple Robe and Anemones* from the Granger Collection.

Figure 1.7 The Victoria and Albert Museum hosted the exhibition "Grace Kelly: Style Icon," which influenced fashion apparel and accessories over the next year.

Box 1.2 Fashion Stylist/Costumer Patricia Field

by Gala Darling, November 16, 2009

Patricia Field is like the fairy godmother of every capricious, madly dressed fashionista on the planet. She is legendary in scope, her name falling in alongside the likes of Betsey Johnson and Vivienne Westwood when it comes to women who do it their way and succeed.

Born and raised in New York City, she has been a Manhattan icon since the late 1970s, when she started her own line of clothing and accessories for club kids, ravers, and other wild personalities. However, she started to really cement her place on the international scene when she began work on the now legendary *Sex and the City*. While she worked alongside other stylists, Field was always at the helm, pointing the way. Her adventurous, creative, and fun ways of looking at clothing and her understanding of how we use clothing to express ourselves suddenly had a worldwide audience and a cult following. As the show became more and more popular, she took bigger sartorial risks, such as adding enormous flowers to garments, mixing high- and low-end fashions, and creating a rainbow palette.

Before Carrie, Samantha, Charlotte, and Miranda made Patricia Field a household name, she owned a boutique in SoHo called Hotel Venus. The goal of the sales associates, who were drag queens and short-shorts-wearin' mamas, was to encourage people to dress up and really enjoy clothing. Years later, the shop was renamed to straight-up Patricia Field and moved to the Bowery, but still with the same mission statement. Diamante-encrusted brass knuckles sit on a shelf alongside sequined pants, a totally mad wig salon resides downstairs, and there are enough rhinestones to thrill even the most discerning magpie.

Field's most well-known work—other than the *Sex and the City* (*SATC*) franchise—was in the movie adaptation of Lauren Weisberger's book *The Devil Wears Prada*, which told the author's story of an allegedly horrifying time working with Anna Wintour at *Vogue*. The styling on *The Devil Wears Prada* was immaculate and quite different than on *SATC*, proving that Field has the vision and the panache to style anyone for any occasion.

What has made Patricia Field so successful? A ton of hard work and gallons of talent combined with a bit of being in the right place at the right time. While a lesser stylist working on *SATC* wouldn't have made as much of an impact, there's no denying that being able to capture millions of eyeballs every week was a huge coup and a boost to her career. The best thing about her, however, is her refusal to rest on her laurels. She is continually pushing boundaries and trying new things. Of her success in the world of film and television, she says, "I never took it for granted and I sustained my business throughout. There is a certain truth about retail. If you listen to the customers, they will tell you."

Source: http://www.chinashopmag.com/2009/11/patricia-field/

Figure 1.8 The wardrobe designer for a television series or film can influence fashion trends. Costume designer Patricia Field clearly influenced fashion through her work in *Sex and the City* and *The Devil Wears Prada*.

Figure 1.9 Celebrities, whether in the news or music, on television or film, have the ability and visibility to set trends.

consumers in weeks (Figure 1.9). Forecasters often watch up-and-coming celebrities and project which newcomers have the star quality and visibility that will make them future stars. Forecasters observe what they wear, who their favorite designers are, how they style their hair, and where they hang out with friends. Since forecasters have to anticipate the actual trends before they happen, identifying the people who will influence future trends is a critical part of the forecaster's job.

- **Fabrics.** Cotton Incorporated is a company that represents the cotton industry and provides trend information to designers and retailers. Fabric companies, such as Springmaid and the Australian Merino Wool Industry (Woolmark), also develop trend information, which is available on their Web sites.

- **Travel.** Vacation hot spots are often filled with people who influence fashion trends. Additionally, certain fashion trends develop in specific geographic locations. China and its fun fur fashions, Belgium with its deconstruction techniques in apparel, Japan and its young and creative street fashions are all examples of the travel destinations where fashion trends have developed (Figure 1.10).

- **Consumer tracking. Consumer tracking information** refers to data that relates to customer spending, such as how much money is spent on clothing, entertainment, or

Figure 1.10
Designer Dries van
Noten and his dog,
Harry, on the rooftop
of his Antwerp
headquarters. Antwerp,
Belgium, with its
vacation appeal and
fashion focus, is an
example of a travel
destination where
fashion trends develop.

food. It can also relate to how a customer makes a purchase—cash, credit card, debit card, or check? Purchases can be correlated with credit card data to examine who is actually buying what.

- **Lifestyle trends.** **Lifestyle trends** refer to a population segment's values, interests, attitudes, dreams, and goals. Think about the following lifestyle trends: an increasing interest in health and fitness, the baby boomers' desire to entertain at home, and couples deciding to have fewer children and to start their families at a later age than previous generations. Next, ask yourself how these lifestyle trends influence fashion. Workout wear sales have increased. Patio furniture, cookware, and tabletop accessories have received a renewed interest in the home furnishings and accessories industries. The number of pieces sold in children's wear has decreased; however, sales in this merchandise classification have increased due to higher unit prices. Two working parents who have launched their careers and waited to have children often have the finances and desire to provide their children with more. Lifestyle shifts influence what the customer wants to buy (Figure 1.11). **Psychographics** take this idea a step further: these include people's lifestyles and behaviors—where they like to vacation, the kinds of interests they have, the values they hold, and how they behave. Forecasters endeavor to become aware of these changes before they occur and identify the products that will meet consumer needs before customers know what they need.

- **Places where people gather.** Airports, concert stadiums, shopping malls, and Times Square on New Year's Eve are some of the locations where groups of people can be

Figure 1.11 Working parents, like Jennifer Lopez, who have launched their careers and waited to have children, often have the finances and desire to provide their children with more. Lifestyle shifts influence what the customer wants to buy.

Figure 1.12 "I watch people anywhere and everywhere," one successful trend forecaster explains. "You never know where a trend will start."

observed. Trend forecasters examine where these people are going, what they are wearing, and from whom and what they are buying.

• **Street scenes.** "I watch people anywhere and everywhere," one successful trend forecaster explains. "You never know where a trend will start." Worth Global Style Network (WGSN), a key forecasting resource discussed later in this chapter, recruits people from colleges and other locations worldwide to submit trend information from their various communities. Every street, from WGSN's perspective, has the potential for fashion leadership (Figure 1.12).

• **Sports.** When a particular sport or activity gains consumer interest, its active sportswear is often imitated or modified for street wear. High-top boxing boots, surfer shorts, and yoga pants illustrate the influence of sports trends on ready-to-wear. As Figure 1.13 depicts, golf is one of the sports currently impacting daytime or streetwear fashion.

The Career Path

Securing a position in trend forecasting does not happen quickly. Typically, many years of industry experience are required. A number of successful forecasters have previously worked as designers or buyers before moving into the fashion-forecasting career field. A few of the fortunate begin with internships or assistantship positions in forecasting firms to gain direct experience, exposure, and contacts in the forecasting world.

Qualifications

Successful trend forecasters often meet or exceed the following qualifications:

- **Education:** At the very least, a bachelor's degree in one of a wide range of disciplines is required. These disciplines most frequently include business administration (e.g., marketing or consumer behavior), visual arts, fashion design, or fashion merchandising.

- **Experience:** Forecasters often begin in entry-level positions in the areas of retail, product development, design, merchandising, or fashion coordination. A number of successful forecasters have held positions in several sectors of the industry, such as design, product development, and retailing.

- **Personal characteristics:** There are a few specific and unique qualities that trend forecasters display. Among them is an excellent understanding of people and human behavior, global population and industry shifts, and fashion trends. Successful trend forecasters have effective visual, written, and oral communication and presentation skills. They are often curious and creative people with superior networking abilities. Most important, they have an exceptional capability to analyze, synthesize, and organize observations into categories that are clearly communicated to clients. Think about viewing 15 couture collection presentations in a five-day period and then identifying the consistent trends among them. Fashion forecasters have the ability to find the common threads and, later, classify and describe these trends for designers, manufacturers, and retailers who use the trend services.

Figure 1.13 When a particular sport or activity gains consumer interest, its active sportswear is often imitated or modified for streetwear.

The Typical Forecaster's Career Path

While the majority of college graduates prefer to start at the top, it is an essential advantage for a fashion forecaster to understand all levels of the industry from a holistic perspective. Even the most entry-level retail sales positions provide valuable experience for future forecasters. As a sales associate, one is directly exposed to the customers' preferences and dislikes. Effective sales associates endeavor to understand who the customers are and identify their buying habits. As future fashion forecasters progress to higher positions within the industry (e.g., product development or merchandising), it is important that they always keep in mind who the customers are and how they are changing. The work experience fashion forecasters have acquired through the years is used on a daily basis when assisting designers, manufacturers, or merchandisers with future purchases for upcoming seasons.

The Job Market for Trend Forecasters

The fashion industry has a limited number of fashion forecasting positions in the areas of color, textile design, apparel and accessories design, and home furnishings. Since fashion forecasting positions are limited, successful fashion forecasters are well compensated for their knowledge and skills. Sometimes, a commission will be paid to fashion forecasters based on how well their companies perform with their assistance.

Career Challenges

The pros of a fashion forecasting career have been discussed, but what about the challenges? Because there are a limited number of successful forecasting firms, there are only a few jobs for a few good men and women. The job of a fashion forecaster requires a tremendous amount of intelligence, skill, and exposure and, perhaps, a sixth sense. Forecasters must be aware of all of the external influences that may affect consumer behavior. The ability to observe, organize, and prioritize these outside influences is a rare skill. Fashion forecasters who consistently identify the right trends develop strong reputations. Many "wannabes" who provide the wrong information for a season or two are no longer hired by clients, who depend on accurate fashion direction to make a profit. It can be stressful for fashion forecasters to identify significant fashion influences seasonally or annually. Additionally, fashion forecasters must be able to market their companies, their ideas, and themselves. The forecaster's knowledge, intuition, and experience truly form the ultimate product.

Examples of Fashion Forecasting Companies

There are a number of successful fashion forecasting companies around the world, with new firms constantly entering the mix. Some focus on a certain target market, such as teens or contemporary men; others emphasize a specific fashion variable, such as color or fabric. Some offer a wide breadth of personal service, while others provide online reports. Whatever your fashion interest, there is a trend forecasting company to fill the bill.

Doneger Creative Services

Doneger Creative Services, based in New York City, is the trend and color forecasting and analysis division of The Doneger Group, located at www.doneger.com/web/dcs_main.htm. Doneger Creative Services offers a broad range of products and services, such as printed publications, online subscriptions, and live presentations. This division addresses the forecasting needs of retailers, manufacturers, and other style-related businesses. Doneger's creative directors, or fashion forecasters, cover the apparel, accessories, and lifestyle markets in the women's, men's, and youth merchandise classifications.

Fashion Snoops

Fashion Snoops is the creator of www.fashionsnoops.com, an online forecasting and fashion trend analysis service that covers the young men's, denim, junior women's, children's, and infant and toddler markets. Fashion Snoops was created in 2001 by a team of designers and merchandisers who have extensive industry experience. The company's goal in bringing professionals together from various sectors of the fashion and licensing industries was to bring practical experience to creative teams. Fashion Snoops has a creative services division that provides consulting and outsourced services in the areas of research, design, merchandising, styling, and graphic art. The company serves hundreds of leading fashion firms in the United States, Canada, Europe, Australia, Asia, and South America.

Worth Global Style Network (WGSN)

Founders Julian and Marc Worth launched WGSN, based in London, in 1998. It is one of the most successful online forecasting services to emerge. WGSN offers research, trend analysis, and news to the fashion, design, and style industries. Members of the 100-person staff travel extensively around the world. The WGSN team includes experienced writers, photographers, researchers, analysts, and trendspotters. **Trendspotters** are people located at universities and other locations worldwide who provide information to WGSN on the latest trends in each locale. The company tracks not only the latest fashion trends but also hot retail stores, new designers, emerging brands, and business innovations. WGSN maintains offices in London, New York City, Hong Kong, Seoul, Los Angeles, Melbourne, and Tokyo. Its client list is long and impressive and includes such designers and retailers as Giorgio Armani, Target, Mango, and Abercrombie & Fitch. The company's Web site is located at www.wgsn.com.

The Zandl Group

Based in New York City, the Zandl Group is a firm that provides trend analysis, consumer research, and marketing direction for businesses and advertising agencies. The company's area of specialization is a big one: 82 million young people between the ages of 8 and 24 in the United States. This market is segmented into the following classifications: young adults, teens, and preteens (also referred to as tweens). The Zandl Group publishes a bimonthly trend report on these market segments called "The Hot Sheet."

SnapFashun

SnapFashun is a source for Los Angeles and European retail reporting, merchandising trends, and original design ideas. The firm monitors up-to-the-minute looks at top-selling items in trendsetting cities. To meet the needs of designers and manufacturers, SnapFashun offers a library of visual images that represents more than 25 years of fashion-reporting experience. The fashion library is updated with new details and silhouettes up to 14 times each year.

Paris Trend Forecasters

There are a number of trend forecasting services and trade shows based in Paris, France. Carlin International is a forecasting firm dedicated to fashion trend information. The company's Web site, www.carlin-groupe.com, is available in English and French. Peclers

Box 1.3 NellyRodi

Since 1985, the NellyRodi consulting agency supports businesses the world over in their processes of creation and innovation. NellyRodi invents the labels, products, and retail modes of tomorrow.

NellyRodi TrendLab, or NellyRodi, is a forecasting agency that has become renowned for its exceptional ability to provide designers with insight into future consumer trends. The agency specializes in publications designed to assist creative teams and manufacturers as they develop future product lines. Among the firm's key publications, trend books are invaluable design resources that include photos, fabric swatches, materials, color ranges, drawings of prints, product sketches, silhouettes, commentaries, and additional inspirational materials.

With expertise in the textile, packaging, automotive, and cosmetic industries, this France-based company has been helping design teams through their creative processes since 1985. The NellyRodi agency features an in-house team of 30 people and numerous freelancers, experts in apparel, beauty, and the art of living. Team members represent a wide range of fashion- and art-related career areas, including fashion artists, designers, sketchers, scenographers, and model makers. Many travel around the world, to 19 countries this past year, detecting and interpreting signs that foreshadow changes in popular culture. By consulting with one another, sharing ideas, and envisioning the future of our world, all of these experts have a strong voice within the ongoing creative interaction of NellyRodi TrendLab. Additionally, the company regularly brings together researchers from such disciplines as sociology, philosophy, and linguistics to brainstorm with marketing directors on social and economic topics.

The Services

One of NellyRodi TrendLab's services is referred to as "made-to-measure consulting." This includes individualized projects in the following areas:

- Presenting trends to fashion directors, buyers, and designers, including creating personalized trend books that cover color palettes, materials, and shapes

- Publishing trendsetters' guides to complement the trend books

- Collaborating with designers, manufacturers, and retailers on the development of product collections or taking charge of collection plan and product design

- Researching brand concepts

- Designing packaging

- Compiling buying guides for distributors

- Researching promotional venues, then creating and organizing press launches

- Developing trend presentations and exhibits for professional trade markets

- Designing visual merchandising projects, such as boutique and window designs

Beauty and Fragrance

With more than 15 years of experience and 70 clients in the cosmetics sector, NellyRodi TrendLab is an international leader of fashion information adapted for the beauty industry. Although for a long time they were limited to cosmetics, fashion influences have recently entered the domains of skin care, perfume, and packaging. NellyRodi assists brands in developing new perfumes and inspires perfumers by suggesting new olfactory directions. With its new division, Scent Factory, NellyRodi brought the company's expertise in perfume to the public. Scent Factory is the first perfume compilation, similar to a musical compilation in that it explores eight extreme olfactory creations conceived by eight perfumers under the direction of NellyRodi.

Source: www.nellyrodi.com

Josh has been a designer and strategist for many years. With a bachelor of arts degree in communications and cognitive science from Hampshire College and a master's in interactive telecommunications from New York University, he began creating mobile device interfaces, Web applications, embedded software, kiosks, installations, and a few T-shirts. When the Internet boom peaked, he was at Razorfish working as the director of mobile solutions. He oversaw the user experience for projects delivered to Vodafone, Citibank, and Adobe, among others. He then went to Motorola to be a lead user interface designer and was in charge of two new software platforms. Later, he was the vice president of product development at Upoc Networks, a software company that develops mobile messaging applications.

In 2003, Josh set out on his own to build a publishing and consulting business focused on design strategy, trend analysis, and mobile marketing for select clients.

Cool Hunting

Since 2003, Josh Rubin's Cool Hunting has been a daily update on happenings from the intersection of design, culture, and technology. Josh started the site as a way to catalog things that inspire him in his practice as a designer and strategist. Cool Hunting is synonymous with seeking inspiration. The company's global team of editors and contributors sift through innovations in design, technology, art, and culture to create award-winning publications, consisting of daily updates and weekly mini-documentaries. Founded as a designer's personal reference, Cool Hunting now has an international audience of like-minded creative people, who find inspiration on www.coolhunting.com and its iPad app, or who follow Cool Hunting on sites like YouTube, Twitter, and Facebook, and subscribe to its RSS feed and e-mail newsletter.

Today, Cool Hunting has grown beyond a personal reference tool—forecasters, designers, consumers, and marketers from around the world visit every day to get their dose of what's cool. As the site became increasingly fueled by contributions from readers, Josh realized Cool Hunting should be a collective. He now serves as editor of the site, which features contributions from a small group of handpicked writers who are out finding great things and looking at all the information readers are feeding them.

Source: http://coolhunting.com

Paris is a fashion trend forecasting service that specializes in textile design, fashion, beauty, consumer goods, and retailing. Première Vision is the world's leading trade show in fabric forecasting, promoting fabric trends for designers and manufacturers in the fashion industry. Première Vision teams with the company Première Vision S.A., a subsidiary of the French Association for the Promotion of Textile Yarns (AFPFT), to produce the Expofil trade show in Paris. The world leader in yarn and fiber sectors, Expofil provides the whole textile industry with fashion information, colors, and materials. Another Paris-based forecasting agency, NellyRodi, is featured in Box 1.3.

Promostyl

Promostyl's mission is to pinpoint fashion, design, and lifestyle trends and help companies adapt to changing trends. The company bases its work on the currents of society, cultures, and lifestyles, believing that society makes fashion. The company creates trend books, develops visual presentations, consults with companies, and maintains an international network of subsidiaries and agents. Three main offices are located in Paris, New York City, and Tokyo.

Color Forecasters

The Color Association of the United States is a color forecasting service. According to its Web site, www.colorassociation.com, it is the oldest such company in the United States. Since 1915, the Color Association has been issuing color reports in fabric-swatched booklets. A committee panel of 8 to 12 industry professionals selects seasonal color palettes. A younger player in the color forecasting business is Color Portfolio, Inc., at www.colorportfolio.com. Started in 1986, Color Portfolio offers color and trend books to retailers, manufacturers, and related industries. The company provides recommendations for colors, trends, and textiles.

Cool Hunting

Cool Hunting, featured in Box 1.4, seeks out trends in the form of "all things cool." Founder Josh Rubin believes that there are no new ideas, just great executions. A self-proclaimed "interaction designer," he is always looking for both creative inspiration and an understanding of the way people do things. In 2003, he decided to start a catalog of what he found and haphazardly named it Cool Hunting. Today, Cool Hunting has a global team of editors and contributors sifting through innovations in design, technology, art, and culture, and then reporting on the coolest of these at www.coolhunting.com.

Trend Union

Trend Union, created by Lidewij Edelkoort, specializes in forecasting trends, consulting, and developing trend books for the fashion and textile industries, as well as architecture, design, interior decor, wellness, and cosmetics industries. With offices in Paris since 1991, Edelkoort is assisted by a highly qualified team of creative professionals: graphic artists, designers, artists, and consultants. Every six months, Edelkoort personally designs the majority of the "notebooks" that become a collection of biannual trend forecasting books setting forth the colors, materials, shapes, and lifestyles for seasons to come. These books are available to Trend Union's clients two years in advance of the major trends in the fields of fashion, textile, and consumption. Twice a year, Edelkoort creates a 20-minute audiovisual presentation of images and music that portray the significant future trends featured in the books. This presentation is shown in Paris to the clients of Trend Union, with sessions in London, Stockholm, New York, Tokyo, Seoul, and Amsterdam.

Leading manufacturers of products for the environmental, automotive, home, office, garden, textile, fashion, and beauty industries seek out advice and creative ideas from Trend Union when developing their own lines, services, and marketing strategies. On its Web site, www.trendunion.com, the company states that its "scope covers the global (international) as well as the local (national) and our vision extends both to the short term (six months to one year) and the long term (three to four years, or even five to ten years)." Some of the industries that employ Trend Union for short- and long-term strategic trend planning include the paper industry, automotive industry (e.g., Nissan), beauty industries from perfume to cosmetics and hair products (e.g., Estée Lauder and Shiseido), food and drink producers (e.g., Coca-Cola and Unilever), high-tech producers, and home products.

Trend Union is a company with a heart—specifically, Heartwear. This is a division of the company created by Edelkoort and a group of her industry friends in 1993. They decided to sponsor a collection of garments utilizing native African skills and adapting the apparel to Western tastes. Profits from this project were returned to the country of Benin to be invested in educational projects. It was the beginning of a not-for-profit association that continues to help artisans in developing countries tailor their products for export without compromising the skill, knowledge, culture, and environment of the region involved. Profits are reinvested in the country with the aim of making the industry independent and generating economic momentum in the region through local and foreign markets. Once a link with a region or a cooperative is established by Heartwear, the association tries to maintain a long-term relationship by developing and advancing local production. To date, Heartwear has developed indigo fabrics for home and apparel with artisans of Benin, ceramics with potters from Morocco, and cotton khadi in India.

Summary

Trend forecasters are central to the fashion industry. Accurate forecasting can make or break a company. Every designer and merchandiser must be aware of trend predictions to ensure their lines will appeal to their specific target market. Trend forecasters may be employed by broad-spectrum firms, fiber or fabric houses, companies specializing in color trends, or businesses that project population trends. They gather information by examining market research firms, couture collections, new designers, trade shows, art, design, e-sources, travel trends, lifestyle trends, entertainment, and street styles. Fashion forecasting is one of the few careers that encompasses all of the aspects of the industry; therefore, it is essential for trend forecasters to possess a strong understanding of the fashion industry, from creative product development to retail selling. Seldom does one gain a position in this field without a number of years of prior experience and education. As a trend forecaster, you may anticipate a challenging career that encourages you to create, read, listen, travel online and off, observe, absorb, organize, and research always!

Key Terms

broad-spectrum firm
consumer tracking information
demographic data
fiber house
lead time
lifestyle trends
psychographics
trend book
trend forecaster
trendspotter

Online Resources

snowinateapot.blogspot.com
us.fashionmag.com
www.apparelsearch.com
www.chictopia.com
www.coolhunting.com
www.cosmoworlds.com
www.cottoninc.com
www.dailycandy.com
www.dailyfashion.com
www.doneger.com
www.elle.com
www.eonline.com
www.fashion.net
www.fashiondig.com
www.fashionera.org
www.fashionica.com
www.fashioninjapan.com
www.fashionising.com
www.fashionsnoops.com
www.fashiontrendsetter.com
www.focusonstyle.com
www.glamour.com
www.handbag.com
www.harpersbazaar.com
www.iconique.com
www.infomat.com
www.instyle.com
www.ivillage.com
www.lebook.com
www.londonfashionweek.com
www.lookbook.nu

www.lotsofstyle.com
www.luckymag.com
www.marieclaire.com
www.millionlooks.com
www.nylonmag.com
www.pantone.com
www.peoplestylewatch.com
www.polyvore.com
www.promadvice.com
www.rachelstyle.com
www.rachelzoe.com
www.seventeen.com
www.shefinds.com
www.shoppingthetrend.com
www.snapfashun.com
www.style.com
www.stylelist.com
www.stylesight.com
www.thefashionspot.com
www.trenddirector.net
www.trendhunter.com
www.trendland.net
www.trendpulse.net
www.trendstop.com
www.trendunion.com
www.vintagetrends.com
www.vogue.com
www.whowhatwear.com
www.wmagazine.com
www.wwd.com

Discussion Questions

1. How conscious are you of current trends? Identify current color, design, art, textile, entertainment, and sociocultural trends for this season and the next.
2. Spot trends within the current season and trace their sources. Did these trends originate from the streets, art exhibitions, new technology, couture collections, or some other source?
3. Analyze the latest issues of fashion magazines and compare the contents with fashion six months ago. Describe three basic trend directions toward next year's fashion.
4. What are some examples of companies outside of the fashion industry that rely on trend forecasting? Why are trends important to these businesses?

Profile of a Trend Forecaster

Know Business, December 3, 2009
By Cecilie Rohwedder
Source: *Wall Street Journal* Digital, http://magazine.wsj.com/features/the-big-interview/know-business/2/)

The clever packaging of prophetic thoughts is not new. When John Naisbitt predicted the might of the information age in his book *Megatrends* in 1982, he helped spawn an entirely new industry—future forecasting. Over the past two decades, the concept of making money out of being able to see what's around the corner has captured the imagination of blue-chip companies from American Express to Coca-Cola; made individuals like Faith Popcorn and the aforementioned Naisbitt wealthy; and put companies like London-based The Future Laboratory on the map.

Li Edelkoort's strengths as a leading modern-day soothsayer are not immediately apparent. A quiet, somewhat stern presence, she lives in a modest house on the outskirts of Paris with her two cats. The distinctive gray accents in her otherwise dark hair and the dark clothing offset by a bright red lipstick are consistent with her art school roots. Otherwise, Edelkoort gives off no clues that she is responsible for helping to guide clients including Nissan, Coca-Cola, Donna Karan, Old Navy, Gucci, Estée Lauder, Gap, and Mattel.

Ivy Ross, now executive vice president of Gap, has been working with Edelkoort for some 20 years. Old Navy's 2006 "pure and natural" line came from Edelkoort's trend forecasts; at toymaker Mattel, Edelkoort helped Ross with the "What's Her Face" doll—a toy with a blank face that children could draw on with washable markers. According to Ross, the feature was a result of one of Edelkoort's presentations, which discussed the public yearning for new beginnings and included a teddy bear without a face. "Other trend services tell you exactly what to do. It is like they give you a rule book," Ross says. "Li's presentations are much more inspirational…she lets you into her world, into her way of thinking. She lets you feel things on a visceral level. Then you can draw your own conclusions." But that doesn't provide much

Figure 1.14 Li Edelkoort of Trend Union

explanation of Edelkoort's methodology. "I'm not a psychic," she says. "I don't see someone's future, I am completely normal." Edelkoort operates, she says, by constantly sampling everything she sees. "I am always scanning. That's how I can see things that are latent, that are sleeping in society, and get early information."

Future forecasting has its fair share of naysayers. "I read it like a horoscope," says Allyson Stewart-Allen, director of London-based consulting firm International Marketing Partners, who reads forecasts, but not Edelkoort's. "If you look at what happened in the last two years, economists didn't get that right and trend forecasters didn't either," says Graham Hales, managing director of

Profile of a Trend Forecaster (continued)

Interbrand, a London-based brand consultancy. Now, he says, it doesn't take a forecaster to know that consumers crave positive stimuli and distraction.

From her airy office in a former glass factory in the south of Paris, Dutch-born Edelkoort runs a small group of companies that employs around 20 people publishing books and magazines on coming trends in color, fabrics, and design, as well as offering consulting services and curating trade fairs. Edelkoort, 59, crosses the globe giving lectures that dissect nascent shifts in the zeitgeist—where they come from and, most crucially for corporate clients, how they translate into future goods and services.

"We make it a point of specializing in long-term trends that merit investment from companies," Edelkoort says. Her trend books—the bread and butter of her business—cost up to $3,400 apiece, and developing a brand can cost up to $240,000. Around a quarter of her clients are American. "A makeup is never just two colors put together," says Dominique Szabo, a former senior vice president for worldwide product development with Estée Lauder, who worked with Edelkoort for over 20 years. "It's always a story, inspired by an exhibit, a film, or a cultural event. Li always knows what that story is."

Back in 2001, when Edelkoort predicted the growing importance of white, she helped Estée Lauder create a skin care product based on milk, called Nutritionist. In 2002, she inspired Nissan to launch five unusually bright color options into the car market in Japan. According to Kei Yoshitomi, of Nissan's Colour Design Department, the range—pale and bright orange, pale yellow, aqua blue, and olive green—sold well and earned an industry award (she also advised Nissan on a later version of the Micra, launched in 2003, as illustrated in Figure 1.15). The company says her long-term forecasts are valuable in the car business, where the life cycle of a car can span 10 years.

In 1999, Edelkoort was elected chair of the Design Academy in Eindhoven, one of the world's most prestigious design schools. Though she gave up the

Figure 1.15 Edelkoort inspired Nissan to launch five unusually bright color options into the car market in Japan. The range—pale and bright orange, pale yellow, aqua blue, and olive green—earned an industry award and retail sales.

role last year, she is recognized as having nurtured some of the best-known names in design, such as Maarten Baas (Design Miami's 2009 Designer of the Year), Hella Jongerius, and Job Smeets. Murray Moss, who co-owns the New York design store Moss and has known Edelkoort since 1994, says, "She trained students to think outside the normal boxes that were imposed by design schools."

It was as a student herself, at the Art Academy in Arnhem, that Edelkoort realized that she was not as artistic as others. Friends would turn to her for style advice, so eventually she started working as a trend scout for a department store. "I somehow always knew what fashion would become. My whole class used me as a forecaster," she says.

If she has a gift, Edelkoort says it is to spot subtle signs of change, filter them out, and give them a name. Edelkoort says she observes people wherever she goes, spending half the year traveling (she's particularly inspired by Tokyo, Stockholm, Istanbul, and New Delhi). In the last two weeks of September, for instance, after presenting new trends for summer 2010 in Paris, she gave a lecture in São Paulo, attended art openings in Los Angeles, and presented a seminar in Kiev, Ukraine.

Profile of a Trend Forecaster (continued)

Colleagues speak of her devouring magazines and newspapers at a fast rate on planes, tearing out articles and images that inspire and leaving the publications behind like carcasses. She's a fan of CNN, which runs all the time in her home and office. Wherever she is, she leaves her hotel to explore, talking to strangers to find out what they are wearing if their look is unique. "We are constantly sampling everything we see. When I go to a lecture I look to see how many people have blond hair? Black hair? How many wearing denim, how many wearing suits? Everything is saved and archived."

Some say Edelkoort doesn't predict the trends, but rather she makes them. "She is a trendsetter," says Reinier Evers, founder of Trendwatching. com. "Because she has so many followers, if she pronounces something, it becomes true. It is a self-fulfilling prophecy." Evers says he respects Edelkoort for her prowess in pinpointing the zeitgeist. She doesn't always get credit for it.

"There is no win for a company to discuss it," says Jane Buckingham, head of Los Angeles–based forecasting company Trendera. "Either the clients have been burned by a trend forecaster or, if they've had success, then they would feel they have to give the credit to the forecaster."

These days, Edelkoort spends much time analyzing the recession. It differs from past crises, she says: "Because the financial institutions screwed up, we don't feel the enormous guilt we felt in former crises. The previous reaction was to go back to frugality, back to basics." This time, Edelkoort says, we are drawn to shine, metallic colors and eccentricity, upbeat trends that are "very unusual for a crisis." Overall, our main reaction to this crisis will be an urgent need for authenticity, "of things that are real," she says, as the shadows lengthen in her serene Paris living room and one of her cats stretches out on a nearby sofa. "It's amazing we are still what we are," Edelkoort says pragmatically. "We have weathered an enormous storm."

chapter 2

Textile Design and Product Development

Have you ever wondered who created the plaid pattern on your shirt or the crazy rubber-ducky print on your bathrobe? Somebody has to be the creative force behind these designs, and that somebody is a textile designer. A textile designer creates original designs for the fabrics used in all sorts of industries. Textile design is a combination of visual arts and technical concerns. **Textile design** is the process of creating patterns, motifs, or surface interest for knitted, woven, or printed fabrics. Pattern and print designs are evaluated in terms of how they can be combined with printing, knitting, weaving, embossing, and embroidery processes. Textile designers often specialize in one type of textile or another (e.g., knits or wovens), and collaborate with textile colorists. A textile colorist works with a design to determine **colorways**, the specific color selections for a particular pattern or print; these are sometimes referred to as a *color palette*. Figure 2.1 provides an example of a colorway for a woven print.

These two creative positions are examples of the numerous career paths in the textile industry, which is a high-touch, high-tech industry. In the high-tech sector of the textile industry, there are a number of other career options, including textile engineering and textile production. A textile engineer works with designers to determine how designs can be applied to a fabric. A textile technician works with the issues that are directly related to the production of piece goods, such as finishing. Newly constructed knit or woven fabric must pass through

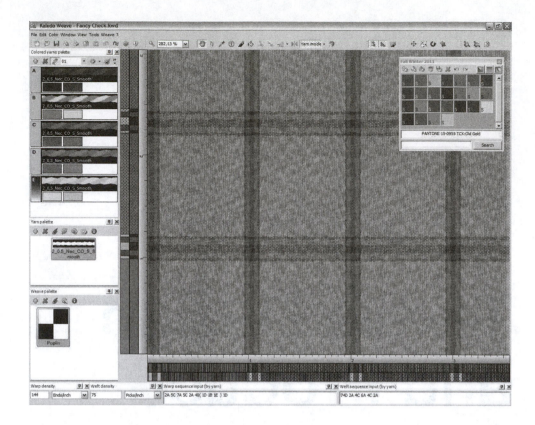

Figure 2.1 Example of a colorway for a woven print.

various finishing processes to make it suitable for its intended purpose. **Finishing** enhances the appearance of fabric and also adds to its suitability for everyday use or hard wear. Finishes can be solely mechanical, solely chemical, or a combination of the two. Finishes that simply prepare the fabric for further use, such as scouring and bleaching in blue jeans, for example, are known as **general finishes**. **Functional finishes**, such as durable press treatments, impart special characteristics to the cloth.

Job opportunities in textile production have dramatically declined in recent years due to inexpensive labor costs overseas. United States fashion companies now, more than ever, outsource much of their production work to companies in foreign countries. **Outsourcing** refers to having an aspect of a company's work performed by nonemployees in another company and, perhaps, in another country. Most outsourced jobs in the textile industry are low-paying production positions in countries with lower labor costs than those in the United States, such as those in the Pacific Rim, as well as South and Central America. The majority of American textile companies design domestically, but they outsource goods internationally to take advantage of the free-trade agreements with low-wage countries. However, the dramatic decline in U.S. production jobs in the textile industry has been offset by creative and scientific tracks in design and product development.

In this chapter, the creative and scientific career opportunities in textile design and textile technology is examined. Whether one has a creative personality and an eye for pattern and color or a scientific mind that excels in engineering and production, there is a job path in the textiles field that can provide a fulfilling career.

Fashion Director

A **fashion director** for a textile company is responsible for determining the trends, colors, themes, and textures for **piece goods**, or fabrics, that the firm will feature for a specific season. Fashion directors are primarily interested in identifying the most important fashion trends for their companies and communicating these trends to textile designers, production managers, and customers. Fashion directors often work with trend forecasting firms to determine trend possibilities in color, form, theme, and, of course, fabric for each season.

Qualifications

The following is a list of qualifications for a career as fashion director.

- **Education:** A bachelor's degree in textiles, fashion design, fashion merchandising, visual arts, or a related field is a minimum requirement for employment as a fashion director.

- **Experience:** The majority of fashion directors moved up the ladder from within the ranks. Many of them were textile designers, product developers, or buyers before obtaining key positions as fashion directors.

- **Personal characteristics:** The fashion director often has similar characteristics to the trend forecaster: curiosity, strong communication skills, a strong visual sensibility, leadership abilities, a good understanding of who the customers actually are, and the ability to work with a variety of constituencies—from designers to production managers to technical assistants.

Career Challenges

The challenges of the fashion director's career relate to two primary areas: securing the job and keeping it. Fashion coordinators are expected to have a strong foundation of work experience in the industry. It takes time, skill, and effort to be promoted through a variety of positions, from technical textile designer to product developer to buyer. The best and the brightest climb quickly up the career ladder. Once in the position of fashion director, there is a great deal of pressure to be right—to be accurate about the color, pattern, style, and theme trends. If, for example, a fashion director determines that olive green is the color for a season and it bombs at the retail level, the company may lose a great deal of money from a high investment in olive green fabrics. As a result of this error, this fashion director may be searching for a new job. Additionally, the fashion director must collaborate successfully with a wide variety of people— designers, production personnel, and clients. It takes a person with a well-balanced personality and excellent communication skills to work effectively with so many different people.

Textile Designer

Textile designers create the images, patterns, colors, textures, weaves, and knits of the fabrics we wear and use, from our clothing and interiors to our automobiles and awnings (Figure 2.2). They can be classified as surface designers; knitters, weavers, or embroiderers for industries ranging from apparel to upholstery. To assist in textile design, there are **print services**, companies that sell art that becomes print designs to mills, wholesalers, product developers, and retailers. Many textile designers utilize **computer-aided design (CAD)**, which is the process of developing garments, prints, and patterns on a computer screen. This process has greatly influenced the field of textile design, as it provides faster, more varied, and more personalized design options in textiles than were possible in past years. Technological advances in CAD software and digital printing, several of which will be presented later in this chapter, offer unlimited creative opportunities to designers. For instance, a customer can now have the photograph of her pet pug transferred to canvas, which will then be used to create a handbag. An image of a Parisian street scene can be scanned and printed on fabric that will later become bedroom curtains. Once the print or pattern is developed, a strike-off is produced by the textile manufacturer. A **strike-off** is a test sample of printed fabric made to show and verify color and pattern before entering into production on larger quantities. Figure 2.3 shows a digitally printed textile design while Box 2.1 provides information on the development of digital textile design and some of its designers.

A computer-aided textile designer likely knows how to paint and draw well, but works specifically on the computer to create designs. There are a number of specialized career paths that a textile designer can take; these include working with wovens, knits, or prints. For example, a textile designer may choose to focus on fibers and processes that are commonly used for knit goods such as sweaters, as illustrated in Figure 2.4. Another textile designer may decide to specialize in creating textile prints for woven fabrics by painting, or using CAD to create a **croquis**, as depicted in Figure 2.5, a rendering or miniature visual of a textile pattern or print for a garment or an accessory, such as a scarf or handbag. The **assistant textile designer**

Figure 2.2 Italian textile designer Donatella Ratti with fabric swatches of her work.

Figure 2.3 A digitally printed textile design by Basso and Brooke.

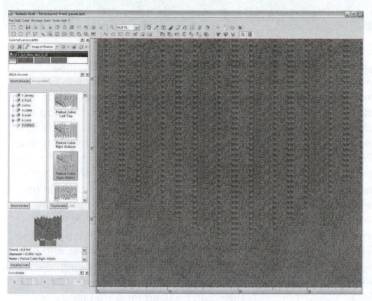

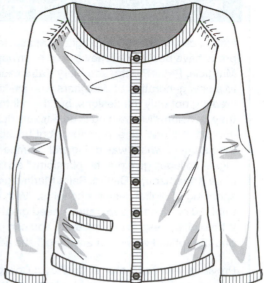

supports the textile designer in accomplishing all these tasks. What is the most important personal trait needed to be a successful textile designer? The key characteristic is to possess a mind that is simultaneously creative, business-oriented, and technically savvy.

Textile Stylist

A **textile stylist** is the creative person who modifies existing textile goods, altering patterns or prints that have been successful on the retail floor to turn them into fresh, new products. The textile stylist may resize the image or develop new colorways for the modified textile print or pattern, and may collaborate with a textile colorist to accomplish this task.

Textile Colorist

A **textile colorist** chooses the color combinations that will be used in creating each textile design. Colorists frequently travel to fashion markets and belong to color forecasting organizations to stay on top of current and future color trends. There is a wide range of industries in which textile designers, stylists, and colorists are employed; they include the following:

- Knitted and woven textiles, used to make clothes and soft-good products, as well as upholstered products, such as home furnishings and automotive seats

- Rugs and carpets

- Prints for wallpapers, paper goods, flooring, or tiles

Box 2.1 Tech Talk: The Fabric as the Designer's Canvas

Lights, cameras, fabrics...Digitally manipulated prints have become big news on the runways. Martin Margiela, Peter Pilotto, and Mary Katrantzou belong to a new generation of designers who are literally creating not only the designs, but the printed fabrics they envision. "My training is as a textile designer and in traditional screen printing, but because of the nature of what I was doing with trompe l'oeil, digital collages give greater plasticity," explains Mary Katrantzou, a Central Saint Martins graduate, speaking of digital design's benefits. "With a screen print, 10 or 15 color separations need great expertise. With digital, there is no limitation. You can print a photographical version of anything," she adds.

Previously an instructor at the Royal College of Art and now a fabric consultant for Louis Vuitton in Paris, Susannah Handley compares the difference between traditional and digitally printed textiles as being similar to that of painting and photography. She tells the *International Herald Tribune*: "Directly from computer to cloth is how many patterns are realized these days—it is a more clinical, faster method with the advantage that an instant result can be achieved."

The inkjet printing technology used in digital printing was first patented in 1968. In the 1990s, inkjet printers became widely available for paper-printing applications. You likely have one on your desk right now. The technology has continued to develop and there are now specialized wide-format printers that can process a variety of substrates, everything from paper to canvas to vinyl, and, of course, fabric. While digital textile printing has been around for decades, it has only recently taken its place in the fashion industry. Digital textile printing provides the ability to print designs on fabric, directly from a PC or Mac. Inkjet printing is done on fabric in the same manner as it is completed on paper, and just as easily. This versatile technology is being used in many apparel and nonapparel markets. Digitally printed textiles can be used for a vast range of applications including apparel, handbags, footwear, umbrellas, flags and banners, exhibition signage, furniture, curtains, drapes, bedding, towels, wall coverings, and carpets or other floor coverings.

For some companies and some products, digital textile printing can significantly reduce the costs associated with screen printing on textiles.

Figure 2.6 Digital printing technologies continue to offer faster production and may grow to become the technology that provides the majority of the world's printed textiles.

Box 2.1 Tech Talk: The Fabric as the Designer's Canvas (continued)

Presently, the textile industry produces the majority of its 34 billion square yards of printed textile fabric by screen printing, also referred to as analog textile printing. However, as we move through the digital age, developments in the digital printing of paper are being adapted more and more for the textile market. Inkjet textile printing is growing, while growth in analog textile printing remains stagnant. As digital print technologies continue to offer faster production and larger cost-effective print runs, digital printing may grow to become the technology that provides the majority of the world's printed textiles. Currently, digital printing on textiles has a number of advantages over traditional textile printing methods, as follow:

- Lower production costs for short runs

- High productivity due to shorter lead times

- Fast turnaround

The only special requirement is that the fabrics used must be pretreated to hold the ink better and reproduce a wider range of high-quality hues. There are various types of treatments according to the fabrics and the inks being used.

Unlimited creative opportunities are often at the top of the designer's list when it comes to digital textile printing. Think about printing photographs on fabrics, using art as inspiration, creating a color palette that is unique to your design collection, and customizing products to meet an individual customer's desires. Digital printing on fabrics has also opened new opportunities for designers, manufacturers, merchandisers and salespersons. For example, it is now possible to print a small piece of fabric, or enough for a garment, to create a sample of a new design.

Sources:

Jessica Bumpus, April 13, 2010. http://www.vogue.co.uk/news/daily/100413-the-digital-print-revolution-.aspx

http://www.suite101.com/content/digital-textile-printing-a215629#ixzz1Ducl0Sg8

http://www.fashion-incubator.com/archive/introduction-to-digital-fabric-printing/

Ujiie, H., ed. *Digital Printing of Textiles.* Centre of Excellence in Digital Ink Jet Printing, Philadelphia University, Woodhead Publishing Series in Textiles No. 53

The responsibilities of textile designers, stylists, and colorists are as follows.

- Interacting with customers (e.g., apparel manufacturers or designers) to understand their needs and interpret their ideas accurately

- Collaborating with marketing, buying, and technical staff members, as well as design colleagues

- Understanding how textiles will be used, what properties textiles need to function optimally, and how the addition of color dyes or surface treatments will affect these properties

- Conducting research for ideas and inspiration, from antique embroidery to modern architecture to children's storybooks

- Experimenting with texture and pattern as it relates to color

- Producing design or color ideas, sketches, and samples and presenting them to customers

- Producing designs or color options for designs using CAD software

- Checking and approving samples of completed items

- Working to meet deadlines

- Working within budgets

- Keeping up to date with new fashions and population trends—current and projected

- Staying on top of new design and production processes

- Attending trade and fashion shows

Textile designers, stylists, and colorists need to consider such factors as how the designs will be produced, how the finished articles will be used, the quality of the materials used, and the budgets. They work standard hours, but they need to be flexible to meet deadlines. They are based in studios or offices. Prospective employers require a strong and relevant portfolio of work for review. Employers include large manufacturing companies and small, exclusive design houses. Some textile designers, stylists, and colorists are self-employed.

Qualifications

Requirements for employment in textile design, stylist, or colorist positions include the following:

- **Education:** A bachelor's degree in textiles, visual arts, computer-aided design, graphic design, fashion design, or a related discipline is a minimum requirement.

- **Experience:** Entry-level design positions provide the ideal starting place for college graduates. Additional experience in technical design (i.e., CAD) and color will assist the candidate in moving up the career ladder. Box 2.2 and Figure 2.7 describe Lectra's widely used Kaledo CAD program for textile design.

- **Personal characteristics:** Flexible computer skills; a strong visual sense for color, texture, and pattern; a creative personality; knowledge of how textiles are produced; effective business skills; an awareness of fashion trends; a practical understanding of skills such as sewing, knitting, weaving, and embroidery; and knowledge of the target consumer help make the textile designer, stylist, and colorist successful.

Career Challenges

The challenges for textile designers, stylists, and colorists are similar. They must interpret the trends designated by the fashion director. Sometimes, converting the words of the fashion director into the images the director envisions can be difficult. Textile designers, stylists, and colorists also must be aware of the technical requirements of fabric development, such as the printing requirements, durability, and application of finishes. Most important, they are often under pressure to meet quick deadlines and work within budget constraints.

Box 2.2 Textile Technology Program: Lectra's Kaledo

Lectra is the world leader in software, CAD/CAM equipment, and associated services designed specifically for industries using textiles, leather, industrial fabrics, and composites to manufacture their products. Its world markets include fashion (e.g., apparel, accessories, and footwear), automotive (e.g., car seats, interiors, and airbags), and furniture, as well as a wide range of other industries. Based in France with 1,400 employees worldwide, Lectra serves 23,000 customers in more than 100 countries. Lectra's products are created for customers to automate, simplify, and accelerate product design, development, and manufacturing. For the fashion industry, the company also facilitates the planning and management of the entire product life cycle.

In 2009, Lectra introduced the new version of Kaledo V2R1. The new Kaledo brings design, product development, marketing, and management teams together, helping them to collaborate on developing trends and collections. Kaledo includes modules to create highly realistic simulations of prints, weaves, and knits, and to develop variations in just a few mouse clicks. "Fashion companies today really have to evolve, as the market has changed. They are under enormous pressure to produce attractive, original styles at reasonable prices, and to do so faster and more frequently than before," explains Daniel Harari, CEO of Lectra. "The result of more than 30 years in technological design solutions and our collaboration with some of the biggest names in fashion, Kaledo is an unprecedented step forward which will allow our customers to reach previously unequalled levels of productivity."

Designers are now expected to produce profitable and technically feasible collections more frequently, while at the same time displaying more creativity.

How does Kaledo help designers and product developers meet this new goal?

- Product developers and designers can develop new items and collections using existing elements, capitalizing on their proven styles while taking new trends into account.

- They can respond to requests for designs or modifications in just a few hours, ensuring quality and fit while limiting costs. Kaledo halves the time designers spent on repetitive tasks.

- Kaledo sits on a platform that unites all of the company's teams and design-related activities, which improves the design process.

- The large files commonly used in the fashion business can now be handled in record time.

- Users are able to save and organize Adobe Illustrator files straight into the Kaledo database.

Time saved, costs reduced, creativity increased, and work efficiency improved—Kaledo is maintaining a leadership position in the textile and fashion design sector of the fashion industry.

Source: www.lectra.com

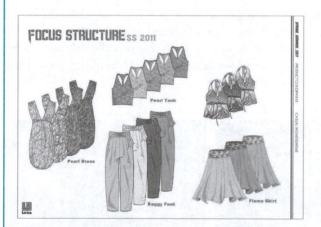

Figure 2.7 Lectra's widely used Kaledo CAD program is used for textile and apparel design.

Textile Technician

A **textile technician** either supervises the production facilities of a company or oversees the production as it is done by a **contractor**, a firm that is hired to manufacture the product line, domestically or abroad. If a textile company owns its manufacturing facility, the textile technician is responsible for the smooth running of the equipment used in textile production to maximize production (Figures 2.8a–c). If a textile company contracts its production out to another company, the textile technician works with the contractor to accomplish these goals. The primary responsibilities of the textile technician are as follows.

- Overseeing the regular routine maintenance of equipment, or the efficient production of the contractor

- Checking performance levels of equipment and/or contractors for optimal production

- Carrying out regular checks on production, spotting any difficulties and dealing with them before they become problematic

In a large textile factory, a technician may specialize in one type of production technique, such as knitting or weaving; however, in a smaller company, the responsibilities of the technician may be more wide-ranging. Technicians work approximately 40 hours a week, sometimes on shifts.

Qualifications

Requirements for employment as a textile technician include the following:

- **Education:** A bachelor's degree in textile technology, textile production, computer science, textile engineering, industrial technology, or a related field is required.

Figures 2.8a–c
A textile technician checks performance levels of equipment and/or contractors for optimal production.

- **Experience:** A number of textile technicians begin in entry-level technical design positions. They may move up into management of a team of technical designers that covers specific merchandise classifications, such as menswear or children's wear. Some technicians move into management or into specialized areas, such as quality control and research.

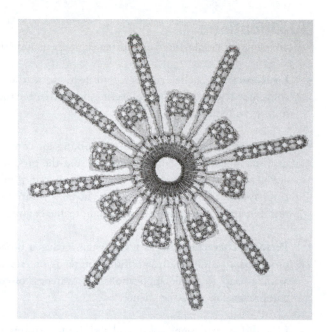

Figure 2.9
Enlarged image
of a crochet-look
bioimplantable
surgical patch.

- **Personal characteristics:** High levels of technical knowledge and computer skills are extremely important personal qualifications in this career path. Strong practical and problem-solving skills are also essential. A thorough understanding of textile applications and usage assists the textile technician in making decisions about product development.

Career Challenges

Textile technicians face the challenge of understanding and anticipating the continually changing technologies in textile design and production. Deadlines are a constant challenge. Communicating and problem solving with a variety of co-workers in different divisions, such as design and production, require a proactive approach, patience, and flexibility by textile technicians.

Textile Engineer

Manufacturers are merging textiles with technology to create new products for the market. For instance, instead of being just wrinkle-resistant, fabrics have become truly wrinkle-free through a process patented by TAL Corporation of Hong Kong. The process involves baking a special coating onto the fabric, as well as innovative use of adhesives along the seams to prevent puckering. Other fabrics are coated with Teflon to resist stains. Materials have been developed to change color with body temperature changes, which is particularly appealing for hospital use. Figure 2.9 shows an additional example of innovative fiber technology. The career path that directly relates to these new products is that of textile engineer. A **textile engineer** works with designers to determine how designs can be applied to a fabric while considering practical variables such as durability, washability, and colorfastness. A person in this position will have a background in textile science that may include chemistry and manufacturing, in addition to textile analysis.

Qualifications

Requirements for employment as a textile engineer include the following:

- **Education:** A bachelor's degree in textiles, textile technology, textile production, computer science, textile engineering, industrial technology, or a related discipline is a minimum requirement.

- **Experience:** Many textile engineers working for companies that own and operate their own manufacturing facilities move up from the production line to this position. Textile engineers working with firms that contract out production may have a greater job emphasis on information technology in their positions. A number of textile engineers begin in apprentice positions as assistant textile engineers.

- **Personal characteristics:** A textile engineer has a broad knowledge of how textiles are produced. In addition, this position requires an understanding of technical considerations as they relate to textile applications, an awareness of consumer wants and needs, and a comprehension of textile science.

In addition to design, color, and technical positions in the textile industry, there are ancillary career paths. The resource room director or reference librarian and the account executive are two career paths that relate to the textile industry, yet require different sets of skills and backgrounds from those of the creative and scientific positions.

Resource Room Director/Reference Librarian

Many large companies maintain a resource room, or reference library, of textile samples, source books and magazines, Internet resources, print and pattern images, and, possibly, actual garments constructed from the company's fabrics or those of competitors. As portrayed in Figure 2.10, these items are used by fashion directors, designers, technicians, and sales representatives for design inspiration and reference. The **resource room director** oversees the procurement, organization, and removal or replacement of these materials. Some companies, such as large apparel manufacturers, fashion publishers, and fiber/fabric houses, maintain reference libraries. The **reference librarian** is responsible for managing the inventory of books and resources and procuring new ones.

Qualifications

Requirements for employment as a resource room director or reference librarian include the following:

- **Education:** A bachelor's degree in textiles, fashion merchandising, fashion design, or a related discipline is a minimum requirement.

- **Experience:** For recent graduates with work experience in fashion retailing and textiles, strong academic performances, and impressive references, these can be entry-level positions. Some resource room directors or reference librarians later move into the design divisions of firms. Exposure to the references of a particular firm helps build the potential designer's background.

- **Personal characteristics:** Strong organizational skills, effective time management, first-rate communication skills, and attention to detail are personal qualities that fit the position of resource room director or reference librarian.

Career Challenges

Managing a resource room or reference library can be a daunting task. There is a constant flow of new acquisitions that need to be inventoried, labeled, and stored, often in minimal space. There must be a high level of organization for the resource room director or reference librarian to be able to pull samples quickly for the fashion director or designer who needs them immediately.

Figure 2.10 Resource rooms, also called reference libraries, hold items that are used by fashion directors, designers, technicians, and sales representatives for design inspiration and reference.

Account Executive

An **account executive**, also referred to as *sales* or *manufacturer's representative*, sells to textile manufacturers and manages accounts. The account executive is responsible for the sales of textiles and usually is assigned to a specific territory, such as the southern or midwestern United States. As illustrated in the classified advertisement of Figure 2.11, account executives can

WANTED: TEXTILE SALES REPRESENTATIVE

JOB SNAPSHOT:
Location: New York, NY
Base Pay: $90,000 to $100,000 per year, plus benefits
Employee Type: Full-time
Industry: Fashion - Apparel – Textile Manufacturing
Manages Others: No
Job Type: Sales and business development
Education: 4-year degree
Experience: At least 5 years
Travel: Up to 50 percent

DESCRIPTION:
A global textile manufacturer seeks sales manager of textiles. Territory is international.

SUMMARY:
This position will be responsible for developing apparel textiles to the apparel industry sector worldwide.

RESPONSIBILITIES:
Receives orders from clients, coordinates with factories based on the orders received, imports finished products, and sells them to clients.
- Develops, implements, and revises sales strategy and tactics for customers.
- Develops and implements both short term and long range plans to expand sales.
- Maintains contact with customers in person, by the telephone, and in writing, to promote the sale and use of the company products in the territory.
- Develops, implements, and revises sales strategy and tactics for customers.

REQUIREMENTS AND PREFERENCES:
- Bachelor's degree in textile or business related field preferred.
- 5 years minimum of sales experience in the textile industry.
- Sales experience in casual wear, sportswear and women's suits preferred.
- Strong communication skills.
- Good computer skills in MS office.
- Chinese language skills are helpful, but not necessary.

NOTE: Please send your resume in MS Word format with your salary requirements.

Figure 2.11
As illustrated in this classified advertisement, account executives are responsible for the sales of a company's textiles and the solicitation and maintainence of accounts.

be paid in several ways: a salary, commission, quota, or a combination of these (examined in Chapter 6, page 132). This is a great career for someone who prefers working independently and enjoys business, budgets, and sales, as well as the textile, fashion, and home furnishing markets.

Qualifications

Qualifications include the following:

- **Education:** A bachelor's degree in fashion merchandising, general business administration, or marketing is preferred.

- **Experience:** Retail or wholesale sales experience is most often required; however, working as an assistant to an account executive is an excellent way to open the door to this career path.

- **Personal characteristics:** A strong understanding of accounting, effective sales skills, good communication abilities, and excellent follow-up skills are important attributes of successful account executives.

Examples of Companies Employing Textile Designers and Product Developers

There are a number of large companies that employ textile personnel, from designers to resource room managers. Many of these firms are located in New York City; some have satellite offices in Dallas, San Diego, and Atlanta, as well as cities abroad. Next, eight of the top textile firms are examined, encompassing fur as a type of textile.

Cotton Incorporated

Cotton Incorporated is an information center for cotton and cotton-blend fibers and textiles. It provides fabric, color, and trend information for textile producers, soft goods and soft-good products for manufacturers, designers, and retailers. Working closely with Cotton Council International, Cotton Incorporated conducts research and promotion for cotton and cotton products with the primary goal of increasing the demand for and profitability of U.S. cotton and its products, as illustrated in Figure 2.12. The company offers technical services, such as fiber processing, fabric development, dyeing and finishing, and cotton quality management assistance. Information services provide data on cotton supply and demand, fiber quality, and consumer research trends. To keep cotton on the runway, Cotton Incorporated's fashion services provide timely trend publications and conduct live trend presentations with leading forecasters, designers, and sourcing specialists, highlighting the company's trend research and supplier information. Cotton Incorporated World Headquarters is located in North Carolina. Offices are located worldwide, including New York, Mexico City, Osaka, Singapore, and Shanghai. The company's Web site, www.cottoninc.com, provides corporate information, research reports, and employment opportunity postings.

Figure 2.12 Cotton Incorporated conducts research and promotion for cotton and cotton products with the primary goal of increasing the demand for and profitability of U.S. cotton and its products.

Australian Wool Services Limited (The Woolmark Company)

With over 60 years of expertise in the wool industry and textile innovation, Australian Wool Services Limited is the world's leading wool fiber textile organization. The company provides unique global endorsement through ownership and licensing of the Woolmark, Woolmark Blend, and Wool Blend brands. The Woolmark Company, a subsidiary of Australian Wool Services, specializes in the commercialization of wool technologies and innovations, technical consulting, business information, and commercial testing of wool fabrics. If you check the label of any quality wool or blended wool item you own, you are likely to find one of the famous Woolmark symbols, as illustrated in Figure 2.13.

These brands and their corresponding brandmarks are protected by strict and extensive control checks to ensure product quality. Australian Wool Services Limited operates globally, working with textile processors, designers, and retailers in both the apparel and interior textile markets.

Fur Council of Canada

The Fur Council of Canada is a national, nonprofit organization incorporated in 1964, representing people working in every sector of the Canadian fur trade. This includes fur producers, auction houses, processors, designers, craftspeople, and retail furriers. The goals of the Fur Council programs include the following:

• Encouraging linkages between designers and other sectors of the fashion industry

• Sponsorship of competitions for both professional designers and students in Canadian fashion colleges

• Promotion of the work of innovative Canadian fur designers through advertising in top national and international fashion publications

• Providing accurate information about the Canadian fur trade to consumers, educators, and the public to counter criticisms that the industry's practices are cruel to animals. For example, in Canada, trappers must pass a mandatory course in which they learn how to use new humane trapping methods and how to apply the principles of sustainable use established by wildlife officials and biologists.

The Fur Council of Canada can be further investigated on its Web site at www.furcouncil. com, as featured in Figure 2.14.

North American Fur and Fashion Exposition

In addition to headquartering the Fur Council, Canada also is the site of a major international fur market. The North American Fur and Fashion Exposition in Montreal (NAFFEM) is the largest fur and outerwear fashion fair of its type in North America and one of the most important fur fashion marketing events in the world. For over 20 years, NAFFEM has attracted thousands of professional buyers from the world's finest specialty boutiques and department stores with its wide array of luxury furs, boutique furs, shearlings, leathers, cashmere, and accessories. During the annual trade show, there are over 200 exhibitors representing designer labels and upscale women's and men's outerwear in fur and precious fabrics. The lines range from formal looks to casual wear, sportswear, and streetwear. More

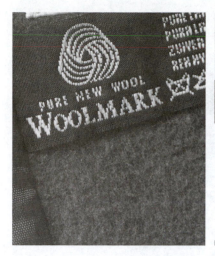

than half of the buyers viewing the lines of these exhibitors come from across the United States and abroad. There is also an area of the trade show that features unique international accessory collections, including handbags, gloves, scarves, hats, wraps, and jewelry. NAFFEM is organized and managed by the Canadian Fur Trade Development Institute (CFTDI) and can be researched online at www.naffem.com.

Mohair Council

The Mohair Council is an organization exclusively dedicated to mohair, the fleece of the Angora goat. Established in 1966, the Mohair Council concentrates on marketing, education, and research as it relates to the mohair industry. The Mohair Council was created for mohair producers and is still financially sustained primarily by producers. It is a nonprofit organization funded by interest and dividend dollars from the now defunct Wool Act, a current voluntary producer mohair assessment program, and funds from the U.S. Department of Agriculture.

The council headquarters is located in San Angelo, Texas, on the edge of Edwards Plateau in the southwest part of the state. This rugged ranching region is prime goat country and has long been home to many of the finest Angora goat breeding flocks in the world. Ninety percent of the U.S. Angora goat population grazes within a 150-mile radius of the Mohair Council's national headquarters, making Texas the primary mohair region of the United States. The United States has developed into one of the three largest mohair-producing nations in the world with an annual production in excess of 2.4 million pounds. The other principal mohair sources are South Africa and Turkey.

The main function of the Mohair Council is to promote American mohair and to find viable worldwide markets for this unique commodity. To market its product, the Mohair Council has a team of 11 professionals who travel the world in search of profitable foreign markets for American mohair. These individuals meet one-on-one with prospective buyers, discover their needs, and then work to put the mohair buyer and supplier together.

Another objective of the Mohair Council is to educate designers, manufacturers, retailers, and consumers about mohair and mohair products, as illustrated in Figure 2.15. For example, did you know that as a decorating fabric, mohair is valued for its flame resistance and high sound absorbency? It is ideal for public places such as theaters, hotel lobbies, and offices, as well as homes. In addition, mohair draperies are effective insulators, keeping heat in during cold

Figure 2.13 If you check the label of any quality wool or blended wool item you own, you are likely to find one of the famous Woolmark symbols, as shown here.

Figure 2.14 The Fur Council of Canada can be further investigated on its Web site at www.furcouncil.com.

Figure 2.15 An objective of the Mohair Council is to educate designers, manufacturers, retailers, and consumers about mohair and mohair products.

Figure 2.16 Cone Industries provides internship opportunities in textile production with a focus on environmental protection.

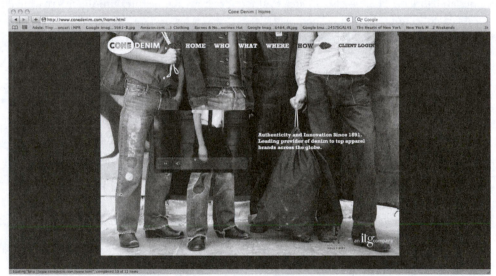

weather and serving as a barrier against hot outdoor temperatures in the summer. The Mohair Council's Web site is www.mohairusa.com.

Cone Mills

Cone Mills, LLC, is one of America's leading textile manufacturers. Cone Mills is a privately held company owned by W. L. Ross and Company as part of the International Textile Group. It is headquartered in Greensboro, North Carolina, with five manufacturing facilities located in North Carolina and Mexico. The company operates regional sales offices in Greensboro, New York, Dallas, Los Angeles, and San Francisco. Established in 1891, Cone Mills aims to be the largest producer of denim fabrics in the world. It has been selling denim and casual sportswear fabrics internationally for over 45 years, serves markets in over 35 countries, and is the largest U.S. exporter of denim and apparel fabrics. Cone Industries has a strong interest in and commitment to safeguarding the environment. The company provides internship opportunities in textile production and environmental protection. As illustrated in Figure 2.16, further information about the company and its job opportunities can be found at its Web site, www.conedenim.com.

Springs Global

Founded in 1887, Springs Global supplies leading retailers with coordinated home furnishings. The company headquarters is located in Fort Mill, South Carolina. Springs Global also produces and markets bed and bath products for institutional and hospitality customers, home sewing fabrics, as well as baby bedding and apparel products. This range of products is truly mind-boggling. Springs's bedding products include sheets and pillowcases, comforters and comforter accessories, bedspreads, blankets, bed skirts, quilts, duvet covers, pillow shams, decorative and bed pillows, and mattress pads. Its bath products include towels, bath and accent rugs, shower curtains, and ceramic and other bath accessories. Its window products include window hardware and decorative rods, blinds, shades, and soft window treatments such as drapes, valances, and balloon shades.

Through licensing agreements, Springs Global has extended its product lines to include kitchen and table accessories, flannel and knit sheets, blankets and throws, and lampshades. As shown in Figure 2.17, Springs Global's licensed brands include Kate Spade, Burlington House, American Lifestyle, Liz At Home, Harry Potter, Mary-Kate and Ashley, Coca-Cola, Serta, and NASCAR. Other major brands of Springs Global include Wamsutta, Springmaid, Regal, Beaulieu, Graber, Bali, Nanik, Dundee, Wabasso, and Texmade.

With such a vast array of product classifications, it is no surprise that Springs Global has approximately 30 manufacturing facilities in the United States, Canada, and Mexico and employs about 15,000 people. Five generations of the Springs family have led this private company. The company's Web site address is www.springs.com.

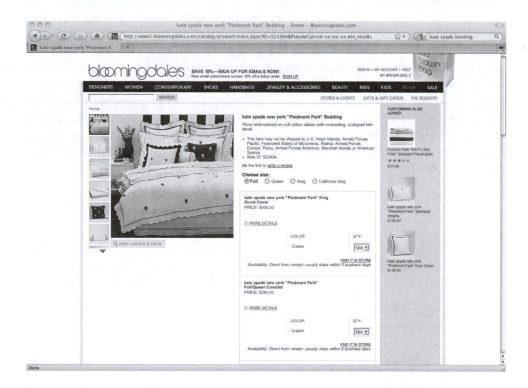

Figure 2.17 Springs Global's licensed brands include Kate Spade, as shown here on the Bloomingdale's Web site.

DuPont

When it was founded in 1802, E. I. du Ponte de Nemours was primarily an explosives company. Today, it is a company that has shown explosive growth. DuPont offers a wide range of innovative products and services for numerous markets, including agriculture, nutrition, electronics, communications, safety and protection, home and construction, transportation, and apparel. DuPont operates in more than 70 countries and employs over 60,000 people worldwide. It is a Fortune 500 company with revenues of $27.3 billion in 2004.

DuPont's mission includes research and development as high priorities. The company has more than 40 research, development, and customer service labs in the United States and more than 35 labs in 11 other countries. The productive results of DuPont's research are illustrated by its products. DuPont's brands include Teflon coatings, Corian solid surfaces, Kevlar high-strength material, and Tyvek housing protective material; DuPont's innovative fabrics run the gamut of uses from hospital and medical care applications to firefighters' gear and sportswear. The company can be located online at www.DuPont.com.

Summary

As fashion companies in the United States now, more than ever, outsource much of their production work to companies in foreign countries, domestic job opportunities in textile production have dramatically declined. The majority of American companies design domestically, but outsource goods internationally to take advantage of the free-trade agreements with low-wage countries. However, the loss in U.S. production jobs in the textile industry has been offset by creative and scientific tracks in design and product development, in addition to textile technology. Some of the key career tracks in the creative sector of textiles include fashion director, textile designer, textile stylist, and textile colorist. In the scientific and manufacturing areas of textiles, career options include textile engineer and textile technician. Additionally, there are ancillary career paths in textiles in a variety of areas such as reference libraries and sales. The director of a resource room or reference library for a fiber association, such as Cotton Incorporated, maintains the fabric samples, garments, books, and trade journals that company employees use for inspiration and reference. The account executive is the sales representative for a fabric producer, selling piece goods to clients, such as the designers and manufacturers of apparel, accessories, or home furnishings. Whether you are interested in sales, technology, or design, there are career opportunities in the **primary level** of the fashion industry, the sector that includes fiber, fabrics, and manufacturing.

Key Terms

account executive

assistant textile designer

colorway

computer-aided design (CAD)

contractor

croquis

fashion director

finishing

functional finish

general finish

outsourcing

piece goods

primary level

print service

reference librarian

resource room director

strike-off

textile colorist

textile design

textile designer

textile engineer

textile stylist

textile technician

Online Resources

www.artdesignfashion.com/textile/

www.dutchtextiledesign.com/

www.larsenfabrics.com/collections/

www.marimekko.com/

www.pierrefrey.com/

www.printsourcenewyork.com/

www.time.com/time/magazine/article/0,9171,1594161-1,00.html

www.texprint.org.uk/

www.textilerepublic.com/

www.textilesource.com/

Discussion Questions

1. In light of the trend toward outsourcing in textile production, what new career options do you believe will develop in the fiber and fabric sector of the fashion industry? What types of knowledge, training, and skills will best equip a job candidate to succeed in this industry over the next decade?
2. What are the differences between the textile designer, stylist, and colorist? The similarities?
3. Using the Internet, locate and describe two new technology programs, one that assists with textile design tasks and another that facilitates textile production.

Interview with a Textile Designer

By Jessie Cacciola, imprintmagazine, November 5, 2008; updated by Diana Martini, January 2011
http://www.imprintmagazine.org/life_and_style/professionals_textile_designer_diana_martini

Diana Martini graduated with degrees in textiles and art and design, which she fueled into a successful career in textile design. She has received multiple awards for her work, and has even been featured in several galleries. On the side, she runs a blog, Please Sir (www.pleasesirblog.blogspot.com), where she shares her daily inspirations.

When did you know you wanted to be a textile designer?

Art and design have always been present in my life, from drawing cartoons as a child to weaving sculptures in college. As a teenager I was surrounded by the large semiannual furniture market that came to High Point, North Carolina. My interest for textile design grew after visiting furniture showrooms and talking to industry leaders in the area. While attending North Carolina State University, I discovered the amazing program for art and textiles. I realized these degrees would allow me to pursue my interest in art and design, which naturally fell into textile design.

What is your day-to-day like?

Each day brings new challenges and learning opportunities. I love starting my day with a cup of tea and reading through design blogs and magazines. This helps to energize and stimulate my creativity. Throughout the day I design new patterns for the home, create storyboards to help communicate design ideas to customers, and follow up with my patterns. My company is fortunate to be attached to a textile plant, so when I design a pattern I can walk to the loom and see it being woven. I've developed a great appreciation for the textile process by having the chance to watch a product from beginning to end.

Was it what you imagined?

Yes and no. Going into textile design I knew I would be creating fabric, but I didn't imagine the paperwork and corporate regulations that came along with it. One thing that impacted me the most was designing for a customer versus designing for myself. I had to accept that there are budgets and the customer knows best! Cutting costs is a big issue for the textile industry due to the difficult economy and continuous outsourcing of textile production overseas.

What does your company do and how much involvement do you have with the creative process?

The company I work for manufactures and distributes textile fabrics to the furniture and upholstery industries. Typically, I receive designs and translate them into fabric. I feel my creativity emerges in the final fabric where I decide on a construction for the design (low or high end) and what type of yarns and colors to utilize. I still have to answer to management, but I've noticed that as my experience builds my involvement in the creative process grows.

How do you stay inspired?

I stay inspired by keeping my senses open to new objects, places, and people. I feel like I'm always working because my mind is continuously soaking up my surroundings and translating them into a pattern or new design project. Even the slightest detail, like the color of a leaf or the material on a purse, can be inspiring. Writing and documenting these inspirations on a blog has helped me expand my creativity and connect with other like-minded individuals. I can't say enough wonderful things about the blogging community; it is truly a breath of fresh air each day. Visiting interesting places like museums or flea markets is another way I reenergize my creative mind. I like to approach design with a childlike mentality and be open to all possibilities…and then push it a step farther.

Any other careers you considered? How would your ability in this one translate?

I enjoy being a textile designer, but I would also like a hands-on career with more creative challenges. Recently, I've been interested in working for a design magazine and trying my talents at interior

Interview with a Textile Designer (continued)

styling. I believe my experience in textile design would be complementary since I've worked on creating eye-catching compositions, color combinations, and building an overall design theme. Going from one design field to another seems exciting since I can bring a fresh perspective and continue to develop my skills. Either that or do something completely different like work on an organic farm! I think one could learn so much about themselves and nature, and then apply it to the world of design.

What are key steps to becoming a successful textile designer?

One of the most important steps to becoming a successful textile designer is having a desire and passion for fabric and pattern. Obtaining an education on the basics of textile design is also important. The world of fabrics is surprisingly complex; it is essential for a designer to understand the technical aspects of a knit, woven, and print pattern. Staying current with the latest textile technology and yarns is also beneficial because of the innovation it brings to the trade. Another key step is networking and playing up your own strengths. The textile community is small, so you should keep all doors open and not burn any bridges along the way. You never know when you might need help from a previous boss, coworker, or assistant.

What have you learned from your career about your life in general, and vice versa?

See and do. I believe there is magic in mixing disciplines, so take a cooking class, join a science club, and travel to new places. Taking yourself out of your comfort zone expands your imagination. Also, I've learned to keep creating. Even when times are tough it is important to feed your creative soul, which also means making time for yourself and doing the things you love.

chapter 3

Sourcing

There is a person whose job is to buy the materials that make up your favorite interview jacket, your great leather belt, or your comfortable reading chair. There is yet another person who locates the manufacturing facility that produces the jacket, belt, or chair. Both of these people are involved in the work of sourcing. **Sourcing** refers to one of two activities: (1) the task of locating the suppliers, or vendors, of components needed to make a product, or (2) the job of securing manufacturers to produce end products and then collaborating with the manufacturer, contractor, or vendor while the products are being created. A **vendor** is any firm, such as a manufacturer or a distributor, from whom a company purchases products or production processes. Sourcing includes the activities of determining the amount of product needed, negotiating the best possible price and discounts, scheduling deliveries, problem solving throughout the procurement and production activities, and following up on actual shipments to make certain that due dates are met and that quality control is maintained. Either way, sourcing takes a product from its conception stage to the sales floor or Web site.

Let's say a designer of an apparel line comes up with several amazing **collections**, or groupings of related styles. According to the designer's sketches, to actually make the illustrations a reality the company will need several tapestry fabrics for jackets, silk chiffons for blouses, and colored denim for bottoms. Additionally, there will be the need for faux fur for the detachable collars, buttons for the jackets and tops, lining fabrics, interfacing, belting, and zippers; the list goes on and on. In some companies, the designer and an assistant will locate the places from which to purchase these items. In larger companies, there may be buyers who source fabrics and related products for the items in the designer's line. The sourcing manager takes the designer's vision and helps turn it into reality.

Sourcing the Product

How do design companies locate the fabrics and other product parts necessary for producing their lines? There are career options that focus on sourcing fabrics and other product components. Fashion production planners, piece goods buyers, and findings buyers are three examples of these career paths. Sourcing may encompass buying goods domestically or abroad. If products are purchased from an overseas vendor and shipped to the United States, they are referred to as **imports**. In contrast, products that are bought by an overseas company from a vendor in the United States and sent out of the country are referred to as **exports**. Imports and exports are examined in further detail in the following discussion of sourcing careers.

Fashion Production Planner

Fashion production planners are sometimes referred to as "raw materials buyers." Their main task is material planning, anticipating all of the parts needed to make the final product. The primary responsibilities of fashion production planners follow:

- Reviewing forecasts of sales generated by the manufacturers' representatives and/or by analyzing past sales performance of line items

- Planning fabric production based on current orders and projected reorders

- Scheduling and monitoring works in progress

- Working with material manufacturers to determine the availability of goods

- Collaborating with key departments, such as design and product development, to anticipate future needs

- Meeting strict deadlines to keep shipments on time

Qualifications

A career as a fashion production planner requires the following qualifications:

- **Education:** A bachelor's degree in fashion merchandising, fashion design, business administration, marketing, international marketing, or a related field is a requirement.

- **Experience:** Skills in a similar role within the fashion manufacturing sector of the industry is a hiring plus. Knowledge of offshore raw materials planning and purchasing as it relates to sales forecasts is essential. Experience in a large and varied manufacturing fashion company would be highly regarded. An internship during college is an added bonus to post-graduate employment.

- **Personal characteristics:** The ability to communicate clearly is essential. Often, fabrics and findings are sourced overseas; therefore, a multilingual background may be extremely valuable. A few of the languages that are currently important in the sourcing field are Mandarin, Cantonese, Taiwanese, and Spanish.

Piece Goods Buyer

The **piece goods buyer** works for a company that uses textiles in the production of its final products. This can be an apparel company, a home furnishings firm, an automotive manufacturer, or an accessories producer. The responsibilities of a piece goods buyer include the following:

- Shopping for textile supplies at trade markets and through textile manufacturers' representatives (Figure 3.1)

- Planning the amount of fabric, referred to as **yardage**, to purchase from various sources or determining from which vendors the piece goods will be purchased and communicating with these vendors

- Coordinating with production managers who advise on the delivery status of purchase orders; a **purchase order (PO)** is a contract for merchandise between buyers, as representatives of their firms, and vendors

Figure 3.1 A piece goods buyer for an apparel manufacturer shops for textiles at trade markets and textile manufacturers' showrooms.

- Communicating with accounts payable on payments and financing, to include proof of payments, wire transfers, and letters of credit; a **letter of credit** is a document issued by a bank authorizing the bearer to draw a specific amount of money from the issuing bank, its branches, or associated banks and agencies. It allows importers to offer secure terms to exporters

- Working with warehouse managers on inventory management, such as availability and accessibility of fabrics

- Monitoring quality control by inspecting shipments and dealing with **chargebacks**, credits for damaged merchandise and returns on defective goods

An **assistant piece goods buyer** often works with the piece goods buyer to accomplish this long list of responsibilities and as training for the position of piece goods buyer in the future.

Qualifications

A career as a piece goods buyer requires the following qualifications:

- **Education:** A bachelor's degree in fashion merchandising, fashion design, textiles, or a related field is a minimum requirement.

- **Experience:** A great number of piece goods buyers are promoted from the position of assistant piece goods buyer; others move into piece goods buying from the textile design track.

- **Personal characteristics:** A piece goods buyer has excellent quantitative skills, which are needed for calculating cost of goods, delivery expenses, and yardage amounts. This person must be able to work effectively under pressure, have excellent follow-up and communication skills, and be a successful negotiator.

Findings and/or Trimmings Buyer

The **findings buyer** is responsible for ordering findings and trimmings. **Findings** include such product components as zippers, thread, linings, and interfacings. Findings are functional and may not be visible when viewing the final product.

Trimmings, however, are decorative components designed to be seen as part of the final product. Trimmings include buttons, appliqués, and beltings. The **trimmings buyer** is responsible for ordering these product components. Locating findings and trimmings is an important job in which timing is critical. Think about the production line, quality control, and the end product. If the findings buyer orders zippers that are too short, either the zippers will be installed and the customers won't be able to get into the skirts or production on the skirts will be halted until the correct zippers are received. If a button shipment is late, the trimmings buyer is held accountable as the entire production has to be held until it arrives. Figure 3.2 shows a photo of Tender Buttons, a well-known boutique in New York City.

Figure 3.2
On a tree-lined street in Manhattan is a tiny brick townhouse, Tender Buttons, the only shop in America devoted entirely to the sale of buttons.

Qualifications

The education, experience, and personal characteristics required for findings and/or trimmings buyers are as follows.

- **Education:** A bachelor's degree in fashion design, fashion merchandising, product development, or a related discipline is a minimum requirement.

- **Experience:** Most findings and trimmings buyers work as assistants to the buyers before moving into this position. Internship experience and employment in either the manufacturing or design sector of the fashion industry are beneficial to securing these positions.

- **Personal characteristics:** High attention to detail is a critical asset to findings and trimmings buyers. Understanding product construction, sewing techniques, and product quality are essential skills. The abilities to locate vendors and negotiate with them are critical, as is following up on deliveries.

Career Challenges

Planners and buyers of raw materials, piece goods, and findings and trimmings share similar job struggles. It can continually be a source of stress to follow up on shipments needed to meet deadlines. Negotiating with vendors for priority shipping and competitive pricing can be a challenge. Written and oral communication skills may be tested when the buyer is putting together a deal with an overseas supplier. Currency exchanges, shipping costs, language barriers, and cultural differences can contribute to communication breakdowns. Attention to detail and written agreements are critical to minimizing these challenges. Finally, the buyer in sourcing is faced with constantly recalculating costs of goods. Shipping prices can change overnight. Handling fees may be added. Taxes may change. The dollar may fluctuate in currency exchange. Reviewing costs is a task that must be reexamined from the time an order is placed until the products reach the receiving dock. Fortunately, most buyers in sourcing enjoy the quantitative work that demands a high level of attention to detail.

Sourcing Manager

In addition to the positions responsible for sourcing materials needed to create the end product, some large companies have a position available entitled sourcing manager, in which an individual is responsible for sourcing production. The **sourcing manager** communicates with the company manufacturing the product, referred to as the **contractor**. Sourcing managers work with overseas or domestic producers, discuss product specifications with them, and negotiate contracts. Next, controls need to be put into place to make certain that production is executed correctly by the outside vendor. After production begins, the sourcing manager monitors quality control and delivery schedules. Throughout the process, there are, more often than not, problems to be resolved.

Qualifications

Sourcing managers should possess the following qualifications:

- **Education:** A bachelor's degree in fashion merchandising, fashion design, product development, business administration, or a related field is a requirement.

- **Experience:** Strong knowledge of sewing and product construction is necessary for sourcing production, fabric, and findings. Also, a general technical knowledge of fabric use and construction is required. This is a position that requires prior work experience. Two to three years as a retail buyer or several years as a wholesale merchandiser provide a good background.

- **Personal characteristics:** Flexibility is often cited as the number one quality for the successful sourcing manager. One has to see far enough down the road to anticipate changes and potential problems and then be flexible enough to keep the work on track. Top sourcing managers are proactive, rather than reactive. Stamina is also a critical characteristic, as there are long hours that require tremendous focus and effort. Frequent travel may be required. Particularly for overseas travel, sensitivity to cultural differences is an asset. The abilities to handle stress, learn from experience, negotiate effectively, and maintain a sense of humor are additional helpful characteristics.

Box 3.1 is a sample of an online classified advertisement for a sourcing manager.

Merchandiser for a Manufacturer

The position of **merchandiser**, or *merchandise planner*, on the wholesaler's or manufacturer's side of the industry is very important to all departments, as this person works as the liaison between the design, production, and sales teams (Figure 3.3). One of the primary responsibilities of the merchandiser is to develop a merchandise line plan by month and by piece count or by **stock-keeping unit** (**SKU**), a type of identification data for a single product. Some of the other duties of the merchandiser for a manufacturer include:

- Determining top sellers, referred to as **volume drivers**, and essential programs, retail pricing, and fabric recommendations for the collections based on past retail selling history

- Shopping the market and competition and, later, presenting a merchandising strategy to the design team

Figure 3.3 One of the key duties performed by the merchandiser is shopping the market.

- Communicating changes in strategy, assortment planning, and allocation to technical, visual, and licensing teams

- Updating and maintaining the purchasing sheets on a weekly basis

- Providing input on budgets, sales, gross margin, and receipt flow

- Recommending line changes at department weekly meetings, based on **actual sales** trends as opposed to the sales plan for each style

- Identifying product opportunities for future seasons by translating trends

- Analyzing the current season's opportunities from retail sales

- Working with the sales teams to make sure their specific products needs are being addressed

Box 3.2 features a classified advertisement for a merchandiser, or merchandise planner.

Qualifications

Merchandise planners should possess the following qualifications:

- **Education:** A bachelor's degree in fashion merchandising, fashion design, product development, business administration, or a related field is a requirement.

Merchandise Planner—New York, NY

An international brand and a leader in the design, marketing, and distribution of premium lifestyle products for more than 40 years in four categories: apparel, home, accessories, and fragrances. Seeking a merchandise planner at corporate headquarters.

Purpose and Scope:

The merchandise planner is responsible for partnering with the merchandising team to create annual and seasonal merchandise plans, forecasting the business based on changes in strategy and business climate, and managing inventory to support forecasts for our newest online business. In addition, this individual will have the opportunity to work on special projects to support the strategic and operating initiatives critical to success of the Web site and our continued growth and profitability.

Responsibilities:

- Forecast sales, margin, and inventory turn by month, at a department/class level, and communicate business performance during the monthly forecast

- Partner with merchant team to analyze current sales trends and on order at a brand level and adjust the forecast accordingly

- Create department and category level quarterly hindsight reports to drive strategic assortment decisions for future quarters and in-season management

- Plan and project receipt flow for basic items to support sales forecasts

- Prepare weekly sales recaps to aid in business analysis

- Track current selling to the plan and provide analysis around promotional events, as needed

Job Requirements:
- Expertise in retail math; strong analytical skills

- Ability to make confident and independent recommendations and accountability for managing and achieving business goals

- Decision-making capability clearly driven by conceptualizing future opportunities and developing strategic business initiatives

- Creative, assertive, and solution-oriented approach when faced with difficult business performance and/or challenging directives from senior management

- Ability to influence, present, and defend a business argument both one-on-one and in a group setting

- Superb presentation and communication skills, both spoken and written

- Ability to prioritize and direct multiple activities

- High level of organizational skills and attention to detail

An equal opportunity employer, offering dynamic career opportunities with growth potential and a generous company discount.

- **Experience:** Strong knowledge of product components and product construction is necessary, as is general knowledge of production capabilities and technology. This position often requires prior work experience as a buyer or assistant merchandise planner. Applicants with work experience in both manufacturing and retailing have an edge over other candidates, as they have the ability to view the product from the manufacturer's and retail buyer's perspectives.

- **Personal characteristics:** Attention to detail, the ability to work accurately with numbers, and a futuring perspective are personal qualities that successful merchandise planners often have.

Career Challenges

The merchandiser (merchandise planner) must continually look ahead, preparing today for tomorrow's sales. It is a daunting task to be able to predict sales trends and to adjust production from slow-selling products into top-selling ones. Strong work relationships and effective communication skills help offset these challenges.

Import Production Coordinator

An **import production coordinator** is the apparel or home furnishings company's liaison with the manufacturer or contractor. The import production coordinator is involved in all aspects of the production process, works closely with the design team, and is the link between overseas factories (e.g., in China, Japan, Taiwan, India, and South America, to name a few locations) and the company's design and buying teams. The import production coordinator's main goal is to ensure on-time delivery and quality of production. This person must have strong analytical skills and materials-planning knowledge to review product forecasts and plan raw materials to manufacture domestically and internationally. Good communication, effective negotiating, and time-management abilities are key attributes, as problems often need to be resolved quickly and with consensus. Import production coordinators negotiate quality, price, and delivery dates of products and track the supply chain from sample production to bulk delivery. A more detailed listing of the main responsibilities of an import production coordinator follows.

- Scheduling sample and line production in collaboration with design team

- Coordinating sample production and communicating any changes to the factory

- Establishing and maintaining strong relationships with offshore suppliers

- Anticipating the length of time it will take goods to be shipped and received from factories abroad

- Knowing import and export laws and how to complete the necessary documents to ship and receive goods and understanding how to work with customs

- Completing final sign-off on samples to begin production

- Managing critical time to ensure on-time deliveries

- Updating in-house computer systems on styling information

- Monitoring the production process and updating management on any changes or needs to create quality products

- Having an eye for detail and quality

- Identifying and resolving issues quickly and with cost efficiency

- Having the accounting knowledge needed to determine **landed costs**, the actual price of goods after taxes, tariffs, handling, and shipping fees are added to the cost of goods

Assistant importers work for the import production coordinator and follow up on orders with overseas suppliers. They also communicate with freight companies and customs agents, process documents, and check pricing agreements. They may also be responsible for arranging payments to overseas suppliers and liaising with internal customers to ensure goods arrive as expected.

Qualifications

The required qualifications for the import production coordinator follow.

- **Education:** A bachelor's degree in fashion design, fashion merchandising, product development, business administration, or a related field is essential.

- **Experience:** To secure this position, a prospective employee will need a number of years in previous import production experience within the apparel or home furnishings industry. Often, the position of import production coordinator requires fluency in a foreign language (Cantonese, Japanese, Spanish, or Mandarin, to name a few). Import production coordinators will also need to have intermediate to advanced Microsoft Office skills; strong candidates are competent in Microsoft Word and Excel. Work experience may be obtained in the position of assistant importer. This position often requires someone who is willing and able to travel extensively. A proven background in importing, shipping, and client relationships is helpful.

- **Personal characteristics:** To be successful, import production coordinators need keen attention to detail, self-motivation, and the ability to work on a team. Excellent written, visual, and oral communication skills are required. They must be highly organized and able to work in a fast-paced environment.

Career Challenges

The sourcing manager, import production coordinator, and assistant importer are faced with the primary challenge of effective communication to ensure on-time deliveries, the best prices, and top-quality products. They are often juggling many balls, working with the numerous vendors, production managers, and designers simultaneously. While global travel may be an exciting adventure in the beginning of these careers, it can become a burden to pack a suitcase, jump on a plane to put out a production "fire," and return to the office, ready to work the next day. It takes a great deal of flexibility, stamina, and organizational skills to rise above the potential stress of a worldwide business operation.

Sourcing Career Options in the Global Community

The world has become one huge global market. Because many countries no longer produce all of the goods and services that they need and/or want, they have come to rely on one another to obtain what they cannot or choose not to produce. As this movement has evolved, the world's nations have become more economically interdependent. **Globalization**, the process of interlinking nations of the world with one another, is a growing trend in the fashion industry. **Global sourcing** refers to the process of locating, purchasing, and importing or exporting goods and services (Figure 3.4). When a retail buyer for a United States store, for example, buys leather handbags from Milan and has them shipped to the United States, his or her company imports them. The country that provides and ships out the goods—in this case, Italy—exports them. Professionals in the sourcing field must understand international trade guidelines for importing and exporting, as well as remain abreast of any updates to those guidelines.

Buyer for a Store-Owned Foreign Buying Office

There are two types of retail organizations that operate **store-owned foreign buying offices**: retailers that are large enough to use and pay for this ancillary operation, and stores with very special images, such as exclusive boutiques and designer emporiums. Buyers who work in store-owned foreign buying offices support and advise other buyers of their respective stores. (In Chapter 11, the career track of the retail buyer is examined.) The buyers for a company- or store-owned buying office survey the market looking for new trends. They recommend vendors and styles, develop catalogs and mailing pieces, and follow up on deliveries. Because they are employed by the retail store, they are, in essence, an extension of it. Buyers in many foreign buying offices are authorized to make purchases from vendors for the company, just as the domestic store buyers are when they shop the local markets. In some situations, the store buyers place purchase orders on the lots procured by the buyers of the foreign buying office. In other companies, the buyers of the foreign buying office place the orders and break down the merchandise to be shipped to the individual retail stores. The **breakdown** of merchandise refers to the segmentation of a purchase order into quantities by sizes and colors to prepare for shipping to specific store branches.

Figure 3.4 Global sourcing refers to the process of locating, purchasing, and importing or exporting goods and services from around the world.

Companies with foreign buying offices generally locate these offices in major fashion capitals such as Paris, London, Rome, Hong Kong, and Tokyo. Saks Fifth Avenue and Neiman Marcus are two examples of major retail operations that maintain store-owned foreign buying offices. Some large mass-merchandise chains also own foreign buying offices; Walmart and JCPenney are two examples. Smaller stores cannot afford to own and operate their own foreign buying offices. Instead, they may choose to subscribe to the services of independently owned resident buying offices with foreign buying divisions. Independent buying offices do not represent retail store competitors in the same city or local area. An example of this type of company is The Doneger Group in New York.

Foreign Commissionaire

Foreign commissionaires, or *foreign-owned independent agents*, usually have offices located in key buying cities overseas. Foreign commissionaires often represent both retailers and manufacturers. They are paid on a fee basis rather than at a monthly or annual rate. Usually, the commissionaires receive a percentage of the **first cost**, or wholesale price, in the country of origin. The **country of origin** refers to the nation in which the goods were located and purchased. While commissionaires provide many of the same services as store-owned foreign buying offices, their offices are often smaller than store-owned offices. They often have **market representatives**, or specialized buyers of individual merchandise classifications (for example, junior sportswear, children's wear, or menswear), who work closely with their client stores, keeping them up to date on new product offerings in the marketplace, recommending new vendors, and assisting them in locating new goods. A great amount of the market representative's time is spent following up on the client's purchase orders to make sure they are shipped on time and as ordered.

Qualifications

The following are qualifications foreign commissionaires should possess to achieve success in this area of employment.

- **Education:** A bachelor's degree in fashion design or fashion merchandising, business administration, marketing, international marketing, or a similar field is a minimum requirement.

- **Experience:** Many commissionaires begin working for a manufacturer, resident buying office, or a retail operation. Experience in wholesale and retail sales, as well as buying, provides a strong background for this career path. The position of market representative is one that requires a candidate with buying experience.

- **Personal characteristics:** The commissionaire must work with people all over the world. The ability and desire to travel extensively and work with persons from a wide range of cultures are important. Strong negotiation skills are valuable. Comprehension of product construction, quality, and design is a necessity. An understanding of import and export laws, shipping options, and finances is critical to this career path.

Importer—Company-Owned

Some retail store buyers may elect to purchase imported goods from United States–owned importing firms. **Importers** based in the United States shop international markets to purchase goods that will come together as their own "lines." The merchandise is purchased with themes, colors, and styling in mind to create cohesive collections that are displayed and presented to the retail store buyers. Shopping the collections of importers, such as those from markets in Morocco and Italy depicted in Figure 3.5, allows store buyers in the United States to purchase foreign fashion merchandise that would not be available to them for one or more of the following reasons: the cost of traveling abroad, the high minimum quantities often required to place purchase orders overseas, and the costs and time requirements of shipping merchandise into the country.

Qualifications
The fashion importer is required to meet the following qualifications:

- **Education:** A bachelor's degree in fashion design or merchandising, business administration, entrepreneurship, marketing, international marketing, or a similar field is a minimum requirement.

- **Experience:** Many fashion importers begin working for a manufacturer, either in sourcing or sales. Others have work experience as a retail store buyer. Retail sales experience during college provides an entry to retail buying or manufacturer's sales. Importers are responsible for their businesses. As a result, knowledge of business planning, finances, personnel, marketing, and operations is essential.

- **Personal characteristics:** Fashion importers must be leaders, people who can manage businesses and position them for growth. The abilities to manage time and stress, sell themselves and their product lines, and monitor finances are critical. Effective negotiation and follow-up skills are necessary. The ability to put a line together each season is a necessity. An understanding of import and export laws, shipping alternatives, landed costs, and different cultures is also critical to this career.

Career Challenges
The career challenges for professionals involved in fashion imports (e.g., a buyer from a store-owned foreign buying office, a foreign commissionaire/agent, and an importer for a company-owned office) include staying abreast of the restrictions and regulations of international trade, managing transactions with overseas suppliers, and planning for extended lead times to accommodate overseas deliveries. Many importers will agree that the best and easiest part of the job is locating great fashion products around the world. However, importers spend a large amount of time investigating the limitations on export quantities, communicating any needed modifications to the manufacturer, and getting the merchandise to their warehouses in the United States in a timely fashion. Building relationships with overseas vendors takes time, and it can make or break the success of an importer.

Licensing and Sourcing

Global sourcing has created a new fashion career path in licensing. Think of European designer names like Christian Dior, Chanel, Versace, and Gucci; American designers such as Donna Karan, Calvin Klein, and Ralph Lauren; American characters like Mickey Mouse,

Care Bears, and Barbie; or manufacturers such as Harley-Davidson, Nike, and Hershey's. All of these companies offer product lines that are not central to their primary product lines. For example, in addition to a Fat Boy motorcycle, you can purchase Harley-Davidson belts, apparel, and sunglasses. Another example of international appeal for character product lines can be found at EuroDisney SCA in Paris, which features a range of Disney character products. The Disney boutique on the Champs Elysées is a prime retail location for the French and tourists alike.

Many well-known celebrities, fashion designers, and companies offer alternative product lines by working with manufacturers to produce goods under their names. For example, Fossil Inc. produces a line of watches for Donna Karan International Inc. The timepiece line fits the Donna Karan image, coordinates with her DKNY clothing and accessories, and features her name; however, Donna Karan International Inc. does not own the watch company. Fossil Inc., owner of the line, is the timepiece company that manufactures this product classification for and pays a fee and/or royalties to Donna Karan International Inc. This arrangement is referred to as a **license**, an agreement in which a manufacturer, the **licensee**, is given exclusive rights to produce and market goods that carry the registered name and brandmark of a designer (e.g., Ralph Lauren), celebrity (e.g., Jessica Simpson), character (e.g., Mickey Mouse), or product line (e.g., Hershey's). The owner of the name or brandmark is called the **licensor**. The licensor receives a percentage of wholesale sales or some other compensation for the arrangement.

Figure 3.5 Shopping the market in other countries, such as Morocco, gives store buyers the opportunity to locate and export foreign merchandise in the apparel, accessories, and home fashions categories that would not be available to U.S. customers.

Figure 3.6 provides an example of footwear licensed under the Jessica Simpson Collection. Camuto Group, Inc., based in Greenwich, Connecticut, coordinates the design, development, and distribution of women's fashion footwear as women's lifestyle brands on a global scale. The company is the master licensee for the Jessica Simpson Collection. Camuto Group, Inc. also develops and manages several exclusive brands for Dillard's, and holds the footwear licenses for BCBGeneration, BCBG Max Azria, Lucky Brand, and kensiegirl.

Today, many companies combine sourcing merchandise from overseas with importing and licensing, as illustrated in Box 3.3. Additionally, a large number of these firms have finished products delivered from overseas manufacturers to retail operations abroad rather than solely importing the merchandise to the United States. It is truly a global market for many licensed products, one that can establish and strengthen brand identity. As international distribution continues to develop, particularly in Asia, manufacturers in the United States need specialists with knowledge of sourcing, importing, exporting, and licensing regulations. These specialists are referred to as licensing directors.

Licensing Director

Figure 3.6 Footwear under the Jessica Simpson Collection label is licensed through Camuto Group, Inc.

Licensing directors are responsible for overseeing the look, quality, labeling, delivery, and distribution of their companies' product lines. Sourcing is an integral part of this job. They work with the foreign and domestic manufacturers of various product lines, the licensees, to make certain that the products are branded correctly. The style, placement, size, and color of

Box 3.3 Sourcing

Canada's Aritzia arrives in New York: A look from Aritzia's spring collection.
by Sharon Edelson
Women's Wear Daily, posted Friday February 4, 2011

New York—As American retail's migration north continues, Target recently said it will open stores in former Zellers units. The Canadian retailer Aritzia is heading in the opposite direction. A temporary location on the third floor of 524 Broadway and Spring Street will debut Sunday, a precursor to Aritzia's permanent 10,000-square-foot bilevel unit opening in May.

Aritzia, a vertically integrated multi-label retailer for women ages 18 to 35, produces eight proprietary brands with such names as Wilfred and A Moveable Feast. All are designed in house and are far from basic. "They're there to stand on their own as individual brands and to complement the other brands," said Brian Hill, chief executive officer. "They're not private label. We have full design, pattern, and technical teams and sourcing capabilities. We can control the fit and there's consistency in the style and quality." So far, Hill has declined to sell the brands to other stores, but it hasn't been for a lack of inquiries. There are plans to wholesale them in the future, he said.

About 25 percent of Aritzia's merchandise mix consists of designer labels. In SoHo, outside labels will comprise 30 percent to 40 percent of the offering, since the store is larger than typical units. J Brand, James Jeans, Athe Vanessa Bruno, Cynthia Vincent, and Rag & Bone are among the labels sold. Aritzia operates 48 units, including stores in Chicago; San Francisco; Portland; Seattle; and Short Hills, New Jersey. Hill said he waited until

Aritzia was ready for prime time before entering Manhattan. "We purposely didn't open there initially because there are a lot of unforeseen challenges with a new business," he said. "Our strategy was to quietly open in some important markets, but not necessarily Manhattan. We had some immigration challenges initially and supply chain issues."

Hill now feels comfortable with the idea of multiple units in Manhattan. "There's a lot of opportunities, including six major ones I see," he said. "Fifth Avenue may be in our cards and is a big project. Some of the other stores will be smaller projects." Aritzia could make things interesting for Intermix and Scoop, two multi-brand retailers with outposts in SoHo. "I'm fairly comfortable with the competition—from Opening Ceremony to Intermix," Hill said. "SoHo is predominantly single-brand stores. It's a testament to how good the real estate is and how good the customers are."

"What gives us the confidence to [expand] in the U.S. is that our product has resonated with the American consumer. Our bestsellers in Canada are also bestsellers in the U.S. Our top colors in Canada are the top colors in the U.S." One difference is the average spend, which is higher in the U.S. than in Canada. Hill declined to disclose U.S. volume but said 2010 comps were up 30 percent over 2009. Total sales were $250 million last year. Aritzia is focusing on the Northeast, Northern California, and the Northwest, due to the similarities with Canada's climate. Six to eight stores are planned for 2011, including a unit at Garden State Plaza in Paramus, New Jersey. "We're focusing more of our energies on the U.S.," Hill said. "We're running out of runway in Canada."

the brandmark and labels must be consistent across all product lines. Additionally, licensing directors make sure product lines meet quality expectations and fit within the design concepts of their company's primary line, whether it be Donna Karan Collection dresses or Kate Spade handbags. For example, if an apparel line for a particular season features black-and-white prints with striped accents, designs of the licensed handbag line should coordinate with similar colors and patterns, as illustrated in Figure 3.7. The results the handbag manufacturer and designer desire are multiple sales to the consumers and a greater presence on retail floors.

Figure 3.7 Licensing directors are responsible for making sure that product lines meet quality expectations and fit within the design concepts of their company's primary line, as with this apparel and accessories.

Qualifications

The job requirements for licensing directors are as follows.

- **Education:** A bachelor's degree in fashion design or merchandising, business administration, marketing, international marketing, or a similar field is a minimum requirement.

- **Experience:** Many licensing directors begin on the showroom floor of a manufacturer or as account representatives. Prior to this, retail sales experience during college provides a solid foundation in working with various product lines and customers. The position of licensing director is one that a candidate is promoted into after showing knowledge and skills in the business.

- **Personal characteristics:** The licensing director must juggle many tasks at one time. The abilities to manage time, stay calm under pressure, and prioritize tasks are significant. Strong negotiation skills are a plus. Comprehension of product construction, quality, and design is a necessity. An understanding of import and export laws, branding regulations, and different cultures is critical to this career path.

Career Challenges

One of the greatest challenges in a licensing career is the need to clearly understand and stay up to date in a wide range of areas. The licensing professional must have a thorough knowledge of design and product development, branding specifications, import and export legislation and regulations, and manufacturing processes—all for a variety of products, such as sunglasses, gloves, sportswear, and footwear. If a product of poor quality that does not reflect the licensor's vision slips out from under the licensing director's radar, the image and sales of the licensor can be negatively affected. Therefore, coordinating the work of many manufacturers located around the world that produce a range of product types is a tremendous task and responsibility.

Summary

From locating vendors to collaborating with manufacturers, sourcing is the process of taking a product from its conception stage to the sales floor. In some companies, designers and their assistants locate the places from which to purchase piece goods. Larger companies may employ buyers to source fabrics and related products for the items in the designer's line. The career options that focus on sourcing fabrics and findings necessary for producing collections include fashion production planner, or raw goods buyer, and piece goods buyer. Production managers, who act as contacts between buyers and vendors, advise on the delivery status of purchase orders. Sourcing managers work with overseas or domestic producers to figure out product specifications and negotiate contracts. An import production coordinator is involved in all aspects of the production process and is often the link between the overseas factories and the design and buying teams.

Today's global market has inspired many companies to combine sourcing merchandise from overseas with importing and licensing. Foreign commissionaires, or foreign-owned independent agents, often employ market representatives, or specialized buyers of individual merchandise classifications. As international distribution continues to develop, manufacturers employ licensing directors, specialists with knowledge of sourcing, importing, exporting, and licensing regulations, as illustrated in Box 3.4.

While education and field experience are important qualifications for a career path in sourcing, the qualifications that are key to success are flexibility, organization, and communication. Knowledge of import and export laws, branding regulations, foreign languages, and different cultures is important to those working within all aspects of the global industry. If you are interested in sourcing as a future career, you must have the ability to work effectively when under pressure and possess excellent negotiation skills. Sourcing is an ideal profession for the curious, creative, and detail-oriented person. It is an exciting and satisfying journey to take a design from dream to reality.

Key Terms

assistant importer

assistant piece goods buyer

breakdown

chargebacks

collection

contractor

country of origin

exports

fashion production planner

findings

findings buyer

first cost

foreign commissionaire

globalization

global sourcing

importer

imports

import production coordinator

landed costs

letter of credit

license

licensee

licensing director

licensor

market representative

merchandiser

piece goods buyer

purchase order (PO)

sourcing

sourcing manager

stock-keeping unit (SKU)

store-owned foreign buying office

trimmings

trimmings buyer

vendor

volume driver

yardage

Online Resources

www.apparelsearch.com/education/books/fashiondex/Sourcing_books_apparel_production_clothing.htm

www.fibre2fashion.com/industry-article/29/2863/global-apparel-sourcing-whats-the-preference-cost-quality-or-lead-time1.asp

www.glassdoor.com/Salary/Polo-Ralph-Lauren-New-York-City-Salaries-EI_IE2937.0,17_IL.18,31_IM615.htm

www.foxnews.com/entertainment/2010/12/07/jessica-simpsons-clothing-line-expected-make-history-billion-sales/

www.wwd.com/business-news/esprit-first-half-net-falls-21-percent-3465415

www.wwd.com/footwear-news/firms-target-sourcing-options-3493333

Discussion Questions

1. How many different components, or parts, make up the clothes and accessories you are wearing today? Determine the fabrics, trimmings, and findings that were sourced to assemble each garment. How likely is it that all of these parts have come from the same producer or even the same country?

2. Research to discover how many licensing agreements your favorite designer shares with manufacturers. Generate a list of three key designers and the licensing arrangements they have by product and manufacturer. Do the manufacturers produce similar lines for other fashion companies?

Box 3.4 Tech Talk: A New Sourcing Platform

Sourcing is the process of identifying, evaluating, and collaborating with suppliers to manufacture products at an agreed-upon price. This collaboration may be close to home or in another country, often referred to as global sourcing. Manufacturing and retailing companies often take their production business overseas to find low-cost production solutions. The goal for the sourcing manager, buyer, or designer is to establish reliable manufacturing partnerships as the critical step in the supply chain. The ten steps to sourcing apparel include:

1. Creating and organizing designs
2. Researching target prices and determining a price point based on wholesale and retail prices preferred and accepted by consumers
3. Considering various distribution channels for the product
4. Creating and distributing a request for quote (RFQ)
5. Receiving quotes and assessing them
6. Performing due diligence with quoting suppliers
7. Negotiating prices when necessary
8. Awarding a quote to the supplier of choice
9. Requesting samples
10. Approving preproduction (PP) samples and placing order with supplier

What is new in sourcing technology? Internet-based platforms are changing the way the global manufacturing industry conducts business. For example, MFG.com provides a customized sourcing platform that connects buyers with proven suppliers, lessening the risk of working with a new manufacturing provider. Whether for samples or million-piece runs, suppliers can quote directly on the production at exactly the moment sourcing managers, designers, or buyers need this information—an on-demand global service. The company matches a buyer's design and specifications to qualified suppliers. Buyers benefit from discovering the suppliers with the appropriate production capabilities with minimal effort. Suppliers find customers with immediate manufacturing needs that they otherwise would not have known about. This simplifies the process of creating, distributing, tracking, and awarding requests for quotes for cut-and-sew textiles and raw materials. In addition, the designer or buyer can invite current suppliers onto the platform to easily transmit and manage designs and quotes between one another. Design collections can be archived entire for access anytime and anywhere. With the development of the Internet sourcing platform, a type of efficient online marketplace, products can be sourced and constructed more easily, quickly, inexpensively, and at higher quality levels.

Source: http://fashionbizinc.org/sourcing

3. Why do piece goods buyers rarely source fabrics and findings from the United States? Construct a list of six reasons for the trend toward outsourcing.
4. Which countries host the largest or greatest number of manufacturing companies for fashion products? In what specific merchandise classifications, fabrics, or production processes does each country specialize? What are some reasons for specialization? Develop a spreadsheet to answer these queries.

Interview with a Sourcing Expert

Sources:
http://www.just-style.com/comment/is-fast-fashion-starting-to-fade_id105258.aspx

http://www.uniqlo.com/us/corp/about/

Mike Flanagan is CEO of Clothesource Sourcing Intelligence, a UK-based consulting company that gathers data in over 100 countries on apparel production, pricing, and trade. For years, fast fashion has been talked up as the "next big thing," but a glance at any major clothing store in Europe or North America suggests that fast fashion has already flooded the industry. What has not happened, however, is the anticipated accompanying shift in production from overseas to local factories. Next, Mike Flanagan discusses why retailers show few signs of sourcing closer to home.

Spain's Inditex, one of the world's largest fashion distributors, revolutionized the fashion industry by continuously modifying the range of products offered in every one of its Zara stores. While giant retailers are getting clothes into their shops more quickly and refreshing their merchandise assortments more frequently, they have managed to do this without moving production to factories near their sales bases—one of the predictions that went hand in hand with fast fashion. Western Europe has moved clothing production to Asia while China's share of Japan's clothes purchases has been falling all year. Throughout the world, retailers and brands are shifting their production away from the "near abroad." So, what is happening?

The Fast Fashion Myth

There was a popular theory about fast fashion. A few blazers went into each of a global fashion chain's shops. Customers told the stores' sales associates that they would like the jackets better with pink buttons. All over the world, the company's sales staff entered the information into their smartphones. Then, in the twinkling of an eye, the chain's factories—located close to where most of those chain's shops were—would make thousands of jackets with the pink buttons. These would be in the shops the following morning, fly out in the customers' arms that afternoon, and a completely different assortment of garments would turn up the following day so that the customers would come back day after day to see what else was new.

Of course, it was never like that. Take Inditex, for example. The corporation still has factories in northwestern Spain, and it still sources half its production from Spain or its near neighbors. The Inditex business generates more money from producing some of its inventory very near the point of sale. The reasons for this are twofold: reaction times are as fast as possible and the cost of maintaining inventory is as low as possible. It is a policy that has made Inditex, by turnover, the largest specialty apparel retailer in the world.

There is, however, a catch. While retailers around the world have learned about keeping merchandise assortments fresh from Inditex, very few have successfully developed mass sales from extensive use of in-country production. Even Inditex does not depend on in-country manufacturing as much as it did. In the 1990s, Asia accounted for practically no Inditex production. Now Asian production accounts for approximately 40 percent of products Inditex sells. Because Inditex sales have more than doubled over the past decade, the volume of its Spanish production has not suffered much.

Refreshing Performance

Most large retailers now update merchandise assortments more often. In fact, Flanagan's research shows that the only retailers who haven't increased the frequency with which they change their ranges have gone out of business. The chains that refresh best also seem to be performing best. Flanagan's studies indicate that, in the United States, The Buckle keeps emerging in monthly retail sales review as the only consistently growing U.S. chain that is not a discounter.

Interview with a Sourcing Expert (continued)

It was recently reported that a substantial proportion of Uniqlo's growth in Japan comes from its ability to keep offering its customers new products. Uniqlo is part of the Fast Retailing group of companies. After opening the first Uniqlo store in 1984 in Japan, the company began its expansion into international markets in 1991. By August of 2010, Uniqlo boasted 808 stores in Japan and 136 stores in other global locations.

Neither The Buckle nor Uniqlo places huge emphasis on getting new designs into stores the day after the designers dream them up. And neither of these businesses shows much sign of wanting to move production closer to home. Interestingly, neither company has followed the recent fads of elaborate networks of overseas sourcing offices or outsourcing their sourcing to one large agent. Uniqlo, which until very recently depended almost entirely on next-door China for all its clothes, is scouting around almost everywhere else in Asia for other places from which to source. It has persuaded a number of suppliers to invest over $80 million in a new Bangladesh production complex, and there are signs of test production going on in a number of Asian countries where it has not previously bought much.

New Attitudes

What has happened in almost every clothing chain has been a profound change in companies' attitudes to offering a continuous flow of new product. Many companies have discovered that it is possible to have a far more frequent program of new garments, but they are not always designing new styles at short notice. Inditex practices what Ken Watson of Industry Forum Services terms continuous flexible flow, defined as "rapid new ideas that turn into real garments on real shelves very fast." Most other retailers who change their ranges often practice what he calls continuous unmodified flow, "where design decisions are taken some time in advance and merchandise assortments change in response to market demand."

If done correctly, continuous flexible flow has the potential to generate higher sale volume, but it is tougher to accomplish. Continually coming up with new concepts, then quickly producing and distributing the goods, presents an array of challenges. As a result, more and more businesses are switching to something closer to continuous unmodified flow, while others mix and match these strategies. As with any new idea, there is no one way that works for everyone. Continuous unmodified flow, in which merchandise assortments change in response to market demand, has not disappeared. Even in a recession, some consumers will always buy more if they see clothes they like at the right time. Continuous flexible flow is here to stay, as it lessens the manufacturers' and retailers' risks. Sourcing continues to be a "moveable feast" as fashion producers continue to follow low prices, better quality, and quicker, smaller production runs around the world.

chapter 4

Production

Some prospective fashion employees find raw materials, such as fabrics and trims, and the construction of products to be two of the most interesting areas of the industry. Others are drawn to the more quantitative tasks, such as buying, costing, and production planning. Many are fascinated with the technical and computer-oriented aspects of the fashion business. Still others are fascinated with the creative and artistic parts of the fashion industry. Whether materials, numbers, computers, or creativity appeal to you, there is a career path in production that relates directly to each area.

The basic stages of the production process can be mapped as follows:

- Sourcing parts and producers for the product

- Securing bids for piece goods, findings, and trimmings

- Costing out the product

- Ordering product components

- Scheduling production

- Creating the production pattern

- Grading

- Marker making

- Spreading and cutting

- Assembling/constructing the product

- Controlling the quality of the product

- Packing and shipping

- Producing and shipping reorders

Production, or manufacturing, of **end products**, the products that will actually be purchased by the customer, is an area that offers several career opportunities. A number of technological and management concepts relative to the fashion industry have created or affected career tracks in this area. These include computer-integrated manufacturing, electronic data interchange, mass customization, supply-chain management, and radio-frequency identification technology. These manufacturing trends will be examined later in this chapter. First, an exploration of career options relating to these concepts, in both domestic and overseas production, will include employment opportunities in the following positions: product manager, production planner, production manager, traffic manager, production efficiency manager, quality control manager, pattern production (pattern grader and marker maker), and spreader and cutter.

Product Manager

Depending on the size of the company, a **product manager** (or *product design manager*) may be responsible for all of the products within a company's product line in a small firm, or for a specific product category within a line for a large company. Product managers often work with one foot in the creative part of the business and the other foot in the production part of the business. On the creative, design-focused side, product managers monitor market and fashion trends related to their assigned product lines. If there is a team of product managers responsible for a variety of the company's product categories, it works to integrate the products for a consistent and cohesive fashion look. Product managers are also responsible for comparison shopping the lines of competitors. They compare assortment, quality, price, and trend representation. They will also shop merchandise lines outside of their product categories, making certain that their product lines will blend with the color, style, and fabric trends being shown for the season in all departments.

For example, the product manager of the handbag division of Coach Leatherware may review the new line for trend representation, optimal fabric selections, and key colors for the season. She may then meet with the product managers of Coach's personal leather goods, jewelry, scarf, glove, knitwear, footwear, and apparel categories to ascertain that all categories have colors, fabrics, and fashion trends in common. The goal is to create a clear and forward fashion image for the company as a whole, as illustrated in Figure 4.1. The product manager will also examine the product lines of other manufacturers that appeal to Coach Leatherware's target market, such as footwear, accessories, and apparel lines that the target customers buy. Each product manager will also review competitive lines, looking for similarities and product voids. **Product voids** refer to merchandise categories in which there are few, if any, items to fill consumer needs and desires. The product manager's objective is to guide the product line to higher sales by creating a timely fashion presence that fits with trends, meshes with the company's total image, and fills a product void.

Figure 4.1 The product manager is responsible for seeing that all product lines present a consistent company image.

On the production side, the product manager will work with sourcing personnel, production managers, and quality control directors, among other departments involved with the manufacturing of the product lines for which they are responsible. The product manager will monitor the manufacturing of his or her product line(s) from start to finish by checking deliveries of product components, overseeing timelines as the products move through the manufacturing process, assessing quality, and assuring on-time delivery to the retailers. The effective product manager has a dual perspective on the product line—the creative viewpoint of fashion trends and a cohesive fashion image, and the business viewpoint of quality and timely production—both combining to place the right products in the consumers' hands at the right time.

Qualifications

A list of qualifications for this career follows.

- **Education:** A bachelor's degree in fashion merchandising, fashion design, product development, production, apparel manufacturing, or a related field is commonly a requirement.

- **Experience:** A sales representative for a manufacturing company may climb the career ladder into the position of product manager. An assistant in a trend forecasting firm may leave that sector of the industry to move up to a product manager position. Large firms have assistant product manager positions, for which product manager positions are the next step up the career ladder.

- **Personal characteristics:** Successful product managers have the ability to analyze their firm's market for opportunities and threats. Assessing competition, communicating fashion trends, and investigating retail trends require the personal attributes of curiosity, observation, and creativity, as well as strong skills in communication, organization, and presentation. They also have an in-depth knowledge of the manufacturing processes for their particular product categories.

Box 4.1 features an interview with a product design manager. Figure 4.2 illustrates a line of products that the product manager may oversee.

Box 4.1 Interview with a Product Design Manager

Interviewee: Jillian Nelson

Job title: Product Design Manager—Ladies Cut and Sew Hats, Bags, and Fleece

Education and experience to move into this career track: I graduated with a bachelor of science degree, with a double major in fashion merchandising and design. In the summer between my junior and senior years, I studied in London through American Intercontinental University, taking a trend forecasting class and interning at the Profile Group on the publication *Fashion Monitor*. I moved to New York City during the summer after graduation. There, I did a short internship with Catherine Malandrino during Fashion Week, and, soon after, I landed my first job at Capelli New York as an assistant in product and design.

If you were hiring someone to work for you, these are the personal characteristics that you would look for in a job candidate: When interviewing, the qualities we look for are a unique sense of style, passion, motivation, ambition, enthusiasm, organizational skills, communication skills, and a positive attitude.

What do you enjoy most about your job: I enjoy the constant mix of business and creativity, managing a small team, and seeing my products' development from beginning to end. The results in the sales percentages in store are a constant challenge and a daily reward. Product development is the perfect mix for someone with a design and merchandising–based mind to be a part of the always-evolving fashion industry.

What do you like the least: In this industry, you work hard and long, and everything is urgent. So I believe you have to have passion about what you are doing; otherwise, it is not worth it.

Industry trends that you believe will affect what you are doing or will be doing in the next five to ten years: The knowledge and experience you gain working in the New York fashion industry are incomparable and things you can carry with you forever. Whether I am still here in New York in the next 5 to 10 years or have moved on to the slower suburban life I grew up with, I believe people will always desire to accessorize themselves in one way or another, and fashion will always have an influence on the way people feel in their lives. So no matter where you are or where you work in the world, these two constants and trends will always need to be fulfilled.

Advice to people interested in entering this career field: My advice for those entering this career field is to have a clear and direct sense of motivation regarding where you are going. Acknowledge and accept gracefully the fact that you need to start at the bottom and work your way up. Have a positive attitude no matter what task you are performing. Let every day build your character into a stronger and more valuable asset to your company. Be assertive, not aggressive; always respect the chain of command; and, most of all, never stop learning.

Career Challenges

Many small companies do not employ product managers; instead, designers are responsible for evaluating competitors and determining fashion trends for the line. As a result, the number of positions in this area is limited to mid- and large-sized firms. Product managers are "under the gun" when it comes to being correct on the fashion colors, styling, and themes that will be featured in product lines. If, for example, rhinestones are the key fashion trend the product design manager chooses for the season and it turns out to be trend a company's target market does not buy, the product manager may be job hunting. Additionally, product managers face great challenges with manufacturing products abroad in terms of quality, fit, and deadlines. Since there is much at stake when a company produces the wrong product or

Figure 4.2 Lee has initiated a new product line with the face of Mike Rowe, led by a product manager who steers the line toward this consumer niche.

ships the right product too late, product managers must conduct detailed research to make accurate decisions, which makes this position exciting, fun, and never dull.

Production Planner

The majority of large manufacturing firms have production planners on staff. **Production planners** estimate the amounts and types of products a company will manufacture, based either on previous seasonal sales or on orders received by sales representatives on the road and in the showroom. There are two primary methods of production planning: cut-to-order and cut-to-stock. **Cut-to-order** is considered the safest method of projecting manufacturing needs. It entails waiting until orders are received from buyers and then working within tight timelines to order product parts, construct product lines as ordered, and ship them to the retail accounts on time. Which types of fashion companies prefer the cut-to-order option? This technique is most often used by designer firms that feature higher-priced, high-fashion merchandise. For these companies, forecasting the sales of products that reflect new fashion trends is more difficult. Also, the costs of being wrong may be much higher than for less expensive, less fashion-forward merchandise because of the more expensive fabrics and, often, more detailed workmanship these high-fashion companies include in their products.

    Cut-to-stock involves purchasing fabrics and other product components before orders are acquired. Production planners using the cut-to-stock method examine a number of variables

Figure 4.3 Garment workers sew at the American Apparel factory in downtown Los Angeles.

before projecting manufacturing needs. They look at the economy and how, when, and on what consumers are spending their money. They investigate what the competition is doing, including new companies entering the market and targeting their customers. They study sales histories of products in the line, focusing on sales by style, color, size, and price for each season. They analyze the strength of new lines by discussing sales potential with the design staff and sales representatives.

What are the advantages of the cut-to-stock option? It enables production to be spread out over a longer period of time. This permits the manufacturer to keep factories in production mode throughout the year, rather than working around "peaks and valleys." Cut-to-stock also allows for a longer **lead time**, the amount of time needed between placing a production order and receiving a shipment of the products. With international production gaining importance, lead times have become longer for manufacturers using overseas factories. Which types of firms find the cut-to-stock alternative to be most efficient and cost effective? A manufacturing company that produces a significant number of basic products, such as a T-shirt company, has the ability to project sales more closely than does the producer of more expensive, fashion-sensitive goods (Figure 4.3).

Qualifications

Whether the production planner uses the cut-to-order or cut-to-stock option, the education, work experience, and personal characteristics needed for successful employment in this career track are similar, including the following:

- **Education:** A bachelor's degree in fashion merchandising, fashion design, product development, apparel manufacturing, or a related field is commonly required.

- **Experience:** Work experience with a manufacturer is needed, possibly beginning in the showroom and later moving into product development or purchasing. An understanding of how products are constructed, the materials they are made from, and the manufacturing processes required to bring them to fruition is critical.

- **Personal characteristics:** The successful product planner has strong quantitative abilities, effective communication skills, excellent time management, and top organizational skills.

Production Manager

Production managers, also referred to as *plant managers*, are responsible for all of the operations at production facilities, whether domestic or overseas locations, contracted or company owned. The job responsibilities of production managers include supervising or completing the estimation of production and employee costs, scheduling work flow in factories, and hiring and training production employees. Production managers are also ultimately responsible for quality control of the products. Think about the number of employees, tasks, and potential problems associated with cutting, constructing, pressing, and shipping a product line. This is a challenging career track, but one that pays well and is critical to the success of a company. Box 4.2 is an example of a classified ad for a plant manager position.

Production assistants often support production managers with detail work, scheduling, and record keeping. Assistants may track fabric, trim, and findings deliveries; help with developing production schedules; and communicate the work flow of the factory to production managers. They also follow up on outgoing shipments, often keeping customers informed on the progress of their orders and expediting deliveries when needed.

Additionally, production managers may have the assistance of traffic managers. **Traffic managers** supervise work flow on factory floors, monitoring products from start to finish. They anticipate problems that may stall production, whether in materials, personnel, or equipment. The goal of the traffic manager is to make certain that the factory employees have all they need to manufacture products with efficiency and in good quality.

Qualifications

The qualifications for a production manager, production assistant, and traffic manager are similar. The production assistant and traffic manager positions usually precede that of production manager.

- **Education:** A bachelor's degree in fashion merchandising, fashion design, product development, apparel manufacturing, or a related field is commonly required.

- **Experience:** Hands-on experience in the industry, which may include work experience in computer-aided pattern design, grading and marker making, product costing, and quality control, is required for this position. The ability to produce flat sketches and specification drawings using a computer is helpful. A production assistant position is often posted as an entry-level position with the potential of moving into a production manager opening. Larger manufacturers offer assistant traffic manager positions as a starting place.

- **Personal characteristics:** Knowledge of raw materials and manufactured products, design and product development, and production technology is required. An understanding of textiles, product construction, the capabilities and limitations of production equipment,

Box 4.2 Sample Classified Advertisement: Plant Manager

Plant Manager—Textile Manufacturing and Production Company

Location: Dallas, Texas

Base Pay: $50,000–$80,000 annually

Industry: Fashion, Apparel, Textile, Manufacturing, Industrial

Required Education: Two-year degree

Required Experience: More than five years

Relocation Covered: Yes

Job Responsibilities

- Manage production facility of approximately 15 employees, consisting of supervisors, drivers, and production crew

- Manage day-to-day operations of the production process, including quality control and productions checks

- Hire, train, review, promote, and discharge employees as required

- Manage service technicians and maintenance crews as necessary

- Meet operational efficiencies by implementing process improvement and monitoring work flow and production

- Create and continuously promote a safe work environment by ensuring all staff understands and adheres to safety-related policies and procedures

- Maintain appropriate safety and waste disposal records/logs

- Resolve day-to-day issues for production facility

- Monitor and order supplies

- Develop and maintain operational budget

Job Requirements

- Management experience within a production/manufacturing facility environment

- Excellent management skills with the ability to delegate responsibilities and tasks

- Solid understanding of budgeting and plant operations

- Associate's degree or higher

We offer a competitive salary, a comprehensive benefits package, incredible growth potential, and learning opportunities. If you have more than five years of management experience within a production/manufacturing facility environment, please apply for immediate consideration.

---

and the principles of patternmaking is essential. The ability to work as part of a team, as well as independently with little supervision, is critical to success. Good communication skills, both oral and written, are also required. Because apparel production workers represent many nationalities, the ability to speak Mandarin, Cantonese, other Asian languages, or Spanish is an asset. An appreciation of cultural diversity is essential.

Career Challenges

What are the challenges for production managers, assistant production managers, and traffic managers? All of them face the obstacles of tight deadlines, sometimes worsened by external factors that are difficult to foresee or control. Manufacturing equipment breakdowns, delayed textile shipments, defective zippers, or thread in the wrong color are types of problems that can halt the work flow of the manufacturing facility and cause the manufacturer to miss shipping commitments. This can be a high-stress area in which to work. Effective communication and excellent follow-up skills are essential to making it in this career path.

Production Efficiency Manager

Some manufacturing firms offer the position of production efficiency manager. These companies are usually quite large and conduct global manufacturing activities. **Production efficiency managers** are responsible for monitoring the speed and output of the manufacturing facilities and for managing waste (Figure 4.4). Often, production efficiency managers work closely with quality control managers to ensure products meet quality standards while costs are under control. For example, the production efficiency manager of a handbag company may find an accessory firm to purchase leather scraps left over from the cutting tables to use them for belts.

Quality Control Manager

Quality control managers, or *quality control engineers*, develop specifications for the products that will be manufactured and they are responsible to see that those standards are met during all of the phases of production, identifying quality problems and working with manufacturing personnel to correct them. The quality control manager works with such issues as fit, fabric performance, construction difficulties, packaging and shipping needs, and production pace.

In large companies, a manufacturer's factories may be located worldwide. The quality control manager frequently travels to a number of manufacturing sites, coordinating production and deliveries, while checking to be certain that quality standards are being met at all locations. Because quality problems can run the gamut from the original product specifications to a

Figure 4.4 Production efficiency managers are responsible for monitoring the speed and output of the manufacturing facilities.

defective button-holer machine, the quality control manager collaborates with personnel in a number of the company's divisions—from the design staff to plant employees.

Qualifications

The qualifications for production efficiency managers and quality control managers are related, with similar requirements in education, work experience, and personal characteristics.

- **Education:** A bachelor's degree in fashion design, fashion merchandising, textiles, production, or a related discipline is needed.

- **Experience:** Knowledge of product construction, textile technology, and manufacturing capabilities is required. A number of quality control managers enter the field from design, merchandising, production, and/or human resources backgrounds.

- **Personal characteristics:** Personal characteristics that enhance the work of quality control managers include organizational abilities, effective time-management skills, and communication skills. Effective quality control managers are strong problem solvers with good follow-up skills and are detail oriented. This position requires human resources skills to gain the commitment of factory workers to produce high-quality products.

Career Challenges

Production efficiency managers and quality control managers face the challenge of working with a wide range of constituencies, from designers and patternmakers to plant workers located in the United States and abroad. It is a significant challenge to communicate with so many people on such diverse levels in, possibly, a number of global locations in different time zones. Strong communication skills and superior organizational abilities are keys to being successful in these two career tracks.

Pattern Production

There are a number of career paths in the area of pattern production. They include patternmaker, pattern grader, and marker maker. The job of a patternmaker will be examined in Chapter 8, which covers design careers. Marker makers and pattern graders share common characteristics: a superior level of accuracy, an understanding of how textiles perform, and an ability to adjust to increasing technological advances in pattern production. Pattern production requires sharp focus and strong attention to detail. If a single pattern piece is one-quarter of an inch too large, the apparel or home furnishing product will likely not flow through the production process. If by chance it does, the consumer will likely not purchase a product that does not fit correctly or look attractive (Figure 4.5). If details and accuracy are in your realm of expertise, pattern production offers a number of career options for you.

Pattern Grader

Working from the **master pattern**, the pattern that evolves after adjusting and perfecting the sample pattern, **pattern graders** develop the full pattern range of sizes offered by the manufacturer. For example, the master pattern may be graded in misses' dress sizes 12 to 20 or sizes 6 to 14, depending on the garment style, the company, and its target market. By enlarging

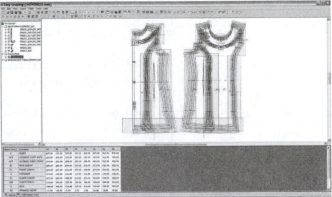

or reducing the pattern within a figure-type category, all of the pattern pieces of a particular design are developed for each size. Pattern grading is technical and precise work. It is often work that must be done at a fast pace under the pressure of production deadlines. While the majority of large manufacturing companies use computers to do grading work quickly, many smaller companies cannot initially afford this technology and/or prefer the hands-on skills of a grader. Figure 4.6 depicts a pattern that has been graded using CAD software.

Qualifications

Pattern graders should have the following background in terms of education, experience, and personal characteristics:

- **Education:** A bachelor's degree in fashion design, apparel production, or a related field is a minimum requirement.

- **Experience:** Effective skills in patternmaking, drafting, and product construction are necessary. Experience in pattern draping is a plus. An understanding of pattern grading technology and related work experience are needed.

- **Personal characteristics:** Strong attention to detail, the ability to work independently and under tight deadlines, and quantitative skills are job requirements for successful pattern graders.

Marker Maker

After the pattern is graded, it is time to develop a marker. A **marker** is the layout of pattern pieces on the fabrication from which the pieces will be cut, as illustrated in Figure 4.7. There are two main purposes of a marker. First, a good marker minimizes fabric waste; secondly, it generates an accurate end design. Fabric prints and patterns, textures and naps, and sheens and matte finishes must be taken into consideration when creating a marker. Think, for example, about a corduroy jacket. If the fabric in the back of the jacket is cut in a different direction from the front, the front and the back will appear to be two different colors. **Marker makers** trace the pattern pieces, by hand or by computer, into the tightest possible layout, while keeping the integrity of the design in mind. In some cases, a marker is generated in hard copy, or print; in other cases, it is stored in the computer.

Figure 4.5 If a single pattern piece is one-quarter of an inch too large, the apparel or home furnishing product will likely not flow through the production process. If by chance it does, the consumer will likely not purchase a product that does not fit correctly or look attractive.

Figure 4.6 A pattern that has been graded using CAD software.

Qualifications

The qualifications required for a marker maker follow:

- **Education:** A bachelor's degree in fashion design, apparel production, or a related field is a minimum requirement.

- **Experience:** Effective skills in patternmaking, drafting, and product construction are necessary. Experience with marker making technology is often required.

- **Personal characteristics:** Like pattern graders, marker makers must have strong attention to detail, the ability to work independently and under tight deadlines, and strong quantitative skills. Additionally, marker makers must have the ability to "see" the product in its final form when determining pattern piece layout.

Spreader and Cutter

After the marker is developed, it is ready to be placed on the fabric as preparation for cutting the pattern pieces. A **spreader** lays out the selected fabric for cutting. The spreader guides bolts of material on a machine that lays the fabric smooth and straight, layer over layer. In mid- to large-sized companies, a machine as shown in Figure 4.8 does this function. In smaller companies or computerized factories that require fewer employees, this job may be done by cutters. A **cutter** uses electronic cutting machines to cut precisely around the pattern pieces through layers of fabric, often several inches in thickness, as shown in Figure 4.9. While firms with advanced technology may use water jets or lasers to cut out garments quickly and accurately (see Box 4.3 and Figures 4.10–4.12), some companies specialize in merchandise classifications that require hand cutting. A bridal wear manufacturer, a firm that produces

Figure 4.7 A marker is the layout of pattern pieces on the fabrication from which the pieces will be cut.

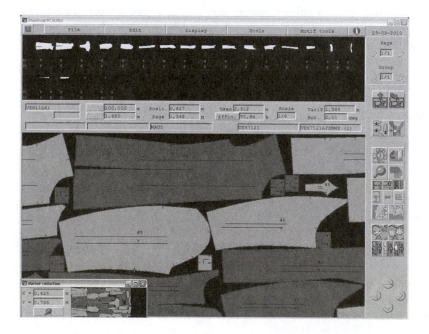

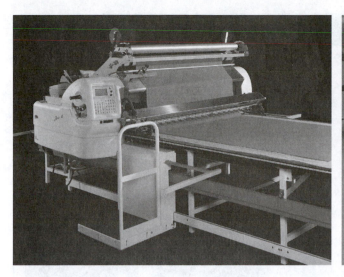

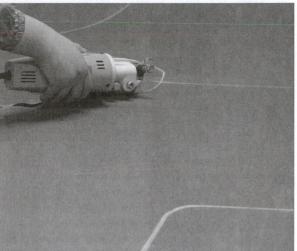

beaded eveningwear, or a couture design house may choose to have fabrications manually spread and cut in consideration of the delicate nature and high cost of the fabrics.

For the spreader and the cutter, vocational training or training with the manufacturer are usually considered adequate. In addition to these positions, there are a number of skilled or semiskilled workers on the production assembly line. These employees run the sewing machines, press or steam the final products, and package them for shipping, among other tasks. The production picture is a broad one with a variety of personnel opportunities.

Example Profiles:
Trends Affecting Careers in Production

At the start of this chapter, five trends in the production of apparel and home soft goods products were mentioned: computer-integrated manufacturing, electronic data interchange, mass customization, supply-chain management, and radio-frequency identification technology. As these trends will undeniably shape the requirements for production careers in the fashion industry of the future, a brief discussion follows.

Computer-Integrated Manufacturing

In many firms, computer-aided manufacturing exists in such forms as computer-aided patternmaking, marker making, cutting, and programmable sewing equipment. As technology develops at a rapid pace globally, the ability to link computers together has introduced amazing advances in production. Computers are being tied together, referred to as **computer-integrated manufacturing (CIM)**, to communicate throughout the entire product development and manufacturing processes, from design to distribution. Computer-aided design and computer-aided manufacturing are linked to form a system in which design and product development activities move smoothly into patternmaking, grading, marker making, cutting, and product construction activities. Computerized information systems concurrently develop costing reports and specification sheets; later, shipping and sales data are analyzed. Examples of manufacturers and retailers using CIM include H&M (Figure 4.13), Talbots, and Zara.

Figure 4.8
The spreading machine lays the fabric smooth and straight, layer over layer, in anticipation of the next step, cutting.

Figure 4.9
A cutter uses an electronic cutting machines to cut precisely around pattern pieces through layers of fabric.

Box 4.3 Tech Talk: Laser Cut Fabric

Laser Cut Fabric is a textile cutting service located in Columbus, Ohio. It is a part of the Laser Cutting Shapes company and provides laser-cutting services for textile and industrial fabrics. The company serves clients across the United States and Canada in such industries as automotive, medical devices, furniture, fashion, and others. Laser Cut Fabric works with an array of fabrications, to include woven and nonwoven fabrics—organics such as silk, wool, cotton, and leather, and artificial materials such as polyesters, nylons, acrylics, neoprene, rubber, pleather, etc. As a partner of Eurolaser in Germany, Laser Cut Fabric uses the fastest and most precise CO_2 laser systems to cut the most intricate details for the fashion industry. One of Laser Cut Fabric's most unique projects is laser-cut acrylic mannequins for Situ Designs

Figure 4.11 Michael Angel's laser-cut neoprene dress.

Figure 4.10 Zac Posen's laser-cut skirt.

in New York City. The mannequins were used for an exhibit in the Phoenix Art Museum. In 2008, the company developed a laser-cut vinyl tent for Design Miami, the paramount international fair for limited-edition design. Design Miami commissioned a temporary structure to house the main body of the show and hired Laser Cut Fabric to create the enormous panels used to cover the facade. In addition, Laser Cut Fabric has laser-cut parts for several designs for Zak Posen and neoprene dresses for Michael Angel.

Why the interest in laser-cut fabrics by designers and manufacturers in an array of industries? The major benefits of laser cutting include:

*   Creative, unique, and proprietary fabric designs can be developed out of most fabrics.

Box 4.3 Tech Talk: Laser Cut Fabric (continued)

Figure 4.12a Laser Cut Fabric's tent panels for Design Miami.

- Shorter lead times can be accomplished with laser cutting. At Laser Cut Fabric, the general lead time for the average project is 5 to 10 days.

- The laser beam seals the edges while cutting due to the high temperature, which reduces or completely eliminates fraying. For most textiles, serging or sewing of the edges is not required with laser cutting.

- Material waste is minimal due to the efficiency of fabric layouts and laser cutting. Laser-cut lines can be extremely close, almost next to each other.

- Software compatibility is easy for designers. Designs are accepted in vector format for laser cutting and bitmap formats for laser engraving. Typical formats are Adobe Illustrator, pdf, AutoCAD files, etc.

Figure 4.12b Marchesa's laser-cut silk dress.

- Intricacy, quality, and accuracy of complex designs that cannot be completed with scissors or blades are consistently implemented through laser-cutting technology. Repeatable clean cuts with unmatched precision are the cornerstone of laser cutting.

Source: http://www.lasercutfabric.com

Electronic Data Interchange

Electronic data interchange (EDI) refers to the electronic exchange of computer-generated information between one company's computer system and another's. Through EDI, manufacturers and retailers share data about the styles, colors, sizes, and price points that consumers are buying or those that are not selling and require markdowns. For example, retail buyers may peruse manufacturers' selling reports and purchase styles that they did not initially order. The manufacturer's representatives, on the other hand, may review the buyers' sales reports and recommend top-selling styles to clients who did not previously buy them. It is an exchange of information that allows the manufacturer to see what is happening on the sales floor.

Figure 4.13 H&M uses computerized information systems to develop costing reports and specification sheets; later, shipping and sales data are analyzed.

Mass Customization

Mass customization is a strategy that allows manufacturers or retailers to provide individualized products to consumers. Today's apparel supplier must look for new ways to offer customers top-quality goods at highly competitive prices. Consumers desire products that can be personalized through fit preferences, color selection, fabric choices, or design characteristics. A solution to the fit preference is a body or foot scanner that takes a customer's measurements digitally, creating what is referred to as digital twin. Based on the exact image, **body scanning** software then defines and captures all the measurements necessary for actually producing the garment or shoe. This data is forwarded online to the manufacturer, whose production technologies ensure an exact fit. The customer then receives the finished product in a very short time. This technological strategy is used today by some fashion firms, such as Custom Fit Footwear. This type of customization is often limited, however, to a select customer with a large budget.

For a broader customer base, Nike provides a Web site, www.nike.com/iD, to give customers the opportunity to design their own shoes. They can select from a variety of athletic shoe styles, then choose colors and add design details from an assortment of options. Figure 4.14 provides an illustration of the Nike custom-shoe process. Levi Strauss has a similar program through which customers provide inseam, hip, and waist measurements; they are then shipped a pair of "better-fitting" jeans within a two-week period. Figures 4.15a–c depict the body-scanning process utilized by Brooks Brothers.

Supply-Chain Management

In the fashion industry, manufacturers and retailers continue to work to decrease the amount of time required from design and the purchase of raw materials to production and distribution of the final product into the consumer's hands. This gallant goal requires a partnership among the supplier, manufacturer, and retailer in which open and honest communication is the key to success. Once these players have developed a trusting relationship that facilitates a constant exchange of accurate information, the results are often increased sales for all. Top-selling products can be reordered and received faster. Modifications of these products give the consumer more options through preferred merchandise assortments. For example, when the retailer reports to the manufacturer that the shipment of a black leather vest sold out within a week, the manufacturer can quickly contract with the supplier to buy the leather for the vest in other colors, to change the topstitching or pocket detailing, or to add a jacket to the mix.

This activity of sharing and coordinating information across all segments of the soft goods industry is referred to as **supply-chain management (SCM)**. Supply-chain management comprises all of the activities required to coordinate and manage every step needed to bring a product to the consumer, including procuring raw materials, producing goods, transporting and distributing those goods, and managing the selling process. The goals of SCM are to reduce inventory, shorten the time for raw materials to become a finished product in the hands of a consumer, and provide better service to the consumer. Collaboration, trust, and dependability are necessary to make SCM effective. Referred to as Quick Response in the past, "SCM goes beyond Quick Response in that SCM companies share forecasting, point-of-sale data, inventory information, and information about unforeseen changes in supply or demand

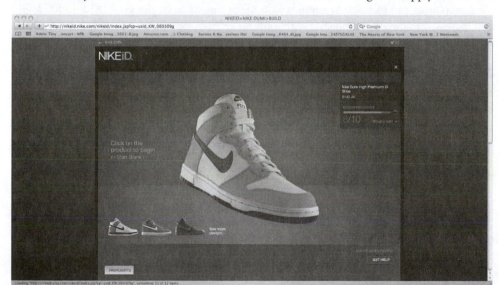

Figure 4.14 NikeiD gives its customers the opportunity to design their own athletic shoes, selecting from a variety of styles, colors, and design details.

Figures 4.15a–c The body-scanning process utilized by Brooks Brothers for "digital tailoring."

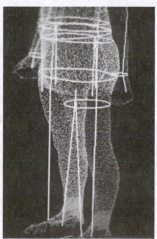
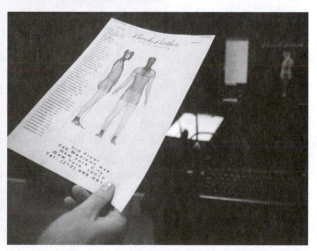

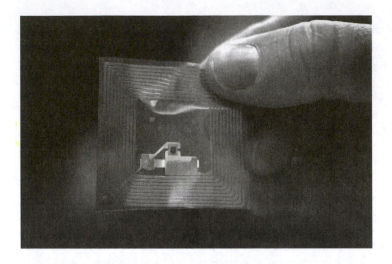

Figure 4.16 RFID tags are referred to as "the next-generation bar code."

for materials or products."[1] As supply-chain management strategies grew, new technologies also increased to provide companies with tools for communication and integration. One such tool is radio-frequency identification technology.

Radio-Frequency Identification Technology

Radio-frequency identification technology (RFID) is referred to as "the next-generation bar code" since its primary functions are to increase supply-chain management through the tagging of containers, pallets, and individual items so that they can be accurately tracked as they move through the supply chain. However, unlike bar codes, RFID tags do not rely on line-of-sight readability. In fact, multiple RFID tags can be read simultaneously; they have memory and, therefore, can store and update data, and they provide fully automated data collection."[2] This technology has proven itself to be so effective that major global retailers, such as Walmart and Target, are requiring all suppliers to apply RFID tags to pallet and case shipments. With these major retailers requiring RFID technologies of their suppliers, RFID equipment, tags, and accessories are becoming more affordable and available to a broader range of companies (Figure 4.16).

Summary

Within fashion firms, large and small, there is a vast range of employment opportunities in the production sector, whether the firms manufacture their lines domestically, overseas, or both. Career tracks exist in production for those interested in fabrics, numbers, or technology. Careers that relate directly to manufacturing include product manager, traffic manager, production planner, production manager, production efficiency manager, and quality control manager. After the designer has created the line, development of the actual product before it goes into production is facilitated by the patternmaker and marker maker. Grading, spreading, and cutting are three phases of production in which computers are quickly impacting job opportunities. Additionally, there are a number of technological trends that will undeniably impact the requirements for production careers in the fashion industry of the future. These include computer-integrated manufacturing, electronic data interchange, mass customization, supply-chain management, and radio-frequency identification technology.

Endnotes

1. Burns, L.D. and N. O. Bryant, *The Business of Fashion: Designing, Manufacturing, and Marketing*, 4th Edition. New York, Fairchild Books, 2011.
2. Ibid.

Key Terms

body scanning
computer-integrated manufacturing (CIM)
cutter
cut-to-order
cut-to-stock
electronic data interchange (EDI)
end product
lead time
marker
marker maker
mass customization
master pattern

pattern grader
product manager
product void
production assistant
production efficiency manager
production manager
production planner
quality control manager
radio-frequency identification technology (RFID)
spreader
supply-chain management (SCM)
traffic manager

Online Resources

www.apparelnews.net/news/manufacturing/

www.apparelsearch.com/technology/software/Production_Management_Software_clothing_production.htm

www.creativejobscentral.com/fashion-internships/Production

www.fashionindustrynetwork.com/group/garmentproduction

www.lectra.com

www.tc2.com

www.vault.com/articles/Fashion-Manufacturing-16702640.html

Discussion Questions

1. Consider apparel and home soft goods production a decade from now. What will be the education, experience, and personal qualities the production manager of a large domestic manufacturer in home furnishings will need? Develop a classified advertisement to recruit a qualified candidate for this position.

2. Select three of the following production trends discussed in this chapter: computer-integrated manufacturing, electronic data interchange, mass customization, supply-chain management, and radio-frequency identification technology. Locate and copy articles that provide illustrations of each of these being implemented in fashion companies for discussion in class.

3. Practice "futuring" by researching manufacturing trends and innovations in technology, not presented in this chapter, that will impact apparel manufacturing over the next decade. Construct a chart of the top five innovations (e.g., software programs or hardware inventions, processes of production, new locations for manufacturing, etc.), their creators, and briefly describe the impact these advances will have on soft goods manufacturing.

Interview with a Sourcing and Production Manager

By Sam Lim, December 3, 2010
Source: http://fashionindie.com/interview-the-row-production-director-joe-karban-2/

The majority of celebrity-turned-designer collections are all about the name behind the brand, but in the case of Mary Kate and Ashley Olsen's luxe line, The Row, it is the fashion that takes center stage. Considering the legitimately esteemed name the line has made for itself in the past three years, it is a wonder to know which capable industry veterans have been behind the sublime silhouettes and clean tailored pieces conceptualized and curated by the young designers.

That is what brings me here today. I am interviewing Joe Karban, the sourcing and production manager behind the brand, and getting a glimpse into his side of the fashion business. Karban has been at the helm of the brand for two and a half years, and the team seems like a family. A 30-year veteran of Ralph Lauren, Tommy Hilfiger, and luxury brand Ginny H, he certainly knows his way around the industry. We chatted about his views on creating the perfect collection, on building the design vision of the Olsen girls, and what qualities it really takes to succeed in the competitive fashion industry.

What is the perspective of the production side of the small luxury house?

The Row works very tightly. It is a close-knit team and a design-driven company. There are no formal rules. We develop procedures and processes that help us produce the vision of the design team, Mary Kate and Ashley. The aim is to create processes that give design the ability to support the vision of the brand. Everything is done in tandem, so production's role is to create processes that marry back to what everyone needs. Everyone here owns their job and every role is crucial. From the interns to the directors, The Row is established so that everyone is as fulfilled as possible.

In terms of developing a collection, walk me through what it is like coming from your point of view as the production and sourcing side.

The Row is different because it is small and very high end. First, we sit and analyze the current collection, we look at how last year sold, and what things are trending against the current season. Then, we build a scorecard. The scorecard is made by merchandising, production, and sales. It determines how much to sell, how much of everything to order, and determines how the line is divided between fashion pieces, foundational pieces, and image/aspiring pieces. Once the scorecard is developed it is given to the design team and they take it to buy all the fabrics and establish the fabric delivery schedule. Then, styles are designed, tech packs and patterns are made; it really is a process that is somewhat mathematical, somewhat inspirational, and somewhat trend. Design marries back to the fabrics that they inspire. As creators, we are more artistic than mathematical; at some point it all blends together, it all happens. Creating the image of the silhouettes, it is all the same energy. From here the samples are made, line sheets are produced, and the clothes go to market. After market, we stock our fabric buys and go through the typical process of fittings, sampling, grading. Every company in the fashion industry is overdeveloped. Your kill ratio from development to production is a lot greater in luxury than it is in the contemporary world. In luxury, it is much more specific. The beauty of this process is that we are such a solid team that works together to come up with a tight collection of the most beautiful pieces.

So you sort of have final say on whether a garment can be made. Does this mean you have input during the design process?

The production and sourcing team gives input on how to produce the designs. We don't change the original designs, rather we come up with the ways to make them possible. I believe that there is no such thing as no—it is all about what your options are and how we can make things possible.

What do you like best about what The Row brand has created?

The simplicity. It is elegant, simplistic, and when a woman wears these clothes, they make her look

Interview with a Sourcing and Production Manager (continued)

beautiful. They make women look magnificent. They are utterly timeless.

What do you find most challenging?
Data flow, communication, and just keeping people talking. You have to tie together production, product development, creative, marketing, and all the moving parts. My main role is in being a navigator, making sure the runway is clear.

What has the experience working with Mary Kate and Ashley Olsen been like and how have they functioned as new designers?
It was really the same as working with anyone else that had the creative vision. The girls live trends. It is easy for them to translate what they live into their vision for the brand. They have been exposed to elegance for a long time, so I really have seen no difference working with them than working with any other veteran of the fashion industry. Great design companies are about incredible vision. We are here on the other side to support the vision of Mary Kate and Ashley. Keeping the philosophy of supporting great design is the nature of it.

How did you end up on the production side of the fashion business?
I started working in the industry 30 years ago when it was growing like crazy. I was lucky because I got to taste every part of the business. I had no idea what I wanted to do, it just evolved into where I am today. I always knew I wanted to marry creative vision with great design. I've always had an eye for fashion and a good business sense; that is also helpful when you're on the production side.

What have you found is the most compelling quality in succeeding as a production leader?
Broad experience in all aspects of the industry is necessary. A good production and sourcing person has to know every aspect of the industry. They need to know what it takes to design, how to develop styles (production), how to spec and structure clothes (technical design), fabric knowledge, how a cutting room works (to know how fabrics perform), cost and time frames (production) and how a line comes together (merchandising). Only when you

master all those aspects can you become a good production and sourcing person.

What advice do you have for other creatives working their way through the industry?
Be a good person and have a good, clean reputation. That is how you will grow and become a great success. If people think that you are skilled, positive, and cooperative, you will go far. This business is all about positive networking and keeping the fun in your business. You also need to remember you are just making clothes. You are making magical, beautiful things, but no one is going to die from what you do.

Figure 4.17 Mary Kate and Ashley Olsen wearing their own design from The Row.

chapter 5

Promotion

Picture a new designer who has recently been featured in newspapers, fashion magazines, on television, and on the Internet. As if it happens overnight, the former Mr. Unknown becomes a significant name and face to fashion industry professionals and fashion followers. When you peruse a fashion magazine, such as *Vogue*, *In Style*, or *W*, you are inundated by promotion in the forms of glossy and often eyebrow-raising advertisements of fashion brands such as Calvin Klein, Diesel, and Gucci. You may also see editorial pieces on celebrities who wear these designs or about the designers themselves. For example, Karl Lagerfeld pushed the envelope when he photographed supermodel Claudia Schiffer for a Dom Perignon advertising campaign in dark makeup and an afro wig, and later as an Asian woman (Figure 5.1).

Other examples of fashion promotion include a home decor article about the pink Manhattan apartment designed by Betsey Johnson (Figure 5.2) and a listing of where the consumer can buy one of Oprah's "Favorite Things," Miraclebody jeans (Figure 5.3). Further, a popup advertisement on the Internet may direct you to a new Web site that will bring designer fashions at discount prices into your home, such as Gilt Groupe. Through a major television series, *Mad Men*, costume designer Janie Bryant placed the spotlight on the late 1950s- and 1960s-era apparel—and the online and brick-and-mortar retailers of vintage clothing—through her selection of sleek and structured suits for the men, curve-hugging dresses and cardigans for the office secretaries, and glamorous gowns and furs for women to wear to swanky dinner parties (Figures 5.4a and b). The magazine articles, advertisements, editorial pieces, and sponsored television series are all forms of promotion. **Promotion** refers to the endorsement of a person, a product, a cause, an idea, or an organization. The ultimate goal of promotion is to encourage the growth, exposure, and development of an image by advancing it to a higher position.

Figure 5.1 Karl Lagerfeld photographed an eyebrow-raising advertising campaign for Dom Perignon featuring supermodel Claudia Schiffer.

Figure 5.2 Part of the Manhattan apartment designed by Betsey Johnson.

Figure 5.3 One of Oprah's "Favorite Things," Miraclebody jeans.

Let's look back at the promotional steps that may have led up to Janie Bryant's wardrobing choices for *Mad Men*. A vintage store owner hired someone to write the press release and to photograph the selections that the store owner wanted the costumer to buy. 1960s garments and accessories were shipped to the television stylist. The store owner then contacted magazine editors and pitched this story. Articles featured the retailer's store and Web site; orders piled in. All of these activities fit into the field of promotion. The major components of promotion involve an understanding of the significance of public relations, the costs and uses of various advertising vehicles, the value of sales promotions, the importance of selling, and the recent impact of sponsorships and partnerships on fashion and businesses and events. The interrelationship between these promotional areas illustrates the teamwork and versatility required by the industry: from glossy magazines through advertising and feature stories to popular media with its backstage administration for shows and events and front-of-house press dossiers and seating plans. The term **promotion product** can refer to an item, such as a press release or an advertisement, or an event, such as a fashion show or music video.

Career opportunities in fashion promotion exist in the industry sectors of apparel and accessories; home furnishings and accessories; publishing, art, and music; image and style consultancy; photography, illustration, and digital visual imagery; and styling of all kinds, from music groups to television and theater celebrities, broadcast media and DVDs, to the Internet. There are general areas of study that provide a strong foundation for future employees in all career tracks within the fashion promotion industry. An understanding of buying, merchandising, and marketing will be used consistently in all fashion promotion career options. Knowledge of computer-aided design and graphics provides an employee in this area of the industry with the skills to communicate a design concept through drawings and board presentations. Fashion forecasting and trend analysis allow the employee to look ahead to cutting-edge fashion, while the study of historical costume enables one to look back and identify which past decades or centuries of fashion cycles and looks are inspiring today's fashion designers. Knowledge of public relations and advertising is a key component of all

Figure 5.4a In *Mad Men*, costume designer Janie Bryant placed the spotlight on apparel from the late 1950s and 1960s through her selection of sleek and structured suits for the men and glamorous gowns for women to wear to swanky dinner parties.

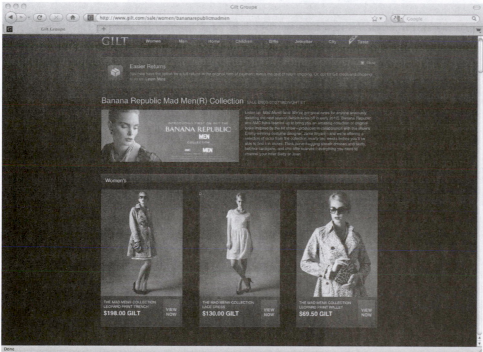

Figure 5.4b Banana Republic's Mad Men® collection for Gilt Groupe translated the hit show's iconic fashions into wearable pieces for consumers.

promotional careers. For some, studies in photography, display, and fashion show production are needed. Journalism skills prepare the fashion promotion candidate for fashion writing, whether in commentary scripts, advertising copy, press releases, or editorial features in consumer or trade publications.

Consumer and Trade Publications

What is the difference between consumer and trade publications? A **consumer publication** is one that is readily available to the layperson, the general customer. The consumer may subscribe to the periodical or purchase it at a bookstore, grocery store, convenience store, drugstore, mass merchandiser, or newsstand. Nearly all consumer lifestyle publications feature some type of fashion content (e.g., *People*, *Town & Country*, and *Travel*); some are devoted exclusively to fashion and interior design. Examples of fashion consumer publications include *Vogue*, *In Style*, *House & Garden*, *W*, *Dwell*, and *Elle*; the list goes on and on (Figures 5.5a and b). Most magazines with a nationwide readership are headquartered in New York City.

In contrast, **trade publications** are periodicals that are designed for readers interested in or employed in specific professions or vocations. These magazines and newspapers are promoted to people in a specific career field. Table 5.1 lists a few major trade journals and the segments of the fashion industry to which they most appeal. There are also publications that provide information about a wide range of merchandise classifications to retailers, designers, manufacturers, and buyers. The top publication in women's apparel and accessories is *Women's Wear Daily*, a print and Web news source that focuses on different merchandise types each day of the week and often features broad-scope fashion news such as general retail trends in sales or mergers and acquisitions in the fashion industry (Figure 5.6).

Figures 5.5a and b
Examples of consumer fashion magazines, part of Condé Nast's collection of publications.

Table 5.1 Top Trade Publications in the Fashion Industry

Industry Segment	Trade Publications
Accessories	*Accessories* *Footwear News*
Beauty	*Beauty Industry Report (BIR)*
Children's Wear	*Childrenswear Business (CWB)* *Earnshaw's*
Interior Design	*Home Furnishing News (HFN)* *InFurniture* *Interior Design*
Menswear	*Gap Press Men's Wear Collections*
Retailing	*California Apparel News* *STORES*
Textiles	*Future Materials* *Nonwovens Report International* *Textile View* *Textile World* *Twist*
Women's Wear	*Apparel Magazine* *Apparel Strategist* *The Business of Fashion* *Gap Press* *Sportswear International* *The Swim Journal* *Women's Wear Daily (WWD)*

Fashion Stylist

A **fashion stylist** is the person who does most of the work before the cameras start shooting, whether for a magazine, film, television series, fashion show, or a personal client. **Fashion photostylist** is the term used to specify the stylist who works with photography. Whether styling for a photograph or a fashion show, a stylist must be aware of the latest trends and bring great resources and a strong personal style to every event. **Fashion shoots**, photography sessions of models and fashions, are a team effort, and the stylist's role is critical to its success. Stylists are responsible for assembling the items, garments, and accessories needed for the event and preparing the people involved in the event, such as the models, dressers, makeup artists, hairstylists, and lighting designers. Stylists must make decisions in minutes, quickly

Figure 5.6 *Women's Wear Daily* is a print and Web news vehicle that focuses on different merchandise types each day of the week and often features broader fashion news such as general retail trends in sales or mergers and acquisitions in the fashion industry.

determining, for example, how various items of apparel are to be combined and accessorized to show each off to the best features. They also handle myriad details, ensuring that the right sizes and colors are available for each model. If the models are celebrities, the appropriateness of the ensembles to each of their images becomes an additional factor. Stylists must be diplomats to win the cooperation of everyone involved in an event. In addition to magazine work, stylists may find employment with advertising agencies, working on print ads or television commercials. Figure 5.7 features a fashion stylist working with a model in a photography studio.

Qualifications

Do you have what it takes to pursue a career in fashion styling? Following is a list of qualifications for a fashion stylist:

- **Education:** A bachelor's degree in fashion design, fashion merchandising, fashion journalism, fashion communication, photography, visual arts, or a related field is preferred.

- **Experience:** An internship with a photographer or stylist is an excellent way to build one's résumé for employment in this industry. Some fashion stylists begin in visual merchandising or as an assistant to a stylist. Fashion stylists are often chosen based on the look of their "books," large volumes of tearsheets from published magazine or newspaper work, as well as Polaroid or digital images that illustrate work they have done with different photographers and/or models. Digital portfolios and computer-aided design skills are beneficial.

- **Personal characteristics:** The attributes of successful fashion stylists include having a network of professionals in photography, hair and makeup design, and the modeling industry; a keen eye for detail; the ability to apply visual art principles to print work and photographs; effective verbal, written, and visual communication skills; strong time-management skills; and the ability to work well under pressure, whether with deadlines or uncontrollable factors, such as poor lighting during an outdoor shoot or models who miss their flights.

Figure 5.7 A fashion stylist working with a model in a photography studio.

Career Challenges

Fashion stylist positions are often only available with large companies or as freelance work. It is a growing, exciting, and potentially profitable career track. Fashion stylists face a number of challenges, including quick decision making and coordinating a multitude of details. Since stylists must ensure that the correct apparel is available for the right models, they must do a great deal of preplanning for the expected and the unexpected, such as broken zippers, a late hairstylist, or models with attitude. "Plan ahead and be prepared for anything" is a motto for successful fashion stylists. Stylists must also work with all types of people and be able to motivate everyone involved in the shoot. It is not enough to have the vision; it is as important to have the skills to implement the vision.

Public Relations Director

Public relations directors are responsible for finding minimal or no-cost ways to effectively promote the company they represent. They develop proposals that will put their company in a favorable spotlight and persuade the media to feature press about the company. Public relations directors work with all types of media representatives, from television and radio producers to newspaper and magazine publishers. There are a number of public relations companies that specialize in fashion and represent a number of designer and manufacturer clients. In addition, many of the designer firms, such as Gucci, Salvatore Ferragamo, and Tod's, have in-house public relations staffs.

Some of the activities that public relations directors develop include charity events such as fashion shows and parties, events that raise awareness for a company or person while generating funds and appreciation for specific causes, press coverage for well-known designers who are presenting new collections, and competitions for fashion students to submit original designs that will be produced by a major manufacturer (Figure 5.8).

Public relations directors attempt to find themes or topics that the media will want to cover and to tie these into the businesses of their clients. For example, a public relations director may work for a major apparel manufacturer/designer, such as Nicole Miller. When Nicole Miller introduces her new home accessories lines of bed linens, pillows, photograph frames, and dinnerware, the public relations director may schedule her to appear at a number of key retail stores around the country. In conjunction with these retail partner arrangements, the public relations director will contact the media and fashion organizations in each city to generate news coverage of the designer's appearances in the retail stores.

Qualifications

Public relations directors should meet the following criteria:

- **Education:** A bachelor's degree in marketing, public relations, advertising, business administration, fashion merchandising, or a related field is a minimum requirement.

- **Experience:** To move into the director position, one usually needs a minimum of eight to ten years of fashion public relations experience and must have an array of excellent contacts within the fashion and lifestyle media. Additionally, a public relations director must compile a portfolio of proposals.

- **Personal characteristics:** Public relations directors must have exceptional writing skills and be confident team players. Successful public relations directors are described as possessing "excellent pitching skills," the ability to sell one's ideas in a persuasive and articulate manner. Budget management skills are also essential.

Career Challenges

A successful public relations director is a great salesperson, frequently selling an image, a company, or an idea. This person must have the ability to stay positive and enthusiastic in a world of repeated rejection. With so much going on in the fashion world, the public relations director is one of many vying for the attention of newspaper and magazine publishers and television producers. Finding creative ways to pitch stories and build relationships with ever-changing media representatives are challenges public relations directors face. This career path is not all about selling, creating, and networking. Public relations directors must have a head for numbers to meet the responsibility for finding cost-effective ways to promote the company. At some point in their careers, public relations directors may be confronted with countering negative publicity. In such cases they must have the skills to work under the pressures of time and stress, quickly developing plans that will put the company in a favorable spotlight and persuading the media to feature positive press about the company.

Advertising Research and Promotion Positions

The major source of revenue for a publication is the sale of advertising space. Those who like to sell may find their niche as **advertising sales representatives**, the people who sell advertising for consumer and trade publications, such as *Glamour*, *Women's Wear Daily*, or *Lucky*. There are a number of other positions in fashion publications; among them are those in advertising research and promotion. Many publications offer positions for those who prefer research. An

advertising research assistant helps sell advertising space in a publication by supplying facts that advertisers will want to know, such as the number of issues sold, the top locations in terms of sales volume, and the profile and buying power of the publication's readers. These facts indicate the publication's ability to reach potential customers for the advertiser. The **advertising promotion staff**, yet another source of job opportunities, develops presentations to help sell advertising space to new and existing accounts. These people often have skills in persuasive writing and creative projects.

A related job option in advertising is that of **media planner**. Media planning is a statistical and mathematical process through which planners determine prices, including quantity discounts, for a media buy that may include several venues, such as radio, television, and newspaper. They determine how advertising budgets are best spent to generate the most exposure and sales.

Qualifications

Following is a list of qualifications for a career in advertising research and promotion.

- **Education:** A bachelor's degree in advertising, journalism, business administration, marketing, fashion merchandising, or a related field is required.

- **Experience:** Working in retail sales is a great way to get started while still in school. Selling is selling, whether it is for an apparel retailer or a newspaper publisher. Some students gain direct sales experience selling advertisements for college publications, such as the yearbook and programs for athletic events and theatrical performances. Some enter the advertising industry through copywriting and/or research jobs with newspapers or publishing firms and then move into the advertising sales representative position. Others gain experience at the retail level through a position in a store's advertising department, writing copy for advertised items, or laying out the actual advertisement.

- **Personal characteristics:** The ability to sell one's ideas is key to success in advertising. An understanding of budgets and accounting is necessary. With a high level of attention to detail, successful advertising professionals are focused on accuracy and fact-checking.

Career Challenges

Advertising research and promotion personnel must gather data from all types of sources and then compile this research to tell a story—why their media vehicle is the best choice for advertisers to spend promotional dollars. This job is not an easy one as it combines the abilities of acquiring and interpreting data with strong writing skills. Advertising is a creative, numbers-based, and fast-paced field. Advertising research and promotion staff members need to stay up to date on all facets of the competition: their target markets, companies that advertise in their publications, and their advertising rates. As competition in this industry is constantly evolving, this is a time-consuming task.

Social Media Director

With the high-speed growth of Internet marketing, fashion public relations is jumping into social media with both feet, and a new career path has evolved—that of the social media director. **Social media** refers to the tools and social Web sites of the Internet that are used to communicate online with others. **Social Web sites**, such as Facebook and LinkedIn, function like an online community of Internet users. **Social networking** is the grouping of individuals into factions with similar interests. Although social networking is possible in person, especially in the workplace, universities, and neighborhoods, it is most popular online. The Internet is filled with millions of individuals who are looking to develop friendships or professional alliances, to gather and share firsthand information and experiences about fashion and news, to find employment, and to market products. Twitter.com indicates that as of September 14, 2010, it had 175 million registered users, and that 95 million tweets were written per day. In Box 5.1, Alexander Wang's entry into the world of Twitter and an interactive Web site is examined.

In addition to social networking, crowdsourcing is another way of meeting potential and current customers online. The purpose of **crowdsourcing** is to tap into the collective intelligence of the public at large to complete business-related tasks that a company would normally either perform itself or outsource to a third-party provider. Not only is free labor a part of crowdsourcing, it enables companies to gain a deeper understanding of what customers really want, as illustrated in Box 5.2.

Facebooking, tweeting, crowdsourcing, and more have led to the development of the career position of social media director. The **social media director** develops, manages, and oversees the implementation of public relations programs in the social media venue. This includes creating content and generating coverage for social media efforts in all forms. Primary responsibilities of the social media director include:

- Managing and initiating strategic and creative planning of public relations campaigns through social media projects

- Integrating projects with marketing, advertising, and promotional divisions

- Managing public relations agencies contracted by the company, if applicable

- Cultivating and developing productive relationships with social media contacts

- Managing press interviews with company executives

- Working to innovate and integrate the use of technology/social media into all public relations efforts

- Managing department resources—personnel and fiscal

By Venessa Lau,
From WWDSTYLE *Issue 03/01/2011*

When Alexander Wang celebrated the opening of his store on February 15, he also made another big debut of sorts: the launch of his Twitter account. "Lauryn Hill is about to go onstage," was the inaugural tweet that night. For a designer so plugged in to what's new, it's a bit shocking that he waited this long. But after noticing—and shutting down—a bunch of fake Twitter accounts under his name, Wang finally took the plunge himself. "I thought we might as well sign up," he remarked.

And beginning today, expect even more behind-the-scenes access when Wang relaunches his Web site, taking it from straightforward to full-on interactive. "We wanted to make our digital world much more engaging for our customer," said the designer, who tapped online design firm Createthe Group, whose client roster includes Donna Karan, Marc Jacobs, Tom Ford, Tory Burch, Gucci, Balenciaga, and Calvin Klein. "The look is still clean and graphic, but not as minimal as before. It's definitely more layered."

In addition to a Collections page (a virtual look book of past and current designs) and a beefed-up e-commerce area (which now sells ready-to-wear, accessories, and the T collection for men and women, and will soon go international), the Web site includes a splashy Studio section that will feature a range of special content, from in-house editorials to video campaigns to the story behind, for example, his first in-house print this season. (It's comprised of random doodles and inside jokes written and drawn by his staff and interns.) Other content will consist of behind-the-scenes documentaries and flashback

moments—"like videos from the old days when I was working out of my apartment," explained Wang—as well as a series of model confessionals. The latter kicks off with Britt Maren, who was filmed before, during, and after Wang's spring show. "It's fittings, hair, and makeup from her point of view and follows her around the city," he said. "We lent her a Flip camera to film moments from home, too."

But perhaps the buzziest of elements here is Wang's collaboration with Terence Koh. The designer tapped the artist to create a special mask for the models to wear while being shot for the e-commerce section. "You usually see their heads cut off because of usage rights," Wang explained. "We thought, let's get creative with this so we can shield the identity but at the same time tell the story of the collection." Inspired by spring's buoyant vibe, Koh created a fluorescent halo to conceal their faces with a faint glow. "It's having fun with these mundane, everyday things," said Wang, who plans to enlist different artists each season.

In two weeks, the designer will unveil yet another collaborative project that combines his recent brick-and-mortar launch with the revamped Web site. He made a video diary, filmed by Gregory Harris, of *Vogue Nippon* editor Anna Dello Russo's experience in Wang's new flagship. What began as a simple taping of her editor's picks turned into a full-on editorial—Wang and Dello Russo played sales associates and camped around as mannequins in the store windows. "There's humor behind the site, of course," said Wang.

Source: http://www.wwd.com/media-news/wang-gets-techie-3528363

Box 5.2 Crowdsourcing

Crowdsourcing Gains Voice in Shoes
By Gerald Flores
From Footwear News *issue 01/24/2011*

The footwear industry is embracing the power of the community. Increasingly, companies are turning to crowdsourcing, the act of outsourcing tasks like design to the general public, as a way to generate fresh ideas.

Simple Shoes, in search of a new brand logo for 2011, recently experimented with a community-driven contest that pooled designs from users on Behance.net. The competition, which garnered more than 600 entries, was the first time the brand used a crowdsourcing model. "Gone are the days where the consumer didn't have a voice," said Simple's strategic outreach manager, Jaime Eschette. "Consumers [speak] through social media and blogs now, and it's a benefit for [the brand] to listen." Eschette said an advantage of crowdsourcing was being able to browse through a large number of designs at one time. Five finalists were each paid $2,500 for their creations, and Simple's new brand identity is scheduled to be unveiled within the next month.

Other footwear companies have experimented with crowdsourcing to find fresh designs for products. Through a collaboration with Local Motors, a car maker that has an online community of more than 8,000 designers, Reebok ran a contest last month to look for a new Zigtech sneaker. Reebok's global creative director, Michael Schaeffer, said the project was beneficial for the brand, even though the winning style will only be distributed on a limited basis. "The goal was to test a strategy that lets a community decide how a product will look and feel," he said. "We found that there's great potential in this model. It's something that's exciting and we're going to continue to look into it going forward." Schaeffer added that community-based design not only helped provide innovative concepts but allowed the firm to tell an engaging story to consumers.

Seeking to leverage the increased interest in crowdsourcing among athletic players, last spring

Brian Bednarek debuted Mesh01, an online platform that has created footwear design competitions for companies including Columbia Sportswear, Hi-Tec, RYZ, Simms, and Callaway Golf. With more than 879 designers in its community, Mesh01 has launched 16 contests in footwear design, which paid an average of $3,000 in prize money to winners. "We're getting very close to a tipping point where [crowdsourcing] will be more permanent," Bednarek said. Users of the site can create a public profile, which companies or potential employers browse.

But there are risks. With a designer's portfolio being readily available for view, what protects their work from potentially being stolen? "There has to be some code of integrity on the site," Bednarek said. "The idea is not to exploit a design community, but to give a company a good quantity and quality of submissions to review." He added that users could also make their profiles private.

Footwear firms who have tapped into Mesh01's services, such as Columbia Sportswear, said they used the platform as a way to broaden their design horizons. But however useful crowdsourcing might be, Jim Gorman, VP of global footwear design manufacturing for Columbia, stressed that it is still important to maintain an in-house design team. "The concept is very interesting, but it's not a replacement for internal design at all because brands need to have their own design perspective," he said.

In addition to marketing and design, crowdsourcing also is manifesting itself in the form of retail concepts. Last year, Jeff Silverman, former head of Steve Madden's custom shoe business, used his industry experience to launch Jeffsilverman. com, a fully crowdsourced e-commerce site that sells directly to the consumer. Through the platform, anyone can upload a sketch or photo of his or her original shoe design and receive that exact product within three weeks. Products are manufactured in China and retail for $125 to $250. And for $100 to $175, consumers can buy existing or tweaked designs. Users of the site also receive a $15 payment when another consumer purchases

Box 5.2 Crowdsourcing (continued)

their designs. The site has produced more than 150 original designs to date. And with all products being made to order, Silverman said he is never sitting on inventory. However, he admitted that users can potentially bootleg well-known designer shoes, but said it's all part of the business. "If you study fashion, what you find is almost every [design] comes from everything else," Silverman said.

While crowdsourcing is still relatively new, experts expect more companies to embrace it going forward. "With the financial crisis, so many retailers have stripped down their selling, general, and administrative expenses and there's not much more they can do to get leaner," said Catherine Moellering, EVP of Tobe Reports, a fashion trend tracking firm. "They're still looking for innovative ways to reduce risk, and crowdsourcing is an initiative that retailers must evaluate." One reason that it hasn't been fully adopted yet is because companies are naturally suspicious of it, Moellering said. "There's a sense that it can replace jobs," she said. "But there are certain aspects of a merchant's, buyer's, or executive's job that can't be displaced." And despite the hurdles, Moellering said she believes there are upsides for the company that can implement crowdsourcing successfully. "We live in an environment where consumers are so powerful," she said. "Crowdsourcing allows retailers to gather so much information about their consumers and basically get it for free. Anything that gets customers engaged is worth looking into."

Source: http://www.wwd.com/footwear-news/crowdsourcing-gains-voice-in-shoes-3443981

Qualifications

Future social media directors should work to acquire the following qualifications:

- **Education:** A bachelor's degree in marketing, computer information systems, public relations, advertising, business administration, fashion merchandising, or a related field is a minimum requirement.

- **Experience:** To move into the director position, one usually needs a minimum of five to seven years of fashion public relations experience with an emphasis on social media. Broad knowledge of social media tools, current and future, is expected, as is a knowledge of traditional fashion press. A comprehensive understanding of competitors and their social networking outreach is a plus. Additionally, the candidate for a social media director position must present a portfolio of proposals.

- **Personal characteristics:** Excellent leadership and management skills are necessary tools. Successful social media directors are described as possessing excellent "futuring" skills, the ability to anticipate the "next big thing" in social networking. Budget management and human resource skills are also essential.

Career Challenges

The social media director is faced with the challenges of updating the social networking efforts of the company by the minute, hour, or day. The work must be ever-changing yet consistent. Conveying the company's image accurately and person-to-person through an online presence is critical.

Fashion Event Planner

Have you ever visited a pop-up shop? Viewed a fashion show production? Attended a trunk show? Participated in a bridal show extravaganza? If so, you have seen the handiwork of a **fashion event planner**, also referred to as a **special events coordinator**. Fashion event planners increase the visibility of design houses, brands, products, or fabrics by coordinating fashion events that provide positive exposure for the company.

Fashion Events

There are many occasions that fashion event planners coordinate to promote an image, an idea, an organization, or a product. As discussed in the next section of this chapter, trunk shows in the designer salon of a department store, for example, may spotlight a new designer line. Another way to create exposure is through tearoom modeling for a women's organization or a community group at a country club or restaurant. A newer development in the fashion event sector, one that takes the fashion show or trunk show a step further, is the pop-up shop.

Whether you call them **pop-up shops** or stores, these projects are like hide-and-seek boutiques that pop up within other retail locations or at vacant retail spaces with few preliminary announcements. They quickly draw crowds, are open for a limited period of time, and then disappear or morph into something else. The designer's or retailer's goals for the pop-up stores are to add freshness, exclusivity, and surprise to their images and product lines, and to sell merchandise. Whether it is tagged mass-exclusivity or planned spontaneity, it is working. In Box 5.3, the reasons and how-tos for opening a pop-up shop are examined. In Box 5.4, examples of pop-up shops in the footwear industry are discussed. Figure 5.9 shows an example of a pop-up shop.

Some of the fashion experiences that fashion event planners develop and participate in follow.

Bridal Shows

Through **bridal shows**, or bridal fairs, wedding product or service manufacturers and retailers are able to get together with auxiliary organizations, such as wedding planners, caterers, florists, and travel agents, to present the season's offerings for brides-to-be and their friends and families. As Figure 5.10 illustrates, the bridal fair is often organized in a convention center with booths that feature each of the vendors and with a fashion show as the main event. These are usually staged in January for the spring wedding season.

Mannequin Modeling

A promotional activity by fashion retailers during the mid-1970s to mid-1980s, this entertainment and promotion activity is back. **Mannequin modeling** involves live models who are hired to stand motionless in the place of regular mannequins in windows or on showroom or retail floors. People often stop to stare, waiting for the models to blink or move (Figure 5.11).

Tearoom Modeling

Tearoom modeling is an informal fashion show that often takes place in a conference center, hotel, or restaurant in which models circulate among the tables as refreshments are served. A women's group or other organization may use this activity as a drawing card for a meeting, or as a fund-raiser for a philanthropic cause. Instead of commentary, printed programs are often left at the place settings to enable guests to read descriptions, prices, and size ranges of the featured garments and accessories so that the meal or the speakers will not be interrupted.

Box 5.3 Why and How to Open a Pop-Up Store

By Jason Del Rey, July 1, 2010

With the national retail vacancy rate at a three-year high, temporary shops are dropping into empty spaces, an attractive option for landlords, business owners, and consumers. Pop-up stores seem to be popping up everywhere. "It's a great way to market your products or your real estate," says Christina Norsig, CEO of PopUpInsider.com, a site that provides available pop-up locations. Here are four reasons that businesses, from new entrepreneurial firms to well-known companies, are opening pop-up stores:

1. To get the word out

While in New York City, Jason Revilla and Jim Grumbine came across some vacant retail spaces being used as pop-up stores. Co-founders of Faith & Fortune, a fledgling online apparel company, they liked the idea and wanted to try something similar in their town of Beverly, Massachusetts. After six weeks of planning and scouting locations, a friend in the real estate industry helped Revilla and Grumbine find an empty store on a street in Beverly with high foot traffic. The space also had wireless Internet access. To publicize the event, the founders sent messages to their Facebook and Twitter followers and handed out flyers around town. Their primary goal was to raise brand awareness. "Since we're a Web-based business, we were looking to get more people to interact with the brand," Grumbine says. "It's great having people come in and see the clothing, because the materials we use are unique, soft, comfortable, and vintage-like." In one weekend, the company sold $1,000 worth of artist-designed T-shirts and sweatshirts; $200 of that was donated to a local charity as part of the company's dedication to charitable causes. After Revilla and Grumbine purchased signage, food, and office supplies, their costs for the event totaled just $150—plus a few T-shirts. The landlord let the founders use the space in exchange for a couple of shirts. "One of the things we found in this economy is that businesses are willing to help each other out," says Revilla. "People are willing to negotiate, and it's something you should take advantage of."

2. To unload dated inventory

Two weeks before a New York City furniture market, Cheri Caso began hunting for space to exhibit the modern housewares she sells through her online store, Merchant No. 4. She considered renting retail space, but she didn't have time to comparison shop, nor the thousands of dollars needed to rent a space. Luckily, a friend who owns an architecture firm agreed to let Caso set up shop in the firm's unused space in its fourth-floor loft. Caso had two objectives in mind: to gain attention for her company's Web site during a time when many potential buyers would be in town, and to sell some products she no longer carried on the site. "We have a lot of odds and ends that are just taking up space in our storage area," she says. Caso spent about $1,000 on the event, including $200 for insurance, $400 for the space, and $400 for the materials she used to build display tables and room dividers. To get foot traffic, she announced the event on Twitter and sent press releases to design blogs and local publications. She also placed a sign on the sidewalk outside the building. Over four days, she gained a small profit and new traffic as about 200 to 300 people passed through the shop. Caso was pleased and sees room for improvement. "Next year, it would definitely need to be in street-level retail space," she says, "so I'll have to start looking for something ahead of time."

3. To test new markets

By 2007, Bobby Kim and Ben Shenassafar had built a strong customer base in Los Angeles for The Hundreds, a clothing company influenced by the styles of California skateboarders. Kim and Shenassafar had a store in the city's Fairfax district and were looking to expand into other cities. Their first target was San Francisco. Opening a pop-up store seemed like a cost-effective way to gauge interest, so they teamed with several other brands to rent a gallery for a day. After the success of that pop-up store, The Hundreds opened a permanent retail space in San Francisco in 2008. Later, The Hundreds opened its own weekend pop-up store in New York City. The event turned a small profit, even with $7,000 in costs. "Not only did we make a little

Box 5.3 Why and How to Open a Pop-Up Store (continued)

Figure 5.9 The Tommy Hilfiger Prep World pop-up cottage in New York's Meatpacking District.

4. To vet a new business idea

For about a year, Dorie Greenspan, a popular cookbook author, and her son, Josh, had discussed opening a cookie shop in New York City. Permanent retail space in the city is pricey, they discovered—as high as $1,725 per square foot per year for prime space. Before making a big financial commitment, they wanted to make sure that people would come. "We needed to figure out if we could physically do this and if people would buy the cookies," Josh says. In late 2009, Josh approached a friend who owned a Manhattan salon and pitched him on the idea of selling cookies there during the days leading up to Valentine's Day. The friend agreed to let the Greenspans use the space for free. He merely asked that they pay the associated fees if they used the salon's credit card swiper. The Greenspans spent about $1,600 to rent a commercial kitchen to bake the cookies and set up a small table near the entrance of the salon. A few fans of Dorie's volunteered to help bake after she publicized the event on Twitter. *Time Out New York* and several food blogs covered the event. In six days, the Greenspans sold more than 4,000 cookies. "It was far beyond anything we expected," Josh says. Not only did the pop-up prove that people would indeed spend up to $3.50 on a single cookie, but it also convinced Josh that a full retail store was unnecessary. He is now looking to permanently rent a sliver of space in someone else's store.

Source: http://www.inc.com/magazine/20100701/how-to-open-a-pop-up-store.html

money and move product," says Shenassafar, "but we were able to market the brand in an area where we didn't have a lot of penetration." That persuaded Kim and Shenassafar to open a third store, set to debut in Manhattan this summer.

Trunk Shows

Through a **trunk show**, a fashion event planner or a manufacturer's representative brings the vendor's full seasonal line to a retail store that carries that particular manufacturer. The planner or representative works with individual customers, educating them about the line and providing personal fashion consultations. The customers can then place special orders. Sometimes, a trunk show in an upscale department or specialty store may feature a well-known designer as well as the designer's latest collection (Figure 5.12).

Box 5.4 Brands Make a Splash with Pop-ups

By Erin Clack
From Footwear News *issue 11/15/2010*

It's no secret that pop-up shops are hot. As the format continues to gain steam, more brands are seeing it as a chance to stand out—and not just to sell shoes. These temporary shops offer an opportunity to generate buzz for a brand, test the viability of operating retail stores, and connect with consumers in a more intimate way—and they're much less risky than traditional stores, which require firms to be locked into a lease.

With their now-you-see-it, now-you-don't allure, pop-up shops have been a bright spot in a dismal retail environment. And the glut of available real estate due to the stagnant economy has meant short-term leases for prime storefronts are much easier to come by. Florsheim, Piperlime, Manolo Blahnik, and Frye are just a few of the footwear companies that have recently jumped on the bandwagon. "The pop-up phenomenon has gone mainstream, and we're seeing a diverse and broad set of companies embracing the format," said Janet Hoffman, managing director of Accenture's retail practice. "[Everyone is] seeking new ways to grab consumers' attention and reignite their desire to spend."

Florsheim opened a pop-up store in September in New York's SoHo neighborhood to showcase newer brand initiatives such as its Florsheim by Duckie Brown collaboration and new mid-priced Florsheim Limited label. According to John Florsheim, president and COO of parent firm Weyco Group Inc., the success of the venture already has the company thinking about pop-ups in other cities. The SoHo shop, meanwhile, is slated to remain open through February, but Florsheim said the brand isn't ruling out staying in the space permanently. "We'll see how things evolve," he said, "but so far, it's been very positive for our brand. The store is exceeding expectations."

"Falling in love with a space and wanting to stay is not uncommon with pop-up ventures," said Christina Norsig, founder and CEO of Pop-up Insider, a national online exchange that connects retailers with landlords seeking to lease space on a short-term basis. "I've seen many examples of companies that intend to stay for only a couple of weeks and then discover it's such a phenomenal location that they go ahead and negotiate a long-term lease," she said.

For online retailer Piperlime, its recent pop-up in New York's SoHo neighborhood was a chance to bring its brand experience to life in a brick-and-mortar format. "It was the first time that Piperlime [was] available in a three-dimensional environment where customers could touch and feel the product," said Piperlime GM Jennifer Gosselin of the shop, which was open for 25 days in September and featured an edited assortment of apparel, footwear, and accessories.

Madison Riley, managing director of consulting firm Kurt Salmon Associates, said the desire to explore beyond the bounds of the Internet is a natural progression for e-tailers, and pop-ups are a way to do that. "Online retailers are always wondering whether [brick-and-mortar stores] can be a long-term profit driver for them," he said. "We'll see more of this."

While many footwear players are leasing freestanding space for their pop-ups, others are

Box 5.4 Brands Make a Splash with Pop-ups (continued)

opting to set up shop inside another retailer's store, creating the feel of an intimate trunk show. Boot maker Frye partnered with one of its biggest Canadian accounts, Ron White, to run a three-week-long pop-up last month at the retailer's flagship in Toronto's Manulife Centre. "Ron White already does very well with the Frye brand and has a loyal customer following," said Michael Petry, Frye's design director. "The pop-up allowed us to boost our brand profile in eastern Canada while giving Ron a chance to reward his best customers, as well as capture new customers."

The pop-up also was an opportunity for Frye, which does not yet have its own retail stores, to tell its entire brand story with a full product assortment. "Normally, Ron's store would show about 80 Frye styles, but for a three-week period, he had 180 styles, including a few limited-edition items and special-order boots," Petry said.

Like Frye, high-end designer Manolo Blahnik chose another store, Liberty of London's Great Marlborough Street flagship, as the site of his first pop-up, which opened in September. Slated to remain open until Christmas, the garden-inspired "World of Manolo" houses a selection of Blahnik's original shoe designs, along with nine limited-edition styles using a dozen prints that Blahnik pulled from Liberty's archives. The designer also created new shoe-inspired prints that are featured on other items, including silk scarves, stationery, and umbrellas. Kristina Blahnik, the designer's niece and collaborator, said Liberty was the right fit because of the type of customers it attracts. "[The store] just feels young, and that's what we want to project, that Manolo Blahnik is a youthful brand," she said. The special, limited-edition aspect of "World of Manolo" is a prime example of what Accenture's Hoffman called the "buy it now or never" appeal of pop-ups. "The temporary nature of these stores and the limited stock create a real sense of excitement and urgency to buy," she said.

The entertainment factor is another significant part of pop-ups' popularity. Companies are coming up with increasingly creative ways for consumers to experience and interact with their favorite brands beyond what is typically possible in a permanent store. Puma has taken the idea to heart in a big way with its pop-ups in Boston, New York, and now Los Angeles. The Puma Social Club LA, which ran October 13–28, combined retail with a nightlife venue, complete with a bar, lounge area, live music, and retro social sports, such as darts, Ping-Pong, and foosball. Puma's elaborate events are a testament to how evolved the pop-up concept has become, as brands up the stakes to garner even bigger buzz.

Still, David Wolfe, creative director of New York–based trend forecasting firm The Doneger Group, warned that companies need to be careful not to take the staging of their shops too far. "I remember some of the early Target ones in New York and how exciting they were because they seemed so temporary," he said. "If you pop something up that looks too planned or like an established venue, then you've lost the point."

Source: http://www.wwd.com/footwear-news/brands-make-splash-with-pop-ups-3382000?browsets=1299093504466&browsets=483044258919

Figure 5.10 The bridal fair is often organized in a convention center with booths that feature each of the vendors and with a fashion show as the main event.

Figure 5.11 Mannequin modeling involves live models who are hired to stand motionless in the place of regular mannequins in store windows to attract walk-by customers.

Party Planning

In some instances, fashion event planners are literally paid to party. **Party planning** involves a manufacturer, a designer, a retailer, or an organization hiring a fashion event planner to put together a party event (Figure 5.13). For example, a textile producer may employ a fashion event planner to coordinate such an event for one of the chapters of Fashion Group International, Inc. The planner arranges to have the showroom open after hours for the party and sends out invitations to the Fashion Group members, offering them a private showing of the new product line during the party. He or she works with the sales manager of the textile producer to schedule sales associates for this evening event and locates a new restaurant and wine shop to serve complimentary appetizers and drinks in exchange for publicity. The planner decorates the entrance of the showroom with Fashion Group banners and locates a desk at the entrance of the showroom to greet and sign in guests, to secure their addresses for future mailings. Door prizes provided by manufacturers that use the firm's textiles are incentives for guests to stay for the entire length of the party. The cost of the event is minimal; the visibility is great as the textile producer showcases its business to the fashion executives. The freelance fashion event planner is then paid well for a job well done.

Educational Events

A fashion event planner, a manufacturer's representative, or an employee hired by a planner may stage an **educational event** to inform an audience about a product. For example, in apparel, the presenter may demonstrate different ways to wear scarves, separates, or evening wear. In home furnishings, a demonstrator may educate an audience by showing how to configure a new sectional sofa for a number of different looks and space needs.

Book Signings

The fashion event planner may organize **book signings**, in which well-known beauty or fashion writers agree to sign copies of their latest books in a book, specialty, or department store.

Complimentary Services

A **complimentary service** is a feature or service offered by a retail operation at no fee to the consumer, with the intent of drawing in and keeping customers. For example, a travel agency may hire a fashion event planner to conduct a workshop on how to pack for an African safari for its clients who have invested in this trip. Matching complimentary services with fashion products and services allows the fashion event planner to generate new contacts and additional revenue.

Fashion Shows

A fashion event planner may execute a fashion show that benefits a nonprofit or charitable organization through its ticket sales or donations (Figure 5.14). This is referred to as a **philanthropic fashion show** or *charity fashion show*. Often community leaders, local celebrities, or executives of the philanthropic organization will model the apparel and accessories, acting as a drawing card for the show. The fashion event planner may also solicit door prizes or auction items from benefactors to generate additional funds for the cause.

Technology has impacted the world of fashion shows. Designers and retailers are featuring their fashion shows online, as illustrated in Box 5.5. Chloé celebrated its fifth anniversary in China by live-streaming a runway show of its spring collection.

Figure 5.12 Designer Stella McCartney greets guests at her trunk show and party at Bergdorf Goodman in New York.

Figure 5.13 The party planner coordinates Opening Ceremony's celebration of Fashion's Night Out.

Duties of Fashion Event Planners

There are many ways to generate interest through fashion events. Because there is much work involved and, in many cases, a great deal of expertise needed, many manufacturers and designers hire freelance fashion event planners to execute them. So, what kinds of activities do fashion event planners do? Here is a sampling:

- Locate a place, make the reservation, and negotiate terms and dates for the event

- Determine lighting, music, sound system, and staging needs

- Assemble merchandise to be featured

- Hire and fit models, arrange lineup, and supervise rehearsals

- Compile commentary, if appropriate, and recruit commentator

- Arrange for printing needs (e.g., tickets, signage, invitations, and programs)

- Arrange for seating, to include setup and breakdown of seats, tables, and staging

Figure 5.14 A fashion event planner may execute a fashion show to benefit a nonprofit organization through its ticket sales or donations.

Box 5.5 Chloé Live-Streams Shanghai Fashion Show

By WWD Staff
From WWDSTYLE Issue 03/01/2011

Chloé just feted its fifth anniversary in China by live-streaming a runway show of its spring collection. And the house has another high-tech project in the works: it plans to launch a global e-commerce site within the next 18 months.

Chloé chief executive officer Geoffroy de la Bourdonnaye said the new site, which will permit orders from China, is part of the house's evolving online strategy. In December, Chloé started a Chinese-language blog, which it claims to be the first of its kind from a Western luxury brand. The site, jesuischloe.com, includes company news and information about various products and collections. Friday's show, which took place at the Shanghai Expo Center, was broadcast live on both the Chinese blog and Chloé's main Web site.

"It is a test, and it is a way to actually innovate," said de la Bourdonnaye of the Chinese blog. "There is no grand plan of doing something with it other than allowing the customers who love Chloé to connect with us and participate in the event in an interactive way, but there might be some other ideas coming up at the end because we will take time to analyze the reaction. We are using technology wherever it serves our purpose."

The Chloé executive said the label has not been able to expand e-commerce initiatives outside of Western markets because of a lack of suitable partners. The company works with Nordstrom, Neiman Marcus, Barneys New York, and Net-a-porter to sell products online. "Honestly, the quality of the experience online has to be comparable to the quality of the experience on the street," de la Bourdonnaye said. "That is why we are not in e-commerce in Japan. Even though Japan is the number-one market, we have no e-commerce there. We are starting to see some partners or stores which provide a luxurious experience, but so far we have not found one." Helen Willerton, managing director for Chloé Asia-Pacific, said

jesuischloe.com racked up 40,000 visitors in its first few weeks of operation.

China has more than 400 million Internet users, according to government statistics. Middle-class consumers, the largest drivers of consumption in China, are almost entirely online, according to a 2010 McKinsey & Co. study. Establishing a presence on the Chinese Internet is becoming increasingly important for retailers seeking a bigger share of consumers here, particularly those living in second- and third-tier cities who have access to the Internet but not necessarily access to brick-and-mortar stores.

Giorgio Armani SpA, for example, launched an online store in China in November. Adidas AG and Uniqlo have flagship e-commerce portals on Taobao.com, China's largest online shopping site, while Lancôme's e-community site, Lancôme Rosebeauty, has become the third-largest beauty forum in the country, according to AdAgeChina.com.

According to a 2010 KPMG study, the in-store experience is still of prime importance to Chinese luxury consumers. The study notes that social media, including blogs, can be an important tool for retailers, including those selling luxury products, to engage potential customers in China. One in five Chinese consumers between the ages of 18 and 44 will not purchase a product or service without first doing online research, KPMG said.

By the end of 2011, Chloé, which is part of Compagnie Financière Richemont SA, will have 13 stores in China. China will overtake Japan to become the number-one market for Chloé within two years, said de la Bourdonnaye, who declined to give any sales forecasts for the brand in China. "They [Chinese consumers] are really catching up," de la Bourdonnaye said. "It is changing extremely fast, and the sophistication of the consumer, they are not buying logo anymore as much as they are in Japan, or in the world. We are not in people's faces. We are in people's minds. You need to get access to their minds or their hearts. It is a long-term initiative. It takes time."

- Recruit backstage help, such as hairstylists, makeup artists, and dressers

- Recruit front-of-stage help, such as ticket sales, concessions, and ushers

- Locate caterers or sponsors for refreshments, if needed

- Handle publicity, which may include invitations, press releases, advertisements, television and/or radio interviews, and other media-related activities

The job of fashion event planner is one of those "chief cook and bottle washer" positions that may have the planner initially doing a little bit of everything to pull the event together. Once more established in the industry, the fashion event planner is able to hire others to handle parts of the larger projects.

Qualifications

This career requires the following qualifications:

- **Education:** A bachelor's degree in fashion merchandising, fashion design, promotion, special events planning, or a related field is required.

- **Experience:** Fashion event planners come from a wide range of industry sectors: retail, design, and manufacturing. Many work as assistants to fashion directors or coordinators in retail operations or manufacturer's showrooms before branching out on their own. Others initially work as assistants to established fashion event planners. Some large retail stores have special events departments through which starting, or assistant, fashion event planners can learn the ropes of fashion event planning and production. Through the positions leading up to becoming a fashion event planner, a large and useful network of contacts related to the fashion industry can be developed.

- **Personal characteristics:** Successful fashion event planners have the following skills and knowledge: an enthusiastic and creative personality, the ability to sell one's ideas and vision, accounting skills to develop and manage budgets, strong organizational and communication skills, and effective time-management abilities.

Career Challenges

The job tasks of fashion event planning require endless attention to detail to ensure trouble-free events. Fashion event planners need a strong sense of fashion, organizational skills, the ability to work well in stressful situations, and the communication skills to work with a wide range of people. Managing a major fashion event can be compared to coordinating a three-ring circus. Frequently, there is a large number of people involved and myriad details to consider. When combining these stresses with the need to keep events on budget and on time, fashion event planners must have the skills to remain calm and collected under pressure.

Summary

Promotion refers to the endorsement of a person, a product, a cause, an idea, or an organization. The ultimate goal of promotion is to encourage the growth, exposure, and development of an image by advancing it to a higher position. Promotion career opportunities in the primary level of the fashion industry include fashion stylist, public relations director, advertising director, advertising sales representative and related positions, social media director, and fashion event planner. While the public relations director, social media director, and advertising representative are usually employed by a large firm, fashion stylists and fashion events planners may choose a career with a retail company, manufacturer, or public relations firm, or decide to open their own companies. In all of these promotion careers, the goal is to sell an idea, an image, or a product—directly or indirectly. It is marketing in its truest form; it is creative, thought provoking, and profitable at its best.

Key Terms

advertising promotion staff
advertising research assistant
advertising sales representative
book signing
bridal show
complimentary service
consumer publication
crowdsourcing
educational event
fashion event planner
fashion photostylist
fashion shoot
fashion stylist
mannequin modeling
media planner
party planning
philanthropic fashion show
pop-up shop
promotion
promotion product
public relations director
social media
social media director
social networking
social Web site
special events coordinator
tearoom modeling
trade publication
trunk show

Online Resources

dailycrowdsource.com/2010/10/10/arts/fashion/crowdsourcing-emerging-in-the-fashion-world/

marquee.blogs.cnn.com/2010/09/24/secrets-from-inside-the-mad-men-wardrobe-department/

www.bnet.com/blog/publishing-style/tale-of-two-retailers-macy-8217s-flies-while-walmart-flounders/1440

www.fashism.com/

www.fashionstake.com/

www.inc.com/magazine/20100701/how-to-open-a-pop-up-store.html

www.mediabistro.com/unbeige/friday-photo-paris-is-a-womans-town_b12103

www.mydaily.co.uk/2011/03/02/chanel-colette-pop-up-boutique/

www.nytimes.com/2011/02/24/fashion/24scouting.html?src=twrhp

www.wwd.com/beauty-industry-news/digital-watch-join-the-crowd-3463469

Discussion Questions

1. How does your favorite designer promote his or her products? Determine the promotional activities coordinated by the company's public relations director. Is the public relations director contracted from an outside firm? If so, what other companies does this firm promote? Are there similarities among its clients?

2. Which do you read more regularly—consumer or trade publications? Read an article from each type of publication and analyze the value of each as it relates to your future career goals.

3. Go online to locate three illustrations each of fashion crowdsourcing and pop-up stores. Set up a spreadsheet to compare and contrast these examples. What are the similarities and differences among these Web sources?

Interview with a Fashion Event Planner

Interview with fashion event planner Nicole Doherty
By Michele Gates | San Francisco Fashion News | Examiner.com
http://www.examiner.com/fashion-news-in-san-francisco/
interview-with-fashion-event-planner-nicole-doherty?render=
print#print#ixzz1BFLCaFvE

Nicole Doherty is a marketing and event services consultant with a knack for getting people inspired and excited about something. Since graduating from Georgetown University with a bachelor's degree in marketing, she has been cultivating her skills passionately. With over 15 years of combined experience in advertising, marketing, sales, event planning, and production, she founded her first company, NicolePresents, five years ago. She has produced all kinds of events within San Francisco, but most notable are her fashion trunk show events, involving cutting-edge DJs, indie fashion designers, and innovative performers of all kinds. She has a talent for producing energetic and creative events in the greatest venues within San Francisco.

Figure 5.15 Fashion event planner Nicole Doherty.

Have you always wanted to go into fashion and event planning?

I stumbled across it. I began with trunk shows in San Francisco. I didn't seek out producing fashion events. It just happened because of my organizational skills. I was in marketing and advertising; my interest evolved from the question: how can I promote and market people in my life, those I like and admire? Getting involved in event planning came from an inspirational stance, rather than from the actual work itself. For instance, if I liked something, I liked to promote it. Right now, I'm interested in yoga. If it's anything involving yoga, I'm the first person to promote it. I like to inspire people, publicize people, and make them aware of what other people are doing. I enjoy connecting people and networking. It's really about people, ultimately.

Was it difficult starting your business in the beginning? What are the challenges then and now?

It's still difficult! Originally, the challenges were having confidence in my work and learning what I needed to do. I just kind of threw myself into it. Reading, reading, reading, and figuring it out. Now the challenge is more the finance and the operations of the business. How to market yourself. It's so easy to get wrapped up in the production of the events, when I also need to be marketing my own business and handling the finances and the accounting. I'm putting on all the hats to run a business and that's a whole new ball game for me.

So what are your assets that help you in developing your business? For example, offhand I know you're a great networker.

I would definitely say networking. I'm also organized. Socially enjoyable. Lighthearted. I don't take anything too seriously. I can laugh at myself.

Do you consider yourself a "type A" personality?

I have some type A personality. You need it to run a business. You have to have the skill set to be organized and manage things. That's type A, right?

But if you take yourself too seriously, you're setting yourself up for disappointment. Because, especially in events, there are so many moving parts and you can't be attached to an outcome. If things arise that aren't expected, you have to just run with it and be solution oriented instead of problem focused. You have to be able to solve things on the fly, and do it with grace and ease and a sense of humor. Otherwise you're just going to break down, and so I think that helped me a lot, too. And yeah, keeping in touch with people always. It just comes back to networking. Knowing so many people in the city and constantly staying in touch with them, through e-mails and Facebook. Fostering the relationship is important.

How did you get started?
I started NK7 Productions with Sean Evans while in the party scene. He was already doing his DJ business and parties, so I kind of organized him and Kollol Huda, a promoter, and we formed NK7, our production company. We focused on underground events. That's also when I actually started doing fashion events. That's how Trunk n' Funk started six years ago, thinking of the pop-up store idea combined with the trunk show idea. It was fairly unique at the time. Now it's more common, you can trip over a trunk show in this city.

What makes yours unique?
Initially it was unique because it involved independent fashion designers and we did have a brunch as part of the experience. There were also DJs, so it was really an all-inclusive shop, hangout, and eatery. Since Sean's background and mine were from music, it ended up as this hybrid type event. And a lot of those people ended up getting introduced to independent fashion and getting excited about it. Back then the pricing was pretty low. Now, the trunk show people are charging a lot more money and it has become a little more mainstream rather than underground indie.

There were few that were doing what we were doing, but they didn't have the brunch aspect or DJs either. Now, everybody does the hybrid. You can get massages, your nails done, etc. In this community, everyone has such a short attention span, you really have to give them everything but the kitchen sink so they'll show up. They have a broad appeal, mass marketed to everybody. There's men's fashion, women's fashion, manicures, pedicures, DJ music, food, everything. You get a little bit of everything.

The Funk n' Trunks over the summer at Triple Crown had makeup and brow shaping. What can you throw in for people, to make it interesting, that they will enjoy. The goal is to have them stick around and to cultivate a relationship with the designer. That's the nice thing about the trunk show. You're able to meet the designer one on one, and then if you cultivate that relationship with them you'll be more loyal to them. You might want to get custom clothing from them. That's what people really want, that level of customer service. In a mass-market economy, you don't get that personal touch. That was our main concept. What can we give people to make their experience unique? We even had on-site hemming. "If you want this outfit, take it and I'll custom fit it for you." It makes the piece memorable. The customer becomes loyal to that designer.

How has the economy impacted the industry?
Designers have had to come down on pricing. We just had an event this past Thursday and there weren't that many people there in relationship to the amount of marketing we did. We were expecting a lot more people. We had four or five different articles written in magazines and also in different blogs. We thought it would be really busy, since we had international designers at the show, but it wasn't that busy.

When you're throwing trunk shows do you get a lot of responses from designers who want to show their collection and is there a selection process you go through?
Yeah, there is a selection process depending on the type of show you are having. You want to know who you're trying to appeal to. Initially, my trunk shows were about getting independent designers exposure to a new audience or broader audience. A lot of them could not get into stores or it was expensive

Interview with a Fashion Event Planner (continued)

for them, or they didn't have enough designs yet. We wanted to help their business.

What's your advice on this situation? I have a girlfriend who is unhappy with her job and she's trying to do something else. She has a lot of different ideas within the fashion industry, but isn't clear on what direction she should take. What should her next steps be?

She needs to figure out where her interests lie and not be afraid to take chances. I've evolved so much over time that I could be a professional development coach. For me, life always changes. I'll start something and really love it and get super into it. Then a couple years later, I'll be "did that, done that" and move on. I'm kind of a rare breed because I'm never one to stick to one thing; when I'm done, I will move on and try something new. There are people out there like me that are risk takers. You also need to be aware that you may not be "successful" right away. You have to take steps, gain skills, keep learning, and keep striving. I'm happy if I'm always learning and experiencing. You don't lose the skills you gain.

I like how things come to you naturally.

One thing I've learned is to set goals and intentions, but don't set things in stone, so that you close doors. My philosophy is nonattachment to an outcome. Be open, let things come, and they will unfold as they will, as long as your goals and intentions are clear. If a project comes to me and it doesn't feel right, then I won't do it. I follow my intuition. I used to take on many projects just to take them on. I would say yes to everything, but I would put myself in positions that made me question why I took them in the first place. We should enjoy our life and work. That's why we're here. To have joy in our lives and to be ever expanding and learning. Why paddle upstream when you can take the river downstream? Life can be easy. When you're doing things that don't feel right, you're resisting and that makes life more difficult.

What has been a common thread for you within your career changes?

I've done lots of different things and it ultimately boiled down to relationships and being inspiring. Anything moving forward in my life will always be about people and relationships. That's why I'm drawn to the healing arts and yoga, getting down to the core of humanity. Finding out what it is that people love to do. What keeps me excited about what I do—the people and creativity. I'm inspired by designers and I love the social, community-building aspect of event planning. I love to see people happy. I love watching people dance at events. I love seeing people inspired by art, fashion, and music. It brings a lot of joy to me.

chapter 6

Sales

You likely know people who are natural-born salespersons.

You probably have worked with this type of person, or you may be one of these people. They have the enthusiasm, drive, and persuasive skills to sell a product, service, concept, or idea. They enjoy the thrill of the chase and the excitement of the closing. The best salespersons are skilled at gaining the attention of customers and, almost instantly, building a rapport with them. Through observation and active listening, sales gurus can determine the customers' needs and desires and then, by emphasizing the benefits of particular products, effectively explain how the products will fit those needs. The finish line is in sight when the customer's concerns are alleviated and the sale is closed. As a grand finale, additional products or services are offered to build the sale. If you have ever purchased an automobile, a cellular phone, a sofa, or a dress from a sales pro, then you know the feeling of a smooth sale.

Some of the top fashion companies are also the employers of the top salespeople. Every manufacturing firm has a person or staff of employees whose primary job is to sell the product line. A product line can be the best in the world; however, if it is not effectively marketed and sold, it will not be manufactured for long. Designer Tom Ford describes the sales potential within the fashion industry: "As a fashion designer, I was always aware that I was not an artist, because I was creating something that was made to be sold, marketed, used, and ultimately discarded."[1]

In this chapter, sales careers in the wholesale businesses of apparel, accessories, soft goods, and home furnishings and accessories will be explored. These include employment opportunities in the following positions: manufacturer's representative, company salesperson, manufacturer's merchandise coordinator, and showroom salesperson.

Manufacturer's Representative

A **manufacturer's representative**, also referred to as a manufacturer's rep, an independent rep, or sales rep, is a wholesale salesperson. If he or she is self-employed, the sales rep is, in essence, often a business owner. Manufacturer's reps sell the product line, or lines, of one or several manufacturers to retail store buyers. Reps who choose to sell a number of lines usually work with noncompetitive product lines and manufacturers. This type of manufacturer's representative is classified as a **multiline**, or multiple-line, **rep**. For example, the manufacturer's rep may represent a handbag line from one manufacturer, a jewelry line from another vendor, and a glove line from yet another manufacturer. Such a rep can call, for instance, on the accessories buyers of retail stores and offer a selection of products that the specialty or department store carries. If the manufacturer's rep elected to represent several lines in the same merchandise classification, the lines could problematically be competing against one another for the same department's dollars. Occasionally, manufacturer's representatives decide to sell lines that are seasonally opposite, such as swimwear and outerwear. This way, the reps have better opportunities to generate sales volume and, subsequently, income year-round. The manufacturer's rep who prefers to sell solely one manufacturer's line as an independent salesperson rather than as a company employee is a **single-line rep**.

The main task of a fashion sales representative is to sell the products manufactured by the company to the buyers of retail operations. The manufacturer's rep holds meetings with prospective clients (i.e., retail buyers of brick-and-mortar stores or Web sites) in order to efficiently facilitate their product purchases and to support them in selling the products to the consumer. Next is a list of the manufacturer's rep's job responsibilities:

- Solicit orders from new and current clients in a specific geographical area

- Provide samples, catalogs, and illustrations of the company's product line

- Handle product inquiries of clients and listen to customer concerns

- Address product-related issues

- Arrange special events, such as employee training or a trunk show, or product launches for new merchandise

- Collaborate on marketing and advertising strategies to increase sales

- Nurture partnerships and build new key accounts

- Maintain excellent customer relations and repeat business

- Survey clients, analyze data, and prepare proposals for new and current clients

Typically, employers look for fashion sales representatives who have strong marketing and advertising skills. Recently, employers have been seeking manufacturer's reps with technology and online skills that allow them to communicate effectively with retail buyers and the ultimate consumer, as in Box 6.1, Tech Talk.

The manufacturer's representative usually works within a given territory, as negotiated with the manufacturer, such as the East Coast, Florida and Georgia, or Europe. Manufacturer's reps will travel to the buying offices of retail companies, the locations of small store operations, and trade marts to sell their lines to retail buyers. **Trade marts**, also called *apparel marts*, house temporary sales booths and permanent showrooms leased by either the sales representatives or the manufacturers. **Market weeks**, also called *trade shows*, are scheduled at apparel and trade marts throughout the year in conjunction with the introduction of the new, seasonal lines presented by manufacturers. The main seasons of the apparel industry are fall I, fall II, holiday, cruise/resort, spring, and summer. While apparel marts are located across the United States, some of the larger ones are situated in New York City, Dallas, Los Angeles, Chicago, and Atlanta. In Figure 6.1, manufacturers' product lines are featured on the runway at MAGIC in Las Vegas, one of the premier trade shows. Manufacturer's representatives arrive at the apparel marts a day or two ahead of the market opening. At this time, the reps set up booths or showrooms, as in Figures 6.2a and b, with the new lines and other materials, such as purchase orders, line brochures, and displays, that will help sell the line. When the market opens, it is showtime. The manufacturer's reps show the line to buyers with whom prearranged appointments have been set or to buyers who stop by, hoping to find new lines that their customers will purchase. Market weeks are key times for representatives to gain new retail clients, meet with current accounts, and secure a part of the retailers' buying dollars.

Figure 6.1
Manufacturers' product lines are featured at MAGIC in Las Vegas, one of the premier apparel and accessories trade shows.

by Eric Busboom on February 12, 2009
www.retailingtogether.com

Line reps are facing a significant technology-driven change in their business that will make some reps much more influential and put many others out of business. The apparel industry is slowly embracing the Internet, and the line reps who profit most in the future will be those who best market and share the information they have always controlled.

Seasoned businesspeople are comfortable with the general idea of a business cycle, even when the cycle is painful. Business decreases sharply, then a year later it surges. But for apparel line reps, this recession marks a significant change, a major shift in how business will be conducted. Over the next five years, many line reps will find business much more difficult, while a few will profit from the changes, gaining substantial influence and additional business.

The shift will create new opportunities for line reps willing to go online. Using Web technologies, they will be able to provide excellent service to more buyers, while reducing costs. The most successful reps will provide their vendors more than sales support, making their roles as educators, mentors, and advisors to buyers more explicit. This will result in more capable buyers who will increase sell-through, to the ultimate benefit of manufacturers and sales reps. The reps who can address this opportunity will displace those who do not, resulting in a future of fewer, but more influential, line reps.

Line reps embracing the Internet and learning how to use technology to develop and enhance, rather than replace their business relationships, will thrive. Line reps who understand how to use Web technologies, and more important, understand how their vendors and buyers want to use the Web, will gain a broad reach. Meanwhile, the laggards will be left with the low-margin scraps. The new opportunities are the result of a confluence of trends and technologies that include:

- High-profile vendors have skipped recent trade shows; many of them are learning how to do business without the shows.

- Vendors are wary of the costs of hiring line reps, but not aware of the full value they bring to the industry.

- Retailers are burdened with many new requirements for success, including advanced skills with merchandising, inventory control, marketing, e-commerce, and online promotion.

- Internet technologies are radically changing how products are promoted and sold.

- The Internet is making meetings less important for business-to-business sales.

Some of the opportunities for line reps are:

- Moving the first stages of the buying process online to reduce costs and make buying more efficient for buyers

- Developing data-driven purchasing guidance, helping buyers know what to purchase based on actual sales data

- Facilitating or delivering retailer training and education

The Confluence of Forces

Vendors are skipping trade shows. Many trade shows are attracting smaller audiences with each market date. Notably absent are some major brands, not only because times are bad, but because the reps realize they can miss the shows. The trade shows are becoming marketing shows, not order-writing shows. Many vendors believe that trade shows are not the best way to spend their marketing budgets. These changes in trade shows may generate even lower attendance in the future; however, the shows won't disappear. They will continue—with a different purpose. Trade shows will have a greatly diminished role in promoting brands and writing orders for larger buyers, but they will continue to be important venues for buyers to discover trends and new products, take educational seminars, and build relationships with business partners.

Vendors want to reduce costs. When manufacturers discover a higher return on investment using other marketing methods, they will reduce their spending on shows. Other manufacturers will follow suit. The result may be a permanent reduction in trade show attendance. Manufacturers and their reps have long complained about the high cost of trade shows, but they felt that they had no options. This recession has given them encouragement to find new options, many of which are online.

Line reps have a powerful and contentious position in the industry. Vendors appreciate the sales work that line reps perform for them, but chafe at their fees. They see line reps as a pure sales cost because they are not aware of the value that line reps have as mentors, advisors, and advocates for buyers. Buyers rely on the line reps with whom they have established relationships for the reps' knowledge, experience, and ability to help independent retailers be better businesspeople. Unfortunately, vendors don't always see the line reps in these roles and value them appropriately.

Modern retailers need many new skills. Today, independent retailers need the experience and guidance of line reps more than ever. Retailers are burdened not only with the business challenges they have had for decades, but they must also learn about inventory control, point-of-sale systems, Web sites, e-commerce, and e-mail marketing. Large integrated retailers handle these issues with dedicated staff, but for most independent retailers, the owner must be proficient in everything. Independent retailers need additional help from all quarters to succeed.

The Internet is pushing change. Weaving itself through all of these issues is a broad range of Internet technologies. Few line reps have Web sites, and even fewer are using Web marketing,

social media, or online video. These technologies, however, are part of consumers' lives. Consumers' use of e-mail, social networks, video, and e-commerce to discover and purchase apparel is flourishing, but the same technologies are rare among manufacturers and line reps. When the apparel industry discovers how to adapt the vibrant consumer technologies to their business-to-business transactions, the resulting shift will create a new set of winners and losers.

The results of these forces, technology and economics, are likely to influence a significant contraction in the apparel industry—a consolidation among businesses and increases in the size and professionalism of the remaining businesses. By embracing new technologies and expanding their traditional roles, savvy reps will be able to provide extraordinary new value for manufacturers, extending their influence and growing their businesses. Because the apparel industry is fragmented, relationships will always be important. An industry with so many businesses requires people to be brokers of trust, vaults of experience, and advocates for common interests. Fortunately, the Internet has not destroyed the value of relationships. It has simply transformed them. As businesspeople become more comfortable with e-mail and Web conferences, face-to-face meetings can be less frequent. Face-to-face meetings are still important to establish a connection, but they are no longer necessary for every business transaction. After a relationship is initially established, business can often be conducted more efficiently

Move the top of the sales funnel online. The first opportunity for line reps will be to move the initial stages of the buying process online, by giving buyers easy ways to identify what lines they should carry in their stores. Blogs, social networks, and new tools like Twitter allow a line rep to develop and maintain contact with many more people, and contact them more frequently than with telephone or e-mail alone. Internet tools make the sales funnel wider at the top and allow salespeople to prequalify buyers with much less expense. These cost savings allow them to give the buyers more personal support later in the sales process. Reps who learn how to use the Internet to manage their sales process will be able to get more leads at a lower cost.

Success will depend on control of information.
It is no secret that we are doing business in an information economy. Line reps gain informal information through their many contacts with manufacturers, retailers, and other sales reps. They know which products are selling now, what will be selling next season, and which products are right for different types of stores. In the future, this information will become even more important, especially when augmented with accurate point-of-sale data.

How to Prepare for the Future
Line reps can prepare their businesses for the future by getting online, learning about Web tools, and

seeing how they fit into their businesses. Some of the technologies that line reps should be exploring are basic Web sites, online photography and video, and social networking. Line reps should become familiar with popular and innovative consumer Web services, such as Daily Candy, Shopflick, and Polyvore. Most of these Web sites help consumers find new brands, and they all have innovative photography, video, and social networking examples.

The Internet has redefined entire industries. With the combination of the recession and the Internet, the manufacturers' reps in the fashion industry cannot hold out any longer. Those who embrace technology now will be best positioned to later capitalize on the post-recession trends and grow their businesses.

Source: www.retailingtogether.com

Compensation

A manufacturer's representative may be paid in a number of ways: commission, quota or a base salary plus commission, or salary. Through **commission**, manufacturer's reps are paid a percentage of the sales volume on merchandise that they have sold that is shipped and accepted by the retailers. For instance, if a rep sells a product line but the manufacturer ships it late, the retailer may refuse it. In this case, the manufacturer's rep often will not receive a commission for the sale. Therefore, a key task for a manufacturer's representative is to follow up on deliveries and to communicate with the retail buyers about orders that may contain style substitutions or arrive a bit late. Commission percents are often negotiable and range greatly, from 3 to 20 percent. **Quota plus commission** refers to a form of remuneration in which manufacturer's representatives are paid commission on sales procured over a specific amount, or baseline, called a quota. **Salaried** manufacturer's representatives are paid set amounts every month. **Base salary plus commission** refers to paying reps a set amount each month and commission payments periodically. Some companies provide bonuses for sales reps with exceptional sales.

There are a number of expenses that manufacturer's reps can incur in the process of doing business. Some manufacturer's representatives are required to purchase their sample lines, often at a discounted price, from manufacturers. A **sample line** includes a prototype of every style within the line. Each prototype is tagged with fabric swatches, color options, sizes available, and its wholesale price, also referred to as **cost price**, or *cost*. Depending on the size of the product line, a sample line can cost a manufacturer's representative thousands of dollars. Some manufacturers buy back the sample lines, possibly to sell at factory outlets. In other cases, reps may sell sample lines independently. Additionally, there are costs associated with showing lines during market weeks. There are rental fees for booths, showrooms, and fixtures, as well as trade organization dues. Some manufacturer's representatives contribute to retailers' advertising costs to build their mutual business. There is also the cost of travel; airfares, automobile costs, lodging expenses, and meals must be paid for while traveling. Manufacturer's representatives who have large businesses may employ administrative and sales assistants. As independent contractors, manufacturer's representatives are business owners who share the risk, potential, and challenges associated with being their own bosses.

The Career Path

Two strategies to gain access to the world of the manufacturer's representative include interning or assisting an established manufacturer's representative. Helping a sales rep during market weeks is an ideal way to receive an overview of presentation and negotiation skills needed to succeed as a manufacturer's rep. Successful reps often hire assistants to work in their showrooms, to take the line on the road to show to smaller accounts, or to "cold call" on prospective accounts. Working as a merchandise coordinator is yet another way to move into a sales rep position. Some manufacturers recruit buyers into sales rep positions, as they have firsthand knowledge of the buyer's responsibilities and needs.

In terms of promotion, manufacturer's reps move up the career ladder when assigned bigger retail accounts or larger territories. Others will secure more prominent and profitable lines when they have developed a successful business that includes strong relationships with the buyers of major retail stores.

Qualifications

Most important, the ability to sell is key. An understanding of accounting is also necessary. Often, the ways to secure this job are through proven sales abilities, knowledge of the line and its retail accounts (existing and potential), and a willingness to travel.

- **Education:** A bachelor's degree in fashion merchandising, product development, business administration, marketing, or a related field is most often a minimum requirement.

Figures 6.2a and b
For market week, the sales reps set up booths or showrooms with the new lines and other materials, such as line brochures and displays that will help sell the line.

- **Experience:** Sales, sales, and more sales are the key experiences needed for a career as a manufacturer's representative. Many students gain work experience in retail sales. Working as an assistant to a manufacturer's representative is an excellent route to understanding the responsibilities of this career and to building a network of industry contacts.

- **Personal characteristics:** Self-discipline, self-motivation, good follow-through skills, perseverance, organizational abilities, and the ability to handle rejection are key attributes of top manufacturer's representatives. Successful reps are highly competitive, believe in the products they sell, and have the ability to maintain enthusiasm for them. They need excellent communication skills, both written and oral. Successful reps are able to establish trust, and, subsequently, good relationships with customers. Knowledge of fashion industry trends and manufacturers' competitors is critical.

Career Challenges

Many manufacturers' reps are faced with the uncertainty of not knowing how much their next paycheck will be. In this career, income is primarily based on sales performance. Sometimes, there are external factors beyond a rep's control that may decrease the amount of money the rep receives. Unshipped orders, late deliveries, and incorrect shipments can reduce the remuneration reps expect based on merchandise they have sold. Also, for some people, extensive travel can be a burden. Traveling to trade markets, sales meetings, and retail accounts costs money. Manufacturer's reps need many of the skills of successful entrepreneurs, as they must manage their budgets to accommodate their costs of doing business.

Company Salesperson

The majority of large manufacturing firms hire company salespeople. The **company salesperson** is a sales representative employed directly by a particular firm who carries just one line, that of the employer. Often, company salespeople have broader territories than manufacturers' representatives may cover. Like manufacturers' representatives, company salespeople travel to retail buying offices, retail stores, or trade markets to show and sell their company's line. Remuneration is often base salary plus commission rather than entirely commission-based. Often, they receive employee benefits, such as health insurance and vacation pay. Employers of company salespeople may also cover some of the expenses that manufacturers' representatives must incur. More often than not, the manufacturer pays for trade show fees, the cost of sample lines, and retail advertising contributions for company salespeople.

When the manufacturer contributes to the cost of advertisements paid for by the retailer, the arrangement is referred to as **cooperative** (or *co-op*) **advertising**. While each manufacturing company develops its own cooperative advertising agreement, there are a number of consistent requirements. An example of a cooperative advertising agreement is presented in Box 6.2.

Most cooperative advertising agreements designate whether or not the retailer must feature the manufacturer's products in an advertisement exclusively, rather than in conjunction with other product lines. Most manufacturers calculate the amount of money that will be

Box 6.2 Annabelle Active Wear Cooperative Advertising Agreement

As we recognize the importance of print, television, radio, and Internet advertising as valuable means of promoting and increasing sales of all Annabelle Active Wear (AAW) products, we offer to our esteemed customers the cooperative advertising plan set forth below. We believe that it will assist our retail clients, our consumers, and AAW in maintaining the very highest standards with regard to the public's perception and awareness of the quality and image of the AAW lines. This plan is in effect until further notice for all ads run on or after June 1, 2011.

1. **AAW and Customer Share.** AAW will share 50 percent of the cost in preapproved advertising vehicles based on the retailer's earned AAW advertising budget, up to an amount not to exceed 5 percent of first-quality, branded net purchases at wholesale for each season. This plan only covers first-quality branded net purchases (applied to all AAW lines).

2. **Charges.** Net cost is limited to actual advertising costs. This agreement shall not include the cost of special preparation, filming, artwork, graphic design, Web development, or any other preparatory advertising and/or production costs. We do not share in the cost of agency fees or special service charges. We do not share in mechanical or production costs for color reproduction.

3. **Enclosure Advertising.** Each season AAW will make statement enclosures available to be included in charge statement mailings. Enclosures are to be ordered on the special forms provided by our advertising department. Minimum quantity orders are necessary to qualify to receive these enclosures. Check with your sales representative for the minimum quantity necessary. A fraction of the actual cost of enclosures will be charged, and this amount will be applied against the 5 percent AAW cooperative advertising limit as set forth in the agreement.

4. **Media.** This plan covers media advertising with those providers that have recognized audited circulation and published rates. Final approval of the content of ads and the AAW dollar amount for share of costs are contingent on our approval. To receive approval, contact your sales representative. After receiving approval, a copy of the approval form, receipt of payment from the advertising provider, and sample of the advertisement must accompany your invoice.

5. **Copy Requirements.**
   a. The AAW product-logotype must appear prominently in the advertisement. For print advertisements, the Annabelle Active Wear name must also appear in the heading or subheading. The use of the AAW product-logotype in the graphics only will not meet our requirements. The name must be as large as the largest type in the advertisement exclusive of the retailer's own logotype. We will supply the Annabelle Active Wear logotype as requested.
   b. Competitive merchandise cannot appear in the same advertisement with the AAW name or product-logotype. If the advertisement shows other merchandise, this other merchandise must be goods other than activewear. In addition to this requirement, the AAW portion of the advertisement must be separate and clearly defined. If any other merchandise is shown in the advertisement, we reserve the right to final approval on such advertisement.
   c. No advertisement in any media shall show a sale price or markdown price on any AAW product. If a price is listed, it must be the full list price, given in an even dollar amount (e.g., $100, $148, and $65). In addition to this requirement, any advertised sale that shows or presents any AAW product or that uses the AAW name must obtain approval from our advertising department.

6. **Payment.** Invoices must be submitted within 45 days of placement of the advertising effort. An advertising credit will be issued for the Annabelle Active Wear share. No deductions are to be made for advertising prior to receiving the credit memo authorizing the amount to be deducted.

contributed to retailers' advertising efforts as a percentage of the dollar amount in orders that the buyer places with the company. Most manufacturers request that the company, line, or designer name be included in the advertisement once or twice, and, sometimes, in the headline of print advertisements. The majority of manufacturers who offer cooperative advertising funds also require proof of advertising, such as a CD-ROM of a television commercial or a tearsheet of a newspaper advertisement. A **tearsheet** is a print page that features the retailer's advertisements, provided by the newspaper's advertising department. Refer to Figure 6.3 for an example of a tearsheet.

Why do some companies invest in hiring an exclusive and salaried company salesperson rather than a commissioned manufacturer's representative? While increased sales are at the top of the list, promotion is another important reason for hiring company salespeople. Company salespeople work closely with their retail clients to promote the product line and build the company's name and image through effective and brand-oriented marketing. They also plan consistent deliveries with buyers, creating a flow of new merchandise that keeps the line looking fresh and its customers coming back. Since many of the firms that employ company salespeople are very large, company salespeople may be working with retailers that have a separate department, and subsequently, an immense investment, for the line in the store. They may assist buyers with fixture selections, signage, and layout of departments. Additionally, company salespeople are often called on by retail clients to educate the store sales and management staff about the product line. If it is a home furnishing line, for example, a company salesperson may be enlisted as a guest presenter at a breakfast meeting for store sales personnel. During this meeting, the company salesperson will show the fabrics featured in the new season; discuss durability and care factors; and provide information about new sofa and chair forms, design themes, and color palettes. The retailer's sales staff leaves the meeting informed, excited, and appreciated, ready to sell the products to the customer. Company salespeople do more than sell the line to retail buyers. They represent the manufacturer in the areas of advertising, marketing, merchandise planning, visual merchandising, and retail sales staff education.

Qualifications

The education, work experience, and personal characteristics needed for successful employment as a company salesperson are similar to those of the manufacturer's representative.

- **Education:** A bachelor's degree in fashion merchandising, fashion design, product development, business administration, marketing, or a related field is commonly required.

- **Experience:** All types of sales experience provide a foundation for future employment as a company salesperson. Working on a retail sales floor or selling advertisements for the campus newspaper provides important knowledge and skills in sales. Work experience with a manufacturer is a plus; one could possibly begin in a showroom as a receptionist and then move into sales.

Figure 6.3 A tearsheet is a page that has been pulled from a newspaper or a magazine that features a product advertisement or a model's shoot.

- **Personal characteristics:** Successful company salespeople are self-disciplined, internally motivated, and excited about their business. Exceptional communication skills, a contagious enthusiasm, and top organizational skills are also necessary characteristics. Understanding how products are constructed, the materials from which they are made, and the manufacturing processes required to bring them to completion helps company salespeople educate their clients, retail buyers in this case, about the product.

Career Challenges

Company salespeople must work under the guidelines of their employers. In some cases, new accounts, trade market participation, and travel plans must be approved by the administration. This position is not as autonomous as that of the manufacturer's representative. When working with a single company, if the product line for a certain season is not strong, the company salesperson does not have another line to rely on for income. If competitive lines become stronger in terms of securing the retail buyers' orders, the company salesperson faces the challenge of staying afloat during a tough sell period or securing a position with a new employer.

Manufacturer's Merchandise Coordinator

In the early 1990s, the number of specialty stores began declining, and large department stores began increasing in size and number of units. Many of these massive department stores did not offer the customer service that most specialty stores provided. In the department stores, there were fewer sales associates. The few sales staff members in the department stores were often part time, seasonal, or "floaters," a term for sales associates moved from department to department as needed, leaving little time for the retail sales staff to get to know the customers and provide personal service. As a result, some of the large manufacturers were compelled to find a way to assist the department stores and, ultimately, help their firms to higher sales volume. These manufacturers, among them Liz Claiborne, Ralph Lauren Polo, and Fossil, developed a new career path in the fashion industry, that of merchandise coordinator.

Merchandise coordinators assist with a manufacturer's line in retail stores and are employed by the manufacturer, rather than the retailer. Merchandise coordinators are hired to service a number of the manufacturer's key retail accounts in a specific geographic area. **Key accounts** are the large retailers, in terms of sales volume, carrying the manufacturer's line. Today, specialty stores have made a comeback as customers seek personalized service. Key accounts can include boutiques, specialty stores, Web sites, and large department stores, depending on the amount of inventory of a particular manufacturer's product line they carry. Merchandise coordinators travel to the retail sites to work with the owners, buyers, management personnel, sales staff, and customers. Most of these retail sites can be visited by car, as they are frequently in large metropolitan areas.

In most cases, it is not the merchandise coordinator's primary responsibility to sell the line to the buyer or customer; coordinators may write **reorders**, fill-ins on merchandise that is selling well. Another service merchandise coordinators may perform is moving merchandise that has been shipped and is waiting in the stockroom to the sales floor. Reorders and stock placement on the floor are commonly referred to as **inventory replenishment**. **Visual merchandising** is another job responsibility of merchandise coordinators. This activity may include changing displays, straightening racks, and resizing and folding stacked goods to present the best possible visual image to the customer. In essence, merchandise coordinators are somewhat like dedicated store owners, except the "stores" are the manufacturers' departments in the manufacturers' key accounts, the retail stores that sell the largest amounts of the manufacturer's line. Some retailers collaborate with merchandise coordinators on promotional events. For example, the merchandise coordinator may be featured in an advertisement as the line's representative, and customers are invited to meet the coordinator for personal assistance with line purchases. The primary responsibilities of a manufacturer's merchandise coordinator follow.

- Act as liaison between manufacturer, sales representatives, store managers, and department managers

- Communicate popular current trends and perform analysis of competition and customer preferences

- Track customer lifestyles, preferences, and requests through customer profile reports in order to communicate market needs

- Motivate sales associates through frequent merchandise updates

- Ensure prime visibility of product line in stores, and merchandise product assortment effectively

- Compile retail sales and inventory levels needed to establish the ideal product assortment within the store

- Develop promotional strategies to ensure product sell-through

---

Box 6.3 Sample Classified Advertisement: Web Site Merchandise Coordinator of Shoes

Detailed Description:

Do you love shoes? Have a passion for fashion retail? The Shoes team is looking for a meticulous and tenacious self-starter to coordinate our merchandising process. The Merchandise Coordinator we are looking for is someone who is highly organized and obsessed with providing excellent customer experiences while continually improving existing processes. This position is a great opportunity for someone with talent, energy, and a love for fashion to join a fast-paced, growing e-business.

Responsibilities:

- Drive smooth execution of Shoes merchandising process from beginning to end

- Collaborate with merchandisers, vendor representatives, designers, and photo studio managers

- Streamline current processes and create efficiencies where needed

- Work cross-functionally to ensure accurate, on-time inputs for promotions

- Coordinate photo shoot samples and create shot lists

- Monitor featured items for receiving and stocking

- Assist with creation and accuracy of keywords, trends, and special features, and content and accuracy of features and site flips

- Produce and distribute weekly merchandising update reports

- Prioritize appropriately when process inputs may be at risk

- Provide support for special projects as assigned

Career Outlook

The future for merchandise coordinators is bright. This career track has been so successful for manufacturers that many large companies have added merchandise coordinator positions. Ralph Lauren Polo employs merchandise coordinators for children's wear, misses' sportswear, and menswear, among other divisions, in New York City, St. Louis, Chicago, Atlanta, and other large cities.

As another example, Jones Apparel Group, Inc., employs about one hundred merchandise coordinators who are trained by their apparel designers to make appropriate recommendations to meet customers' tastes. According to Jones Apparel Group, the key benefit of the merchandise coordinators is that they are the link between the showroom and the stores, providing invaluable feedback regarding customer preferences. The growth in merchandise coordinator positions is not limited to brick-and-mortar retail specialty and department stores; online companies are offering these positions as well. Box 6.3 is a sample classified advertisement for a merchandise coordinator of footwear with a major online retailer.

Qualifications

Successful merchandise coordinators may meet or exceed the following criteria:

- **Education:** A bachelor's degree in fashion merchandising, fashion design, product development, business administration, marketing, sales, or a related field is commonly required.

- **Experience:** Hands-on experience in the industry, which may include work experience in retail or wholesale selling, is required for this position. Many companies hire new college graduates with strong selling skills and an enthusiasm for the manufacturer's line.

- **Personal characteristics:** Knowledge of the product line and marketing is required. An understanding of sales, visual merchandising, textiles, and product construction is helpful. The ability to work independently with little supervision and guidance is critical to success. Strong communication skills, both oral and written, are also required.

Career Challenges

Merchandise coordinators walk a fine line between several parties—the manufacturer, the manufacturer's sales rep, the retail buyer, the retailer's sales staff, and the consumer. This career requires strong attention to the goals of all parties. Merchandise coordinators are constantly challenged to find ways to help retailers generate sales, while keeping their focus on their manufacturer's profits. There may be many client stores in a merchandise coordinator's territory, requiring carefully scheduled travel plans and exceptional time management. Additionally, they have a large number of tasks to complete in each retail location. It is a fast-paced job; however, it is an excellent position for someone who enjoys crossing the line between retailers' and manufacturers' worlds.

Showroom Salesperson

As depicted in Figure 6.4, the majority of large manufacturers in the apparel and accessories industry have showrooms in New York City, Dallas, Chicago, Atlanta, and Los Angeles, as these are the major metropolitan areas featuring large fashion trade markets. **Showrooms**, unlike typical apparel, accessories, furniture, and fabric retail stores, rarely sell merchandise from the floor. Items are generally for display only, to allow the buyers to see pieces that would otherwise be visible only in a catalog or online. The buyers then order the items they believe their customers will purchase.

Showrooms come in all types. In the home interiors industry, they showcase kitchen and bath fixtures, hardware and cabinetry, fabrics and wallpapers, interior and exterior furnishings, flooring materials, lighting, antiques, paintings, and other accessories. Some interior design showrooms offer only one type of item, while others may have fabrics, furnishings, lighting, and accessories all together under one roof, as depicted in Figure 6.5. This type of showroom is similar in the wholesale level of the apparel and accessories industry, where merchandise is displayed for ordering. Some showrooms carry a variety of merchandise classifications, and others feature a single product type or manufacturer's line.

Showroom salespeople, also called *showroom representatives*, work at a manufacturer's or designer's showroom, where they meet with visiting retail buyers and present the latest product line to them. Once buyers agree to purchase the manufacturer's products, the showroom sales representatives are responsible for working with the buyers in placing their purchase orders. They must make sure that the purchase orders are accurate and the buyer is aware of shipping dates. The showroom sales representatives will later keep the buyers informed on new items added to the line, top sellers, and off-price, or sale, goods when they become available. In the home and interior design industry, showroom sales representatives are located on-site and are usually assigned to specific designers. They are responsible for

helping the designers by finding fabrics, providing suggestions, inputting orders, checking stock, and supplying price quotes. Once designers have decided on a certain fabric, they will call showroom salespersons with the quantity of fabric needed and the dye lot, if applicable. The showroom reps will check the inventory or call the factory, then let the designers know whether the fabric is available, and if so, determine the lead time (that is, time from when payment is received until the fabric is expected to arrive) and which **cuts**, or yardage amounts, are available. On occasion, only a group of small cuts are available at a given time. If those are not adequate because a designer needs one large length for a window treatment, as an example, the designer must decide whether to wait for the next supply of new goods or to select an alternate fabric. Fabric yardage may also be needed to match a certain dye lot. If a designer has previously used a fabric on a sofa, for instance, and now needs more of the same fabric for a new chair in the same room, it is important to ensure the fabric comes from the same dye lot or is similar enough in color to ensure continuity. Showroom salespeople are responsible for making sure that designers receive written quotes with shipping charges and a **cutting for approval (CFA)**, a fabric sample also called a *memo*, if requested. Maintaining a good relationship with each client through efficient follow-up and a positive personality is imperative to ensure ongoing sales.

One of the tools that supports showroom sales reps in communicating regularly with clients and providing up-to-date information on orders, shipments, and top-selling information is the computer. Knowledge of technology, such as spreadsheets, Web site development, and social media, gives the showroom salesperson an edge in communicating with customers, organizing data, and promoting the showroom's lines, as illustrated in Box 6.4.

Figure 6.4 The majority of large manufacturers in the apparel and accessories industry have showrooms in New York City, Dallas, Chicago, Atlanta, and Los Angeles, as these are the major metropolitan areas featuring large fashion trade markets.

Figure 6.5 In the Lee Joffa fabric showroom, interior designers can view fabrics both on wings and in samples of upholstered furniture. A designer can request memos of selected fabrics from a showroom salesperson to share with clients before placing an order.

Box 6.4 Showroom Sales Representatives and Technology

Bluebird Showroom Melds Tradition and Technology

When Aimee Moss founded Bluebird Showroom in 2004, she didn't know she was crafting a new direction for the apparel industry and its use of technology. But years later, Bluebird Showroom is notable not only for the lines it carries and the strong relationship it has with its buyers, but also for its extensive use of Internet technology. Unlike many companies that use technology to insulate themselves from customers, Bluebird Showroom uses the Web to build relationships, not to avoid them.

The Bluebird Showroom Web site has two parts: the public pages presenting the look of the lines they carry and introducing potential buyers to the showroom and its staff, and a private area serving as a virtual showroom for buyers. Between the two parts is a relationship between the buyer and the showroom that is established "the traditional way" with phone calls, in-person meetings, and the occasional e-mail. The public pages of the Web site are very well designed, setting the proper tone for the showroom's market niche. The excellent Web site design of bluebirdshowroom.com instantly establishes the feel of the showroom on the homepage with a slideshow of high-quality images for each of the lines they carry.

The Collections page shows logos for 12 lines, and the Press page is a scrapbook that includes scans of offline magazines and screen shots of Web sites that have featured the lines they carry. The most interesting public page is the About page, the first About page we've seen that is entirely a video. The video instantly humanizes the showroom owner and staff, giving buyers who have never visited the showroom or met any of the staff the feeling they are already acquainted. Because of the video, Bluebird Showroom quickly shifts from being a corporation to being a local business that is run by people the buyer already knows and likes.

The private pages are accessible only after a buyer has contacted the showroom and the showroom staff has gotten to know the buyer. These internal pages give buyers access to line sheets, order forms, photographs, and video of the lines: much of the material that other showrooms still communicate through mail and fax machines. The showroom also has a MySpace page that has links to the pages of many of their lines and retailers.

Despite the well-developed Web site, Moss isn't a technologist who puts computers before people. She prefers to build a business on relationships, so the Web site doesn't give too much information away. Moss would rather use the site to start a relationship with the buyer, not to substitute for a relationship, and developing and maintaining relationships is the core of Moss's business. "Relationships are the crux of any great showroom hoping to maintain their brands' appeal over time," says Moss, who sees herself as "a diplomat, a liaison between my lines and buyers."

Bluebird has established its business on a combination of tradition and innovation, a critical combination in a 180-year-old industry that is just beginning to address the Internet era. In an industry as large and fragmented as the apparel industry, with 41,000 apparel manufacturers and 91,000 clothing stores, developing and maintaining relationships is a requirement for conducting business. Because they have to work between the manufacturers and retailers, the best line reps are masters of building relationships, and Moss and Bluebird are a great example of how to incorporate relationships with technology, and a pointer to the future of sales in the apparel industry.

http://www.retailingtogether.com/posts/2009/1162-bluebird-showroom-melds-tradition-and-technology; written by www.retailingtogether.com staff on February 26, 2009

Qualifications

As illustrated by Figure 6.6, a career as a showroom salesperson may be achieved with the following qualifications:

- **Education:** A bachelor's degree in interior design, textiles, fashion merchandising, fashion design, business, or marketing is preferred, but not always required. Graduates with good communication skills and the right personality have a good chance of being hired right out of college, particularly if they have interned in this area.

- **Experience:** Previous retail sales experience is helpful. The traditional career path for showroom sales assistants is to move up to the position of showroom sales representative to showroom sales manager. Showroom salespeople should expect to work long hours during the fashion market weeks. Showroom salespeople often have the opportunity to increase their pay through commissions on orders and bonuses based on their sales performance.

- **Personal characteristics:** Successful showroom salespeople are enthusiastic, friendly, and outgoing. Effective listening skills, excellent communication and presentation abilities, knowledge of the manufacturing and retail sectors of the fashion industry, as well as good organizational and computer skills, are all assets.

Career Challenges

The showroom salesperson often works long hours, crisscrossing the showroom floor, writing orders for buyers, and contacting suppliers. When not selling the line, the showroom representative is following up on product availability, ordering shipments, and checking delivery options. It is a highly detailed business in which products are often expected and

Figure 6.6 A showroom representative meets with a retail buyer to present the latest product line.

needed quickly. If, for example, the incorrect color number of a tile is posted on an order, a kitchen renovation can be delayed for weeks by the arrival of the wrong product. Or, for example, if a jacket cannot be delivered on time for an advertisement the retailer is planning to run, the showroom salesperson may lose the order, the commission that comes with it, and the retail account. For some, it can be stressful to work under such details and deadlines in a fast-paced environment. For others, it can be motivating.

Summary

Manufacturing firms, possibly titled under a designer's name, are prevalent in the apparel, accessories, soft goods, home furnishings, and home accessories industries. The designer's name, the company's name, or the brandmark may be well known, but if it is not effectively marketed and sold, it will not be manufactured for long. These companies employ or contract a person or a staff of employees whose primary job is to sell the manufacturer's product line. Within this wholesale level of the fashion industry, the main career paths include the manufacturer's representative, the company salesperson, the merchandise coordinator, and the showroom salesperson.

A manufacturer's representative, or sales rep, is an independent salesperson who may represent the lines of several manufacturers, often working exclusively on commission or commission with a salary component. The company salesperson is a sales representative employed directly by a particular firm who carries one product line, that of the employer, and usually works on a salary plus commission or bonus basis. The manufacturer's merchandise coordinator is employed by the manufacturer and works in the retail stores, servicing key accounts in a specific territory. Merchandise coordinators travel to the retail sites to work with the owner, buyer, management personnel, sales staff, and/or customers in the areas of visual merchandising, inventory replenishment, retail sales staff training, and promotional events. Finally, the showroom salesperson works at a manufacturer's or designer's showroom, meeting with visiting retail buyers to present and sell the latest product lines to them.

Sales are critical to a fashion company's success. No matter how exceptional the product line is, there has to be a sales force behind it. With each season, with every trend, and with the ever-changing customer, there is a new opportunity to sell fashion.

Endnote

1. http://www.brainyquote.com/quotes/quotes/t/tomford209396.html

Key Terms

base salary plus commission
commission
company salesperson
cooperative advertising
cost price
cut
cutting for approval (CFA)
inventory replenishment
key account
manufacturer's representative
market week
merchandise coordinator

multiline rep
quota plus commission
reorder
salaried
sample line
showroom
showroom salesperson
single-line rep
tearsheet
trade mart
visual merchandising

Online Resources

fashionablymarketing.me/2009/10/how-to-find-a-fashion-showroom-represent-product-line/

thegiggleguide.com/rep-wrapup/2010-08/sandra-martinez-leads-team-whose-work-always-play

http://www.associatedcontent.com/article/5955060/interview_with_krystyna_schexnayder.html

www.fashion-schools.org/fashion-sales.htm

www.vault.com/wps/portal/usa/vcm/detail/Career-Advice/Industry-Overview/Jobs-in-a-Design-Showroom?id=648

Discussion Questions

1. Visit a large department store and find a national brand sold within the store. Are these products merchandised differently from other products within the store? Is the department store staff knowledgeable about this national brand's merchandise?
2. In what types of sales environments are commissions, quota plus commissions, or salaried methods of payment most effective? Why? Provide examples.
3. What constitutes a successful sale? Recall your sales experiences as a customer or salesperson and determine why each was positive or negative and why.

Interview with a Buyer on the Keys to Success for a Sales Representative

Interview with a Buyer by Gail McInnes, Fashion Magnet.com

Source: http://fashionmagnet.ca/2010/03/02/interview-with-a-buyer/

Juan Carlos Gaona is the owner of Magnolia, a stylish boutique opened in 2008 in Toronto. A strong supporter of local talent, Magnolia's spring 2010 racks include Lucian Matis, Carrie Hayes, Paris Li, and Izzy Camilleri (made-to-order and small leather accessories). The international labels include Designers Remix, Hoss Intropia, Tara Jarmon, By Malene Birger, Pringle 1815, Drykorn, American Retro, Love Moschino, and handbags from Badgley Mischka. Prices range from $30 for accessories to $1,000 and up for custom-made pieces. Next, Gaona shares thoughts on the process he takes when he is selecting lines to carry in his store.

How did your store get its name?

Magnolias, aside from being one of my favorite flowers, embody what I wanted for the boutique itself and what I see in our customers: a strong, elegant beauty that is unique in many ways.

How do you select the lines that you carry?

There are lines that I admire and personally love, so I contact them directly. There are lines that I've seen in showrooms and have caught my attention. There are lines that have been recommended by people I trust (sales reps, friends, stylists, photographers). There is just one case where the designer came to me directly with a look book and I agreed to carry the line. The only thing that all of these decisions have in common is the line has to have an appeal to me and what the store stands for. It is the emotional connection that makes the sale, and that's what our customers want. They are tired of mass-market fast-food clothing; they want garments that mean something, in quality, inspiration, beauty, uniqueness!

What steps do you take when buying a line?

1. *Introduction:* Someone tells me about a line.
2. *Research:* I go to their Web sites and browse through their present and past collections, looking for what they stand for, and what is their overall style, price points, and aesthetic. (If a designer contacts me directly and I am interested, I ask for previous look books and line sheets.)
3. *Collection preview:* I go and see the collection they intend me to buy, and see how it works—both in the store and with the other labels we carry. Also, I do a quality check (I am immediately attracted to lines that pay as much attention to the inside as the outside). If they put on a fashion show, I try to attend to see what they are about as a whole and also I try to get guests' feedback.
4. *Collection edits:* I put together a mock order with what I feel are their stronger pieces, or what defines the brand. Here is where the main decision comes. If I can get their "stronger looks" from other designers I already have, I don't pick them. Same goes if their pieces don't look good with the other collections in-store.
5. *Final order and first season:* If I decide to add the label to our inventory, I place an order and see how they do, not only in terms of sales, but I look for their real values: quality (sampling and production can be very different), delivery timing, hanger appeal, sizing, fit, and real customer feedback. This defines entirely if they will be carried further ahead. I can personally love one label, but if customers have issues (e.g., pricing, quality, originality, fit, etc.), then it will only collect dust on our racks.

How would you advise manufacturers' reps or sales reps to approach retailers to carry their lines?

When sending a request to a retailer (especially a boutique type) try to make it as personal as possible, do some research, ask for the name/contact for the buyer/manager. There is nothing that makes me laugh more than e-mails (directed to info@magnoliaonline.ca) with the greeting "Dear info." True story, and, sadly, very common.

Why do you believe working with the sales rep is important?

I was at an appointment and the sales rep asked me if I was interested in carrying another line. I declined

Interview with a Buyer on the Keys to Success for a Sales Representative (continued)

to even look at it, since I was about to go over budget. I had an appointment with them next week, so I came back. The mannequins at the entrance of the showroom were styled impeccably. I asked what they were wearing; obviously it was the line they had offered before. I loved it so much, I decided to risk it and went a little over budget with it. It has become one of my bestsellers. Moral: Sales reps know the tricks, they have a better relationship with the retail world, and they know by heart what their clients (and their clients' clients) want.

What are common mistakes sales reps make when approaching a retailer to buy their lines?

1. *No market research:* One of the biggest and most common mistakes. Thoroughly investigate your retailer, their vision, customers, prices, sizing, labels, etc. before offering your line. I've had people sending me look books of lingerie, bathing suits, sleepwear, and shoes; needless to say, I don't carry any of that.

2. *Less-than-spectacular look books:* Companies need to realize 90 percent of your chances (especially on a higher-end market) are based on first impressions; you need your look book to be your strongest selling point. That is what will make me curious or excited about your label as a whole and your particular collection that season.

3. *Too many adjectives:* When introducing a line, the use of too many adjectives is also a big mistake to me. Let the clothes speak for themselves; let the customers hear what your line has to say, before you try to put words in their minds.

4. *Cocky attitudes:* Some reps have contacted me to tell me their lines are what my store needs to make it big or that it's a mistake not to have them. Some have treated me with very poor manners until they realize I am the buyer. That speaks tons about you, both professionally and personally.

5. *Unannounced visits:* People have come through the door with their collection in a suitcase. Nothing wrong with that, you do what you can. But coming in unannounced during a time when the retailer has customers is very disrespectful.

6. *Double dipping:* If you already sell across the street, you should not approach another retailer in the area. It is one of the unspoken rules of retail, and sometimes it's actually illegal to do that (another reason to have a sales rep that can help you with distribution areas and these little inside things).

7. *Bad-quality samples:* If your samples are not finished the right way, it makes buyers anxious. At an appointment there's only so many times you can hear "this (e.g., color, sizing, length, closure, lining, zipper, etc.) will not be like this in production" without wondering if the dress you're looking at will still look like a dress when it's delivered.

How should the sales rep follow up with the retailer?

Take into consideration that buyers and retailers get harassed every season by tons of people. Be persistent, but learn the difference between being persistent and being pushy (no means no, not maybe). Buyers are very busy during showroom season, so it's very common if they take a day or two to return your call or e-mail. Don't call the next day every hour to see if they've read your materials or to ask what they think. I find this to be one of the most recurrent problems my buyer friends have.

How should the sales rep respond to buyer feedback?

If you can't take the good and the bad, don't ask for feedback at all. Life lessons are not free. The knowledge of a buyer has usually cost them one way or another. Be sure you have some sort of a relationship before asking for someone's expertise.

chapter 7

Resource Management: Finance, Accounting, and Human Resources

In the back offices of the manufacturer's showroom, behind the scenes, there are two departments that are critical to the success of the fashion company. The people in these departments are not surrounded by trend boards, garment samples, and slick advertising images; instead, they work in a world of financial reports or personnel files. The two company divisions examined in this chapter have a common thread; resource management. These resources are the money upon which the company operates and the employees who run the company—(1) finance and accounting and (2) human resources. To begin, we will examine the finance and accounting division and the career opportunities within it.

Finance and Accounting

You may wonder, "Why would anyone choose a finance and accounting career in the fashion industry, rather than any other career path in the field?" When many people think fashion, they envision color and style trends, new designs, and action-packed runway shows. When they think about accounting, two words may come to mind: boring and tedious. Add to this the image of a bespectacled person wearing a pocket protector and crunching numbers in a sparse, little room (Figure 7.1). It is a fact—accounting has had an image problem; however, that is the past. While the geek stereotype may have been the field's image, it no longer represents an accurate picture of this career track.

Accounting functions are increasingly becoming automated through technological advances. There are a number of career tracks in finance and accounting that are at the top of the career ladder in large fashion firms. Accountants are focusing more on analysis, interpretation, and business strategy. Many designers, such as Isaac Mizrahi and Diane Von Furstenberg (Box 7.1), have learned through tough times that a focus on the accounting side of the business could save a company.

What are the advantages of a career in accounting? Accounting is a field that provides adaptability to many functions (e.g., purchasing, manufacturing, wholesaling, retailing, marketing, and finance). As the collectors and interpreters of financial information, accountants develop comprehensive knowledge about what is occurring and close relationships with key decision makers, and they are increasingly being called on to offer strategic advice. As a result, career options and promotional opportunities are readily available in the area of accounting. In

Figure 7.1 The image of accounting has changed; no longer considered "bean counters," good accountants are critical to the success of a fashion business.

"Once upon a time, there was a princess with an idea. The idea was a dress. Not a taffeta ball gown like the ones fairy-tale heroines usually wear—this was a drip-dry, cotton jersey dress that wrapped in front and tied at the waist....And even though the princess was a member of the jet set, famous far and wide as a glamorous party girl, her dress was seen as evidence of an uncanny knack for identifying with her customers: they felt that she must have understood them to have invented something so comfortable and practical, so suitable to their own everyday adventures and to their newfound sense of independence."

Holly Brauchbach of *The New York Times*

Designer Oscar de la Renta described fashion in the 1970s this way: "Today, there is no fashion, really. There are just . . . choices. Women dress today to reveal their personalities. They used to reveal the designer's personality. Until the '70s, women listened to designers. Now women want to do it their own way. There are no boundaries. And without boundaries, there is no fashion."[1] There was one designer, however, that women of the '70s heard loud and clear, and she is Diane Von Furstenberg.

In 1972, Von Furstenberg caused an explosion in the fashion world with a simple yet radical fashion mantra: "Feel like a woman. Wear a dress." By 1976, she had sold millions of her famous knitted jersey wrap dresses and was featured on the cover of *Newsweek*. Over the next decade, it was a bumpy ride of bouncing sales and extensive licensing that led to the need for a break from her company and a hiatus. In 1985, Diane stepped away from the fashion limelight and moved to Paris. Here, she built a different type of company, a French-language publishing house, moving back to the United States in 1989. She couldn't stay away from the fashion world, and reentered it in 1992 with Silk Assets, a pioneer in television shopping. With Diane at the helm promoting her line, the debut collection sold out on QVC in less than two hours. Five years later, Von Furstenberg relaunched her clothing line, and the iconic wrap dress found a warm reception once again. This time, it was the '70s fashionistas and their daughters welcoming the wrap dress into their wardrobes.

Today, the original jersey wrap dress is in the collection of the Costume Institute of the Metropolitan Museum of Art and the Smithsonian Institute, and DVF is a global luxury lifestyle brand that includes sportswear, beauty, and accessories lines. The full range of accessories extends to shoes, handbags, small leather goods, scarves, eyewear, fine jewelry, watches, and luggage. In 2011, DVF introduced its home collection composed of tabletop, bedding, and rugs, and Diane, the fragrance. DVF is currently sold in 72 countries and 61 shops worldwide.

The company's flagship store is a cornerstone in the fashion quarter of New York's Meatpacking District, functioning as a boutique, design studio, and pied-à-terre for Von Furstenberg. New York City's Landmarks Preservation Commission has heralded her flagship building on 14th Street as a "new model of adaptive reuse for the city" for blending an original structure with new design incorporating recycled materials and sustainable elements. Home is where her heart is, as is her family. Diane is married to Barry Diller. She has two children, Alexandre and Tatiana, and three grandchildren. With all of her successes, Diane happily states, "My children are my greatest creations."

Footnote:
1. Quoted in an interview with Lynn Hirschberg, *New York Times Magazine*, May 26, 2002, 5.

Sources:
http://www.chinadaily.com.cn/cndy/2011-04/07/content_12282874.htm

http://www.dvf.com/Diane/about-diane,default,pg.html

http://www.fashioncollections.org/fashion-designers/dian-von-furstenberg/

http://nymag.com/fashion/fashionshows/designers/bios/dianevonfurstenberg/

this chapter, finance and accounting careers in the wholesale businesses of apparel, accessories, soft goods, as well as home furnishings and accessories, will be explored. These include employment opportunities in the following positions:

- Chief financial officer

- Controller and assistant controller

- Senior, intermediate, and entry-level accountants

- Accounts receivable personnel

- Accounts payable personnel

Chief Financial Officer

The **chief financial officer (CFO)** directs the overall financial plans and accounting practices of an organization. This executive oversees finances, accounting, budget, and tax and audit activities of the organization and its subsidiaries and is responsible for determining the financial and accounting system controls and standards. This includes ensuring timely financial and statistical reports used by management and the board of trustees. The CFO holds the top finance and accounting position within an organization.

Qualifications

Following are qualifications for a chief financial officer:

- **Education:** A bachelor's degree in accounting, finance, or a related field is a minimum requirement. In some companies, a master's degree in business administration, accounting, or finance is required. Most firms require that the CFO have a certified public accounting (CPA) or equivalent certification.

- **Experience:** A minimum of ten years of administrative experience in finance and accounting is often required.

- **Personal characteristics:** Successful CFOs have strong managerial abilities, effective oral and written communication skills, a quantitative aptitude, and organizational expertise. They have the ability to synthesize and summarize financial data for constituencies of the company, from management to stockholders. They are skilled at making strategic projections for the company based on an in-depth knowledge of the company's financial transactions.

Career Challenges

The CFO commonly works long hours, often more than 60 per week. CFOs are generally required to travel extensively to attend meetings of financial and economic associations and visit subsidiary firms or divisions of the corporation. They work in a leadership position of high visibility, one that requires a broad range of business and people skills (Figure 7.2).

Figure 7.2
Jean-Jacques Guiony, chief financial officer at LVMH Moët Hennessy Louis Vuitton, presents financial reports to the management team.

Interpersonal skills are important because this position involves managing people and working as part of a team to solve problems. A broad overview of the business is also essential. Being able to shift from problem solving in financial issues to concerns with personnel in moments takes practice, focus, and skill. Financial operations are increasingly being affected by the global economy, so CFOs must continually update their knowledge of international finance.

Controller

A **controller**, also referred to as a *comptroller*, is responsible for a company's financial plans and policies, its accounting practices, its relationships with lending institutions and the financial community, the maintenance of its fiscal records, and the preparation of its financial reports. This position may be the top level in a mid-size company or report to the CFO in a very large company. If there is no CFO, the controller is, in essence, the top gun in accounting. Controllers direct the financial affairs of organizations by preparing financial analyses of the companies' operations for management's guidance. In some companies, they have the final responsibility for providing effective financial controls for the organization. In others, the CFO has this responsibility.

While most people recognize that the controller works with the company's finances, many do not realize that the position requires working effectively with people, too. In large firms, controllers may supervise a staff of accountants in several accounting divisions, from general accounting and property accounting to internal auditing and budgetary controls. They are responsible for evaluating the performance of accounting, determining training requirements, and, in some firms, recommending that personnel be hired, promoted, or removed from the accounting divisions. The essential functions of the controller are as follows.

- Develop, analyze, and interpret statistical and accounting information to evaluate profitability, performance against budget, and other matters that affect the fiscal health and operating effectiveness of the organization

- Maintain the company's system of accounts to include books and records on all company transactions and assets; consolidate all budgets within the company

- Establish major economic objectives for the company and prepare reports that outline the company's financial position in the areas of income, expenses, and earnings based on past, present, and future operations

- Read industry news for current trends and ideas on how to better the company

- Coordinate and direct development of the budget and financial forecasts, develop policies and procedures for financial planning and control, and analyze and report variances to ensure budget compliance and improve company efficiencies

- Oversee tax planning and compliance with all federal, state, local, corporate, payroll, and other applicable taxes

- Revise and update useful and efficient internal reports and furnish external reports as necessary

- Evaluate and recommend insurance coverage for protection against property losses and potential liabilities

- Allocate funding to support management decisions on projects with the highest priorities

- Ensure the adequate allocation of funding to the various business departments

Qualifications

The necessary education, experience, and personal characteristics for employment as a controller may include the following:

- **Education:** A bachelor's degree in business administration (e.g., accounting, finance, control, or marketing) or a related field is a minimum requirement. Some firms require a master's degree in one of these disciplines. Often, major companies will also require the controller to complete post-graduate studies in a finance or control area and CPA certification or an equivalent licensure.

- **Experience:** For this executive position, many corporations require a minimum of five to seven years of relevant experience in financial management.

- **Personal characteristics:** The person in this key financial position must have very strong analytical skills, effective computer skills, and excellent communication abilities, both oral and written. In an international company, skills in a foreign language may be required. For example, Adidas requires fluent written and spoken English and German language abilities for its controller position.

Career Challenges

The career challenges for the controller are similar to those of the CFO: long hours, the necessity of shifting quickly from one issue to another, and the need for a deep understanding of the financial needs of the business.

Assistant Controller

In large firms, there may be a position for an assistant controller. The **assistant controller** supports the company's controller in directing budget and cost controls, financial analysis, and accounting procedures. This person may be called on to manage financial statement preparation, organize and plan auditing schedules, and develop policy and procedure manuals for the accounting department. This position requires a bachelor's degree in accounting, finance, or a related field and four to six years of relevant experience.

Senior Accountant

The senior accountant has extensive experience and depth of knowledge in the accounting field. In large firms, some of them directly supervise accounting associates who may be responsible for a variety of functions. **Senior accountants** are responsible for establishing, interpreting, and analyzing complex accounting records of financial statements for management, which may include general accounting, costing, or budget data. They also analyze variances in monthly financial reports, forecast finances, and reconcile budgets. Preparation of tax and audit schedules quarterly is often part of the senior accountant's tasks.

Qualifications

The following list of qualifications is applicable to the senior accountant position:

- **Education:** A bachelor's degree is required, preferably in accounting or finance.

- **Experience:** Work experience, such as an internship with an accounting firm or in the accounting department of a company, is a door-opener to the accounting profession. Experience in fashion, whether in retail sales or merchandising, provides an advantage to the accountant interested in employment with a fashion firm. Three to five years of general accounting experience is usually required to obtain a senior accountant position. Proficiency with computer programs, such as Microsoft Excel and Word, is required. General ledger experience is expected. Supervisory experience is a plus.

- **Personal characteristics:** Strong communication (both written and oral) and analytical skills are needed. Senior accountants must be detail oriented, organized, and capable of prioritizing their own workloads, as well as the workloads of other accounting staff, to complete multiple tasks and meet deadlines.

The **intermediate** or *mid-level* **accountant** prepares and maintains accounting records that may include general accounting, costing, or budget data. Intermediate accountants analyze and interpret accounting records for the purpose of giving advice or preparing statements. They have completed a bachelor's degree in accounting, finance, or business, followed by two to four years of relevant accounting experience. Often, this previous experience may be as an entry-level accountant.

An **entry-level accountant** maintains records of routine accounting transactions and assists in the preparation of financial and operating reports. This involves helping with the analysis and interpretation of accounting records for use by management. This position is a great starting place for college graduates with a bachelor's degree in accounting, finance, business, or a related field.

Career Challenges

Most accountants generally work a standard 40-hour week, but many work longer hours, particularly if they work for a large company with many divisions. Tax specialists often work long hours during the tax season. People planning a successful career in accounting must be able to analyze, compare, and interpret facts and figures quickly. Accountants must stay up to date on accounting software. Because financial decisions are made on the basis of their statements and services, accountants should have high standards of integrity, as they carry a legal responsibility for their reports.

Accounts Receivable Personnel

What does the term "accounts receivable" mean? **Accounts receivable** refers to the amount of money owed to a business that it expects to receive for goods furnished and services rendered, including sales made on credit, reimbursements earned, and refunds due. It is imperative for a business to monitor accounts receivable and collect funds due to stay in business. There are a number of career opportunities related to this accounting department. An **accounts receivable manager** supervises the accounts receivable division within an organization's established policies. Job responsibilities include arranging and overseeing the completion of all accounts receivable work, including posting, processing, and verifying receipts, credit claims, refunds, interest charges, or other similar records (Figure 7.3). In addition to producing regular or special written reports, the accounts receivable manager suggests improvements to increase effectiveness of units. The **accounts receivable supervisor** oversees record keeping in this department. This person ensures that cash receipts, claims, or unpaid invoices are accounted for properly and calculates and enters charges for interest, refunds, or related items, then produces account statements or other related reports. The **accounts receivable clerk** verifies and posts accounts receivable transactions to journals, ledgers, and other records. The clerk is responsible for sorting and filing documents after posting and preparing bank deposits.

Figure 7.3 The accounts receivable clerk verifies financial transactions, such as sales and the company's credit card payments.

Qualifications

The qualifications for personnel in the accounts receivable department of an accounting division are as follows.

- **Education:** To secure a position as an accounts receivable manager or supervisor, a bachelor's degree in accounting or finance is a minimum requirement. Some firms will hire a candidate with an associate's degree as an accounts receivable clerk.

- **Experience:** The accounts receivable manager position usually requires four to six years of relevant accounting work experience. Two to four years of relevant work is expected for the position of accounts receivable supervisor. Accounts receivable clerk is an entry-level position. This position requires an understanding of bookkeeping procedures and one to two years of relevant work experience. Work experience should be in general accounting procedures and related computer programs; however, those interested in obtaining employment in the accounting division of a fashion firm should gain work experience in retail or merchandising.

- **Personal characteristics:** Strong attention to detail, strong organizational skills, and a high quantitative aptitude are critical to success in this position.

Career Challenges

Accounts receivable personnel deal with a continuing cycle of financial analyses that must be accurate and completed within tight deadlines. There are several times of the year, such as when preparing for a board meeting or preparing tax returns, when the accounts receivable staff works many hours of overtime. To some, the work is never-ending, as it is difficult to see the end of a project when many are ongoing every year. These career challenges for accounts receivable personnel are similar to those for accounts payable personnel, as discussed next in this chapter.

Accounts Payable Personnel

Accounts payable is defined as the monies owed to creditors for goods and services; often, it is the amount owed by a business to its suppliers or vendors. Analysts look at a company's relationship of accounts payable to purchases as an indication of sound financial management. An **accounts payable manager** directs the accounts payable division of a company under the organization's established policies. This person arranges and oversees the completion of all accounts payable work by examining records of amounts due and making sure invoices are paid and discounts taken on time. He or she directs invoice processing and verification, expense coding, and the drafting of payment checks or vouchers. Developing written reports and suggesting improvements in processes to increase effectiveness of the accounts payable unit are key responsibilities of this position. Working under the accounts payable manager, an **accounts payable supervisor** oversees accounts payable record keeping by looking after the recording of amounts due, verification of invoices, and calculation of discounts.

The entry-level position in this division is that of the **accounts payable clerk**. The accounts payable clerk reviews invoices for accuracy and completeness, sorts documents by account name or number, and processes the invoices for payment. The clerk may also be responsible for posting transactions to journals, ledgers, and other records. A classified advertisement for an accounts payable clerk is presented in Box 7.2.

Qualifications

The qualifications for personnel in the accounts payable department of an accounting division are as follows.

- **Education:** To secure a position as an accounts payable manager or supervisor, a bachelor's degree in accounting or finance is a minimum requirement. For an accounts payable clerk position, some firms will hire a candidate with an associate's degree.

- **Experience:** The accounts payable manager position usually requires four to six years of relevant accounting experience. For the accounts payable supervisor position, two to four years of relevant work is expected before hiring. For the accounts payable clerk, work experience in general accounting procedures is required; however, for people interested in securing employment in the accounting division of a fashion firm, work experience in fashion retailing or merchandising is a plus. Computer knowledge is important, particularly knowledge of Microsoft Excel.

- **Personal characteristics:** A strong attention to detail, good organizational skills, and a strong quantitative aptitude are critical to success in these positions.

Human Resources Development

Human resources (HR) refers to the department in charge of an organization's employees, which has responsibilities including finding and hiring employees (Figure 7.4), helping them grow and learn within the organization, and managing the process when employees either leave or are fired (Figure 7.5). **Human resources development (HRD)** refers to the activities of recruiting, training, maintaining, motivating, and managing—in essence, growing—the people who work for a business or organization. Viewed as a group, all of the employees or staff within a company are known as **personnel**. Sometimes, the human resources division of a company is called *personnel* or, for example in reference to a modeling agency, *talent management*. The HR staff takes care of employees from the time they are interested in an organization, and often long after they leave.

Figure 7.4 A human resources manager interviews a prospective employee, often using a position description and job requirement listing to formulate the right questions.

Figure 7.5 HR managers are responsible for firing employees whose work doesn't meet company standards.

One of the primary responsibilities of **human resources management (HRM)** is gauging the staffing needs a company has and will have, then deciding whether to use independent contractors or hire employees to fill these needs. HRM is also responsible for recruiting and training the best employees, supporting them to be high performers, dealing with performance issues, and ensuring that personnel and management practices conform to various regulations. Tasks also include overseeing the management of employee benefits and compensation, as well as employee records and personnel policies. Effective human resources offices always ensure that employees are aware of personnel policies that conform to current regulations.

Some people distinguish between HRM as a major management activity and HRD as a profession. Those people may include HRM within HRD, explaining that HRD includes the broader range of activities to develop personnel inside of organizations, including, for example, career development, training, and organizational development. HRD includes employment opportunities in positions such as human resources manager, hiring manager, recruiter, and trainer.

Human Resources Manager

Human resources managers, or *human resources directors*, play a leadership role in the employee-related parts of a company's business strategy and related legal compliance. They identify human relations issues in the workplace and meet with supervisors and managers to determine effective solutions. They also provide guidance and counsel to managers, supervisors, and employees on a variety of issues, including conflict resolution, interpersonal communications, and effective group interaction. Another responsibility is negotiating contracts with vendors for programs, such as health insurance, and then managing the relationship between the vendor and the company. HR managers prepare annual operating budgets and monitor costs to ensure compliance with budgetary guidelines. They represent the organization at personnel-related hearings and investigations, providing information and coordinating responses for legal issues and interpreting changes in laws, guidelines, and policies as representatives of the firm.

In small to midsize companies, HR managers recruit, interview, and select employees to fill vacant positions. They may plan employee orientation seminars to help new employees meet company goals. HR managers recommend procedural changes to adjust to the changing needs of the organization. They work with other departments to make certain that there is a consistent application of policies and procedures and access to available training and development opportunities. HR managers are ultimately responsible for ensuring a safe and comfortable work environment for all employees. A list of job responsibilities for an HR manager follows.

- Promotes the ongoing role of HR and operations

- Creates development opportunities for HR consultants and provides coaching

- Establishes department goals and action plans

- Monitors and reports on progress in the HR division

- Provides coaching and training opportunities for HRD staff and personnel

- Identifies and proactively raises organizational issues and trends; diagnoses processes, structures, and approaches; recommends alternatives for improved effectiveness

- Clarifies present and future skills and competencies needed by employees

- Acts as "external search" consultant in skills and talents to be brought to the company

Assistant Human Resources Manager

Assistant human resources managers often are responsible for maintaining records and files on all injuries, illnesses, and safety programs within a company. They ensure that all reports are maintained to meet regulatory requirements and corporate policies, and they maintain records of hired employee characteristics for governmental reporting, such as the number of minority employees. Their responsibilities may also include preparing employee separation notices and related documentation and conducting exit interviews to determine the reasons for separations. Box 7.3 provides an example of a classified advertisement for an assistant human resources manager.

Qualifications

The following is a list of qualifications for human resources managers.

- **Education:** A bachelor's degree in organizational development, human resources, or a related field is a minimum requirement. Some firms specify a master's degree as a preferred qualification.

- **Experience:** Seven to ten years of related experience in HRD is usually required. On-the-job experience in interviewing, hiring, and training employees; planning, assigning, and directing work; appraising performance; rewarding and disciplining employees; and addressing complaints and resolving problems is required for this supervisory position.

- **Personal characteristics:** Successful HR managers have the ability to maintain a high level of confidentiality when dealing with highly sensitive issues or information. They must be able to present information effectively and respond to questions from groups of employees, administrators, customers, and the general public. Strong leadership skills, effective interpersonal relationship skills, and conflict resolution abilities are important characteristics. HR managers must also have excellent written and oral communication skills, the ability to manage multiple projects simultaneously, excellent decision-making and analytical skills, and strong coaching and consulting skills.

Career Challenges

The HR manager has the big responsibility of overseeing all of the personnel needs for a company. It is challenging to stay on top of all of the government hiring regulations, the firm's current and future employment requirements, internal company conflicts, employee satisfaction, and personnel budgets. The HR manager is a budget manager, a negotiator, an evaluator, a

Box 7.3 Sample Classified Advertisement: Human Resources Assistant

Contemporary fashion apparel company is seeking an HR Assistant. Candidate needs to be comfortable working in a fast-paced, time-sensitive, minimally structured, constantly evolving environment—supporting the creative, sales, technical, and administrative staffs. The ideal candidate will be a welcoming, available, and responsive resource for employees. He or she will take a proactive lead in interviewing, staffing and recruiting, and implementing HR policies and procedures. He or she will also assist in handling employee relations. The candidate will report directly to the HR Managing Director and will be responsible for the following:

- Assist in maintaining all employee records including compensation and benefits, vacation, leave, job descriptions, etc.

- Implement and organize the internship/training program for all departments

- Enter and maintain employee data, assist with developing and updating personnel policies, company chart, and employee manual as needed

- Process employee paperwork (e.g., new hires, changes, and terms) and properly maintain personnel files

- Assist with recruiting including job postings to our Web site and external job sites, as well as screening résumés, and scheduling and conducting interviews

- Participate in new employee introductions and setup

- Coordinate with all department managers in developing salary/grade/title adjustment policies and procedures

- Coordinate benefits enrollment meetings

- Assist with hiring and termination processes

- Respond to employees' and managers' HR-related inquiries and work to resolve any issues

- Coordinate employee events and activities

- Contribute toward developing and implementing HR programs and processes

- Coordinate with finance team to manage payroll and other related requests

- Contribute toward developing and implementing new and existing HR programs and processes

- Assist with other projects and tasks as requested

Please send résumé to: jobs@company.com with "HR assistant" in the subject line.

Position Requirements:
- Bachelor's degree

- 2+ years HR administration and recruiting support experience, ideally in a similar environment

- Proficiency in Microsoft Word, Excel, PowerPoint as well as experience managing/inputting data

- Must have excellent verbal communication and written skills

- Interest in fashion a plus

- Positive "can do" pitch-in attitude is a must (no room for "it's not my job")

- Ability to develop and maintain professional relationships with both employees and management and to professionally and effectively interact with all levels within our company communicator, and a motivator. It is a huge task to manage and respond to all of the employees in a company; yet, ultimately, this is the HR manager's job. A new tool on the horizon to assist HR directors with hearing from and answering employees is social media, as depicted in Box 7.4.

Hiring Manager

In some companies, the HR manager is responsible for recruiting and hiring employees. In larger firms, there may also be a hiring manager and a recruiter or a team of recruiters. The **hiring manager** is responsible for making the decisions on whether or not a job opening will be filled and who will fill it. A job opening comes about in one of two ways: either someone has left the position or a new position has been created. If an existing position needs to be filled and has been proven over time to be an essential role within an organization, the hiring process can go relatively smoothly. The hiring manager reviews the job description and the budget for it and then posts the job on internal and external listings, such as a classified advertisement in newspapers and trade publications and on Web sites that feature job listings. The hiring manager or recruiter is the first company representative to review the applications of potential candidates. Once applications are reviewed, or screened, the hiring manager will schedule interviews with select applicants. The applicants may need to interview with several other people in the organization. It is the hiring manager's job to determine with whom these interviews will be and then to schedule them. It is also the hiring manager's responsibility to know which types of interview questions are appropriate and legal to ask. If a new position needs to be filled, hiring managers will work with others in the organization to develop a job description and salary package for their ideal candidate. Once job candidates are located and interviewed, the hiring manager is responsible for recommending the top applicant for the position, offering the position, negotiating its terms to the applicant, and then following up on the hire.

Qualifications

What does a hiring manager need in terms of education, experience, and personal characteristics to succeed in this career track? A list of qualifications follows.

- **Education:** A bachelor's degree in organizational development, business administration, human resources, or a related field is a minimum requirement. Some firms specify a master's degree as a preferred qualification.

- **Experience:** Five to seven years of experience in HR is usually required. On-the-job experience in interviewing and hiring employees is required for this position. Some hiring managers begin as an assistant to the HR manager. If interested in a hiring manager position with a fashion-related firm, then work experience in a fashion company is a bonus. For example, candidates who worked part time during college in fashion retailing are likely to have insight on the skills needed for various positions in this type of company.

- **Personal characteristics:** Successful hiring managers are good at reading people and asking the right questions to discern whether or not a person is prepared and able to handle a specific job. Strong communication skills, the ability to manage multiple projects simultaneously, and excellent decision-making skills are necessary qualifications to be successful in this position.

Box 7.4 Tech Talk: The Future of Human Resources and Social Media

By Sharon Lauby, November 2010, mashable.com

Some industry professionals are late adopters when it comes to anything technology related; however, the popularity and possibilities of social media have caused quite a stir among human resource professionals who are using it for social recruiting. While part of HR's role is to educate and evaluate employees, mitigate legal risks, and anticipate future hires, another very large responsibility of the job is to help support and cultivate the corporate culture. As social media becomes more prevalent in the business world, human resources professionals have a significant opportunity to leverage this powerful medium in many aspects of their businesses. Next is a look at how social media will likely affect the human resources field.

1. *Resources for professional growth at your fingertips.* Regardless of the career path, using social media allows people to expand their networks. Human resource professionals are no exception. One minute the human resource director is planning a company social event, and the next he or she is terminating an employee. Having the ability to interact with colleagues around the world about the challenges facing human resources is a huge help. In terms of professional development, HR pros can use Twitter to keep up with industry conferences, information, and articles for their jobs and certifications.

2. *Finding new (or recycled) talent.* Staying connected has the extra benefit of possibly finding new talent for the organization. Victorio Milian, human resources generalist for global fashion retailer H&M, points out that social media allows human resources to stay engaged with former employees. "I worked with our public relations and marketing departments to create a LinkedIn Alumni Group for former H&M employees. This allows the company to continue to keep the brand in the forefront of their minds. It also helps to reduce the amount of knowledge that gets lost when an employee leaves. Lastly, it's a potential pool of rehires for H&M."

3. *Balancing productivity and value.* Many human resources pros remember when using the Internet at work became popular. Organizations were convinced that employees would spend all day surfing instead of finishing their work. Human resources departments are still fighting that battle. This time, it is social media. Milian emphasizes the importance of understanding value. "Human resource professionals must understand which social media tools and strategies will give them the most bang for their buck. Just because many of these tools are free or low cost doesn't mean they're worth investing in. That lack of cost makes it easy to dive into social media without considering what you want to get out of it."

4. *Connecting with the workforce.* It is important to create value not only for the business, but for the internal workforce and the industry. Some HR directors use Facebook to give employees fun facts and news they can use, such as information related to the fashion industry, community activities, and fun events that go on in the company. Social media can attract an internal following of employees that are more engaged with their coworkers, a possible strategy for reducing employee turnover.

5. *Opening up the culture.* When human resources departments begin to include employee involvement in their corporate social media strategy, it also means working with senior leadership to create a culture that supports the change. Encouraging employees to become involved with the company on Facebook will open the door for employees to contact HR regarding work matters. While using social media tools provides convenience for human resources professionals, establishing appropriate metrics to measure results will be key. Just as other aspects of the business like public relations and marketing are searching to

quantify social media, human resources is doing the same.

6. *Taking time off from social media.* Using social media can change levels of expectation. Before Facebook and iPhones, it was understood that there are times when people just weren't available. Even though we now try to encourage "disconnect" time, it is still essential for organizations to set expectations and manage those expectations where using social media is concerned. This not only applies to employees using social media, but to customer service. HR pros have to work closely with marketing, sales, and operations to understand customer demographics and needs.

Social media can also drive the business to be able to respond to the needs of their customers faster and more efficiently. This is critically important, as customers are using social media to speak their minds if they are unhappy with a business. We have all seen the power of a negative tweet or YouTube video by an irate customer. On the flip side, companies like Zappos have proven that social media can be good for business.

7. *Supporting innovation.* There is tremendous potential in social media tools for collaboration and the sharing of real-time ideas or solutions with team members. Internal conferences or team development and meetings can save time and expense and provide a platform for all team members to participate. Training cohorts by providing educational opportunities via social media is yet another collaborative option. Human resources professionals realize that in order to accomplish business goals, individuals must be encouraged and rewarded for using nontraditional thinking. The more we use social media tools, the more we're going to learn and grow in our roles. We are just now at the starting gate. The challenge for human resource directors is integrating a cohesive, relevant, and effective strategy for social media that works at every level of the organization.

Source: http://mashable.com/2010/11/08/human/resources/social/media/

Career Challenges

The hiring manager is held accountable for finding the right people for the positions the company needs to fill. If poor job and personnel matches are made and if there is excessive employee turnover, management turns to the hiring manager. It can be difficult to find excellent employees, particularly in certain geographic locations and if the positions require specialized skills or the organization is offering less than competitive salary ranges.

Recruiter

Recruiters generally work for a specific employer or are in business for themselves and have several companies as clients. Companies such as Ralph Lauren, Jones Apparel Group, and Levi's, to name a few, all have recruiters that they employ directly. **Recruiters** seek out job candidates at college campuses, job fairs, other companies, and online to apply for positions the company is seeking to fill. The duties of a recruiter include:

- Understanding the employer's staffing needs in terms of open positions and the types of candidates that will fit with corporate strategy and culture

- Developing sources for locating the best applicants, including **cold calling** (contacting businesses or people without a personal reference or previous contact), developing leads, and networking

- Locating and implementing tools (e.g., interview strategies or tests) that reveal an applicant's strengths and weaknesses

- Screening candidates

- Keeping up to date on workforce trends

Qualifications

What backgrounds and personal characteristics fit the career track of a recruiter? Following is a list of qualifications.

- **Education:** A bachelor's degree in human resources, business administration, or a related field is a minimum requirement.

- **Experience:** Some companies hire recent college graduates as recruiters, particularly if the companies send recruiters to college campuses to recruit job candidates for them. On-the-job experience in some facet of HR, such as an internship, is a plus.

- **Personal characteristics:** The recruiter is a cheerleader for the company, selling the firm and its opportunities for professional and personal growth to top candidates. This person also has a knack for identifying which candidates would best fit the company culture and the specific job openings. The ability to effectively present information and respond to questions is a key attribute. Strong interpersonal skills, a high energy level, and a love of travel are important traits for recruiters.

Career Challenges

The recruiter often has strong competition for the top job candidates. At job fairs, there are often a large number of recruiters, some working for more widely recognized companies and companies offering more attractive salary and benefit packages. The recruiter is challenged with marketing the company and its positions, selling the firm to prospective employees. Once the recruiter has identified and persuaded top candidates to apply for openings, the hiring manager takes over. If there is not a quick response by the hiring manager, the recruiter is back to square one.

The Hiring Manager and the Recruiter as Partners

In most successful companies, a recruiter and hiring manager spend time together researching and crafting job descriptions for open positions. Through this process, it is likely that their efforts will result in quicker and better-quality hires. Smart recruiters understand that their key objective is to bring hiring managers the right candidates, and good job descriptions help accomplish this goal. When developing a job description, three questions are key:

- What are the specific skills required for the position?

- What are the goals to be accomplished by the person in the position?

- Is there something unique and exciting about the job that can be presented to the candidate as a compelling selling point?

A recruiter may want to ask a hiring manager one specific question: "Can you tell me about someone who works for you and is particularly great?" In the employee or employees named, both the recruiter and hiring manager will identify the attributes of the ideal candidate by noting the behaviors and characteristics of the valued people in the company. In addition to the laundry list of desired qualifications, such as education level, employment background, and certification, there are qualifications or personal characteristics that tend to be a better fit for the company.

Trainer

A **trainer** either directs employees or recruits an expert to work with them on certain areas of knowledge or skills to improve employees' performances in their current jobs. Training sessions, or seminars, are designed to develop the company's workforce (Figure 7.6). Development is a

Figure 7.6 Employee training seminars are designed to develop a company's workforce in such areas as multicultural awareness and effective communication.

broad, ongoing, multifaceted set of activities created to bring an employee or an organization up to another threshold of performance, often to perform some job or new role in the future. Training and development for an employee or a group of employees can be initiated for a variety of reasons:

- When a performance appraisal indicates performance improvement is needed

- As part of an overall professional development program

- As part of succession planning to help an employee be eligible for a planned change in role within the organization

- To pilot, or test, the operation of a new performance management system

- To educate employees about a specific topic

Current topics of employee training that have resulted from a global marketplace include diversity, human relations, communications, and ethics. **Diversity training** usually includes an explanation about how people of different cultures, races, and religions, for example, can have different perspectives and views. It includes techniques to value and expand and multicultural awareness in the workplace. **Human relations training** focuses on helping people get along with one another in the workplace. Conflict management is often part of this training seminar. **Communications training** has become an important topic in workplaces for several reasons. Employees in many companies must work together from different locations. Accelerated productivity requires effective and quick communication. Staff turnover is reduced when employees are "in the loop" and are part of the decisions made within the company.

Figure 7.7 Sexual harassment training equips employees with the knowledge of which behaviors are and are not appropriate for the working environment.

Other current trends in training topics include sexual harassment, safety, customer service, quality initiatives, and technology. Sexual harassment training usually includes careful description of the organization's policies concerning sexual harassment, what are inappropriate behaviors, and what to do about them (Figure 7.7). **Safety training** (Figure 7.8) is critical in situations where there are employees working with heavy equipment, hazardous chemicals, and repetitive activities, such as in an apparel factory or textile mill. Increased competition in today's marketplace makes it critical for employees to understand and meet the needs of customers; therefore, an emphasis on customer service training is significant. **Computer skills training** (Figure 7.9) is becoming an ongoing necessity for conducting administrative and office tasks and for communicating with other departments in a company. **Quality initiatives training** examines such programs as total quality management (TQM), quality circles, and **benchmarking**, the activity of identifying competitors and organizations in other industries with features or skills in areas that the company does not currently have and would like to have. Once benchmark organizations are identified, managers of the HRD division analyze how the company compares in terms of such variables as number of employees, salaries and benefits, employee retention, job descriptions, and other factors. Benchmarking allows HRD administrators and trainers to see how their company compares to firms that they believe are strong competitors.

Figure 7.8 Safety training is critical where there are employees working with heavy equipment, hazardous chemicals, and repetitive activities, such as an apparel factory or textile mill.

Figure 7.9 Computer skills training is becoming an ongoing necessity for conducting administrative and office tasks and for communicating with other departments in a company.

What are the goals of the trainer in developing and coordinating these training seminars? Increased job satisfaction, motivation, and morale among employees are prime objectives that often result in reduced employee turnover. An effective training program can enhance the company's image, both internally and externally. Effective training can also produce increased efficiencies in processes, resulting in financial gain for the company, as well as greater innovation in strategies and products. For example, the capacity to adopt new technologies and methods is a common result of an ongoing computer training program for employees at all levels.

Qualifications

A trainer is expected to have the following qualifications:

- **Education:** A bachelor's degree in human resources, psychology, education, or a related field is a job prerequisite.

- **Experience:** An internship in the human resources department of a major company is an excellent way to open the door to a trainer's position. Most companies expect two to four years of experience in human resources as background for this career path.

- **Personal characteristics:** The trainer is, first and foremost, an excellent communicator in all areas: writing, speaking, and listening. Teaching abilities, presentation skills, and enthusiasm for the subject matter characterize the successful trainer. Additionally, the trainer is an effective networker, able to recruit experts for the various programs that the employees will need.

Career Challenges

The trainer must motivate, inform, and educate employees from all levels of the company on an ever-changing range of subjects. The wide range of audiences and training topics requires trainers to continually find new ways to present information effectively and to educate themselves constantly. Developing alternative methods of training delivery (e.g., online training, video productions, and guest speaker presentations) can be a full-time job in itself. There can be a great deal of pressure to get the job done in a timely and entertaining fashion.

Summary

Today's accountants focus more on analysis, interpretation, and business strategy than accountants have in the past. Accounting employment opportunities in the wholesale businesses of apparel and accessories include the positions of chief financial officer; controller and assistant controller; senior, intermediate, and entry-level accountants; accounts receivable personnel; and accounts payable personnel. The chief financial officer holds the top accounting position in a large company, directing its overall financial plans and accounting practices. In smaller companies, the controller may hold the top position. Senior, intermediate, and entry-level accountants may be responsible for a number of functions ranging from analyzing and interpreting complex accounting documents to maintaining records of routine transactions. Accounts receivable, the amount of money owed to a business that it expects to receive, and accounts payable, the amount owed to creditors, are accounting departments that offer manager, supervisor, clerk, and bookkeeping career opportunities. Every business needs good accounting personnel and practices to succeed in its industry, and fashion companies are no exception. Rated as one of the most desirable professions available, the accounting job track offers good compensation, autonomy, and significant employment demand.

Human resources development (HRD) and human resources management (HRM) professionals work in the field of business focused on recruiting, hiring, training, maintaining, motivating, and managing personnel. Human resources is a field that is gaining importance in businesses around the world, as business owners agree that employees are a company's greatest resource. Building and maintaining a strong workforce are critical to the success of every fashion organization. If supporting people to be their best in an optimal environment is your dream job, then HRD offers a range of opportunities to fulfill this dream.

Key Terms

accounts payable
accounts payable clerk
accounts payable manager
accounts payable supervisor
accounts receivable
accounts receivable clerk
accounts receivable manager
accounts receivable supervisor
assistant controller
assistant human resources manager
benchmarking
chief financial officer (CFO)
cold calling
communications training
computer skills training
controller
diversity training
entry-level accountant
hiring manager
human relations training
human resources (HR)
human resources development (HRD)
human resources management (HRM)
human resources manager
intermediate accountant
personnel
quality initiatives training
recruiter
safety training
senior accountant
trainer

Online Resources

jobs.wwd.com/careers/jobsearch

www.fashionnewspaper.com/articles/1233/1/American-Apparel-Provides-Update-on-Status-of-Accounting-Evaluation/Page1.html

www.payscale.com

www.referenceforbusiness.com/encyclopedia/Cos-Des/Costing-Methods-Manufacturing.html

Discussion Questions

1. Major fashion companies may require their accountants to have worked for one of the "Big Four" accounting firms in the United States. Research to find the names and backgrounds of these firms and determine why this experience is important. Which of the "Big Four" is most appealing to you? Why?

2. Develop a list of the activities a small apparel manufacturer conducts that require accounting assistance. Payroll, for example, is one of these; purchasing materials for the finished products is another. You may be surprised at the length of your list.

3. Go online to locate an example of a fashion manufacturing company with a human resources department that uses social media vehicles to connect with employees and consumers. Find and print illustrations of the company's online activities in recognizing employee efforts, building a team mind-set, and informing employees on industry trends.

Interview with a Human Resource Director

HR careers: Interview with Ann Pickering, HR director at O2
By Louisa Peacock, Jobs Editor 1:48PM BST 26 Aug 2010
Source: http://www.telegraph.co.uk/finance/jobs/7959909/HR-careers-Interview-with-Ann-Pickering-HR-director-at-O2.html

Describe your job in a nutshell.
I lead a team of HR managers who make sure that O2 has people with the right skills and attitude, who have the opportunity to drive our business forward.

What are you working on right now?
A major transformation of the HR function. We're looking at how to hire based on "mind-sets" rather than experience, looking at qualities rather than qualifications.

What's the greatest risk you took to get where you are today?
I left university and joined the Marks & Spencer graduate training scheme, specializing in HR. My big break came through working for IT company Xansa, now known as Steria. I worked closely with the chief executive on several major projects, including the purchase of an Indian software house. I developed my commercial acumen and learned a great deal about being a woman in a commercial world.

What three words would you use to describe yourself?
Passionate, loyal, direct.

What is the main challenge facing HR over the next five years?
In a tough economic environment, HR must keep making as strong a case as possible for maintaining investment in training, learning, and development. The service sector will increasingly rely on people with the right skills to help it grow and HR will be central to that.

What is the most annoying piece of management jargon?
"They left the company to pursue other opportunities."

What's the best piece of advice for anyone looking to make it in HR?
It's a great career for someone who wants to work in business and make tough, commercial decisions every day. It's not an easy option.

What skills do you need to be successful in HR?
Recruit for attitude, you can train for skill.

What is the worst thing anyone can do at a job interview?
Come underprepared without having researched the company.

Sum up your philosophy on life in one sentence.
You get one shot at life, live it.

chapter 8

Fashion Design

Who creates the billions of dresses, suits, shoes, and other apparel and accessories purchased every year by consumers? Fashion designers and their teams do. How do they do this month after month, year after year? From all around the world, fashion designers share their imaginations, personalities, and aesthetic preferences as they develop their creations. They put themselves out there each fashion season. Think about Betsey Johnson, who has a love for detail and design that is evident in everything she has done in life and in business for the past 45 years (Figure 8.1). She says, "Making clothes involves what I like, and color, pattern, shape, and movement, and I like the everyday process and the people, the pressure, the surprise of seeing the work come alive walking and dancing around on strangers."[1] Fashion design is about knowing your customer, as described by footwear designer Manolo Blahnik (Figure 8.2): "About half my designs are controlled fantasy, 15 percent are total madness, and the rest are bread-and-butter designs."[2] Fashion design is about creativity, self-expression, and change—always change. Karl Lagerfeld (Figure 8.3) explains this: "Fashion keeps me designing: the love of change, the idea that the next one will be the right one, the nonstop dialogue."[3]

Fashion design is the development and execution of wearable forms, structures, and patterns. Just as fashions have changed over the years, the field of fashion design has changed dramatically. The move into outsourcing (or overseas production), the customer's need for speed in purchasing new looks, and the advent of technology in design and manufacturing have generated new career opportunities in fashion design. In the career sector of fashion design, there are now a number of new positions in addition to that of the fashion designer, assistant fashion designer, and patternmaker. Among them are the career paths of the technical designer and specification technician. In this chapter, all five career paths are explored, beginning with the fashion designer.

Figure 8.1
Betsey Johnson.

Figure 8.2
Manolo Blahnik.

Figure 8.3
Karl Lagerfeld.

Fashion Designer

Working as a **fashion designer**, an artist dedicated to the creation of apparel and accessories, can mean supervising a team of design assistants at a swimwear company, working under the label of a big-name designer or manufacturer, freelancing for others while creating your own line, or producing a line under your own name. Although the first two options may not appear to be as alluring as the others, they may be less stressful and, quite possibly, more lucrative. Designing and manufacturing your own label takes a great deal of money, time, dedication, and hard work.

There are as many different ways designers embark upon a fashion career as there are styles of design. Ralph Lauren started with a small tie collection that he sold to Bloomingdale's. Helmut Lang opened his own clothing store because he couldn't find "the right" T-shirt. Michael Kors (Figure 8.4) built a following of customers selling his designs in an NYC boutique. Menswear designer Hedi Slimane (Figure 8.5) completed a degree in art history and began a career in fashion design interning at Martin Margiela and working as an assistant designer for Yves Saint Laurent Homme. Six months later, he was the head designer for Yves Saint Laurent's menswear before becoming the highly praised designer of Dior Homme from 2000 to 2007. (Karl Lagerfeld comments on the phenomenon: "I lost 200 pounds to wear suits by Hedi Slimane."[4]) After stepping away from Dior, Slimane has pursued other artistic endeavors on the fringe of fashion, designing furniture for Comme des Garçon, designing costumes, and focusing on his photographs for magazines and his Web site. Nicolas Ghesquière (Figure 8.6) is a globally recognized fashion designer who is currently creative director for the house of Balenciaga owned by the Gucci Group. He learned the job hands-on as an assistant at Jean-Paul Gaultier. The paths in fashion design are diverse; however, most people find that the best foundation for a design career is a college degree and the work experience needed to truly know what it takes to be a fashion designer.

Fashion designers can work in the merchandise categories of men's, women's, and children's apparel, including casual wear, career wear, sportswear, dresses, formal wear, bridal wear, outerwear, maternity, sleepwear, and intimate apparel. Footwear designers create different styles of shoes and boots. Accessory designers create such items as handbags, belts, scarves, hats, hosiery, and eyewear. Jewelry designers work in the areas of costume jewelry or fine jewelry using precious stones and metals (Figure 8.7). While most fashion designers specialize in a specific area of fashion (e.g., knitwear, wovens, fur, children's wear, handbags, etc.), a few work in all areas. Regardless of the merchandise category in which a designer works, the steps in the design process are very similar.

From conceiving the initial design to producing the final product, the design process can take between 18 and 24 months. Listed next are the general steps the fashion designer takes to place a new collection or line in the retailers' hands.

Figure 8.4
Michael Kors.

Figure 8.5
Hedi Slimane.

Figure 8.6
Nicolas Ghesquière.

Figure 8.7
Jewelry designer
Alexis Bittar
in his studio.

1. Researching current fashion and making predictions of future trends. Some designers conduct their own research, while others turn to fashion industry trade groups or trend forecasters who publish trend reports that project the particular styles, colors, and fabrics for a season.

2. Sketching preliminary designs. Many designers sketch initial designs by hand; more and more make use of computer-aided design (CAD) software to transfer these hand sketches to the computer, or to draw first sketches, as discussed in Box 8.1.

3. Attending trade shows or visiting manufacturers to peruse fabrics and procure samples in order to decide which fabrics to use

4. Determining a color palette

5. Designing the styles to be part of the new collection or line, knowing that some of these will later be eliminated due to cost or merchandising decisions

6. Costing out styles to make certain they fit within the price range of the line

7. Creating a prototype or sample of the garment and then trying the sample on the fit model for design adjustments

8. Creating the full collection or line of samples and reviewing the full line for styles to keep or delete

9. Having sample lines constructed to market to retail buyers in the showroom or at trade markets

10. After buyers have placed their orders, distributing the garments to retail operations and identifying top-selling items for the next collection

Trend information, technology, and creativity combine to create fast and simple visuals in fashion flat sketching for fashion and education. For over 30 years, SnapFashun has compiled a vast archive of vector-based fashion flats that cover all aspects of the apparel business. SnapFashun flats allow for fast design generation that is fun, easy, and cost effective. Designers can produce more efficient vector silhouettes that travel seamlessly from design room to boardroom to patternmaker to production tables. Fashion students and fashion professionals can use the archive as a way of expanding their knowledge of what is possible, as well as learning the correct names of details and silhouettes. Entrepreneurs can use the archive to develop or build apparel-related "co-creation" Web sites.

SnapFashun provides members with access to an archive of vector sketches and flats, based on retail, street, and runway reporting from the fashion capitals of the world. SnapFashun works with Adobe Illustrator to provide an interactive reference library, as well as a browser to store sketches. SnapFashun libraries include both details and items that can be "snapped" together, manipulated, altered, and resized. Also, it quickly and easily teaches the indispensable tools of Illustrator that the fashion industry requires. This knowledge, teamed with learning the correct names of fashion details and silhouettes, lays a foundation for the verbal and technical skills required to work in the industry.

Source: snapfashun.com

Qualifications

The qualifications for a fashion designer are presented in the following list.

- **Education:** A bachelor's degree in fashion design or product development is commonly required. Supplementing a fashion design degree with a business, marketing, or fashion merchandising degree or minor gives a job candidate an edge.

- **Experience:** A fashion designer needs basic skills in drawing, sewing, and patternmaking. Fashion designers are expected to present a portfolio of work at interviews. Industry experience is necessary. Many fashion designers started out as patternmakers or design assistants for more experienced designers. Salaried designers as a rule earn higher and more stable incomes than self-employed designers. However, a small number of self-employed fashion designers who have become very successful earn many times the salary of even the highest-paid salaried designers. The highest concentrations of fashion designers are employed in New York and California. Designers with many years of experience under their belts can earn much greater than the average national salary, in addition to bonuses or commissions for exceptional seasonal sales.

- **Personal characteristics:** A strong eye for color and detail, a sense of balance and proportion, aesthetic appreciation, and knowledge of historical fashion are important competencies for a designer. Fashion designers also need effective communication and problem-solving skills, as well as sketching and/or computer-aided design abilities. Strong sales and presentation skills and knowledge of the business end of the fashion industry are vital to a successful fashion design career.

Depending on the size of the design firm and the designer's level of experience, fashion designers have varying levels of involvement in different aspects of design and production.

In large design firms, fashion designers often are the lead designers who are responsible for creating the designs, choosing the colors and fabrics, and overseeing technical designers who turn the designs into a final product. (Technical designers are discussed later in this chapter.) Large design houses also employ their own patternmakers who create the master patterns for the design and sew the prototypes and samples. Designers working in small firms, or those new to the job, usually perform most of the technical, patternmaking, and sewing tasks, in addition to designing the clothing. A small number of high-fashion designers are self-employed and create custom designs for individual clients. Other high-fashion designers sell their designs in their own retail stores, specialty stores, or department stores.

Yet other fashion designers specialize in costume design for performing arts, film, and television productions. While the work of costume designers is similar to that of other fashion designers, it is different in that costume designers often perform extensive research on the styles worn during the period in which the performance takes place, or collaborate with directors to select and create appropriate attire. They sketch the designs, select fabric and other materials, and oversee the production of the costumes within the costume budget. Costume designers are discussed in Chapter 13.

Career Challenges

A fashion design career is not for the meek. Fashion designers must be able to work in a high-pressure environment with an assortment of personalities—with the common goal of meeting tight deadlines. Those entering this occupation must be willing to work as part of a team. Designers are expected to handle criticism, and critics in this field can be brutal. Successful fashion designers know how to learn from a critique while maintaining their individual styles. Many designers tend to have sporadic working hours, often needing to make adjustments to their work day (or work night) to accommodate company deadlines (e.g., market week timing, fashion show plans, production due dates, etc.). Constant interfacing with suppliers, manufacturers, and co-workers throughout the world requires excellent communication skills and patience. Most fashion designers can expect frequent travel. Finally, they must stay on top of consumer and fashion trends, competition, and how their lines are performing at retail. As trend reporter and marketer Jason Campbell states, "Spotting trends is an ongoing exercise."[5]

Assistant Fashion Designer

In the fashion design field, as well as any other career field, you have to start somewhere. This is where assistant designers, or design assistants, come in. **Assistant fashion designers** support designers by helping them create new materials, styles, colors, and patterns for fashion brands and labels. Like fashion designers, design assistants usually specialize in a particular line, such as woven garments, knitwear, footwear, or accessories. The design assistant uses product knowledge and, in some firms, strong patternmaking skills to create prototypes or to modify existing garments. The assistant designer may also be responsible for managing parts of the design process, for example, making certain products arrive on time by working closely with factories and suppliers.

The duties of an assistant designer typically include:

- Assist the design and development teams to execute the seasonal concept direction, line plan style needs, margin requirements, and completion of product

- Communicate with vendors and other departments under the direction of the designer, such as sourcing fabrics and trimmings

- Participate in meetings with vendors, sales representatives, representatives of other company departments, and retail clients, as determined by the designer

- Communicate technical and creative ideas to designer, using sketches, fabrics, and trims

- Assist the designer in creating the product collections at the beginning of each season

- Prepare development creative packages and specification packets under the direction of the designer, such as clear and detailed technical sketches

- Assist in the preparation of seasonal product review meetings

- Create new artwork for trims, appliqués, and such for items in the collection

- Support the design and development team by preparing necessary visual tools (e.g., sketches, presentation boards, fabric swatches, color standards, etc.)

- Check for quality by inspecting products during the design process and when a product is completed, ensuring that samples are constructed accurately and on time

With experience, the assistant designer may take part in seasonal market research to help the design team develop a new product range and forecast trends for the following season. Some companies hire interns and, often, it is the assistant designer's responsibility to supervise and guide them. While the assistant designer usually works in a studio, he or she may have the opportunity to travel and visit manufacturers or go on research trips to art galleries, trade shows, or particular places or countries that inspire a design theme (Figure 8.8).

Figure 8.8 While the assistant designer usually works in a studio, he or she may have the opportunity to travel and visit manufacturers or go on research trips to art galleries, trade shows, or particular places or countries that inspire a design theme.

Qualifications

The qualifications required for an assistant designer position vary with employers; however, there are two common prerequisites: training in patternmaking and experience in **computer-aided design (CAD)**. CAD is increasingly being used in the fashion design industry. Although most designers initially sketch designs by hand, a growing number translate these hand sketches to the computer or draw completely on the computer. CAD allows designers to view apparel styles on virtual models and in various colors and shapes, saving time by requiring fewer adjustments of prototypes and samples later. A listing of qualifications commonly required for an assistant designer follows.

- **Education:** A bachelor's degree in fashion design and/or product development is commonly required, to include coursework in patternmaking, illustration, and CAD. Training in draping, tailoring, and specialized merchandise categories (e.g., swimwear, menswear, children's wear, etc.) is a plus when it matches the employer's product line.

- **Experience:** The assistant designer should have computer skills in design-related software, such as in Adobe Illustrator, Excel, Kaledo, and Photoshop. Working on CAD updates and color, color cards, fabric swatches, and tech pack updates requires strong computer skills. Experience in design or product development with some background in fit, fabric development, finishes, and construction details is often required. Experience often separates the candidate who receives the job offer from other applicants. This can begin in the form of volunteer work, such as costuming for a community theater, and end with an internship with a design or manufacturing firm during college years.

- **Personal characteristics:** Excellent organizational and verbal communication skills are needed. A high level of attention to detail and accuracy is important. The ability to work as part of a team is mandatory. A strong aesthetic sense and abilities in color, proportion, and fit are critical skills for the assistant designer.

Technical Designer

Technical design is a relatively new career path. As the majority of apparel and accessories production was moved to overseas manufacturing facilities, these offshore manufacturers began producing a wide range of products across several categories. Many of the products were new to the manufacturers. Someone was needed to oversee what the factories were doing—the measurements they were using, the construction techniques that were being applied, the dates products were going through the different stages of production, and more. A specialist was needed to provide product specifications and to communicate with the various contractors. Technical design was born.

Technical design (also called *tech design*) refers to using drawings, measurements, patterns, and models to develop the "blueprints," or technical plans, needed for the manufacturing of products. Technical design includes determining specifications of trim colors, construction, and components of products as needed by the manufacturer. Fashion is a perfect fit for technical design because the manufacturer's work with overseas contractors mandates strict oversight of specifications to ensure consistent quality, good fit, and standardized sizing. In addition, technical design impacts manufacturing efficiency and cost effectiveness through reduced errors and quicker turnaround.

The day-to-day tasks for one technical designer may be very atypical for another technical designer at a different company, but they all have the same goal at the end of the day: to produce a well-fitting garment at a marketable price. Next, an insider's view of the daily work as a technical designer is provided by 39thandbroadway.com.

My mornings usually start off with reading e-mails from the factories to see what issues or questions they might have or what they need from us. From there, I begin my day and focus on my priorities. I may be sending comments or production tech packs out to the factory, doing a fitting with the design team, and/or correcting a pattern. We also have meetings with the sales staff to go over new styles or a meeting on production issues that need to be solved with the production team.

Most technical designers work very closely with the factories, and, sometimes, we get the opportunity to fly over to meet the people we speak to overseas on a daily basis. Unfortunately, these days it's very rare to see that happen, due to the economy, but I think once the industry picks up, we will be able to experience that once again.

The working hours can be very exhausting, but each position is quite different. My hours do not allow for any personal time. I am always one of the first to arrive, and the last one to leave, with about a 10-minute lunch that requires me to swallow food whole while still reading e-mails. It's tiring, to say the least. That is why it is very important to like the people with whom you work; in this respect, I have been very fortunate.

Source: http://www.39thandbroadway.com/interview-technical-designer/

Today's technical designer essentially does parts of the job that designers used to do when companies were smaller and production was completed domestically. In years past, the technical design position did not exist because companies had their own production facilities. Their products were similar and used the same types of construction and, often, these processes were standardized in house. As production crossed borders and oceans, the designer needed help—badly. The technical design position allowed the designer to design again.

A **technical designer** is the liaison between the designer and factory, responsible for working closely with the designers to communicate their specific product requests to the factory overseas. An apparel technical designer's focus is on the fit of the garment, more than the actual design of it. Technical designers are, in essence, the architects of fashion products. They work with flat measurements, construction, and pattern corrections from the first sample to production. They are responsible for creating the prototypes and patterns and work with the manufacturers and suppliers during the production stages. Technical designers may also work with the sales team to figure out how they want the fit executed, depending on the trend for that season. In Box 8.2, a day in the life of a technical designer is explored.

Responsibilities of the technical designer vary with each company, as with any industry. Some companies require the technical designer to be more involved with design and computer work in such programs as Adobe Illustrator and Kaledo, while others require the technical designer to work heavily with patterns. The general responsibilities of the technical designer follow.

- Manage the fit process of production garments from first sample fitting through stock delivery

- Ensure garments adhere to the company's quality and fit standards

Primary Objectives for Technical Designers

- Acquire basic computer skills and program-specific skills (e.g., PDM, Excel, Adobe Illustrator, and Kaledo)

- Facilitate (not complicate) the product development process

- Focus on quality

- Understand the world of patternmaking

- Know how to fit a garment

- Understand and communicate effectively with manufacturing partners

- Develop clear and simple specification packages

- Know how to illustrate construction or fit details and changes

- Know how to use illustrations to analyze fit details or changes and show solutions

- Understand tolerance standards for style, construction details, and graded measurements

- Recognize the pros and cons of various measuring methods

- Grasp the importance of measuring manuals or diagrams to convey methods of measuring

- Appreciate the differences between auditing and evaluating

- Understand how garment measurements are related and how they can be interpreted

- Realize when to revise a spec and when garment specs are truly achievable

- Identify and solve basic balance and fit problems

- Conduct fittings and issue all fit corrections

- Resolve construction and fit issues to ensure consistent fit and quality

- Generate complete and accurate production specifications and corrections

- Organize and track production samples

- Interface with manufacturing to identify any issues that may prevent timely fit approval

- Monitor/resolve any testing issues

- Provide care-labeling instructions

- Conduct stock review

- Communicate daily and troubleshoot with overseas offices

- Oversee adherence to design and production calendar, responding to change as appropriate and, if applicable, partner with design and manufacturing team to ensure timely delivery of line

Box 8.3 provides a list of basic training, or objectives, for the technical designer.

Qualifications

The qualifications for the position of technical designer are as follows.

- **Education:** Technical designers are typically required to have at least an associate's degree, likely a bachelor's degree in fashion design. Basic training includes computer skills in common programs (e.g., Microsoft Excel, etc.) and program-specific skills (e.g., Adobe Photoshop, Illustrator, and Kaledo).

- **Experience:** Patternmaking and CAD experience are expected. Many technical designers are hired from the position of specification technician. An internship with a fashion design firm and work in the technical design department can help open the door to a position in this area. A strong portfolio of a person's best work is the best showcase of his or her creativity and can go a long way toward convincing potential employers that the person would be an asset to their business.

- **Personal characteristics:** An understanding of numbers, business, and technology can be very helpful to a technical designer, as are an eye for detail and strong interpersonal skills, since this position often requires working with a cross-disciplinary team. Technical designers often work within specialized niches, gaining field-specific knowledge as they continue to climb the professional ladder. As companies continue to outsource their work, often expanding overseas in the process, there will also continue to be a growing demand for technical designers. Since technical designers work in specialized niche fields, demand will also fluctuate with the performance of those fields.

Specification Technician

The typical duties of a **specification technician**, or a *spec tech*, are to attend the fittings of the sample garments, take measurements, and compile these measurements into packets to hand off to production. These packets are referred to as **spec**, or *tech*, **packs** and contain detailed information taken from the designer's sketch, translated into measurements in order to ensure desired fit and styling details, such as the placement of pockets, the length of zippers, the size of buttons, etc., as illustrated in Figure 8.9. Spec tech is usually an entry-level position, because the primary responsibility of the spec tech is to measure the product. Spec techs are usually promoted to technical designers after they gain a few years of experience, depending on their situation. The qualifications for a spec tech are equivalent to those of a beginning technical designer.

Patternmaker

Patternmakers play a key role in the design and production processes. They are responsible for translating the design concept into a pattern for the actual garment. Patternmakers develop a **first pattern**, which is used to cut and sew the **prototype**, or first sample garment. The first pattern is made in a **sample size**, the size used for testing fit and appearance in addition to selling purposes. For juniors, sample sizes are 5, 7, or 9; for misses, they are 6, 8, or 10; and for women's wear, sample sizes are 18 or 20; depending on the line and its target market. For

Figure 8.9

Spec packs contain detailed information taken from the designer's sketch, translated into measurements in order to ensure desired fit and styling details, such as the placement of pockets, the length of zippers, the size of buttons, etc.

CUSTOMER :								SEASON :	
DESC. OF SAMPLE :	WOMEN'S SS KNIT SHIRT POLO							DATE :	
STYLE : KN21								MODIFY:	
QTY : (PCS)								VENDOR:	

DESC.	S	M	L	XL	1X	2X	3X	TOLERANCE
CHEST (1" BELOW ARMHOLE)	38	41	44	47	52	55	58	+ / - 1/4
SWEEP	38	41	44	47	52	55	58	+ / - 1/2
BACK LENGTH (FROM COLLAR SEAM DOWN)	25.5	26	26.5	27	27.75	28.5	29.25	+ / - 1/4
FRONT BODY LENGTH (FROM HIGH POINT)	26	26.5	27	27.5	28.25	29	29.75	+ / - 1/4
ACROSS SHOULDER	16	16.5	17	17.5	19	19.5	20	+ / - 1/4
ARMHOLE (CURVE)- HALF	9	9.5	10	10.5	11	11.75	12.5	+ / - 1/4
SLEEVE LENGTH (FROM CENTER BACK)	17	17.5	18	18.5	20	21	22	+ / - 1/4
SLEEVE OPENING (ON THE HALF)	5.5	6	6.5	7	7.25	7.5	7.75	+ / - 1/4
NECK OPENING	19.25	20	20.75	21.5	23	23.75	24.5	+ / - 1/4
COLLAR HEIGHT (CENTER BACK)	2.5	2.5	2.5	2.5	2.5	2.5	2.5	+ / - 1/8
FRONT NECK DROP	3.25	3.5	3.75	4	4.25	4.5	4.75	+ / - 1/8
BACK NECK DROP	1	1	1	1	1	1	1	+ / - 1/8
FRONT PLACKET WIDTH	1	1	1	1	1	1	1	+ / - 1/8
FRONT PLACKET LENGTH	4.5	4.5	4.5	4.5	4.5	4.5	4.5	+ / - 1/8
SLIT HEIGHT AT BOTTOM	2	2	2	2	2	2	2	+ / - 1/8
HEM HEIGHT	1	1	1	1	1	1	1	+ / - 1/8

menswear, sample sizes are 34 for trousers and 38 for tailored suits. For infants' apparel, size 3–6 months is the sample size; for toddlers' apparel, size 2 is often the sample size; in children's wear, it is usually a size 7.

Patternmakers can use three techniques to develop the first pattern: draping, flat pattern, or computer-aided patternmaking. With the **draping method**, patternmakers shape and cut muslin or the garment fabric on a dress form, or model, to create a pattern, as shown in Figure 8.10. Draping is the preferred strategy for soft, flowing designs. It allows the patternmaker to adjust the design as it evolves three-dimensionally, as with a piece of sculpture. When the designer approves the look, the patternmaker removes the muslin from the form and then draws the pattern on heavy paper. Alternately, the **flat pattern method** uses angles, rulers, and curves to alter existing basic patterns, referred to as **blocks** or *slopers*. The term "block" is used to describe a pre-pattern template for which additional manipulation is required at the end to generate a pattern (e.g. changing the bust dart, adding seam allowances, etc.) for a variety of other garments. Finally, computer-aided patternmaking is utilized by **many** large firms that can afford the expense of the equipment and software programs. With **computer-aided patternmaking**, patternmakers can manipulate graphics of pattern pieces on a computer screen or make patterns manually using a **stylus**, a computerized pen, or a **puck**, a mouselike device. Another tool in computer-aided patternmaking is the **digitizer**, a program integration feature used to make or alter patterns. Patternmakers and technical designers can copy and paste measurements to a design, as well as grade patterns. With a digitizer, they can also import appliqués, screen graphics, and embroideries from other programs for pattern placement. The digitizer can also be used to create or alter markers. Whether draped, created by flat pattern, or developed on a computer, the first pattern must accurately reflect the style, proportion, and fit the designer had in mind when conceiving the product.

Qualifications

Following are the qualifications for a patternmaker.

• **Education:** A bachelor's degree in fashion design, product development, apparel manufacturing, or a related field is commonly required.

- **Experience:** Preparation for the career of patternmaker includes knowledge of draping, flat patternmaking, and computer-aided design. Most patternmakers begin their careers as an assistant patternmaker or a pattern grader.

- **Personal characteristics:** Patternmakers must have an understanding of mathematical calculations as they pertain to sizing and fit. They must have keen eyes for proportion and line, as well as the ability to achieve perfect fits. The successful patternmaker is a design technician with a critical eye for detail and accuracy.

Figure 8.10
With the draping method, patternmakers shape and cut muslin or the garment fabric on a dress form or model to create a pattern.

Summary

What are the differences in the careers of a technical designer, patternmaker, and specification technician? A technical designer's responsibilities encompass most of the duties that a pattern-maker and specification technician would have. If a company offers all three positions (technical designer, patternmaker, and specification technician), the team will work together, each with a different focus. The patternmaker will focus on adjusting patterns, correcting and balancing them so the garment will fit properly. The technical designer will work with measurements. The specification technician will prepare the spec pack.

Endnotes

1. www.betseyjohnson.com/about/
2. www.brainyquote.com/quotes/quotes/m/manoloblah110627.html
3. www.brainyquote.com/quotes/quotes/k/karllagerfeld.html
4. www.vogue.co.uk/celebrity-photos/080208-karl-lagerfeld-famous-quotes/gallery.aspx#/imageno/11
5. dianepernet.typepad.com/diane/2010/05/page/2/

Key Terms

assistant fashion designer
block
computer-aided design (CAD)
computer-aided patternmaking
digitizer
draping method
fashion design
fashion designer
first pattern
flat pattern method
patternmaker
prototype
puck
sample size
spec pack
specification technician
stylus
technical design
technical designer

Online Resources

dianepernet.typepad.com/diane/2010/05/page/2/

jcreport.com/

online.wsj.com/article/SB10001424052748703584804576144640148103236.html

princetonreview.com/Careers.aspx?cid=63

www.fashion.net/howto/fashiondesigner/

www.hintmag.com/hinterview/hedislimane/hedislimane2.php

www.stylecaster.com/search/results/?q=fashion+design+careers

www.youtube.com/watch?v=QFOGN8SiJUw

Discussion Questions

1. Select one of each: a new and relatively unknown designer, a current contemporary designer, and a legendary designer of the past. Construct a report examining the following aspects of these designers' careers: background (e.g., birthplace, education, experience, etc.), career startup and path (e.g., internships, jobs, and current position), signature looks, licenses in other product areas, and future plans.
2. Select three well-known apparel manufacturers that would likely require a patternmaker to have exceptional abilities in one of each of the following skill areas: draping, making flat patterns, and computer-aided patternmaking. Why did you choose these manufacturers?
3. Compare and contrast two classified advertisements for technical designers. How are the position descriptions similar and different? Among many other Web sites, you can locate classified ads for the fashion industry at http://www.wwd.com/wwdcareers, http://www.stylecareers.com, and http://www.fashion.net/jobs/.

Interview with a Patternmaker

By Oriana DiNella, July 2009
Source: www.39thandbroadway.com/interview-pattern-maker/

Are patternmakers a dying breed? Laura Moore is a self-taught patternmaker currently living in New York City who has been in the industry since the late 1970s. She teaches hand tailoring at Pratt Institute, which is one of the most advanced classes in the curriculum. She is still trying to figure out if she can make it as a patternmaker in New York City. She considers herself a bit of a dinosaur because of her old-school handwork and couture-level construction. She works, as they say, on the table. This market all but dried up years ago in the United States, but Laura stresses it is important to know the basics of how things work because this will make you a better designer. Oriana DiNella delves into the life of the lost art of creating a pattern by hand with one of the industry's masters.

Eight years ago, when I found myself for the third time in my career having to leave a major job, I decided that I really wanted to teach. I still do freelance patternmaking and hold a position as a part-time professor at Pratt Institute. Nothing I have ever done thrills me as much as teaching does. I have been a sample maker, production manager, tech designer, and assistant in the tech design department.

What are the day-to-day activities in a freelance world?

No two days ever resemble each other. As a freelance patternmaker, I have a diverse and ever-changing group of clients. One day I will work on jeans, the next day on a tailored blazer, later on a wedding gown, and then possibly swimsuits. Being a freelancer requires one to be more diverse and well rounded. Back in the day, patternmakers had more specific jobs (e.g., children's wear, swimwear, etc.) because there was barely any freelancing. It is exciting because I get to vary the type of product I work on. This is a great benefit. The downside is I don't know week to week how much work I will have, or if I will have enough money coming in. In the good old days, I worked at the same pattern table for the same label every day. The flexibility is wonderful in freelancing, but job security is not there. As there is not a lot of job security in the fashion industry in general, being able to wear many hats has kept me going.

I also do product development and consulting for potential startup companies. I have told many not to go forward because I was looking out for their best interests. If someone is consulting with me and they do not have the backing and business knowledge for a fashion line, then the company they are trying to make will not get there.

Startup businesses are expensive and time consuming! If a concept is too far removed from reality, it's a no go. What I get a lot is many new moms wanting to design a line of baby clothes. We have all worn clothes our entire lives and a lot of ordinary people think they can be clothing designers. I don't understand why someone would go into a field they know nothing about! There were times when I interviewed people about working in the fashion industry and asked them why they wanted to get into it, and they replied, "I watch the fashion channel all the time." Good luck to them.

The whole *Project Runway* phenomenon has been interesting. Daniel Vosovic wrote a book, *Fashion Inside Out*, in which he profiled quite a few industry professionals. He gave me a chapter. I commend him on his book, because it is geared for young people who might be considering a career in fashion and it tells what that work and life entail. I talk to students at Pratt about it a lot. No one ever says they came to Pratt because of how much they love *Project Runway. Project Runway* is fun for seeing what people do when you put them in a creative situation; however, I do not think it draws people into the industry.

Due to the current economic climate, have there been fewer jobs for patternmakers and seamstresses in New York City?

I am a patternmaker who works on the table and I consider myself a dinosaur. The Fashion Institute of Technology (FIT) stopped offering a major in patternmaking a few years ago, which shows how

Interview with a Patternmaker (continued)

many patternmakers are no longer out there and how low the demand is for them.

FIT needs to place graduates, and if there are no jobs in patternmaking, the school is not going to focus on this area. A lot has to do with the economy, of course. In the last 20 years, there has been a whole generation shift of doing patterns. I teach fashion design, which is a two-semester fashion class. It is vital for the students to take this—not so they can get jobs as patternmakers, but so they can communicate while working in the industry. It is easier to communicate about something if you understand it.

Do you feel that more manufacturing services have been outsourced?

Many years ago, factory owners realized they could make their services more appealing if they offered patternmaking for free. It is much less costly to have patternmakers abroad. Because of this, a huge demand for tech designers has resulted. I have also worked as a tech designer.

A good patternmaker understands the importance of shapes. A designer can give a sketch with the same measurements to five different patternmakers and get five different garments. One garment will make a person look thinner, one heavier, etc. Everyone wants the perfect pants! When drawing patterns there are a lot of different ways to make numbers fit. No matter how great the tech pack is, if a less than great patternmaker is on the other end, you will *not* receive a great pattern. One needs to have an amazing patternmaker to translate the tech pack into gorgeous garments.

Very few jobs for patternmakers are left. They have been replaced by tech designers or computers. That doesn't mean the skill of patternmaking has gone away. I do not use a computer; all of my patterns are done by hand. I make original patterns on paper and consider myself more of a craftsperson. What I do use technology for is to have the patterns digitized to keep the originals safe. I can then e-mail the originals to whoever needs them.

Tech designers began to evolve in the 1980s, reaching their heyday in the 1990s. The emergence

of tech design meant that manufacturers no longer needed a pattern department and a sample room. Companies just needed a couple of tech designers and then would send information to overseas factories. With the economic downturn, jobs for tech designers are now decreasing.

Do you see things coming back to the heyday of the Garment District with the onset of the slow fashion movement and eco clothing taking off?

No, because we have various forces in society that encourage the consumer to want cheap, disposable products that cost as little as possible to make. I am hopeful for the current generation that is concerned about the environment. Consumer behavior is beginning to evolve, but has a lot more evolving to do.

To average consumers, an amazing garment that may cost 20 percent more isn't worth the price, because they will not see the difference and are not willing to pay the extra money. I am excited and encouraged with the eco brands, such as Restore, and companies that are active in the Save the Garment Center, a movement to revitalize what has become a dying industry. The Garment District has made a ton of progress, but will not see its heyday again. This is not possible now due to the emergence of China; it is a global economy.

Where do you foresee things going with the Garment District in general?

I am optimistic and believe it will not dry up and go away. I think that more startup businesses are interested in being small, staying local, and doing the "right" thing. I am hopeful that it is not going to die. I do not think it is going to flourish in the next couple of years, nor is any business for that matter. New York City has recognized it is smart to not turn all manufacturing business sites into multimillion-dollar apartment buildings. Construction is leveling off and the owners of spaces currently zoned for manufacturing will not be fighting to get them zoned for residential—which will allow them to keep making things here in New York City. It is wasteful and expensive to buy goods that are shipped from here to overseas and back. This is why there are $300 shirts at Barneys.

Interview with a Technical Designer

Behind the Scenes with a Technical Designer
June 23, 2009
www.39thandbroadway.com/scenes-technical-designer/

An often overlooked arena of the fashion business is the field of technical design. For those of you not in the business, a technical designer handles issues relating to measurements, fit, patterns, and more. Below is our interview with Morgan, an FIT graduate who moved from Tennessee to New York City to become a technical designer. She currently works for a large multibillion-dollar company as a technical designer and has been kind enough to share her experience with us. And, regarding her answer to the second question, yes, it is a fact that many designers do their own specing and communicating with factories.

What is your educational background and do you feel it helped prepare you for the fashion industry?
I went to the Fashion Institute of Technology. I have an associate's degree in patternmaking technology, and in my second year concentrated on technical design. I also have a bachelor's degree in international trade and marketing (ITM) for the fashion industry. Both of my degrees prepared me for the fashion industry and my technical design career. I use skills from my patternmaking degree daily, and since it was only a two-year program I chose to do ITM for my bachelor's, which gave me a broader education on all different aspects of the industry. FIT no longer offers patternmaking technology because they are working on offering a four-year technical design program, so I think that will be even more beneficial for this growing field.

You are a technical designer. For those not familiar with the title, what exactly is a technical designer?
The easiest way to explain a technical designer: he or she is the liaison between the designer and the factory. Since most apparel is now made overseas, the technical designer is responsible for working closely with the designer and conveying their ideas to the factory overseas with flat measurements, construction, and pattern corrections, from the first sample to production.

For a young person wanting a career in tech design, how would you recommend they proceed?
I think the first step if you would like to make tech design a career is enrolling in a patternmaking or a technical design program. Every day as a technical designer you are working with patterns, making corrections and fitting samples, so it is very important that you have a good understanding of patterns and correcting patterns after fittings. I would also recommend taking sewing and tailoring classes to become familiar with the construction inside different garments. Technology-wise it is important to be proficient in computer programs such as Adobe Illustrator, Photoshop, Microsoft Excel, Word, and Outlook. Any knowledge of pattern programs, such as Gerber, is also a big plus. However, the best education is through experience, so intern, intern, intern as much as you can.

Can you describe the basic day-to-day responsibilities of a technical designer?
For every company and depending on your position, the day-to-day responsibilities of a technical designer vary. Basic responsibilities include going over sketches with the designer; producing flat measurements and general construction from the sketches; specing garments; conducting fittings; correcting patterns based on fitting corrections; creating tech packs (which include corrections, construction, measurements, trims, etc.); and conveying all corrections, issues, and details to overseas vendors as clearly as possible.

What is your opinion of the working conditions in the fashion industry/Garment Center and is there anything that you would like to see companies improve on?
I work for a very large company, and I think the conditions are pretty good. I have great benefits, I work in a clean, spacious building, and the hours are typically 8 a.m. to 6 p.m. Technical design can be very stressful, lots of deadlines, and there have been nights I have stayed until 10 p.m. It is really

Interview with a Technical Designer (continued)

about time management and organizing your work. One complaint I have of the fashion industry as a whole is the amount of waste that almost all fashion companies have. I would really like to see the fashion industry and Garment Center work on being more eco-friendly. I think if the fashion industry could move in that direction, it could make a huge impact globally.

For those not familiar with the technical side of fashion design, can you generally explain the difference between a technical designer versus a patternmaker, tailor, spec tech, etc.?
The technical designer, at my company, has to basically be proficient in patternmaking, tailoring, specing, flat sketching, etc. As a technical designer, your job is to give as much information as possible from a designer's sketch to the overseas vendor so that a sample can be created and, through several fittings, an entire line produced. To me, the general difference is that technical design isn't one specific focus, but a combination of all of these jobs, and a technical designer must be proficient in each area.

What is the one thing you wish you had known before entering the fashion industry?
Honestly, I wish I had known more about technical design and the process of creating apparel. During my patternmaking degree, there were only three technical design classes, which were all very broad on the subject. I became interested through those three classes and took a job the following year, which is where I really learned the most about technical design. I think there are very few people, including fashion students, who understand the process it takes to create one garment.

Interview with a Fashion Designer

By Bridget Foley
Wednesday, May 12, 2010
From WWD Milestones issue
Source: www.wwd.com/fashion-news/vera-wang-a-life-in-fashion-3068440

From the moment she unlaced her competitive figure skates for the last time, Vera Wang set her sights on a life in fashion. In the 40-plus years since, hers has been a singular ride, one that took her first to *Vogue* magazine, where she learned that no one disturbed the calm of Mr. Penn's set with chatter, to Ralph Lauren, where she experienced the creative joys of limitless resources, and finally, 20 years ago, to her own company.

From its modest beginnings as a small bridal boutique, Vera Wang the firm has grown into an important licensing-based operation, and Vera Wang the designer into a major force. Long the go-to goddess for aisle-bound superstars, as of this fall, Wang begins a relationship with the marrying masses via her recent deal with David's Bridal. In ready-to-wear, she has dared to be different, adhering steadfastly to her luxe-casual bohemian aesthetic—even though she acknowledges that a more mundane approach might play better at retail. But then, Wang didn't get into this business for the money. "For me, fashion was sheerly for the love," she says. "It was never about the money. And unfortunately, now it has to be. That's the big adjustment I had to make in my life. You can't survive with a fashion company if you don't make any money. That's just a silly little reality we all want to sweep under the rug, but it's true."

Figure 8.11 Vera Wang.

Twenty years in business—a moment for reflection. You've also looked backward for some recent speaking engagements. Any intriguing self-revelations?
As I looked through, it became very apparent that my life has been defined far more by my failures to attain things, my goals or desires or hopes or dreams, than by anything you could perceive as success.

That sounds harsh.
I fell in love with figure skating when I was about six....Skating was my life. It was more than just

a passing fantasy. I was always fourth [in competition] and they only took three....So when I didn't make the [1968 Olympic] team, this was such a part of my life, I was devastated. That was the first lesson I learned in life.

What was the lesson?
That nobody's going to get your dreams. It's not necessarily about winning or having your dream come true. It's about what you learn along the way. It's a process; it's not just the end result. And then it happened again at *Vogue*.

What happened at *Vogue*?
I started after college as a rover, and then became Polly Mellen's assistant.

Interview with a Fashion Designer (continued)

What was Polly like?
Oh, killer. Killer. And she knows it. She was a total perfectionist. She was an artist in her own right and, like many artists, they have to work themselves into a fevered pitch to get the result. What I learned from watching Polly was that Polly made the model feel like a queen.

But there was a lesson of disappointment?
I was there for 17 years. I became a senior editor. Eventually, I just didn't see where I was going. I did some really nice work with most of the photographers of that era. But I wasn't shooting with Penn and I wasn't getting Avedon because Polly was getting them. And so I decided to leave.

And eventually, after several years working as an accessories designer for Ralph Lauren, your father decided to back you in business. Why did he insist on bridal?
It would be manageable, he thought. He said, "The inventory level seems low. You custom-make a dress, it's controllable. A nice boutique."

So rather than a passion, bridal was merely a way into fashion design?
It became my passion because as I got better at it and I began to grow it, I could express myself in a way that I hadn't been able to in a long time. I've put everything into it for 20 years. I trained myself on the job. I didn't know how to work in lace. One day I just said, "I'm going to master the technique of lace, whether I have to cut it out, piece it, drape it, line it." Bridal became my passion....It didn't start that way.

What did you bring to bridal that was missing?
I think I brought a fashion sense that changed bridal. I think we really changed the vocabulary of it. I've spent 20 years of my life doing that and investing in it financially and with physical energy.

What was your first big celebrity wedding?
The first really big one was Max Kennedy's, Ethel Kennedy's son. The bride, Victoria, was heaven. She was a law student and she was beautiful. I didn't go, but from what I heard, the dress was destroyed within 10 minutes because they were playing football after the ceremony. Victoria Kennedy was the first really big name, social-slash-celebrity, and from there on we got very lucky.

Why do you think you connected so strongly with the celebrity set? There were and are other major names in bridal....
I think what connected was the single-mindedness of it. There was nothing else. I could focus all that energy into how to cut a veil. I didn't have an empire. I looked for inspiration just as I would for ready-to-wear, in film, or something else that resonated for me.

Let's move to where you are now. How do you assess your business today?
My business today is definitely based on the licensing model. That's where we have grown the most, that's where we've spent a lot of energy, and I think we've been very successful. I don't want to ever appear like I think I'm really successful because a) it isn't true, and b) whenever I say I'm feeling good, the next day I come down with strep throat. It's been a good model for us, but we've also worked hard at it. I think my licensees have grown to depend on my participation, which is a challenge because I'm one person. But I do control those businesses carefully, as much as I can.

What have been the biggest challenges?
Each one of the businesses is different, and I've had to come up to speed on them all. I've had to understand what the market will bear and yet I try not to let go of my own aesthetic. It's that constant challenge that is very, very difficult. At Wedgewood alone, there are 15 categories that I have to satisfy — the crystal, the sub-crystal, the plates, the gifting, the picture-frame business.

It seems a great deal radiates from bridal.
[It's about] the credibility, the dedication, the singular energy, the fact that we work with brides, we fit brides. This isn't ready-to-wear—you really are involved. You have to deliver a perfect dress. They don't have three in the closet—they're depending on you. That responsibility never escapes me in bridal, and I think [it crosses over]

to all the licensees. I mean, I said to Wedgewood, "I want the weight of the stainless to be heavy because there's nothing worse than a fork you can bend, and most people don't use sterling." I said, "Make sure that the stainless is heavy enough that people feel there's value." Defending all that on every level is a full-time job.

Figure 8.12 Vera Wang meets with her staff.

While most designers start with ready-to-wear, your collection is only six years old. What is its great challenge for you?
It's trying to push a contemporary—I don't mean a contemporary business, but a more contemporary, younger feel. Why should women at any age, young or old, have to dress old? It's been challenging.

For most designers, ready-to-wear is the nucleus around which they build their brands. For you, the bridal is the nucleus. How important is ready-to-wear to your business?
It is [important] because it expresses who I really am as a woman, as a person, and as a designer. It's important for me to be able to wear my own clothes, which is not a small thing to me after all the years of work and investment. I like to wear my knits. I like to wear my T-shirts. I'm doing things, finally, that are real to me.

How difficult is it to balance your casual attitude with the realities of the business?
That's always been my problem—how do you reconcile who you are as a person and as, I would say, a fashion professional after all these years? And what do you have to do to be really successful, if it doesn't come naturally to you?

You've talked about your life having been defined by things that didn't go as planned.
Relating that to the business, getting established in contemporary had been problematic. We've tried three times, the most recent time with Lavender. We got too big too fast—too much distribution. And then the economy turned and the combination of the two—a double whammy. Lavender was only a year and a half old, and I just said this isn't the time to continue this.

Conversely, Kohl's is working.
I'll tell you why—because Kohl's has tremendous distribution. I'm able to be myself within the world of Kohl's, the context of Kohl's. They're really moving into fashion—that's been their big goal. That was the whole reason they brought me on. And they've always had a great juniors business.

Interview with a Fashion Designer (continued)

Otherwise, besides Lavender, how has the recession impacted the Vera Wang business?
It affected bridal. At the same time, I made sure that I got away from any fabrics that were $40 to $50 a yard. You have to also realize that Neiman's and Saks closed bridal doors. In the major cities— L.A. or Dallas or Chicago—that's where I was. When you're at the upper end and you lose, let's say, 15, 16 doors in the key cities in the U.S., that's a bit of a blow. I heard it from WWD before I heard it from the buyer.

What do you see as the recession's residual effects, both bottom line and psychologically?
Financially, I was okay because I have a very, very good licensing business. But in terms of our business, we had to shave costs; we had to adjust everything. We had to change some leases. For example, I had a bigger store slated for L.A. because I was doing bridal and ready-to-wear, and bridal takes a lot of room. I gave up on that lease and took the smaller store, which is the one we're in now. But—I can't do alterations out of that store. I had to get another, less expensive space for alterations, which brings in other issues in terms of functionality and how you get it done. Welcome to my world. I've had to make the toughest decisions. I'm actually very proud to say this because I like change in clothes, but I don't like change in my life. We've had to make big changes, but I think we're in a good place. We're in a solid place. I'm not

being boastful or anything, because you know, I'm never going to be Ralph.

In between *Vogue* and opening that first bridal shop, you worked for Ralph. What was that like?
I was design director for accessories. I just adored it because you could just be creative. You don't have to worry about getting it made, you don't have to worry about pricing it, you don't have to worry about whether we can duplicate this [or] are we spending too much money? It was kind of like being in a candy store. The amount of product we created—it's just inconceivable.

What's next for Vera Wang?
Retail is a very important component for us. I don't need 30 stores. I'm not trying to be an empire at the upper end, but I would like four or five stores in America. After that, what we want to do is a line somewhere between high and low. I think there's room for women in America to have something that isn't at Kohl's and isn't more elitist.

Do you feel at all daunted? So many people in fashion say that starting out, they were too ignorant to be scared.
I was ignorant and scared. I may have been a neophyte bridal designer, but I wasn't a neophyte in fashion. Because when you work for *Vogue*, you see businesses come and go. And when you work for Ralph, you see what it takes.

2

Careers in Product Development and Sales for the Fashion Retailer

Some retailers purchase finished fashion merchandise from manufacturers or wholesalers. Others also develop and manufacture products specifically for their clientele. As a result, Unit 2 begins with a discussion of product development and design by and for the fashion retailer, in Chapter 9. A number of large retail operations own a product development division that functions as a design and production source exclusively for them. Whether the fashion product is created and manufactured by the retailer or purchased from a manufacturer or wholesaler, it must be marketed to appeal to the consumer. In Chapter 10, we see that the promotion division of a retail operation does just that through such professionals as the advertising director and art staff, visual merchandiser, special events coordinator, Web site developer, and personal shopper. Chapter 11 explores the merchandising division of the retail operation, the buying and marketing of products. Merchandise managers, buyers, allocators, and planners work on the selection, pricing, and placement of merchandise on retail sales floors. In Chapter 12, management careers in the retail sector are examined, to include store (regional, store unit, associate, and assistant), operations, and customer service managers. Finally, there are the all-in-one retail specialists, the entrepreneurs who own and operate their retail organizations, whether brick-and-mortar, brick-and-click, or solely e-retailing.

chapter 9

Product Development and Design by the Retailer

What is product development?

Product development is the creation, production, and marketing of a product, such as a dress, belt, or chair, from start to finish. This is not a new process. Manufacturers in every industry, from fashion to automobiles to household appliances, have always engaged in product development. In the 1980s, it became very popular for retailers to develop products of their own instead of simply selling the lines of manufacturers. The Gap, for example, used to carry a variety of national brands, such as Levi's. Now it carries only Gap-branded merchandise that is designed and developed in house.

Product development may be the function of one department in a retail operation, or a division within an organization. For example, Macy's, Inc., with corporate offices in Cincinnati and New York, is one of the nation's premier retailers, with fiscal 2010 sales of $25.0 billion. The company operates about 810 Macy's department stores and furniture galleries in 45 states, the District of Columbia, Guam, and Puerto Rico, as well as macys.com. The Bloomingdale's brand includes 41 stores in 12 states, four Bloomingdale's Outlet stores and bloomingdales. com. The diverse workforce of Macy's, Inc., includes approximately 161,000 employees. [1]

Within Macy's there is a division called Macy's Merchandising Group (MMG). MMG is responsible for conceptualizing, designing, sourcing, and marketing private label and private branded goods sold at Macy's and, in some cases, at Bloomingdale's. Some of MMG's 15 highly successful private brands are I.N.C., Charter Club, American Rag, Alfani, Style&co., and Hotel Collection. MMG's private brand merchandise exceeded 19 percent of Macy's total sales in 2009.[2]

Whether it is for a single department or a division of a retail firm, a number of steps are taken when developing a line, though the details may change depending on the type of product, on whether the line is to be produced overseas or domestically, or if the company has an in-house sample department. The general steps that are taken for each season are as follow.

1. Inspiration sources (e.g., fabrics, art and museum exhibitions, travel destinations, films, color palettes, and so on) are reviewed. Market research is conducted. The previous year's sales and markdowns are analyzed. Product categories are decided.
2. Trend forecasts are discussed. The preliminary line is planned. The company decides "what it believes in." Color stories are selected.
3. Fabrics and trims are researched, then selections are made. Prints are designed.
4. Concepts are developed, storyboards are created, and designs are sketched. Sample fabrics and trims are ordered. Labdips, colored samples of selected fabrics, are requested.
5. Merchandising meetings are held. The line may be edited from sketches.
6. Specifications are written, and technical packages are compiled.
7. Sourcing is completed. Samples, or prototypes, are constructed, and preliminary costing is requested.
8. Patterns and first samples are produced by a sample room or contractors. Often 20–50 percent more designs are made than those that actually will be manufactured. Factories advise on costs.
9. Samples are fitted, edited, and adopted into the line during a line review. The fitting process continues until the sample is approved or dropped. Costs are negotiated. Quantity may be an integral part of cost negotiations, or it may be determined when orders are generated. Quantities may be finalized and orders may be placed at this time, depending on factory lead time.
10. Samples, or prototypes, are produced. Private label goods may require only a meeting sample. Costs are finalized. Photo and production samples are requested.
11. For a private brand in a retail operation with decentralized buying, the styles will be "sold" internally to buyers who quantify the purchase. **Decentralized buying** refers to the process used by individual stores or groups of stores within a retail chain that have a buyer who selects from the company's primary buyer's purchases.
12. Production fabric and trim are ordered as soon as the factories receive orders.
13. Production goods are manufactured, and quality control is completed.
14. Goods are packed and shipped to the retailer.
15. Merchandise is received by the retailer and delivered to the warehouse or selling floors.[3]

In the fashion industry, there are three key types of businesses that produce merchandise: manufacturers, contractors, and retailers. As discussed in Unit 1, manufacturers are companies that create, produce, market, and distribute product lines on a continual basis. This may be a designer who owns a company or a company that employs designers. Manufacturers may own their own factories or use contractors to construct their products. Contractors, factories that make and finish goods as shown in Figure 9.1, may be domestic, meaning in the United States, or offshore, such as those in China, India, or Taiwan. **Retailers** are businesses that sell products to the ultimate consumer and may include the vast range of brick-and-mortar

Figure 9.1 Many retail product development divisions hire contractors, factories that make and finish goods, for production.

stores (e.g., department stores, mass merchants, specialty stores, boutiques, discount stores, and outlet stores), as well as catalogues, brick-and-click stores, and online stores. **Brick-and-mortar store** is a term that refers to retail operations in a facility, such as a building or a store in a mall. **Brick-and-click store** refers to a retail operation that offers products both through actual stores and online. Some retailers sell through all or several of these channels. JCPenney, Saks Fifth Avenue, and Nordstrom's, for example, sell their product lines through brick-and-click stores and catalogues. Nearly all of the large retailers are currently engaging in some form of product development. In this chapter, the focus is on the product development and design activities of retail operations.

Why Retailers Became Designers

There are four main reasons why retailers moved into the business of developing their own products or lines of products. First, retailers wanted to be able to satisfy specific customer demands. Sometimes the retail buyers were unable to locate the products, looks, prices, or fit their customers' needs. The second reason retailers went into the business of creating products is fashion exclusivity. **Fashion exclusivity** refers to a company having merchandise that is unique to that particular company (Figure 9.2). You may have remarked or may have overheard a customer saying, "Everything in the mall looks the same. I cannot find anything unique." Retailers that wanted to project fashion images unique to their particular companies established product development departments or divisions. Most important, product development provided new profit margins. Retailers reasoned that by producing directly through contracted or company-owned factories instead of buying from manufacturers, they could make more money on each item, even while charging the customers less than they charged for nationally branded merchandise. Finally, retailers needed to reduce lead time between ordering new merchandise and receiving it on the sales floor. This trend is referred to as fast fashion.

Fast fashion is a term used to describe apparel and accessories trends that are designed and manufactured quickly, and in an affordable way, to allow the mainstream consumer to take advantage of current fashions at a lower price. This philosophy of quick manufacturing at affordable prices is considered the "success story" of a number of large retailers such as H&M, Forever 21, and Zara. Fast fashion is achieved through the retailers' understanding of the target market's wants, in that variations of products the customer is buying are delivered to the sales floor as fast as possible. The product developer's first objective is a high-fashion-looking garment at a mass-market price. His or her second objective is to create modifications of the items that sell and have these manufactured quickly. The product developer, buyer, and manufacturer collaborate to maximize sales and profits by satisfying customer needs. Fast fashion brings more product options to the consumer more frequently.

Initially, retailers who developed their own product lines ran into a few problems. There is a long tradition in the fashion business of knocking off the hot or successful designs offered by top designers, rather than creating new looks. A **knockoff** is a copy of another style, often of lesser quality and with minor modifications. Knockoffs of Hermès' Birkin and Kelly bags, carried by celebrities like Victoria Beckham and Sarah Jessica Parker, can be found at midpriced retail stores. (Figure 9.3) While it is less common today, retailers were historically known for creating private label lines that were collections of knockoffs. **Private label** refers to a line name or brand that the retailer develops and assigns to a collection of products. Since many of the retailers were knocking off products that were already on the market, the majority of the private label products lacked fashion newness. Retailers also had to take responsibility for securing fabrics, avoiding fit problems, and shipping goods. Another obstacle was that many overseas factories required retailers to open letters of credit to pay for goods. As a result, retailers were faced with tying up large amounts of their operations' dollars in advance of shipping, rather than paying for merchandise 30 days after they received shipment.

Figure 9.2 Fashion exclusivity refers to having merchandise that is unique to a particular company, such as Material Girl at Macy's.

Figure 9.3 Knockoffs of Hermès' Birkin and Kelly bags can be found modified at midpriced retail stores, or copied by counterfeiters.

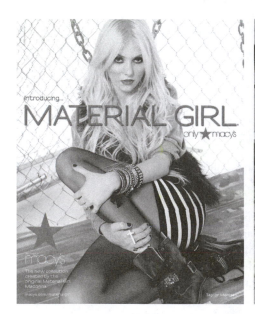

As retail-driven product development matured, retailers began to build highly skilled design and merchandising teams to forestall some of the previously mentioned problems. Some major retailers do not attempt to develop products in certain specialized apparel categories because these areas are too precarious or too dependent on major brand names. A few of the product categories that retailers place in product development are: basic apparel, because of ease of fit; jeans, because of the low risk and ease of entry into the market as a price-point alternative (lower and higher) to major brands; and product categories that have a lower level of competition from major brands. Many retail operations prefer to leave development of highly specialized apparel, such as swimwear and hosiery, or categories that require major advertising investments, such as cosmetics and fragrances, to the major brand manufacturers. As styling in basic products makes it difficult to distinguish a major brand from a private label, some retailers have found that they are safer developing this type of merchandise. Other retailers choose private label lines to create unique and exclusive products that are not available in the market. Most retailers take a big risk when trying to develop trendy, high-priced merchandise because customers often prefer a designer name attached to their investment purchases.

Types of Product Development Businesses

A number of product development classifications have evolved as retailers engage more and more in the customizing of product lines. These classifications include retail label, private label, private brand, direct market brand, and licenses. A **retail label** is a brand with the retailer's name on it, such as Neiman Marcus, Custom Interiors, or Saks Fifth Avenue. A retailer may negotiate with a manufacturer to put its label on a group of items instead of or in addition to the manufacturer's label, though the retailer may not have had anything to do with the design or development of the items. Some of the items carrying a retail label may be **exclusives**, or items that only one retailer carries. In some cases, a retailer may negotiate to be the only one in a geographic region to carry a particular item or the only one in the country to carry a particular color. For example, the label may read, "Burberry Exclusively for Neiman Marcus."

Similar to a private label, yet with a greater level of market penetration primarily through advertising, a **private brand** is a name owned exclusively by a particular store that is extensively marketed with a definite image, such as Target's Mossimo and Isaac Mizrahi brands, Macy's brand I.N.C. (Figure 9.4), and JCPenney's brand Stafford. A **direct market brand** describes a brand that is the name of the retailer. Often, this is a specialty store chain, such as Ann Taylor, IKEA, or Gap (Figure 9.5). A license agreement, discussed in Chapter 3, is a contract with a company that owns the rights to the name of a designer, a celebrity, a sports star, an animated or storybook character, or a distinctive design. Retailers pay royalties to develop lines under those names. Licensees typically must receive approval from the licensor on the design direction of the line, but they are responsible for financing all of the line development, marketing, and sales of the products.

Today, large retail companies are major employers of product development staffs. The career paths in this field include the following: director of product development, merchandiser, sourcing staff, designer, retail trend forecaster, colorist, textile technical designer, patternmaker, and quality control manager.

[handwritten margin notes: free people, forever 21, anthropologie, zara]

[handwritten margin notes: mossimo → ann taylor, j.crew, IKEA]

Figure 9.4 Macy's displays clothing from I.N.C., International Concepts Collection, which is a private brand.

Figure 9.5 Gap features a full merchandise assortment of its own direct market brand.

Director of Product Development

A **director of product development** is ultimately responsible for the strategic planning of the division, specifying exactly what it is the company will make and market, as well as when it will do this. After selecting a general product category, such as junior T-shirts, the director of product development must narrow the focus. The fashion market is extremely segmented, with each brand filling its particular niche. It is not enough simply to decide to create a line of junior T-shirts, because that is far too broad a category to allow for effective line development. Instead, the director of product development will decide, for example, to create vintage-inspired T-shirts for fashion-forward, young female customers in junior sizes extra-small (XS) to large (L). A key product segmentation decision is specifying the target market niche, and that can be accomplished only by knowing the customer well—who she is, what she likes, and where she lives, works, and plays. Other product segmentation decisions that product development directors must make relate to the product, price, size, and taste level. Next, they will work to create a brand by creating an image or personality for the line. An image is the way the product developer wants the brand to be perceived, the way that will best attract the target customer. With the abundance of fashion products on the market, image may be the only means of product differentiation. Carefully defining target customers will allow brands to develop images and product lines that will appeal to them.

There are two main approaches the director of product development may take toward the branding of a line: a design-driven brand or a merchandising-driven brand. A **design-driven brand** is one that is led by a designer who is expressing a personal artistic vision and sense of taste. This type of brand appeals to customers who relate to the designer's particular style and flair and includes most brands with designer names. These apparel brands tend to be more original and creative. Design-driven brands also have the peculiar distinction of representing both a particular designer's viewpoint and a line of products. In the case of a manufacturer's line, such as Ralph Lauren's home accessories, the brand has several faces including English gentleman, East Coast aristocrat, African safari adventurer, and Western individualist, as shown in Figures 9.6a–c.

Merchandising-driven brands, or *void-filling* brands, do just that. These market-based brands search for a void in the market or an underserved customer and create a product to fill that void and appeal to that distinct customer. Styling decisions are based on careful monitoring of past sales successes and failures in conjunction with customer desires. Customer comfort and competitive pricing are of utmost importance to merchandising-driven brands. Many private labels are merchandising-driven brands.

The director of product development has an important overall task. Retailers' brands must have a fashion image consistent with that of the customer the operation attracts. It is the responsibility of the director of product development to make certain that the designed products add up to a marketable line that matches the image of the retail operation. If, for example, a retailer of women's conservative career wear brings in a private label line of Indian cotton bohemian blouses and skirts, the customer may be turned off by the confusing look of the inventory.

Market knowledge is as critical to the success of a fashion brand as is customer knowledge. The director of product development must examine the competition. **Direct competition** is any other brand producing a similar product at roughly the same price point, targeted toward the same customer or market niche. It is important for product developers to be attentive to

Figures 9.6a–c
A few of the many faces of designer Ralph Lauren's lines: English gentleman (a), world adventurer (b), and Western Americana (c).

what direct competitors are doing, if only to refrain from duplicating their products or brand image. These direct competitors are fighting to be the consumer's choice. Ideally, a company wishing to grow a brand will have such a great product and know its customers so well that customers feel they must buy it. In a broader sense, competition is any other brand vying for consumers' retail dollars.

Types of competition change as retailing venues change. Think about the Internet as a shopping mall of new competitors. As the face of retail changes, a brand's product line may be competing with brands online, at different price ranges and from global companies. Consumers are less loyal to retailers today, as there is no stigma attached to cross-shopping. **Cross-shopping** refers to the customer's inclination to purchase a wide variety of products in an array of brands from any number of providers—directly from the manufacturer, in a resale store, at a flea market, or through a couturier (Figure 9.7). For today's consumer, it is cool to buy smart. The new consumer mentality puts added pressure on the director of product development, who must now be aware of price, quality, and look of products in all categories, not just one narrow market niche.

Qualifications

The qualifications for the position of director of product development include the following:

- **Education:** A bachelor's degree in fashion merchandising, fashion design, product development, or a related field is required.

- **Experience:** The director of product development holds an executive position that often requires five to seven years of successful work experience as a merchandiser or designer.

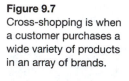

Figure 9.7
Cross-shopping is when a customer purchases a wide variety of products in an array of brands.

- **Personal characteristics:** Creativity, a strong marketing sense, and an understanding of consumers, quantitative skills, and networking abilities are key attributes for directors of product development. They are excellent communicators—orally, in writing, and visually. Also, the director of product development has other diverse characteristics: curiosity, leadership abilities, and the ability to work with a variety of constituencies, from designers to merchandisers to colorists.

A classified advertisement for a director of product development is featured in Box 9.1.

Career Challenges

The director of product development is the leader of the pack. It is a high-pressure job in which one must be a motivator, guide, and, sometimes, the "take charge" person. It takes a strong person with vision to manage a team of executives.

Merchandiser

A merchandiser's responsibilities vary widely depending on company requirements. A product development **merchandiser** collaborates with the director of product development in deciding what to produce and then organizes and manages the entire product development process. Merchandisers are responsible for the development of a balanced, marketable, profitable, and timely line. In some companies, merchandisers oversee the design function and may serve as liaisons between design and sales. They will create the initial line plan and project target wholesale costs by analyzing sales from previous seasons, fashion trends, and customer wants. As Figure 9.8 illustrates, merchandisers work closely with designers on seasonal themes and guide designers on the development of cost-effective and marketable styles. In some companies, merchandisers may also have responsibilities in sourcing and marketing functions. In other companies, there is a sourcing staff to locate the suppliers and manufacturers for the product.

The merchandiser is responsible for constructing the **merchandising calendar**, the product development team's schedule. The goal of the calendar is to deliver the right product (i.e., correct style, quality, and price) at the right time. When creating a new line, developers carefully plan how often they want goods to flow into the stores. Once they complete the delivery schedule, merchandisers create a calendar by working backward from in-store delivery dates, listing all of the tasks in the product development cycle, with deadlines for each. Next, merchandisers develop detailed line plans. The **line plan** shows the number of styles in the line, the number and general types of fabrics and yarns to be used, the colors per style, the anticipated stock-keeping units (SKUs), and the approximate preferred costs. The line plan not only gives product developers guidelines from which to work and focuses their efforts in a distinct direction but also takes into account fabric and yarn minimums and lead times. Merchandisers often work on different phases of several seasons at once.

Typical responsibilities of the merchandiser include the following:

- Researching the market, including tracking market trends and attending trade shows

- Fashion forecasting

- Attending consumer focus groups

- Shopping the competition

- Scouting fabric and trim markets

- Analyzing past sales, markdowns, and market trends within the retail operation

- Developing the merchandising calendar and line plan

- Creating design concepts with the product developers

- Calculating cost estimates for new products

- Directing and participating in line presentations

Figure 9.8
A merchandiser
discusses design and
color concepts with
a product developer.

- Choosing and quantifying which styles will actually be produced, sometimes prior to sales (referred to as **production authorization**)

- Sourcing, in some cases

- Fostering a creative environment so technical design and sourcing staffs can do their best work

Qualifications

To achieve a career as a retail merchandiser, consider obtaining the following qualifications:

- **Education:** A bachelor's degree in fashion merchandising, fashion design, retailing, or a related field is required.

- **Experience:** The merchandiser is sometimes promoted from within the product development department or division, having worked on the sourcing or technical design staff, for example. Three to five years of on-the-job experience in product development is preferred. In some cases, highly skilled people from the retail side of the business may be trained for this position. After all, who knows the customer better than someone who has worked successfully with the retail operation's clientele on a daily basis?

- **Personal characteristics:** The merchandiser is an excellent communicator, orally and in writing. Thorough market knowledge, a keen fashion sense, strong analytical skills, creativity, and an astute marketing instinct are essential characteristics. Successful merchandisers are continually cognizant of the market environment and the target customer and make well-informed decisions quickly and confidently. In companies that manufacture the majority of their product lines overseas, fluency in the languages of the countries where production takes place can be very helpful.

Career Challenges

The merchandiser is a planner. You know—or perhaps you are—this type of person, with your schedule drafted months in advance, telephone numbers and addresses at your fingertips, and a to-do list in a constant state of addition and completion. The merchandiser thinks creatively and quantitatively. The product lines are viewed from many perspectives—what will be in fashion, how much will it cost to manufacture a product, which items will the customer purchase or not, and what is the competition doing. The successful merchandiser must be a sponge, soaking up all of the variables that affect whether a product will sell or not.

Sourcing Staff

Sourcing, locating components and producers of the final product, was discussed in Chapter 3 as it relates to the primary level of the industry, manufacturers of fashion merchandise. Sourcing in product development for the retailer is much the same as it is for the manufacturer. The primary difference, in most cases, is that the retailer often finds and hires contractors to produce private label lines, rather than building or purchasing factories to manufacture the lines. The sourcing staff of a product development team is responsible for finding the best possible fabrics, findings, trims, and manufacturers to make the designers' lines reality. Members of the sourcing staff may specialize in specific categories, such as belting or trims. They may also travel extensively to locate parts of the product or a manufacturer for the product.

The sourcing staff often works with a sales forecast to determine the amount of product components needed. A **sales forecast** is created by the product development director and merchandiser, in conjunction with the sourcing staff. It includes projections of sales by category, style, color, and size based on historical data and statistical analysis. This information may be used to place preliminary fabric and trim orders and block out production time in factories. As the sourcing staff must often place orders early, an accurate sales forecast is critical to deliveries made at the right time and in the right amount.

Qualifications

To become a member of a company's sourcing staff, one should fulfill the following qualifications:

- **Education:** Usually employers require a bachelor's degree in fashion design, fashion merchandising, product development, or a related field.

- **Experience:** In many corporations, sourcing personnel are promoted from the technical design staff or are hired with assistant designer experience from outside of the company.

- **Personal characteristics:** Sourcing personnel pay attention to detail and have efficient organizational skills and strong written and oral communication abilities. They are "born to shop," comparing quality, price, and availability in product parts and production requirements.

Career Challenges

Sourcing staff personnel face the task of finding the best product or product parts at the best price, in the right quantity, and in a timely fashion. Many are required to travel globally and frequently. Negotiations can be tough when working with people from different cultures, with or without an interpreter. The abilities to shop until you drop and then communicate effectively and negotiate successfully take a great deal of flexibility and stamina.

Product Development and Private Label Designer for a Retailer

Product development designers (also called *private label designers*) are the creators of the product line for the retailer; they are trend forecasters in their own right by determining what the customer will be ready for next. They go through the design process with each new season. Table 9.1 shows monthly activities for product development by season. The **design process** refers to the conception of a style, to include its inspiration or theme, color palette, fabric selection, form, and fit. Private label designers must be adept at synthesizing a variety of fashion influences while acknowledging marketability and fulfilling customer wants and needs. An important designer trait is the art of compromise. These designers must balance the desired fashion look of a product and the highest possible quality standards with a price tag that is desirable to the target customer.

After determining the style, color, fabric, and trend concepts, designers begin sketching individual styles, usually with a particular form, or silhouette, in mind that epitomizes the fashion trends for the upcoming season. They may repeat versions of this silhouette throughout the line. Some styles may be completely original, but sometimes designers will adapt a style from an actual garment found on a shopping expedition or in a magazine. Most lines include at least a few **carryovers**, bestsellers from a previous season. The designers will be careful to include important basics and to balance each group with the help of the merchandiser. Many companies ask for estimated costs from factories before samples are made so that styles can either

Table 9.1 Product Development Activity Calendar

Activity	Fall	Holiday/Resort	Spring	Summer
Design/Development	January/February	April/May	July/August	November/December
Selling and Show Dates	February/March	June/August	September/October	January
Producing Orders Begins	May	August	November	February
Shipping Starts	July	October	January	April
Shipping Completed	September	Early December	Early March	Early May

be dropped or adjusted when the line is still in sketch form. Oversampling is quite expensive, so the merchandiser will generally try to keep it under control. When a complete group of styles is finalized, all of the sketches are placed on a line sheet so the group may be seen at a glance. Typical tasks of the designer may include the following:

- Shopping the retail market, sometimes with merchandisers or a member of the sourcing staff, for design ideas and knowledge of the competition; buying samples

- Shopping the fabric, yarn, and trim markets

- Attending trend forecasting meetings

- Developing **color palettes**, groups of colors, and **colorways**, combinations or pairings of colors

- Determining the styling direction of the line and creating concept boards or storyboards

- Shopping the print market and buying print paintings for textile development

- Developing styles through sketching garments by hand or on a computer

- Recoloring garments or prints

- Designing embroideries, screen prints, and appliqués

- Writing specification sheets

- Corresponding with factories or in-house sample departments regarding drapes, patterns, and garment construction

- Attending fit meetings

These tasks vary, of course, often depending on the size of the company for which the designer works. Some of the larger companies may assign some of these tasks, such as writing specifications or developing color palettes, to more specialized personnel, such as technical designers or colorists.

Qualifications

Designers on product development teams of retailers are likely to have the following qualifications:

- **Education:** A bachelor's degree in fashion design, product development, fashion merchandising, or a related field is a minimum requirement.

- **Experience:** Employment as an assistant designer or technical designer is an excellent stepping-stone to the position of designer. These entry-level positions provide knowledge of fabrics, construction, and fit. Additionally, the designer needs prior experience in PC software, such as spreadsheets, databases, and word processing. Many employers require designers to have CAD experience.

- **Personal characteristics:** Successful designers have excellent organizational skills and pay attention to detail. They can create an image of the final product, either on a drawing pad or on the computer. Because much business is conducted in Asian countries, foreign language skills in languages such as Cantonese, Mandarin, or Japanese are a plus.

Career Challenges

The successful designer must know the retailer's customer well because knowing the customer's likes and dislikes minimizes the designer's fashion risks. Designers must be able to multitask with the best, often working on two or more collections at one time. Working with color, silhouettes or forms, fabric, and trend themes, they are challenged to create collections. It may be difficult to find new sources of inspiration and find a common theme to weave among the items in a collection.

Retail Trend Forecaster

Retailers must continually research their customers, products, and markets through consumer, product, and market research. In Chapter 1, the trend forecaster employed in the primary level of the industry was discussed. In this chapter, the career track of the retail trend forecaster is examined. The **retail trend forecaster**, or *retail fashion director*, researches many sources to create formal reports that summarize important fashion trends in a particular season that will appeal to the retailer's clientele. These reports are presented to the product development team members to ensure the development of consistent looks across all departments. Retail trend forecasters in the product development divisions of retailers identify the fashion trends and then interpret them for the retailers' particular customers, or markets. Additionally, they project looks for the retail operations' customers for upcoming seasons.

Qualifications

The following are education and experience goals, as well as personal characteristics, of the successful retail trend forecaster.

- **Education:** A bachelor's degree in product development, fashion design, fashion merchandising, visual arts, or a related field is a minimum requirement.

- **Experience:** The majority of retail trend forecasters move up the ladder from within the ranks. Many are textile designers, product developers, or buyers before obtaining the key position of retail trend forecaster.

- **Personal characteristics:** Curiosity, an awareness of global population shifts and consumer interests, and a fascination with fashion trends are important characteristics of a retail trend forecaster. Additionally, the abilities to synthesize, categorize, and prioritize key fashion trends are critical attributes. Most important, an understanding of the retailer's customers in terms of fashion taste is required.

Career Challenges

Predicting fashion trends of color, form, and theme is just one of the challenges facing the retail trend forecaster. An equally significant challenge is determining which fashion trends the retailer's customers will actually buy. One's personal tastes have to be set aside in this career track. The retail trend forecaster must know where in the fashion life cycle the customer is most comfortable, how much the customer will spend, and what will entice the customer to buy. Trend forecasting is simply one part of the job; customer forecasting is another.

Colorist

A **colorist** in product development chooses the color combinations that will be used in creating the product lines. Colorists frequently travel to trade and fashion markets and subscribe to color-forecasting publications to stay on top of current and future color trends. They observe what the customers purchase, or do not buy, to understand their needs and interpret their color preferences accurately. Colorists collaborate with marketing, buying, and technical staff members, as well as design colleagues, on color trends and preferences. They often conduct research for ideas and inspiration, with topics ranging from historical costume to modern architecture. After determining a color palette for the season, the colorist produces boards, swatches, or other visuals to present the color ideas to the product development team (Figure 9.9). Finally, the colorist is responsible for checking and approving samples of completed items.

Colors and patterns are constantly changing in the fashion industry. There is special language to describe this area of product development: labdips and strike-offs. As soon as colors and fabrics have been determined, a company must decide whether any of the colors will be custom dyed in any of the fabrics. If so, original color standards must be sent to the dyeing mills or fabric companies so that dye formulations may be created. The mills will send **labdips**, small swatches of the dyed fabric, to the product development team for color approval prior to dyeing large yardages of fabric. Organizing and approving labdips may consume a significant amount of a colorist's time. Printed fabric may be purchased from a number of companies, but sometimes, a designer will want to include a print on the line that is exclusive to the company. This requires that the company buy a croquis, a painting of the print, have it printed into repeat, and decide colorways or the color composition. When these projects are finalized, the painting is sent to a printing mill. The mill will print a few yards of fabric, called a **strike-off**, and send them to the product developer (i.e., colorist, designer, and sample maker) to be made into a sample.

Colorists need to consider such factors as how the design will be produced, how the finished article will be used, how good the quality of materials is, and how big or limited the budget is. They work standard hours but need to be flexible to meet deadlines. They are based in studios or offices. Prospective employers require a strong and relevant portfolio of work for review.

Qualifications

Following are the qualifications for a successful colorist.

- **Education:** A bachelor's degree in visual arts, fine arts, computer-aided design, graphic design, fashion design, textiles, or a related discipline is a minimum requirement.

- **Experience:** Technical designers, particularly those with experience in textiles, may move into the position of colorist. An understanding of how a textile will be used, what properties it needs in order to function optimally, and how the addition of color dyes or surface treatments will affect these properties is critical to the colorist's work. Two

Figure 9.9 An example of a dress design and the fabrics selected to construct it from Todd & Duncan and Pitti Textiles.

to five years' experience in design is often a prerequisite for this position. One of the paths to move into the position of colorist is to work as an assistant to the colorist. Some fortunate college students are able to secure internships in the color department of a product development division.

- **Personal characteristics:** The colorist must keep up to date with fashion and population trends—current and projected—while staying on top of new design and production processes. Flexibility, computer skills, the ability to meet deadlines, and effective business skills make colorists successful. They have an exceptional eye for discerning and recalling colors. A strong network of color expertise, from trade organizations to publications to peers, supports the colorist's own expertise. The successful colorist has the ability to identify color trends that evolve from such external influences as major art exhibitions, timely couturiers, and popular travel destinations.

Career Challenges

The colorist is part chemist, part artist, and part fashion forecaster. It takes a wealth of skills in many areas. This person must maintain extremely high standards and pay careful attention to detail. It is critical that the colorist be an effective communicator. Think about describing a specific color to someone and explaining it so effectively that this person can actually mix the paint for the exact color. It is not an easy task.

Textile Technical Designer

A **textile technical designer** creates new textile designs or modifies existing textile goods, altering patterns or prints that have been successful on the retail floor to turn them into fresh, new products. The textile technical designer will develop color alternatives for a modified fabric print or pattern or work with a colorist to accomplish this task. Most textile technical designers work on computers to create or modify designs. An example of a popular fashion product and textile design software program is Kaledo by Lectra, as shown in Box 2.2 and Figures 9.10a and b. There are a number of specialized areas in which technical textile designers can work; among these are wovens, knits, or prints. For example, a technical textile designer may work primarily with either sweater knits or woven shirtings. The textile technical designer who specializes in prints will often use a computer-aided design program to create a croquis.

Qualifications

The following is a list of qualifications for the career path of a textile technical designer.

- **Education:** A bachelor's degree in textiles, textile technology, fashion design, computer-aided design, graphic design, or a related discipline is a minimum requirement.

- **Experience:** Many textile technical designers begin in this position after college graduation. An internship in the technical design division of a retail corporation is an ideal way to open the door to this field.

- **Personal characteristics:** A textile technical designer has knowledge of computer-aided design and an understanding of technical considerations as they relate to textile

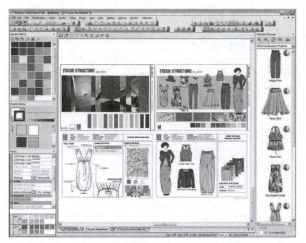

applications. An awareness of consumer wants and needs and an eye for color and patterns are essentials. The successful textile technical designer is simultaneously creative and technologically savvy.

Career Challenges

Textile technical designers live in a high-touch, high-tech world. They must understand the technical features of CAD and the production aspects of knit, woven, print, and textured fabrics. In addition, they must understand the feel, or hand, of a diverse array of fabrics and the application of each. Which types of fabrics are best suited for which products? How do these fabrics wear? What are the care factors for each? There is much to know in this field, in which new fabrics, computer technology, and manufacturing techniques arrive daily.

Figures 9.10a and b
Kaledo is a popular software program developed by Lectra, used for fashion production and textile design. These illustrations represent Kaledo's Collection Multiboard.

Product Development Patternmaker

Technical design and follow-up are parts of a patternmaker's responsibilities on a product development team. The **product development patternmaker** takes accurate measurements and develops a pattern, using either draping or flat pattern methods that, if correctly written, ensures the designer's vision will be implemented. Specification lists, commonly referred to as **spec sheets**, typically provide detailed measurements and construction guidelines. Designers may give patternmakers sketches and a few measurement specifications for guidance or may actually drape a garment to get the exact form they envisioned. Following the designers' approval, patternmakers will develop detailed spec sheets. A spec sheet includes a technical sketch, all of the measurements and tolerances, type and yardage of fabrication, and trim information. Different companies have their own spec sheet formats; however, all of them have similar components. Each item on the spec sheet can have a critical impact on cost and on production of the item. The components of a spec sheet are illustrated in Figure 9.11.

Some retail product developers have additional challenges. They often do not employ in-house patternmakers and do much of the manufacturing in faraway factories where the factories' patternmakers do the work. They frequently have to complete whole spec packages to send overseas that tell factories every detail of what will be required to engineer a style.

Figure 9.11 Kaledo is a popular fashion product and textile design software program developed by Lectra. These illustrations represent Kaledo's Collection Multiboard.

Dress Spec Sheet

NAME:			DATE:		
SEASON: SPRING		STYLE: CHEONG SAM	SIZE: 14 PRETEEN		
DESCRIPTION: MANDARIN COLLAR, CAP SLEEVES, FRONT FROG DETAILS AND BACK ZIPPER CLOSURE					
FABRICATION: 97% POLYESTER, 3% SPANDEX					
ACCESSORIES:		TRIM: 1-19" INVISIBLE ZIPER, 2 FROGS W/ 15 LIGHE KNOTTED BUTTONS			

		FRONT	BACK	TOTAL	COMMENTS
1	NECK DROP	2.75	0.25		
2	NECK – WIDTH	7.00			
3	NECK CIRCUMFERENCE	9.00	8.00	17.00	
4	SHOULDER – LENGTH	4.00			
5	ACROSS SHOULDER			14.50	
6	LENGTH *				
	a. HPS	32.00	32.00		
	b. CF/CB	29.25	31.75		
	c. Side			23.50	
7	ACROSS BACK		14.00		4" FROM CB
8	ACROSS CHEST	16.50	16.50	33.00	
9	WAIST – LENGTH *				
	a. CF/CB	11.25	13.75		
	b. HPS	14.00	14.00		
10	ACROSS WAIST				
	a. Relaxed	15.50	16.00	31.50	
	b. Extended				
11	HIGH HIP	16.00	16.50	32.50	3" FROM WAIST
12	LOW HIP	17.50	18.00	35.50	6" FROM WAIST
13	BOTTOM EDGE OPENING (SWEEP)	20.00	20.00	40.00	
14	HPS TO UNDERARM	9.50			
15	ARMHOLE CIRCUMFERENCE	8.50	9.50	18.00	
16	UPPER SLEEVE – WIDTH				
17	SLEEVE – LENGTH *				
	a. Overarm	3.50			
	b. Underarm				
	c. CB		11.00		
	d. HPS		7.50		
18	ELBOW				
19	SLEEVE HEM/CUFF OPENING				
	a. Relaxed	5.00	4.00	9.00	
	b. Extended				
20	DEPTH OF SLEEVE HEM			0.25	
21	CUFF HEIGHT				
22	DART				
	a. Placement – CF/CB to top of dart	3.50	3.50		.
	b. Placement – HPS to top of dart	10.50	10.00		
	c. Placement – CF/CB to bottom of dart	3.50	3.75		
	d. Placement – HPS to bottom of dart	18.00	18.00		
	e. Dart – Length	7.50	8.00		
23	BINDING WIDTH/HEM			1.00	
24	BUTTON PLACEMENT	SEE FROGS			

REMARKS/OTHER SPECS/STITCHING: All measurements in inches; all graphs drawn at .125" = 1" scale

COLLAR STAND - FRONT/BACK 1"

YOKE SEAM - LEFT SIDE ONLY
CF TO ARMHOLE L - 6.5"
HPS TO YOKE TOP 3.25"
HPS TO YOKE BOTTOM 5.5"

SIDE SLITS 2"

2 FROGS
L - 2.25"
W - .875"

FROG 'A'
CF TO TOP - .75
CF TO BOTTOM 2"
HPS TO TOP 3"
HPS TO BOTTOM 5.25

FROG 'B'
CF TO TOP 4.75"
CF TO BOTTOM 3.75"
HPS TO TOP 4"
HPS TO BOTTOM 6.25"

STITCH - SN .25" FROM EDGE -
ARMHOLE SLEEVE HEM,
SIDE SLIT

SN AT EDGE - YOKE

SN - HEM

BAR TAC - TOP OF SLIT

* Circle method for measuring   Abbreviations: high point of shoulder (HPS), center front (CF), center back (CB), single needle (SN)

Many times spec sheets are used to calculate estimated costing so that items can be adjusted or canceled before a costly sample is made. If the company does not employ the technical staff to write specifications, it can contract with patternmaking and CAD companies that will write specs and prepare detailed spec sheets.

Qualifications

Following are the qualifications for a patternmaker of a product development team.

- **Education:** A bachelor's degree in fashion design, product development, or a related field is often required.

- **Experience:** If a position as a patternmaker's assistant is available, this position is often an entry for college graduates. Some technical designers and sample makers move into the patternmaker slot. Two to five years' experience is usually required for a key patternmaker position. Effective skills in draping, flat patternmaking, and CAD are necessary.

- **Personal characteristics:** The patternmaker is, in essence, an engineer. A keen attention to detail, the ability to construct almost every type of garment, and a focus on accuracy are necessary characteristics of successful patternmakers.

Career Challenges

Patternmakers must work with accuracy and speed on details. If a pattern piece is one-eighth inch smaller than it should be, the entire garment may not be able to be produced. Even if it can be manufactured, it may not fit or it may have a design flaw. That is a large responsibility to bear. Many of the people who are interested in patternmaking enjoy methodical and detailed work—engineering of sorts. What they often do not enjoy is the pressure of deadlines.

Quality Control Manager

A **quality control manager** of a retail product development team is responsible for the final inspection of garments from the manufacturer, checking fabric, fit, and construction for quality and adherence to product specification guidelines. This person is responsible for training new and existing quality control employees and for developing specific guidelines and standards for the department.

Qualifications

The background and characteristics of a successful quality control manager in the retail setting are as follows.

- **Education:** An associate of arts degree in fashion design, product development, or a similar field is required. A bachelor's degree is preferred.

- **Experience:** Two to four years of experience in quality control are expected as a prerequisite for this supervisory position. The quality control manager must have a solid understanding of garment construction, garment specifications, and spec sheets.

- **Personal characteristics:** The quality control manager should possess an excellent eye for detail and a commitment to high standards. Bilingual skills may be necessary, depending on the location of the manufacturing facilities. Excellent communication and people skills are important.

Career Challenges

The quality control manager must maintain excellent standards and oversee every detail of production from beginning to conclusion. It can be a high-pressure job with little recognition. The product development team, the retail personnel, and the customers assume that products will be made correctly and will perform well. When this is not the case, the white-hot spotlight shines on the quality control manager.

Summary

Product development describes the processes needed to make a product, from conception and manufacturing to marketing. In this chapter, product development conducted by the retailer was examined. The three main reasons retailers moved into the business of developing their own product lines included satisfying specific merchandise needs of their customers, creating exclusive products unique to their particular companies, and generating new profit margins. The result is private label merchandise, lines for which the retailer develops brands that are assigned to collections of products. A number of product development classifications have evolved as retailers engage more and more in the customizing of product lines. These classifications include retail label, private label, private brand, direct market brand, and licenses.

As a result of this move into product development, large retail companies are major employers of product development staffs. The careers in this field include director of product development, merchandiser, sourcing staff, designer, retail trend forecaster, colorist, textile technical designer, patternmaker, and quality control manager. The director of product development is ultimately responsible for the strategic planning of the division, specifying exactly what it is the company will make and market, as well as when it will do this. The merchandiser collaborates with the director of product development in deciding what to produce and then organizes and manages the entire product development process. The sourcing staff of a product development team is responsible for finding the best possible fabrics, findings, trims, and manufacturers to make the designers' lines a reality. The product development designer is the creator of the merchandise lines for the retailer. The retail trend forecaster creates formal reports that summarize important fashion trends with seasonal themes. The colorist chooses the color combinations that will be used in creating the product lines. Using this color direction, the textile technical designer creates new fabric designs or modifies existing textile goods by altering patterns or prints that have been successful on the retail floor to turn them into fresh, new products. The pattern-maker uses draping or flat pattern methods to develop a pattern that uses these textile options and implements the designers' vision. The quality control manager reviews the final product for fit, durability, and overall quality. Together, the product development team brings exclusive merchandise developed specifically to appeal to the retailer's target market from conception to reality.

Endnotes

1. http://www.macysinc.com/AboutUs/
2. http://www.macysinc.com/search/default.aspx?zoom_query=MMG
3. Kirsteen Buchanan, Stephens College, Columbia, Missouri, 2011.

Key Terms

brick-and-click store
brick-and-mortar store
carryover
color palette
colorist
colorway
cross-shopping
decentralized buying
design-driven brand
design process
direct competition
direct market brand
director of product development
exclusive
fashion exclusivity
fast fashion
knockoff
labdip

line plan
merchandiser
merchandising calendar
merchandising-driven brand
private brand
private label
product development
product development designer
product development patternmaker
production authorization
quality control manager
retail label
retail trend forecaster
retailer
sales forecast
spec sheet
strike-off
textile technical designer

Online and Print Resources

Alford, Holly and Anne Stegemeyer. *Who's Who in Fashion*, 5th ed. New York: Fairchild Books, 2010.

Armstrong, Jemi, Lorrie Ivas, and Wynn Armstrong. *From Pencil to Pen Tool: Understanding & Creating the Digital Fashion Image*. New York: Fairchild Books, 2008.

Brannon, Evelyn L. *Designer's Guide to Fashion Apparel*. New York: Fairchild Books, 2011.

Keiser, Sandra J. and Myrna Garner. *Beyond Design: The Synergy of Apparel Product Development*, 2nd ed. New York: Fairchild Books, 2008.

fashiontech.wordpress.com/2008/02/08/ibm-presents-the-future-of-shopping/

hbswk.hbs.edu/archive/4652.html www.apparelsearch.com/terms/P/Product_Development_Process.htm

Discussion Questions

1. What are your predictions for the future of private label merchandise by retailers? Will it increase, decrease, or remain the same, and why?

2. This chapter mentions that a few of the product categories retailers place in product development include basic apparel, jeans, and product categories that have a lower level of competition from major brands. Provide specific examples of brands in the latter product categories (those with less competition from national brands), and identify retailers that have succeeded in these merchandise classifications.

3. Develop a line plan for a small private label jean line. Specify the season of the line, then identify the number of styles, colors, size ranges, and price points that are in your line. Provide word descriptions and visuals for the line, such as magazine clippings, Internet images, or sketches.

Interview with a Product Developer

Interview by Martin Gibson, Embody 3D (3/22/2010)
Source: http://embody3d.com/2010/04/09/interview-%E2%80%93-michelle-chung-chinelas-by-michelle/

Michelle Chung is the Director of Chinelas by Michelle, a foldable ballet-flat shoe that girls can wear after a long night out on the town, or if they just want comfortable and beautiful footwear. Michelle studied design at UTS in Sydney, Australia, and has started her own business revolving around this footwear product at her Web site—http://www.chinelasbymichelle.com.

To get started, could you please give me a quick introduction to yourself and Chinelas by Michelle?
I graduated from Industrial Design at UTS in 2003 and worked in the fashion industry doing graphics and product design for a few years, as well as in the souvenir and toy industry. After my product development manager position was eliminated, I realized that it was a great time to start my own business, developing an idea for a gap in the market—which is how Chinelas by Michelle folding shoes were born.

My innovative range of foldable footwear came from the social concept of women wearing high heels that became too uncomfortable to wear for long periods of time. Creating a product that was durable, compact, and hygienic enough to go in the handbag is the concept behind the brand, and I did a lot of self-study in business, marketing, and PR to get it to where I wanted it to be.

Small minorities of industrial designers decide to start their own business once they've finished university, often based around a product they've designed themselves. What made you decide to take this leap of faith and a very steep learning curve, rather than perhaps working for a consultancy or a manufacturer?
I definitely recommend working in the industry for other companies before taking the plunge yourself—it gives you so much invaluable insight and experience. It's very difficult to run a business. If all you want to do is design products, I would not recommend running a business on your own. If you did want to have your own company

Figure 9.12 An example of product development is Chinelas by Michelle, a foldable ballet-flat shoe to wear after a long night out on the town in stilettos.

I would suggest finding a business partner who can run this side of things while you work on the product development. It's often very difficult to do everything yourself (as I found for myself) but I really liked learning and implementing the business and sales side of it, as I wanted to grow my skills in this area. Also, the fact that I was released from what I thought was a secure, great job in 2007 made me not want to rely on others for my career or financial security. I did a lot of research on how to secure my future with investments (hence the reason why Chinelas shoes are patented, with the plan to earn royalties as a form of passive income).

Interview with a Product Developer (continued)

Do you have any general advice for students studying design and product development who are perhaps contemplating starting their own business once they've finished?
I would recommend working for someone—especially a small business so you can see firsthand how someone else runs it. It really depends on what kind of business you want—offering design services, for example, is much simpler and more straightforward. But for those who want to manufacture their own products—this is a massive job that usually requires a handful of experts in such areas as production, marketing, sales, and financials. Unless you have all those skills yourself, you will need to find someone who does.

Or you can develop your own products and sell or license them to trading companies who will take them to the world market and pay you royalties if they do well. You need to be very careful here too, to ensure you find the right people to work with and a proper license agreement so you don't get ripped off.

What do you tend to spend the most time on with Chinelas by Michelle? Designing and making corrections? Communicating your ideas and working with manufacturing? Or just simply trying to sell and market your product?
It depends what phase of the business, but definitely sales is an ongoing job. Designing is only 10 percent of what needs to be done, but if we don't make enough sales, we won't have the cash flow to continue business operations.

Could you tell me a bit more about the design process for Chinelas by Michelle and how you ended up with the design in its current state?
I knew that the execution would be the most important factor in ensuring this project would be a success. First, I had a few brainstorming sessions with my friends from the university. We came up with a whole bunch of crazy concepts, eventually (taking months) developing a concept that was essentially practical and functional yet simple. There was no point designing the most amazing design, if the user could not figure out how to use it.

I made some molds using silicone and polyrubber outsole samples initially and then some rapid prototypes once I was happy with the initial ideas. I took them to a manufacturer (ensuring I had a confidentiality agreement), who further developed it into something easily manufacturable.

I understand you spent a lot of the design process optimizing the hinging and locking of the shoes. What were the main challenges there?
Making sure the manufacturer was able to replicate the working sample cheaply and that it would still work! The company's technology was not very advanced and a lot of things are handcrafted.

What styles and colors do the shoes come in and how much do they cost?
They come in just one style for now, in black, silver, red, and purple. I wanted some practical colors as well as fashion colors. They cost $39.95.

You also run a design entrepreneurship blog that can be found at michellechung.uwcblog.com, which is loaded with great firsthand advice around starting your own business, importing, sampling, marketing, just about everything. Could you tell me more about the blog?
There are two main reasons I started the blog—to help other designers get some great, practical information from someone who's done it all and can share what works and what doesn't. The second reason is to help bring a targeted audience and provide quality links to the Web site.

Do you have any last thoughts for our readers?
Don't be scared to start your own business but do make sure you are prepared and well researched. You can always go back to a job if it doesn't work out, but you do need the determination and motivation to succeed.

SAN FRANCISCO
ONE WAY
BAY BRIDGE
PERFECTION LUMIÈRE
LONG-WEAR FLAWLESS FLUID MAKEUP SPF 10
PERFECTION HAS NEVER BEEN SO SIMPLE
CHANEL
CHANEL.COM

chapter 10

Promotion in Retailing

Promotion in retailing has entered an entirely new world with the growth of the Internet and the advent of its social media opportunities. If you peruse a fashion magazine, e-shop on the Internet, or window-shop in a mall, you are part of a fashion promotion audience. If you Facebook or tweet (and who doesn't?), create sets on Polyvore or Couturious, or play Retail Therapy, you may be actually participating in fashion promotion, retailing, and design activities. Take, for example, Polyvore and its partnership with Rebecca Minkoff, one of the designers who engaged with the Polyvore community through a number of creative contests. The "Style the Rebecca Minkoff Runway" challenge gave winners the opportunity to help style her runway at New York Fashion Week and led to 22 million impressions. Minkoff also pushed the envelope by asking Polyvore users to design a new version of her iconic "Morning After Clutch." This design challenge resulted in more than 6,500 entries, and the new "Dee" clutch designed by a Polyvore member debuted in Minkoff's runway show during New York Fashion Week, arriving in stores around March 2011. About the impact of Minkoff's collaboration with Polyvore, she says, "Partnering with Polyvore ... has been a remarkable process. Our customers are consistently seeking new and convenient ways to access the brand, and Polyvore has been a great tool in their next step. Having my customers and Polyvore users be a part of my fall 2011 collection has shown that they not only understand my aesthetic but my design theory as well."[1] Polyvore is further examined in Box 10.1 and Figure 10.1.

This chapter examines the fashion careers in retailing that relate to the promotion of the retail operation—internally and externally, as a whole and for its individual products, as well as online and in the brick-and-mortar operation. **Promotion** refers to the activities that

Box 10.1 Fashion Democracy: The World of Virtual Anna Wintour

by Alexandra Jacobs, March 29, 2010

Last summer, subscribers to *Harper's Bazaar* received their September issues with the androgynous model Agyness Deyn on the cover. She was dressed in an expensive designer homage to Michael Jackson: Balmain tuxedo pants with a matching sequined jacket; special-order Repetto oxford shoes; a four-hundred-dollar black fedora by Albertus Swanepoel; and a glittering Givenchy glove. Within days, the image was copied from the Internet by a sixteen-year-old named Antonia in Croatia, on the fashion Web site Polyvore.com. Antonia pasted the photo of Deyn into an online collage—or "set," as Polyvore calls it—she was making, layering on pictures of cheaper clothing, including a studded blazer ($140 at Topshop), a purple leopard-print skirt from a store in Japan, and a Vanessa Bruno tank top. She finished by adding the vaguely Michael Jackson–inflected caption "Tomorrow can wait. Dance all through the night." In Indonesia, a student found the *Bazaar* cover similarly inspiring. Her Polyvore set included a Vivienne Westwood skull-print dress, an Alexander McQueen cuff bracelet, an Alexis Bittar bubble ring, Louboutin ankle boots, a Victoria's Secret mascara wand, all under the headline "Think Black."

The Louboutin boots also caught the fancy of Gail Helmer, a forty-three-year-old marketing consultant and Polyvore user in Calgary, who put them in two different sets that season. Since she discovered the site two years ago via Facebook, Helmer has visited Polyvore daily, and she has become one of the site's most popular creators, with thousands of followers. Each morning, she signs on as MyChanel and begins every set with an electronic scissor called the Clipper, saved to a browser's toolbar, which allows the user to collect pictures of merchandise and other visuals from all over the Web. Her choices are stored in her virtual closet, which is open to inspection by any of the 6.6 million people who visit Polyvore monthly. Helmer's closet currently contains more than 5,000 items, including accessories, jewelry, and cosmetics.

Polyvore is a lot like playing paper dolls with pictures of real clothes. Some people spend an hour on each set. It's the rare Internet pastime that feels productive—even if the product is just an online collage that you e-mail to a friend, with the message, "I made this outfit for you!" After dragging and dropping enough images for an ensemble, a user may paste in a background and then garnish the set with a lipstick or a bottle of perfume, and give it a soundtrack. "I'll find an item and it kind of tells me what it goes with. What shoes, what bags," Helmer says. Polyvore permits a maximum of fifty items in each set, but Helmer usually limits herself to a dozen, which she enlarges, shrinks, or rotates at her pleasure, perhaps adding a phrase in a decorative typeface.

Polyvore's site has 1.4 million registered users, 200,000 who are, like Helmer, dedicated "creators," amateur stylists of whom put together sets every day and post them on Facebook, Twitter, and their personal blogs. "Our mission is to democratize fashion," Jess Lee, Polyvore's vice-president of product management, states. "To empower people on the street to think about their sense of style and share it with the world."

Polyvore once collaborated with Barneys on a contest called "Barneys Obsession." Users put merchandise from the store's Web site into sets that were then judged by Barneys' fashion director. Other recent judges include the pop stars Katy Perry and Lady Gaga; and the designers Vivienne Tam and Tory Burch. It's a start to Polyvore's profitability. About a third of the company's revenue comes from commissions arranged with online retailers. The other two-thirds come from a combination of traditional ads; contests like the Barneys event; and sponsored sets, like the one posted by Calvin Klein. Each item in the CK set was invisibly tagged so that Polyvore could track for CK how often it was "touched" by online hands. Recent sets were filled with products from Nike, which sponsored a contest, or "community challenge," on Polyvore. Polyvore's most valuable asset is the intelligence that it gathers about its users' preferences. Every day, in a section called Zeitgeist, the site presents top-twenty lists of users' favorite brands, trends, and celebrities. Part of the company's business plan involves selling the statistics it's tabulating to designers and to store buyers, in order to manage inventory more effectively.

Polyvore's co-founders, Pasha Sadri, Guangwei Yuan, and Jianing Hu, are software engineers who started the company in 2007, after working together at Yahoo. Sadri, who is thirty-five, was born in Iran. "I grew up playing Legos," he said. "I think that was an important factor in shaping the person that I am. When you put on clothes, you are making that sort of assembly from pieces that you have—this is the Lego analogy—and it's highly integrated with your identity." Asked what inspired the site, he replied, "I felt that it would be great to work on something that has a visual component. If you look at all the different types of visual media, images are the ones your brain processes the fastest."

In 2010, Sadri announced that the former president of Google's Asia-Pacific and Latin-American operations, Sukhinder Singh Cassidy, would replace him as CEO. It was the beginning of a hiring binge intended to double the size of the company, based in Mountain View, California. Singh Cassidy, who once sat on the board of J. Crew, seems determined to raise Polyvore's profile. "I love style," she said.

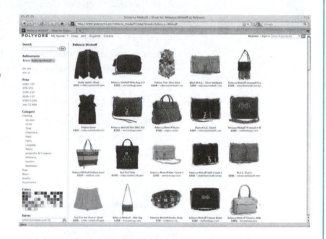

Figure 10.1 This is just a peek at the huge number of products Polyvore's site features for its "sets."

"I love décor, I love design, I love fashion—and, most importantly, I love the idea of finding women beautiful things." She sees her task as solving "the problem of curation and discovery." She ventured that Polyvore may start to participate more directly in e-commerce. ("People write to us a lot asking, for example, 'Do you have this in a size 8?'" Lee noted.) Singh Cassidy said, "We're a platform that helps the user aspire, inspire, and ultimately, I hope, fulfill."

Source: http://www.newyorker.com/reporting/2010/03/29/100329fa_fact_jacobs?printable=true#ixzz1Ilt40aqY

communicate the company's or product's attributes to target consumers. Promotion for a large national or regional chain store organization often requires a full-time staff. In contrast, promotion for a small, local retailer may be conducted by the store owner or an advertising agency hired for this purpose. Promotion consists of two primary channels: publicity and advertising. **Publicity** is, in essence, free press; it refers to the mention of a company or its merchandise in the media for which the company does not pay a fee. For example, when a retailer hosts a well-known guest designer and receives television, radio, newspaper, and Internet coverage because of the designer's visit to the store, the result is publicity. The event or news will likely involve some expenditures, but the retailer does not pay for the media coverage; the retailer's image is enhanced by the recognition. In contrast, **advertising** is paid, nonpersonal communication. Examples of advertisements are abundant in newspapers, magazines, online, and on the radio. Think about how many advertisements interrupt your favorite television shows. Whether it is publicity or advertising, the primary goal of any promotional campaign is to raise visibility in a positive fashion and, ultimately, to increase sales volume. To promote effectively, a retail business first needs to determine the message it wants to convey and to whom that message will be sent. The first question the organization should ask when developing a promotional activity is, "What does this business want or need to communicate?" A young and trendy fashion image? Community involvement? Exclusive merchandise and superior service? The answer to these questions will help ensure that the company is using its promotional efforts effectively. A company knows its promotions are effective when increases in consumer traffic and sales volume are significant, such as experiencing an increase in orders placed through the company Web site or by tracking sales of the specific product promoted through an advertising campaign. A successful promotional message accomplishes the following:

- Generates attention

- Stimulates an interest

- Promotes a desire

- Induces action

Think about the parts of a promotional message and how they relate to retailing career tracks in promotion. If you are looking for a field of action, then promotion may be your fast track to success in the fashion industry. The following careers in retail promotion are explored within this chapter: promotion director; publicity/public relations director; special events coordinator; Internet promotions director; advertising director; art staff (illustrator, photographer, art director, and Web site developer); store planning director; visual merchandiser; and personal shopper.

Promotion Director

A **promotion director** guides the marketing activities of the retail operation. Have you ever thought about how you learned that a new product or fashion line was available in your town? Did you watch television, surf the Internet, read a magazine or newspaper, or see a billboard on your way to class or work today? If so, you were exposed to marketing that was designed to persuade you to enter a store, view a Web site, or buy a product or service. Think about a specialty retailer, such as White House/Black Market (WHBM), and its range of promotional activities. In a WHBM store, there is signage throughout the store that promotes new products. These signs may be designed to create a mood for new products, such as a floral-bordered strawcloth board announcing the arrival of new tank tops. There are also subtle promotions at WHBM in the forms of window and in-store displays, hangtags, and shopping bags. You may also be one of those customers who receive e-mails announcing the arrival of new merchandise or clearance sales from WHBM, yet another form of promotion. An introduction to WHBM, and a promotion by the retailer, are provided in Box 10.2 and Figure 10.2.

Ultimately, if the promotion for the store and its products is a success, the retailer sees an increase in the number of customers shopping at the retail operation, often resulting in higher profits. There are many types of promotional campaigns: television commercials,

A Letter from Donna Noce, brand president

What I love about the beginning of White House/Black Market is that it says everything about who we are today.

We began in 1985 as a single, tiny neighborhood boutique in Baltimore, Maryland. We called ourselves The White House, and we offered unique, individual collections of fabulous clothing and

Figure 10.2 The White House/Black Market exterior and interior reflect its product lines and promotions for a cohesive image.

accessories in shades of white and ivory. It was a special, very personal place...for us and our customers.

And as we grew we made sure each new boutique would be just as special. Expanding on our original theme, we opened Black Market in 1995, and in 1997 we combined our boutiques into one concept, and White House/Black Market was born.

Throughout everything, our passion has always been to make women feel beautiful. That's what we're about. And our clothing remains a symbol of who we are: the honest simplicity of black and white, and the remarkable individuality of the different styles we build from it.

Today we have over 300 boutiques, and in each one we're dedicated to helping you feel that every place you go is more beautiful...simply because you're there.

The WHBM Promotion: Put Your Name in Our Little Black Book

Members whose purchases online, by phone, and in our boutiques have reached a total of $300 are entitled to all our Black Book benefits, including 5% off every merchandise purchase; free basic shipping; birthday bonuses; exclusive VIP invitations and offers.

Source: http://www.whitehouseblackmarket.com/store/page.jsp?id=24

radio spots, print publications (e.g., magazine ads, flyers, and catalogues), billboards, and the Internet. Because there are so many options, many retail companies seek the guidance and expertise of an advertising agency. An **advertising agency** is an outside firm that may be contracted by the retail organization to help choose the right promotional vehicles that will reach the company's target market and maximize its advertising budget. The advertising agency may also be contracted to create the advertisements. The promotion director may collaborate with an advertising agency or may make the media and budget decisions independently.

The promotion director is expected to know which media types are most effective for different types of promotions. For example, television and radio are considered best suited for institutional advertising. In many retail operations, promotion directors, with their overview of the organization, focus on institutional advertising. **Institutional advertisements** are promotional activities that sell an organization as a whole, as a fashion leader, community supporter, or provider of the best value for the dollar, among other images.

Qualifications

What are the personal characteristics, skills, education, and experiences that would best support a candidate in climbing the career ladder to the position of promotion director? Following is a description of the preferred backgrounds and characteristics for successful promotion directors:

- **Education:** A bachelor's degree in promotion, advertising, fashion communication, fashion merchandising, or a similar field is a minimum requirement.

- **Experience:** Becoming a promotion director does not happen overnight; usually, many years of industry experience are required. A few candidates start at the most entry-level position, sales associate. Others begin in an advertising department, and then move to the promotion department.

- **Personal characteristics:** An excellent understanding of fashion marketing, the ability to communicate fashion trends, an understanding of consumer behavior, strong communication and presentation skills, and a great networking ability are key personal characteristics of the successful promotion director.

Career Challenges

The promotion director has the difficult challenge of differentiating the retail organization from its competitors. Meeting this challenge requires a keen understanding of the market, its customers, and the media—not a small task. Promotion directors are challenged with creating cost-effective and eye-catching marketing activities that communicate an organization's personality and generate sales. Throughout these activities, the bottom line is always in sight, as they must generate more profit than the activities cost. As a result, promotion directors are constantly under pressure to come up with innovative ideas that fit within their budgets. Additionally, they coordinate all of the marketing efforts of their company to communicate clear, consistent company images. There are many people involved in this collaboration and many days when creative ideas are not forthcoming.

Publicity and Its Director

Publicity is the dissemination of information about people, places, special events, or other newsworthy topics through a variety of communications media. As previously noted, there are no media costs for publicity, which is why it is often difficult to obtain. Media editors choose the topics they publicize based on information they believe will be of most interest to the public. Publicity helps sell fashion merchandise by making a style, trend, designer, or retailer better known to the consumer. The **publicity director** is responsible for securing publicity for the retail operation and may collaborate with other departments to create events, such as fashion show productions or celebrity personal appearances.

The publicity director provides the media with information about such events or people, with the goal that the media will publicize them. Summaries of the important facts relating to these events, called **press releases**, or *news releases*, are formatted specifically for the media and sent

Figure 10.3
A press release from Target announcing their limited-edition collection by Calypso St. Barth.

directly to them by the publicity director (Figure 10.3). If photographs and related information are included with the press release, such as news articles from similar events in other cities or background information, the parcel is referred to as a **press package**, or *press kit*. The publicity director is responsible for directing the press package to the media whose audience would be most interested in its message. The press release and press packages may be intentionally designed to provide different perspectives to ensure that each medium has a different angle on the story.

Qualifications

Following are the qualifications for the publicity director of a large company:

- **Education:** A bachelor's degree in promotion, advertising, fashion communication, journalism, fashion merchandising, or a similar field is a minimum requirement.

- **Experience:** A number of publicity directors began in the advertising department, then transfer to assistant positions in the public relations department. Others gain experience working in one of the media fields before moving into retailing.

- **Personal characteristics:** An excellent understanding of media alternatives, journalism, and marketing provides a solid foundation for public relations work. Exceptional communication and presentation skills, attention to detail, and a strong networking ability are common personal characteristics of successful public relations directors.

Career Challenges

The publicity director is always searching for a "free ride." The "ride" is publicity, positive mention of the company in the press. It takes a great spin master to create a new way of looking at something old. Take, for example, the in-store visit of a designer. The publicity director must find a way to make this event appear new and fresh by tying it to a fashion show that benefits a charitable cause or a model search for an in-store informal show. It is challenging to create new perspectives, find publicity opportunities, and communicate effectively with the various media contacts.

Special Events Coordinator

Special events refer to designed occurrences that are intended to communicate particular messages to a target audience. A **special events coordinator** develops and executes events that are fashion related, such as fashion and trunk shows, as well as fashion presentations at clubs and for organizations. Additionally, the special events coordinator creates and directs activities that are not fashion related, but put the company in a favorable light in the public eye. A company's participation in Habitat for Humanity, its sponsorship of a sporting event to raise money for a local school, or a fund-raising drive among company employees for survivors of hurricanes or other natural disasters are illustrations of special events that may be coordinated as public affairs activities to support the local or world community.

Special events coordinators collaborate with the promotion and public relations directors to develop events that will either feature merchandise or enhance the company's image. They are effective at finding opportunities to accomplish both. They may work with promotion directors and retail buyers on sales promotion events. **Sales promotions** often feature short-term incentives that encourage the sale of particular products or categories of merchandise. Examples of sales promotion techniques include free samples, coupons, gift-with-purchase giveaways, point-of-purchase displays, contests, sweepstakes, and games. An example of an externally sponsored sales promotion is *Teen Vogue*'s back-to-school fashion show. *Teen Vogue* provides funding for the retailer to sponsor the event, such as advertising monies and door prizes, as well as gifts for students who audition as models. In exchange, the retailer features merchandise advertised in *Teen Vogue* in the fashion show.

The special events coordinator is adept at planning activities, recruiting partners (e.g., country clubs, community clubs, and philanthropic organizations), finding assistance for events, working within budgets and schedules, and recruiting press coverage. It is not an easy job, but it can be exhilarating and fulfilling.

Qualifications

What does it take to be a special events coordinator? Following is a list of qualifications.

- **Education:** A bachelor's degree in public relations, fashion merchandising, fashion communication, or a related discipline is a common requirement.

- **Experience:** Between two and five years of experience in advertising, public relations, or fashion coordination are required. Retail or sales experience can be obtained during the educational years to help open a door to this field.

- **Personal characteristics:** The special events coordinator has the ability to create enthusiasm and drama for a product, line, or activity. A person in this position is creative in finding new and exciting venues to introduce the retail operation and its products to consumers. The successful special events coordinator remains well organized and detail oriented while working effectively with others and staying calm under pressure.

Career Challenges

The special events coordinator must be a jack-of-all-trades; for instance, directing a fashion show to introduce a new season's merchandise, coordinating a fashion show that raises funds for a charity, and hosting a luncheon for women executives—all in the same month. Time-management skills, attention to detail, and strong organizational abilities are essential for this position, but are not the only necessary personal traits. Additionally, special events coordinators must be able to motivate all of the people involved in the events. It can be a huge task to juggle several events and a large number of constituencies at one time; yet the best special events coordinators do so with grace.

Internet Promotions Director

The **Internet promotions director** is responsible for developing and communicating the company brand and its products through technology. Key responsibilities for the Internet promotions director include guiding the company's digital presence through communications, the online calendar, display and search advertising, and social media outreach. Development and maintenance of social media connections, such as Facebook, Twitter, and Foursquare, are a significant part of the Internet promotions director's job. The Internet promotions director works with other departments in the company to feature compelling content, maximizing the opportunities of the online venue. Every content contribution is developed to have a consistent voice and messaging. The Internet promotions director also works with agencies on creative development, makes media buys, and analyzes the results of the media efforts.

Qualifications

Following is a list of the education, work experience, and personal characteristics that an Internet promotions director is expected to have.

- **Education:** A bachelor's degree in business, marketing, computer information systems, or fashion merchandising (with an emphasis or minor in computers) is strongly preferred.

- **Experience:** Three to five years of experience are often required. Proven, successful digital experience is required. Retail experience is an excellent asset that will make a candidate stand out.

- **Personal characteristics:** This is the position for a person who has a passion for all things digital. He or she must be an excellent project manager with the ability to multitask multiple priorities and timelines. The person who has a strong understanding of the fundamentals of interactive marketing and an ability to think analytically and strategically will have a strong advantage in this field.

Box 10.3 features an article on social media platforms and retailers that are using the Internet to build customer relationships and to market their products. Careers in e-commerce will keep evolving, proliferating, and gaining influence in the fashion world.

Box 10.3 Social Media Rewrite the Rules for Brands

By Lauren Benet Stephenson
Posted Wednesday June 24, 2009 from WWD issue 06/24/2009

Gucci is doing it. So are Oscar de la Renta, Donna Karan, Target, Urban Outfitters, Louis Vuitton, and Rachel Roy. Fashion houses, designers, and retailers are rushing into the free social media phenomenon that is reshaping not only interpersonal communication, but how fashion products are marketed and sold. Companies are tweeting, blogging, and updating their profiles in an effort to mold their brand personalities on real-time global platforms and form relationships with a community of customers, particularly consumers for whom the Web is as important as an arm or a leg. "Customers can feel like they are part of the brand's extended family, and therefore the brand itself, while the interactive element further deepens that relationship," said Alex Bolen, CEO of Oscar de la Renta. A key component of social media, Bolen states, "is real-time feedback—an ability to accurately measure marketing results."

Designers and retailers, such as Rachel Roy and Charlotte Ronson, share immediate snapshots of their personal lives and their company's activities via social media. Brands including Gap, Victoria's Secret, Ralph Lauren, Calvin Klein, Nike, and Adidas also have tapped into YouTube, MySpace, and other sites, where their videos, commercials, behind-the-scenes footage, and fashion shows are posted. Examples of social media efforts in fashion retailing follow.

- Charlotte Ronson updates her Twitter fans at least daily, "letting them know if something new comes in or something sells well. It's a good way to keep everyone connected." In the Twitter-as-marketing technique, one tweet said, "Just got in some great Rag & Bone items… hats, ties and belts…come check it out!!!" In a Twitter-for-building-relationships strategy, another tweet reported, "I'm watching *Funny Face*, the musical with Audrey Hepburn and Fred Astaire…Need I say more…"

- Rachel Roy combines promotional tweets, such as, "The entire RR 2010 Resort Collection Look Book has been posted on Rachel Roy's official Facebook Page. Check it out," with more personal tweets—"I found some cute wellies by Hunter for my daughter and I—green for me and purple for her. Here's a link to more." The juxtaposition is engineered to nurture ties with customers. "I hope that my relationship with customers will become more intimate as they get to know me beyond my designs," she said.

- Gucci first became involved with Facebook in 2008 after noticing that about 50,000 fans had signed up for a Gucci page started by a person unaffiliated with the fashion label. So Gucci decided to launch a company page and substantially raised the fan count to its current total of over four million followers. The weekly updated page contains original video uploaded to the site, photos from events, and new product announcements.

- Target has used its Facebook page for advertising its latest designer collaborations. To publicize its philanthropic efforts, the company launched the "Bullseye Gives" campaign that allowed its users to vote on the charity to which Target should give money. When users choose a charity, they are offered the option of publishing their choice to their own news feed. There is also a "wall" where the company and its fans can post messages, photos, and video; a tab for information about the company, and additional tabs where a firm can add everything from sale promotions to trailers for new ad campaigns.

- When American Apparel and its CEO, Dov Charney, were embroiled in a lawsuit filed by Woody Allen over unauthorized use of his image, the company used its Twitter and Facebook pages for direct access to customers by posting its official statement on Facebook and linking to Twitter. "We were able to speak and reassure customers," said an American Apparel spokesperson.

- Juicy Couture launched an interactive social media platform on its own site, called Club Couture. The technology allows consumers to put together looks from the collection and share the outfits with friends, who can then rate the outfit and create their own.

The result of social media usage by retailers and designers is two-way communication with their consumer. Reggie Bradford, CEO of ViTrue, a social media consulting firm, believes it's important to view the situation in reverse, saying a brand will ultimately be "measured in growth or losses by being there [on social media] or not being there." More than any marketing medium, including print, where advertising is suffering, social media give brands a chance to be a part of a dialogue about their own companies. The best of these social media merchants leverage their presence on social networks through great content, frequent updates, and tools for engagement and conversation. Fashion brands can represent consumers' personalities, or how they want to be perceived. Connecting with others through social media is a real opportunity for retailers to reach out to potential customers as free advertising, to bring current customers together, and to be a human voice for the brand. "The fashion world is shifting, needs are changing, and people's shopping habits are changing....It's clear that [consumers on social media] are part of the overall fashion conversation," Rachel Roy says. "And I don't think that is going to change." It appears certain that social media platforms will keep evolving, proliferating, and gaining influence in the fashion world.

Advertising Director

An **advertising director** of a retail operation develops and implements the company's advertising strategy for the purpose of increasing sales. Designed to serve different purposes, there are five primary types of advertising: institutional, brand, sales, classified, and advocacy (Figure 10.4a). As mentioned previously, institutional advertising is intended to build the organization's image and create community goodwill. **Brand advertising** promotes a particular label or manufacturer, while **sales advertising** announces specific value items. **Classified advertising** disseminates information about a sale, service, or event. These advertisements are usually presented as small ads in specific sections of print publications. **Advocacy advertising** supports a particular cause. For example, a home-building retailer may run a newspaper advertisement that entirely features green design merchandise, all composed of sustainable resources or recyclable products, in support of environmental awareness. Figure 10.4b provides an example of an advocacy campaign advertisement for the Hanes Sock Drive. The goal of the promotion was to engage consumers in social media through a philanthropic initiative with the purposes of 1) growing the Hanes Facebook page, 2) making a charitable donation of 500,000 pairs of socks to the Salvation Army, and 3) building a connection in consumers' minds between Hanes and the Salvation Army, or world community goodwill in general. With the insight that socks are the number one requested items in homeless shelters, Hanes developed an online promotion and empowered consumers to help donate socks to the Salvation Army with a simple mouse click on Facebook. This initiative catapulted Hanes onto AllFacebook.com's list of "The Most Explosive Facebook Pages" for the week the Hanes Sock Drive was introduced and generated enough buzz for Hanes to end up with over 800,000 followers, thousands of comments and likes, and over 1 billion impressions.[2]

Figure 10.4a Since it began in 1996, Lee National Denim Day has raised more than $83 million for the fight against breast cancer and unites nearly one million supporters nationwide each year.

Figure 10.4b The Hanes Sock Drive on Facebook gleaned a barrage of new followers and 500,000 pairs of socks for the Salvation Army.

In addition to determining which type of advertising best suits a product, line, or event, the advertising director also selects the venue for the advertisement, called the media form. Advertising **media forms**, or simply media, include magazines and newspapers, television and radio, outdoor displays, direct mail, novelties (e.g., calendars, pencils, and memo tablets), catalogues, directories, and circulars. After deciding the media form of an advertisement, advertising directors work to position their companies relative to the competition. They first determine the goal of the advertisement. Is the objective to get consumers to make buying decisions in the near future? Is the goal to introduce a new product or service? The goals of advertising campaigns influence which media forms advertising directors will choose to convey messages.

The advertising director will likely work with support departments to develop a promotional campaign that is within the company's advertising funds. Support departments can include graphic design, illustration, photography, and printing. For example, an advertising director may work with an illustrator to develop drawings depicting a promotional concept for television, magazine, or newspaper ads. The ideas would then be evaluated by looking at concept boards to determine whether the promotion is likely to be successful. The selected concept would then be implemented using whatever resources are necessary to complete the project. In a print ad, for example, a fashion photographer may be hired to shoot the necessary pictures. Finally, the advertising director measures the outcome of advertising efforts, in terms of sales volume, customer traffic generated, and units sold, to determine the success of the advertisement. The most common form of advertising evaluation is an analysis of sales and profit impact before, during, and after the promotional effort occurs.

Qualifications

Here is what you need to know and do to become an advertising director for a retail organization.

- **Education:** A bachelor's degree in advertising, fashion merchandising, fashion communication, or a similar field is frequently a minimum requirement.

- **Experience:** An entry-level position in advertising, such as sales associate or copywriter, is an excellent starting place. The advertising director has completed a minimum of between three and five years' experience in promotion and retailing.

- **Personal characteristics:** An excellent understanding of fashion trends, customers, and retail competition is extremely helpful. The ability to sell is a critical skill. The advertising director has mastered the skills of persuasion and communication.

Career Challenges

Advertising directors of large companies must develop expertise in a wide range of media sources, from print advertising in magazines and newspapers to television and radio commercials to Internet advertisements. Each media type requires different strategies and skills. Maintaining strong attention to detail while managing quick deadlines can be a challenging task.

Art Staff

Art directors, illustrators, photographers, and Web site developers may be categorized as members of an art staff. Large companies usually employ a full art staff, while small retailers hire an advertising agency or freelance personnel to do these jobs. As an **art director** develops and implements the creative concepts for advertisements, catalogues, mailers, and so on, the goal is to provide an overall and consistent visual view with regard to the retailer's graphic design execution, including signage, photography, direct mail, packaging, and advertising illustrations. **Illustrators** often work within the advertising departments of major retailers to sketch garments for print advertisements. Illustrations can show more detail than photographs, may be less expensive to create, and can take less time to execute than a photography session. Many illustrators begin in a freelance capacity, with the hope of future full-time employment with a large retailer. Today, a number of them work with computers to develop or finalize drawings. Adobe Photoshop, Kaledo, and Illustrator are important CAD programs for illustrators. Many large retailers also employ **photographers** in their promotion division. Figure 10.5a is of photographer Dan Lecca on the runway; Figure 10.5b shows Lecca's photo from a recent fashion season, featuring the Calvin Klein Collection by Francisco Costa. Retailers with a major Internet presence will hire **Web site developers**, or designers, to construct, maintain, and grow the company's Web site. Box 10.4 presents e-retailer Bluefly's introduction of social gaming to build customer patronage on its Web site.

Qualifications

If you are interested in an art-related position with a retailer, here are an employer's expectations in terms of education, experience, and personal characteristics.

- **Education:** A two-to-four-year college degree in fashion illustration, fashion design, fine arts, photography, or computer science is often a minimum requirement.

- **Experience:** An outstanding portfolio should be developed to show one's ability to work with a variety of products in a range of styles. Two to five years of experience in freelance work can open the door to these positions. Most companies expect candidates to have skills in computer-aided design applications.

Figure 10.5a Fashion photographer Dan Lecca behind the lens.

Figure 10.5b One of Lecca's favorites of all the shots he took this season, from the Calvin Klein collection by Francisco Costa.

- **Personal characteristics:** A solid background in visual design is necessary. The abilities to work quickly, adapt to different viewpoints, and work with a range of mediums are important. Members of an art staff must be able to work independently and meet deadlines.

Career Challenges

Members of the art staff, whether they are illustrators, photographers, or Web site developers, are confronted with the challenges of acquiring and understanding new technology on a regular basis. Most illustrators work on computers, even if simply to finalize hand drawings. Computers have become vital instruments in the photographer's world as well. The Web site developer is likely the most comfortable with technology; however, the influx of new innovations in Web site retailing keeps the developer in constant training as well.

Store Planning Director

A **store planning director** develops a plan that details fixture placement, lighting, dressing rooms, restrooms, windows, aisles, and cash and wrap areas of a store. Store planning directors keep several goals in mind when laying out store floor plans. Aesthetic appeal, image consistency, visibility and security of merchandise, comfort and ease of staff and consumers, and merchandising flexibility are among these objectives. Once a floor plan is finalized, all of the **supplies** (e.g., hangers, bags, and tissue) will be purchased, along with the **equipment** (e.g., four-way fixtures, T-stands, slat walls, mirrors, and computer registers) to set up the retail floor. All of this must be accomplished within a predetermined budget.

The store planning director often works with the visual merchandising director to design the store layout. Window and interior display areas and cases to exhibit small goods, fixtures, and mannequins are of interest to both. The store planner who has work experience in visual merchandising often has an edge over one who does not.

Qualifications

What else does it take to have a successful career in store planning? Education, experience, and personal qualifications are the following:

- **Education:** A bachelor's degree in fashion merchandising, interior design, retailing, or a related field is a minimum requirement.

- **Experience:** Between two and five years of experience in retail management, visual merchandising, interior design, or buying are preferred.

- **Personal characteristics:** Store planners are detail oriented, computer literate (CAD), and task oriented. They have effective communication skills—oral, written, and visual. Additionally, they have strong quantitative skills, as space allocation and budgeting are core responsibilities of someone on this career path.

The job outlook for this field is good. Most large retail operations rely on store planning directors for updating facilities, setting up new departments or stores, and keeping the equipment and supplies for the retail floor in stock, up to date, and safe.

Career Challenges

The store planner has a great deal to consider when designing or remodeling a retail operation. Store managers, buyers, sales associates, customers, receiving clerks, and maintenance staff have specific space needs and desires. While working under the control of a budget, the store planner must consider the comfort and safety of all constituencies while keeping in mind the main goal of the retailer—selling merchandise. Designing a space to meet all of these objectives takes observation, patience, and perseverance.

Figures 10.6a and b
Bold color and interesting
layout designs separate
these interior displays
from the norm.

Visual Merchandiser

Promotions are not limited to print ads, television commercials, and billboards. Promoting the image of the store through visual merchandising is another way retailers market their products to prospective customers. What is visual merchandising? Often called the "silent salesperson," **visual merchandising** refers to the design, development, procurement, and installation of merchandise displays that enhance the ambiance of the environment in which the displays are shown. Effective visual merchandising aims to create an image that reflects the company and sells the company's product lines. Some visual merchandising efforts are institutional, such as Macy's large boulevard windows that feature holiday extravaganzas of mechanical dolls and a twelve-foot tree made of glass lollipops. Others are product-driven, such as Tiffany's shadow-box windows that highlight new jewelry pieces.

Visual merchandisers are the people responsible for window installations, in-store displays (Figures 10.6a and b), signage, fixtures, mannequins, and decorations that give a retail operation aesthetic appeal and a distinct image. Visual merchandisers have the ability to look at the merchandise selected by the buyers and, through their creativity and expertise, create an image of the store that entices customers to enter the store and purchase merchandise. Think about an outfit displayed in a retail window or on a mannequin. As a result of seeing the presentation of the garment and accessories, you may have decided to buy the items on display. This purchase is due to the successful work of a visual merchandiser.

The visual merchandiser is responsible for a number of key tasks:

- Designing an aesthetically appealing environment that reflects the company's image, sometimes including floor, wall, and furnishing selections

- Creating exciting visual displays to educate customers and to sell merchandise

- Presenting the merchandise in ways that will maximize sales, such as displaying the full range of colors of a new handbag and matching footwear

Most often, the visual merchandiser consults with the retail operation's buyers to determine which merchandise should be featured. Since one of the main goals of visual merchandising is to increase revenue, merchandisers will ask the visual merchandiser to create displays for new, key items that have been purchased in depth, as in Figure 10.7. Alternatively, the buyer may ask the visual merchandiser to feature products that are not selling well to increase sales on the items so that the merchandiser will not have to mark them down, thereby decreasing the retailer's profit. Some visual merchandisers have numerous job responsibilities in addition to designing and installing window displays. They also place inventory of the sales floor stock and set up new stores for openings. They locate and purchase props and fixtures for installations and create signage for display windows and the sales floor.

Qualifications

Are you a person who is artistic, resourceful, and loves creating visual displays? This may be the career path for you if you have the following qualifications:

- **Education:** A two- or four-year college degree in fashion merchandising, fashion design, interior design, retail planning and design, fine arts, or visual merchandising is often a minimum requirement.

- **Experience:** Many visual display directors begin as members of a visual merchandising crew, installing window and interior displays. Others may come from the field of fashion stylist. One of the best ways to prepare for the job search is to build a portfolio of work:

Figure 10.7 Kate Spade's in-store display represents lifestyle merchandising with its array of related products.

photographs of displays created for local merchants, class projects, or internships in visual merchandising. Most visual merchandisers have experience in drafting, allowing them to sketch concepts before executing them.

- **Personal characteristics:** The successful visual merchandiser requires a breadth of skills and knowledge: an understanding of fashion marketing and merchandising; an eye for color, line, balance, and proportion; a theatrical aesthetic sense; a strong sense of fashion; the ability to develop and follow time and budget schedules; computer-aided design skills to develop schematics of displays; and the ability to rethink and reuse props, mannequins, and other display components. The effective visual merchandiser is not only self-motivated but also able to take directions to execute concepts and work as a member of a team. This position requires one to be able to work well under pressure.

Career opportunities in this field are increasing because the retail industry understands how important visual image is to the consumer. It is significant to note that the job of visual display is one that can be accomplished at the primary level of the fashion industry. There are a number of companies outside of the retail industry that hire visual merchandisers as part of their staffs. These include home furnishings and accessories manufacturers, beauty and cosmetics firms, apparel and accessories manufacturers, trend forecasting firms, and fabric and notions representatives or suppliers. In addition to employment with a primary-level firm, there are also opportunities to work as a freelance visual merchandiser in all levels of the fashion industry.

Career Challenges

People interested in pursuing a visual merchandising career often start at the first rung of the career ladder as a display associate, paid a fairly low hourly wage. The job does not consist solely of selecting beautiful merchandise and designing attractive displays. It includes vacuuming the floors of the store windows, cleaning the glass, refurbishing props to stay within budget, and working evenings to install displays when customers are not in the store. After paying their dues in this position, display associates may move into assistant visual merchandising director positions and upward to the position of director.

Personal Shopper

Imagine a retail apparel company paying you a high salary for shopping for its customers—pulling together wardrobes for their cruises, weddings, or new career positions. Perhaps you want to work in the home interior industry. Here again, retailers hire personal shoppers to help their customers select home furnishings, wall coverings, flooring, and home accessories. Yes, there is actually a fashion career in shopping—that of personal shopper. The stereotype of the personal shopper is of a person who works part time for the rich and famous; however, this career track is rapidly changing. Today's society places great demands on family life. More often than not, both parents are working full-time jobs, and their children are participating in extracurricular activities. This leaves little time for the parent/professional to shop, whether it is for food, clothing, or home furnishings. Personal shoppers of a retail operation free up time for the family. They may freelance or work for a boutique, an upscale department store, or a specialty store. These **personal shoppers** assist customers with individualized attention and service. They maintain a log of sizes, preferred brands and styles, and special-occasion dates for each client. Personal shoppers may assist customers in selecting an entire season's wardrobe or an outfit for a specific occasion, based on the needs of the customers, including their budgets, activities, and personal styles.

The ultimate personal shopper may be referred to as a **stylist**. This person consults with clients on hair, makeup, footwear, jewelry, and apparel to create total looks, often for specific events. Perhaps the most well-known stylist is Rachel Zoe, the creator of many celebrity wardrobes (Figure 10.8). Being a stylist in the world of the rich and famous means that Zoe helps prominent people (mostly young actresses, such as Cameron Diaz and Kate Beckinsale) choose what to wear to red-carpet events, photo shoots, or sometimes just to the local coffee shop. Though not a retailer, photographer, or magazine editor, Zoe has become one of the most powerful women in fashion, as the fashion apparel and accessories she chooses fill the pages of magazines and add millions to the profits of the designers and retailers she recommends.

An impetus for the increase in personal shopper positions in the world of the mass market is the fact that we, as a society, are living longer, more active lives. Today's "baby boomers" have more disposable income (and, often, more energetic lifestyles) than any generation before them. They may welcome assistance with the constraints of shopping, which involves time and traveling. Personal shoppers can assist with buying clothing and gift items for the clients, their families, and their business associates. The increase in the number of personal shoppers is also a result of the interest in this area by business clientele. Executives who work for large companies may hire personal shoppers to find the perfect gifts for important clients, holiday gift giving, special events, and conferences.

Qualifications

If you love to shop, understand a customer's needs, work well with people, and enjoy attention to detail, then the personal shopper position may be designed for you. Following are the requirements for securing this position.

- **Education:** A two- to four-year college degree in fashion merchandising, fashion design, retailing, or a similar field is preferred.

- **Experience:** Successful retail sales experience in a variety of departments is key to securing a personal shopper position. The top sales associates in a retail operation are usually recruited for these openings.

- **Personal characteristics:** Personal shoppers are effective communicators, active listeners, and strong record keepers. They are strong at networking, poised and tactful, and up to date on fashion trends.

This career path is wide open. The customer's preference for more individualized attention while shopping and more personal or free time has made this a career choice in demand. Most personal shoppers are paid on commission, a percent of the merchandise sold; some are paid a salary; and a few receive a base salary plus commission.

Career Challenges

The successful personal shopper needs to combine the skills of a top-notch salesperson with the abilities of a retail promoter. This person is required not only to sell the store's merchandise but also to sell the store as the place for the customer to make all fashion purchases. This skill enables the personal shopper to build a customer base of repeat patrons. It is challenging to maintain detailed customer records, contact customers when new merchandise arrives without appearing overly aggressive, and continually add new customers to the clientele list. Additionally, the successful personal shopper knows how to effectively collaborate with the retail buyer to secure the products the clientele desires.

Summary

Retail promotion refers to advertising and publicity efforts that communicate the retail company's or product's attributes to the target consumers. The promotion director guides the marketing activities of a retail operation. Working with the promotion director, the publicity director solicits publicity, or free press, for the company. The special events coordinator develops and executes events that are fashion related, such as fashion shows, and those that are not

Figure 10.8 Rachel Zoe, stylist to the stars and the masses.

fashion related, such as a company's participation in Habitat for Humanity. It is the advertising director who develops and implements the company's advertising strategy. Advertising differs from publicity in that it is paid-for, nonpersonal communication delivered through mass media. Working with the advertising director, the illustrator creates sketches used in print and electronic advertising. Some companies also employ in-house photographers for promotional activities; others also have positions for an art director and a Web site developer.

Promotion also occurs within the retail store. A store planning director develops the layout that details fixture placement, lighting, dressing rooms, restrooms, windows, aisles, and cash and wrap areas of a store or department. Once the store layout is constructed, the visual merchandiser is responsible for the window installations, in-store displays, signage, fixtures, mannequins, and decorations that give a retail operation aesthetic appeal and a distinct image. Many large retailers promote products through the assistance of personal shoppers, who select merchandise to meet the needs of personal clients.

Promotion is successful when the customer is affected by the communication and then purchases merchandise from the retailer. The customer walks out of the store with a smile, shopping bag in hand, and a good feeling about both the purchase and the source of the purchase, the retailer.

Endnotes

1. Agathous, Amalia. The Rise of Polyvore: Trendsetting Goes Social. http://thenextweb. com/socialmedia/2011/02/19/the-future-of-polyvore-the-webs-largest-fashion- community-interview/.
2. Hanes Sock Drive; http://competition.s3.amazonaws.com/hanes.html.

Key Terms

advertising
advertising agency
advertising director
advocacy advertising
art director
brand advertising
classified advertising
equipment
illustrator
institutional advertisement
Internet promotions director
media form
personal shopper
photographer
press package

press release
promotion
promotion director
publicity
publicity director
sales advertising
sales promotion
special event
special events coordinator
store planning director
stylist
supplies
visual merchandiser
visual merchandising
Web site developer

Online Resources

4fashionistas.wordpress.com/category/social-media-marketing-thought-leaders-in-fashion-industry/

fashionscollective.com/

mashable.com/2010/02/13/fashion-industry-social-media/

mediasiteinc.com/how-fashion-retailers-are-redefining-e-commerce-with-social-media/oursuburbancottage.blogspot.com/2010/05/demystifying-polyvore.html

thenextweb.com/socialmedia/2011/02/17/the-rise-of-polyvore-trendsetting-goes-social/

www.wwd.com/fashion-news/buyers-flock-to-fashion-weeks-in-india-3591844

www.fashionablymarketing.me

www.guardian.co.uk/business/2008/mar/21/asda.retail

www.prcouture.com/2009/06/26/top-fashion-pr-links-29/

www.rachelzoe.com

www.wwd.com/fashion-news/king-of-the-pit-1342815

Discussion Questions

1. Using a print source, such as a newspaper or magazine, or the Internet, locate and copy an example of an institutional advertisement for a retail operation. Attach to the ad a one-page summary of your perception of the retailer's image based solely on the advertisement. How does the image differentiate this retailer from its competitors?

2. Locate a print source, such as a newspaper or magazine, or the Internet, that provides an example of publicity for a retail operation. Copy the publicity illustration and develop a one-page press release that could have been used to solicit the publicity among media sources.

3. Assume that you are the promotion director for an Internet retailer. How would you promote your company? Construct a list of promotional activities that you would implement to market your Web site.

4. Develop a list of special events that could be used to introduce a new brick-and-mortar home accessories store to your community. Include partnership promotions, externally funded events, and activities that would likely attract publicity.

5. Consider a variety of retailers and note those that excel in visual merchandising. Which visual elements are used to strengthen their company image? Provide examples of current visual merchandising trends implemented by these retailers.

Interview with a Retail Promotion Director

"We All Need a Little Retail Therapy; Interview with Brian Sugar"
By Macala Wright Lee, Founder, FashionablyMarketing.Me (http://www.fashionablymarketing.me) on 08/18/2010
Source: http://fashionablymarketing.me/2010/08/retail-therapy-interview-with-brian-sugar/

In mid-July, Sugar Inc. expanded its women's media network with the launch of its first social online game, called PopSugar's Retail Therapy. The online game made a strong debut, featuring popular brands such as Banana Republic, Barneys New York, Diane Von Furstenberg, Gap, Juicy Couture, Topshop, and Tory Burch. Macala Wright interviewed Brian Sugar on the game's astounding success.

About Retail Therapy

PopSugar's Retail Therapy allows players to merchandise and design their own fashion boutiques, letting them dress characters in the hottest styles and brands. Retail Therapy is available on Facebook and can be played for free.

Beginning with a small and empty boutique, players are challenged to stock their stores with clothing from PopSugar's Retail Therapy brand partners; they're also challenged to design their store layout. The virtual clothes are replicas of real items that players can buy. By carrying the best fashions, players earn virtual money to customize their stores with stylized furnishings, or they can grow their stores into giant department stores.

In addition to running their own boutique, players can shop at their friends' stores or stores hosted by brand-name retailers. Players can also download their personalized characters and outfits to social networking sites in order to share their style with their network of friends. "Our goal is to constantly add innovative offerings that entertain and delight our large audience of women. We wanted to create an addicting game that would appeal to one of their greatest areas of passion: fashion. Retail Therapy allows women to mix and match dream outfits from their favorite retailers and feel the experience of running their own high-end fashion boutique," states Brian Sugar, founder and CEO of Sugar Inc.

Interview with Brian Sugar

By creating Retail Therapy, Sugar has made gaming's potential to fashion understandable and extremely enticing. You've done this by making the products engaging and providing transactional links. That's a win in itself. But could this be taken a step further, offering retailer merchandise forecasting opportunities? Do you think that Retail Therapy could drive sales of limited-edition apparel or virtually created clothing collections?

What you're asking is absolutely possible with Retail Therapy. Designers will be able to host virtual pop-up events, hold sample sales, and test product colors and collections. Let's say a designer tries a skirt she or he was going to release in blue, black, and green. If it ends up that the skirt in blue or black was virtually bought most, while green didn't receive any attention, the designer could cut the color from the collection or buyers could alter their orders from that designer.

What do you look for in acquiring Web sites or when you're incorporating new tools for reaching new audiences? What trends in the media do you look for? What trends in the analytics of a Web site do you look for?

We look for sites that offer great technology or great services (as seen with our most recent site Fresh Guide). Most of the sites we acquire are sites that should spend money on marketing but have yet to spend any. These are great companies for us. Their growth potential, coupled with Sugar's target audiences, offer us huge advantages.

What are five favorite Web sites for information on the Web, for business or pleasure?

Hacker News, Silicon Alley Insider, Daring Fireball, Kottke.Org, and of course OnSugar. I'd have to say Buzz and Tres Sugar are my favorites.

What are your picks for the next social networks? Foursquare? Dailybooth?

Interview with a Retail Promotion Director (continued)

Foursquare. It's getting past early adoption now. People I know on Facebook who aren't on the trendsetting curve are now "checking in."

Afterthoughts

With Retail Therapy, Sugar has taken all the successful elements of marketing brick-and-mortar stores and made virtual extensions. We'll be excited to see how social shopping games can integrate geo-social activities and how retailers will want to take virtual consumers/user interactions offline. Sugar has always been ahead of the curve in Web site acquisition (ShopFlick/ShopStyle) and in its explorations in digital mediums like video, mobile apps, etc. Sugar's content is very mainstream and includes big brands, big retailers. Will Sugar turn its attention to indie fashion (smaller, emerging brands) as well? We'll be watching to see if (or when) Sugar will soon move toward cashing in on the indie fashion social commerce wave.

chapter 11

Merchandising for the Retailer

How simple is it to find a new pair of jeans to buy?

All you have to do is go to the nearest department store or specialty shop, or order the jeans online at your favorite apparel Web site. Have you ever wondered how the dozens or even hundreds of pairs of blue jeans ended up at the retail store or Web site in the first place (Figures 11.1a–c)? Who decided which brands and styles of jeans the retailer would sell and which ones it would not? Chances are, a buyer indirectly influenced your wardrobe. The merchandise found in a fashion retail operation has likely been purchased either by the business owner or a buyer who is employed by the business owner. In large operations, the buying tasks are performed by specialists who have acquired in-depth knowledge of the merchandising function of a specific department or a group of related departments. In small operations, the buying function may be one of many carried out by the company's owner. Alternatively, the small business owner may employ a buyer to purchase merchandise for all of the departments in the retail operation.

As discussed previously, **merchandising** refers to all of the activities involved in the buying and selling of the retailer's products. The major responsibilities of the merchandiser, or the buyer, are to locate and purchase products, with the preferences of the consumer in mind, and then to sell these products at a profit. The selection of products available for sale in a fashion operation is commonly called its **inventory**, or *merchandise assortment*. Who are the people involved in selecting the merchandise assortment, and how do they do it?

In this chapter, merchandising positions for the retailer are explored. The career options that are discussed include general merchandising manager, divisional merchandising manager, buyer/fashion merchandiser, assistant buyer, planner, distribution manager/allocator, and merchandising trainee.

Figures 11.1a–c
Have you ever wondered how the dozens or even hundreds of pairs of blue jeans ended up at the retail store or Web site in the first place?

General Merchandising Manager

A **general merchandising manager (GMM)** is the boss of the buyers' boss. The GMM leads and manages the buyers of all divisions in a retail operation. This key administrator is responsible for setting the overall strategy and merchandise direction of the retail operation. The GMM develops the buying and selling strategies that will, hopefully, maximize business performance and profitability. The GMM ensures that pricing decisions, promotional strategies, and marketing activities support the financial objectives of the merchandising team. To accomplish this, the GMM must understand not only the competitors' strengths, weaknesses, and strategies, but also the customers' demographics, wants, and needs, as well as merchandise trends in all departments.

GMMs set the merchandise direction to ensure a focused continuity on the selling floor. They work with the divisional merchandising managers and buyers to develop competitive merchandise assortments that appeal to customers at the right prices and at the right fashion level. They also assist the buying staff with securing the best merchandise exclusives, product launches, and deliveries available in the market (Figure 11.2). They collaborate on which manufacturers or designers, fashion items, and merchandise categories will be carried in depth by the retail organization.

Figure 11.2 The GMM assists the buying staff with securing the best merchandise exclusives, product launches, such as Bieber's new fragrance line with personal appearances and giveaways.

General Merchandising Manager (GMM)—Juniors' Apparel Retail Chain

Job Responsibilities:

The general merchandising manager is a senior position with a private, regional, midsize retailer of junior apparel/shoes/accessories. Responsibilities include:

- Developing and managing strategic plans

- Planning merchandise assortments

- Maintaining vendor relations

- Monitoring retail pricing, along with analysis of what competition is doing

- Promotional planning to achieve financial goals

- Identifying, recruiting, challenging, and developing buying staff

Job Requirements:

- Four-year college or university degree in business, fashion merchandising, retailing, or related field

- Ten-plus years experience in apparel

- Excellent established vendor relationships in the apparel industry

- Negotiation skills

- Strategic planning skills

- Specialty store buying experience preferred

- 25 percent travel required

Other:

Position reports directly to the president. Excellent benefits including life, medical, dental insurance; 529, 401(k), profit-sharing plan; a generous merchandise discount; and possible annual bonus based on performance and net profit. Relocation assistance will be provided as needed.

GMMs manage, coach, and develop the buying staff, creating an environment that promotes the professional development of the divisional merchandising managers and buyers and enhancing morale among the entire buying team. While collaborating with the divisional merchandising managers in developing merchandise assortments that support the needs of the customers and the financial objectives of each merchandise division, GMMs are ultimately responsible for overseeing merchandise selection and procurement of goods by the buyers. Box 11.1 is a classified advertisement seeking to fill this position.

Qualifications

What does it take to be at the highest level of the merchandising career ladder? While it takes intelligence, perseverance, and high energy, the retail employer will expect the following educational background, experience, and personal characteristics as well.

- **Education:** A bachelor's degree in fashion merchandising, retailing, retail merchandising, business administration, or a related field is necessary. A master's degree in fashion merchandising or business administration may be required.

- **Experience:** A minimum of ten years of retail management, divisional merchandise management, or extensive buying experience in a full-line department store or specialty store chain is usually required for this key position. Experience in multi-location retail stores as a merchandiser or with multiple delivery systems (e.g., brick-and-mortar, Internet, and catalogue) and product development is preferred.

- **Personal characteristics:** Strong leadership, communication, and organizational skills are necessary. The ability to change priorities and work topics quickly is a needed personal quality. Being able to manage teams and relate to all levels of employees is important. Effective negotiation skills are critical for the successful GMM, as are being able to plan ahead and be an analytical problem solver.

The number of GMM positions is limited, as these are top leadership slots available in midsize and large retail operations. Some companies offer GMMs supplementary packages, such as bonuses or stock options, based on increases in the company's sales volume and gross margin.

Career Challenges

As the leader of the merchandising staff, the GMM must understand and oversee all merchandising personnel and all merchandise classifications. It is an important job to be able to move quickly between buyers and their respective departments and be up to date on each of their areas. As a leader, the GMM is challenged to keep all merchandisers on the same path in terms of merchandise selection, price ranges, fashion trends, and similar variables. The GMM needs to know when to push or pull back buyers who are not meeting sales-volume goals or buying into the fashion trend statements that the retailer will feature.

Divisional Merchandising Manager

Once you have mastered the buying side of the fashion world as a fashion merchandiser, you may be ready for advancement. Before a buyer becomes a GMM, the next step up the career ladder is to the divisional merchandising manager position. A **divisional merchandising manager (DMM)** works under the GMM and provides leadership for the buying staff of a division, or a related group of departments, such as menswear, women's wear, or home furnishings. DMMs coordinate teamwork among the buyers and delegate responsibilities to the buyers, assistant buyers, and planners. They collaborate with the buyers on future purchases, marketing and promotional efforts, merchandise expenditures, and inventory management. The main objective of the DMM is to keep profits up and losses down by maximizing sales and minimizing markdowns. They also study the fashion industry through shopping the competition, forecasting trends, attending markets, and working with buyers on the right fashion directions for the upcoming season. Box 11.2 is a classified advertisement seeking a DMM.

In general, DMMs oversee the buyers' merchandise selections for a particular department of the business. Specifically, their job responsibilities include the following:

- Developing merchandise strategies in support of the total company

- Managing, coaching, and developing the buying staff, to include associate and assistant buyers

Seeking a seasoned, creative, enthusiastic, and friendly individual to join our merchandising team as Divisional Merchandise Manager of Men's Sportswear. The Divisional Merchandise Manager of Men's Sportswear partners with the GMM in the development and implementation of merchandising strategies, new business initiatives, and key item strategies to drive top line sales, sales per square foot, and profit growth for the Men's Sportswear department. This position has profit and loss accountability and responsibility for the merchandising, inventory control, and private label development for this evolving Men's Sportswear business. This role will also focus on overall direction, market penetration, assortment, and vendor mix to meet the needs of the demanding customer base, as well as the development and management of private label within the department.

Our Benefits:

In addition to a dynamic and friendly work environment, where dedication and hard work are recognized and rewarded and work/family balance is valued, the company also offers the following benefits:

- Relocation assistance

- Generous incentive compensation plan

- Generous associate discount

- Paid holidays

- Paid vacation, sick, and personal days

- Medical/dental/vision plans

- Short/long-term disability plans

- 401(k) retirement plan

- Employee stock purchase plan

- Flexible spending account

- Life insurance

Requirements:

- Bachelor's degree in business, retail merchandising, or related field preferred

- Five to seven years of applicable corporate retail merchandising/buying expertise and leadership experience within the Men's Sportswear category

- Solid track record of success in growing and enhancing businesses within the Men's Sportswear category

- Experience working with various technologies including Oracle/Retek Retail Merchandising systems

- PC skills to include proficiency with Microsoft Office and Outlook e-mail applications

- Merchandising skills, negotiating skills, retail math skills, and project management skills

- Ability to research and analyze large amounts of data

- Results-oriented personality; willingness to follow through, make informed decisions, complete tasks, and problem-solve

- Demonstrated abilities in learning new skills, change/variety in work, and creativity

- Should display a strong fashion sense and understanding of quality/value relationships

- Travel requirements: some amount of travel is required

- Mentoring and fostering an environment that promotes the development of buyers and their businesses as a divisional buying team

- Setting the overall strategy and merchandise direction for the division

- Directing buyers to develop assortments that support the needs of the customer and the financial objectives of the merchandise division

- Ensuring that pricing, promotional strategies, and marketing support the financial objectives of the merchandise division

- Working with the planning organization to develop by-store assortment plans that support the overall plan for positioning key merchandise categories, selected trends, items, and vendors

- Working with the buyers to strengthen market relationships and knowledge of market trends

- Understanding competitors' strengths, weaknesses, and strategies

- Facilitating and promoting timely communication and cooperation between branch stores, merchandising functions, and resources

Qualifications

Are you looking for a leadership role in the buying division? What educational background, work experience, and personal characteristics combine to make the best candidate for this position? A list of the qualifications for a top-notch DMM follows.

- **Education:** A bachelor's degree in fashion merchandising, retailing, retail merchandising, or a related field is necessary. A minor or elective coursework in business administration and fashion design is a plus. A master's degree in apparel merchandising or business administration may be required.

- **Experience:** A minimum of 5 to 7 years of retail management or buying experience in full-line department stores, specialty store chains, or e-retailers is usually required for this key administrative position. Experience in merchandising for multi-location retail stores or in trend forecasting and product development is a plus. The successful DMM will advance to the position of GMM.

- **Personal characteristics:** Strong leadership and organizational skills, as well as the ability to adapt to quickly changing priorities, are needed personal qualities. Excellent communication skills, the ability to work well with all levels of management, and effective negotiation skills are critical characteristics of successful DMMs. They should be articulate and enthusiastic, and they must be analytical thinkers and effective problem solvers, particularly in mathematical applications.

Advancement into this career level is good with broad executive experience and the right credentials.

Career Challenges

The divisional merchandising manager faces many of the same challenges as the GMM. Leading a group of diverse buyers working with a wide range of merchandise classifications requires a great deal of multitasking and prioritizing. The DMM is often held accountable for the accuracy of the numbers the buyers submit, such as planned sales and inventories. This executive must specialize in a variety of areas—fashion, merchandising mathematics, vendor negotiations, and personnel management. All of these areas demand the time and attention of the DMM, who must decide how much time to focus on each and when.

Buyer or Fashion Merchandiser

Are you someone who enjoys the thrill of the shopping hunt? Do you enjoy trend forecasting and being involved in product development? Are attending markets and purchasing the newest trends to sell to customers enticing job tasks for you? Then you may want to pursue a career as a buyer/fashion merchandiser. **Buyers**, or *fashion merchandisers*, are typically responsible for all of the product purchases for a company or particular department of a company within a certain budget. Buyers monitor the fashion trends and determine which seasonal items their customers will buy. They search for the items (often traveling to do so) that best fit the seasonal theme and their customers' preferences (Box 11.3). They locate the right merchandise suppliers, and negotiate prices, shipping, and discounts. They sometimes work with other departments in the retail operation, such as advertising and visual merchandising, on promotions and product placement. The ultimate goal of a buyer is to recognize trends that fit with the target market in terms of taste and price, procure merchandise that reflects these trends, and translate them into a profitable business plan for the retailer. Buyers select and purchase products from designers, manufacturers, or wholesalers for retail sale to their customers. They use their fashion sense, knowledge of trends, and understanding of their target customers' wants to purchase desirable merchandise assortments at markets for their retail businesses (Figure 11.3). Due to the length of time it takes for a designer or manufacturer to fill orders, buyers often make their purchases three to six months in advance, or longer if they are high-fashion goods. Buyers must be effective at budgeting and planning their assortments so that a good selection of products is always available to the consumer. Buyers for larger retail operations usually specialize in a merchandise classification, such as men's tailored apparel or home tabletop fashions.

A fashion merchandiser may work for a specialty chain (e.g., Gap, The Limited, or Charming Charlie), a department store (e.g., Nordstrom's, Macy's, or Saks Fifth Avenue), or a privately owned store or boutique. A fashion merchandiser also does extensive research on the department's or store's customers, trying to predict what the customers will want to buy for the upcoming season. To get started, a buyer will develop a buying plan, usually six months to one year before the merchandise can be purchased by customers. The **buying plan**, or *six-month plan*, is a financial plan that takes into account past and projected sales, inventory, markups and markdowns by department, and profit, or **gross margin**. After developing the buying plan, the buyer will track and analyze market trends, calculate how much will be spent on new products, and then go to markets and meet with manufacturers to preview apparel that will be produced (Figure 11.4). Once the manufacturers' lines are reviewed, the buyer will place orders for merchandise to arrive in the future, from one month for reorders to as much as one year in advance for new merchandise.

Box 11.3 Buyer's Preparation for a Market Trip

What to Bring
Buyers should bring several copies of the following:

- Tax identification number for business

- Bank reference (letter from bank)

- Business cards

- Resale license/permit

- Appointment schedule

- Purchase order forms

To make filling out forms fast and easy, bring a rubber stamp or computer labels with the following information: business name; street and e-mail addresses; phone and fax; contact person; and tax identification number.

Preparing for Market
- Make travel arrangements well in advance. Ask about special buyer rates at partner hotels.

- Allow time for seminars, fashion shows, and comparison shopping.

- Review directory of exhibitors, product categories, maps, and floor plans to help you organize your schedule while at market. You can request a printed version of the directory or locate it online.

- Attend a new buyer orientation. During market orientation, you will learn the building design and layout, the showroom numbering system, the location of merchandise, how to use the market directory, and the locations of various buyer amenities, such as restaurants.

- You may want to save time by going directly from the airport to the mart. If you have any luggage with you, check it at the mart.

- Take time to walk the building and familiarize yourself with the product layout.

- Take advantage of free buyer lounges to network with buyers from other locations or to take a break.

Quick Tips for Covering Market
- Arrive prepared with open-to-buy figures by department. Have a buying plan, a general description of the types and quantities of merchandise to be purchased.

- Bring extra business cards to distribute to sales reps and retailers with whom you've networked.

- Make appointments with showrooms before the market begins.

- If possible, set aside at least one day for "just looking."

- Wear comfortable shoes for all-day walking and line viewing.

- Visit tried-and-true vendors first, allowing time to find new vendors and items. Be sure to shop the temporary floors to discover new trends and up-and-coming designers.

- Prepare a list of questions for each vendor you visit.

- Write orders as soon as possible to ensure on-time deliveries.

- Never pack uncompleted orders or line sheets in luggage you check with the airlines.

- If you are loaded down with line sheets, order forms or copies, samples, brochures, etc., send them home ahead of time via UPS or FedEx.

Figure 11.3
Barneys' buyers use their fashion sense, knowledge of trends, and understanding of their target customers' wants to purchase desirable merchandise assortments at markets.

Figure 11.4
After developing the buying plan, the buyer will go to markets and meet with manufacturers to preview apparel that will be produced.

Being a fashion merchandiser or buyer is like being a product developer, with a twist. Instead of reinventing the wheel every season, the buyer takes the retailer's bestsellers from the previous season or year and finds the item with slight changes. The buyer may locate an item that was a bestseller with an updated color or new styling detail. The result is a new item with a good sales history for the upcoming selling season. A fashion merchandiser also makes decisions on new, fashion-forward merchandise. The buyer always wants fresh, trendy looks to welcome customers into the department.

Job Responsibilities:

- Manage, update, and review open-to-buy

- Select/place seasonal market orders

- Project seasonal sales

- Review weekly sales reports, ensuring planned sales and inventory levels are achieved

- Place and confirm reorders as needed

- Manage return-to-vendors

- Review and follow up with deliveries

- Manage stock placement for new merchandise

- Update and manage purchase orders

- Place and confirm special orders as needed

- Manage inventory for store events

- Recap show and incentive results

- Make stock projections; review sales and net receipts

- Oversee stock balances

- Review sales results on advertising campaigns and catalogue styles

- Prepare and review fast/slow sellers report

- Prepare and review sell-through report

- Provide end of season (EOS) product analysis and final sales report

- Provide EOS final sale reports

Skills and Competencies:

- Ability to effectively manage merchandise coordinator

- Strategic agility

- Excellent organizational skills and drive for results

Job Requirements:

- Four to six years prior merchandising experience; luxury retail preferred

- Availability for frequent travel

- Strong knowledge of Microsoft Office programs (e.g., Excel, Access, and Word)

This career path, however, is not all about shopping. The fashion merchandiser is accountable for the bottom line. The company wants to know whether the merchandise selected for customers to buy has made a profit. Fashion merchandisers are responsible for the financials of their departments and the resulting profit or loss. It is a daily task for fashion merchandisers to track the sales of merchandise and decide whether items need to be reordered or put on sale. They also spend time talking with vendors and negotiating the best wholesale prices so that higher profits can be achieved. Since most fashion merchandisers have worked their way through the ranks, they also know how important it is to communicate with the department and store managers and solicit feedback about what customers are seeking, buying, and rejecting. A career as a fashion merchandiser is a very exciting and rewarding one for a high-energy person, as shown in Box 11.4, which features a classified advertisement for the shoe buyer position with a luxury retailer.

The most important task performed by the buyer is selecting merchandise for the retail operation. This responsibility encompasses determining which goods are needed, calculating the size of purchases and from which vendors the goods should be bought, recognizing when merchandise should be ordered for timely delivery, and negotiating the prices and terms of a sale (Box 11.5). From a planning perspective, the buyer projects sales and inventory levels by month for each department and, subsequently, determines the amount of funding to be spent on inventory. Another part of the planning process is determining merchandise assortments in terms of color, size, and style. The amount of money allocated for new merchandise purchases each month is referred to as **open-to-buy**. With open-to-buy as the lead factor, the buyer determines which lines will be carried in large quantities and which ones will be stocked in smaller quantities. Those manufacturers' lines featured as the greatest proportion of a retailer's inventory are called **key vendors**. Lines carried in smaller quantities are referred to as **secondary vendors**.

Buyers have a great number of responsibilities in addition to locating the vendors, selecting and purchasing the right amount of the right merchandise, and setting prices on the merchandise. They also assign floor space for items or lines, select specific merchandise for visual displays and advertisements, and manage or collaborate with personnel in various areas of the business. For example, a buyer may hold training seminars to educate sales staff on the newest trends and product lines. In multi-unit retail operations, the buyer advises store personnel on how many units of a product should be transferred to one branch store or another. With the advertising department, the buyer determines marketing plans and promotional calendars for each month. Collaborating with the visual merchandising department, the buyer develops visual presentation guidelines for the stores, to support seasonal strategies (Figure 11.5). For example, the buyer may meet with the director of visual merchandising to discuss color trends, specific manufacturers' lines, and key fashion items that should be featured in windows and interior displays to give the retail operation a strong, fashion-forward look and, ultimately, sell products.

Qualifications

Do you love to travel, enjoy searching for a specific item, and have proficient mathematical and analytical skills? You may consider the career path of buyer. What are the education and work experiences you will need to secure a position in this field? Which personal characteristics are significant to the success of a buyer? The answers to these questions are as follows.

- **Education:** A bachelor's degree in fashion merchandising, retailing, retail merchandising, or a related field is required. A minor or additional coursework in business administration and fashion design is very helpful.

- **Experience:** Two to five years of work in the apparel industry is required for a buyer, including retail or sales experience. Retail sales experience is very helpful because understanding customer buying behavior is a key part of being a successful buyer. The common step into a buyer position is from assistant buyer. To move up the career ladder, buyers gain experience buying for a variety of departments, usually moving from one department to another of higher sales volume.

- **Personal characteristics:** Successful buyers love fashion and have knowledge of fashion history and trends, as well as an understanding of the fashion industry as a whole. They have good analytical, mathematical, and computer skills (e.g., Microsoft Excel), particularly in budgeting, planning, and inventory management. Successful buyers are good negotiators, possess excellent communication and organizational skills, are detail oriented, and are able to deal well with deadlines and stress.

Figure 11.5
Collaborating with the visual merchandising department, the buyer develops visual presentation guidelines for the stores, to support seasonal strategies.

The outlook for career opportunities in buying is very good to excellent. The number of new buyer positions available is expected to remain stable, and existing positions will become available because of internal promotions or transitions. One can grow on the job by being promoted to the buyer's position in a larger department with greater sales volume.

Career Challenges

There are a good number of buyer positions available in the fashion industry; however, buyers excel by showing maintained profitability and growth within their departments and making good buying decisions for their particular target markets. Because the numbers tell the story, buyers are under pressure to reach or surpass sales-volume goals while maintaining the planned inventory levels—every single month. If a line does not sell, the buyer is expected to negotiate with the vendor for returns, exchanges, or a reduced price to cover the cost of markdowns. Items planned for advertising can be a source of stress if they are not delivered as planned. The buyer has a multitude of tasks to juggle, and all of them require high attention to detail and quick turnarounds.

Assistant Buyer

An **assistant buyer** works directly for the buyer of a department or group of related departments. Assistant buyers primarily work with the six-month plan, open-to-buy, and inventory, taking cues from buyers. In some companies, they will accompany buyers to markets. They often work hands-on with the merchandise assortment, transferring items from one retail location to another as needed, and placing special orders. In most companies, the assistant buyer is in training for a buying position in the future.

Qualifications

Following are the education and work experience requirements for assistant buyers, as well as necessary personal characteristics.

- **Education:** A bachelor's degree in fashion merchandising, retailing, retail merchandising, or a related field is usually required. Some companies will accept an associate's degree in these disciplines. Additional coursework in business administration and fashion design is very helpful.

- **Experience:** Two to three years of apparel industry experience, including retail or sales experience, is required. Experience in accounting and budgeting is extremely helpful. Some companies have an executive training program to prepare entry-level employees for a merchandising career, often beginning as an assistant buyer.

- **Personal characteristics:** Assistant buyers understand the fashion of today and yesterday—its history and current trends. To move up the career ladder, they must have both a sense of what is fashionable and of who the customer is. Additionally, they should have knowledge of retailing and sales and strong analytical, mathematical, and computer skills (e.g., Microsoft Excel software), as their responsibilities include extensive work in budgeting, planning, and inventory management. Assistant buyers who are self-directed and motivated will advance quickly. Effective communication and organizational skills, attention to detail, an eye for accuracy, and the ability to work well under pressure are significant attributes.

College graduates who begin at the assistant buyer level and have the right skills, personal qualities, and ambition have a good chance of becoming full-fledged buyers within three to five years.

Career Challenges

Many assistant buyers describe their job responsibilities as "doing what the buyer does not want to do, or does not have time to do." The key word in the job title is "assistant," as this person is employed to help the buyer accomplish all merchandising tasks. Some buyers believe it is a part of their responsibilities to educate assistant buyers on all it takes to become a buyer; others do not. Some buyers do not want to retrain a new assistant and, consequently, prefer to keep their assistant buyers in this position. It can be a challenge for the assistant buyer to learn all of the ropes of merchandising and earn the support of the buyer to move into a buying position, but it can be accomplished. Anticipating what needs to be done and doing it well and independently are keys to succeeding in this position.

Planner

In large companies, a **planner** works in collaboration with a buyer to develop sales forecasts, inventory plans, and spending budgets for merchandise to minimize markdowns and achieve the retailer's sales and profit objectives. Using past sales data and sales projections based on fashion trends, planners construct merchandise assortments for specific departments. The merchandise assortment plan can include sizes, colors, styles, price ranges, and classifications. For example, a planner in a junior sportswear department may construct a chart, referred to as a planning module, for top-to-bottom ratios. In this **planning module,** the planner will project how many blouses, T-shirts, and tank tops to purchase and how many pants, shorts, or skirts need to be purchased for a given season. Today's junior customer, for instance, buys two to four times as many tops as she does bottoms. The merchandise assortment needs to reflect this proportion to be profitable. Using the planning module, planners recommend product flow (e.g., tanks, tees, and long-sleeved shirts) by department and by month or season. They also project markdown dollar budgets by month or season, based on actual markdowns during prior seasons, and assist buyers in determining how much money will be available to spend on new merchandise by providing seasonal buying budgets and monthly open-to-buy dollars by department and by season.

In addition to planning at the start of a season, planners in multi-unit retail firms review sales and stock performance by retail location as it compares to plans. They also ensure that key vendor plans are in place and that there is adequate inventory for the sales of major lines. Throughout each season, the planner coordinates communication to and from stores with regard to merchandise performance and sales plans. A department manager in the retail store may, for example, contact a planner for additional types of items that have sold out in the store. The planner will transfer the preferred merchandise into this store from a branch store that has not sold the items as well. Box 11.6 is a classified advertisement for a planner.

In partnership with the buying staff, the planner's main goal is to accurately anticipate and control inventories at the retail locations to maximize sales, inventory, and profit. The

Company Description
High-end Intimate Apparel Boutique in Miami, Florida

Job Responsibilities
- Regularly manage, update, and review open-to-buy plan

- Prepare detailed daily, weekly, monthly, seasonal sales analysis based on history and current trends in order to strategically forecast future orders

- Prepare replenishment orders as needed

- Place and confirm special orders as needed

- Develop and place seasonally appropriate merchandise assortment, while paying special attention to merchandise classification structure

- Serve as a direct liaison between vendors and the company

Required Qualifications, Skills, and Knowledge
- University or college degree in fashion merchandising

- Three or more years of buying/planning experience in a small fashion company

- Excellent retail math skills

- Knowledge of Retail Pro software, Excel, and related computer programs

- Must be honest and accountable

- Must have strong analytical, financial, strategic, and planning skills

- Must be a team player who can work effectively in a fast-paced environment and possess ability to multitask

- Must be a go-getter, with a can-do attitude and a true excitement for business

- Must have a strong sense of style with a keen understanding and interest in fashion and trends

- Must have excellent communication skills

planner works to keep all store locations in stock of key items by directing the distribution of goods through reorders and transfers of merchandise. If you enjoy working with numbers, are accurate, and want to move into buying, the position of planner is a great place to begin.

Qualifications

A listing of the educational background, experience, and personal characteristics needed for the job of merchandise planner follows.

- **Education:** A bachelor's degree in fashion merchandising, retailing, accounting, finance, or a related field is a prerequisite. Some companies hire candidates who have completed a two-year associate's degree in one of these fields for the position of assistant planner.

- **Experience:** Gaining retail sales experience is an excellent way for the future planner to start. The person who understands the customer's desires as they pertain to sales and inventory is a step ahead of job candidates without this work experience.

- **Personal characteristics:** Planners must be detail oriented with strong analytical skills. They must be quick, accurate, and able to work with advanced spreadsheet applications. Effective interpersonal and communication skills are important in this position, as is the ability to work well with all levels of employees of the organization.

Some larger retail organizations offer the position of planning manager. A **planning manager** provides leadership, direction, and support at the merchandise-division level to plan, distribute, and monitor inventory appropriately within the company's various retail locations to maximize sales. The planning manager supervises planners and partners with the DMM in the financial planning process.

Career Challenges

The planner is a number cruncher, and this may be a challenging job for the fashion graduate entering the merchandising field. While being a planner is an excellent entry-level position for the future assistant buyer or buyer, it can be a tough tour of duty for those who are interested in working with the actual merchandise. The important thing to remember is that those numbers represent the merchandise, and there is much to be learned in the planner's position. Accuracy is a critical part of this job, as one decimal point off can equal thousands of the company's dollars.

Distribution Manager/Allocator

Have you ever thought about how merchandise gets to the retail floor for customers to purchase? A **distribution manager**, or *allocator*, is responsible for planning and managing merchandise deliveries received from vendors, as ordered by buyers, to the retail locations. In some companies, this position is referred to as *replenishment analyst*. The merchandise is held in a central distribution warehouse to be allotted to the right store, at the right time, and in the right quantities to meet customer demands and maximize sales for the retail stores. Figure 11.6 depicts an allocator assessing inventory of merchandise prior to distribution. Distribution managers oversee merchandise receipts from manufacturers, shipments to the retail stores from the distribution center, and shipments from one store to another via the distribution center. They arrange for the transportation of merchandise to the retail outlet locations and may work for catalog and Internet distribution centers where they are responsible for keeping items in stock in the warehouse. Their main job is to be certain that merchandise is available when a customer stops by a store, or orders an item over the phone, by mail, or via the Internet. Distribution managers have some of the responsibilities of buyers. They must study sales and inventory reports and then analyze the needs of each individual retail store to determine the correct quantities to distribute to the stores.

Qualifications

If you are detail oriented and organized, and enjoy working with merchandise and numbers (while not on a sales floor), this career path may be ideal for you, if you meet the following criteria:

- **Education:** A bachelor's degree in fashion merchandising, retailing, business administration, or a related field is usually required. Some firms hire employees with associate's degrees in these fields.

- **Experience:** One of the most important backgrounds for the distribution manager may be surprising. It is retail experience. Working on the sales floor, observing the flow of merchandise, and getting to know the customer provide a future distribution manager with a solid foundation for this career. An internship in a distribution department is an

Figure 11.6 An allocator assessing inventory of merchandise prior to distribution.

ideal door-opener. Merchandising experience, such as being an assistant buyer, is another way of going into distribution management.

- **Personal characteristics:** Good problem-solving skills, detail and deadline orientation, the ability to coordinate scheduling, and strong math skills are important personal characteristics for distribution managers. Effective communication skills are important as well.

Opportunities for distribution manager positions can be found throughout the industry with major retailers of all kinds.

Career Challenges

If merchandise is not on the selling floor, then it will not sell. A distribution manager, or allocator, is under pressure to push products out of the distribution warehouse to the correct retail store quickly and in the right amounts, after it is tagged correctly. During pre-holiday times, when there are huge amounts of merchandise receipts and many buyers calling to check on the distribution of their orders, this is particularly challenging. Speed, organization, and accuracy must go hand in hand in this career track.

Merchandising Trainee

One avenue college graduates often choose to move into a merchandising career track is through an executive training program. Many retailers, particularly larger ones, offer these programs, which help graduates work their way up to buying positions. For example, the executive training programs at Neiman Marcus and Bloomingdale's prepare participants for jobs as assistant buyers and, ultimately, buyers for the company (Figure 11.7).

A **merchandising executive training program,** or *merchant executive training program*, is designed for new hires, former interns, college recruits, or current employees who have shown skills in merchandising, to prepare them for their first assignments as assistant buyers. Through on-the-job and classroom training, trainees gain the necessary skills needed for analyzing financial data, planning assortment selections, and developing vendor relationships to achieve business goals. The executive training program is a structured development program of classes, guest speakers, and projects. The trainee must show active participation and successfully complete all of the training assignments within the time frame of the program, which can range from six weeks to twelve months.

Qualifications

What do you need to know to become a merchandising trainee?

- **Education:** A bachelor's degree in fashion merchandising, retail merchandising, retailing, business administration, or a related field is often required.

- **Experience:** A retail sales position and, possibly, an internship with a retail organization are work experiences that make a potential merchandising executive trainee appealing to a retailer. Many companies require trainee candidates to complete tests that reveal proficiency in the areas of mathematics, case study analysis, writing, and presentation skills.

- **Personal characteristics:** Merchandising trainees exhibit strong analytical abilities, effective computer skills, organizational skills, and excellent communication skills—written, oral, and visual. Effective time management, flexibility, and the ability to react

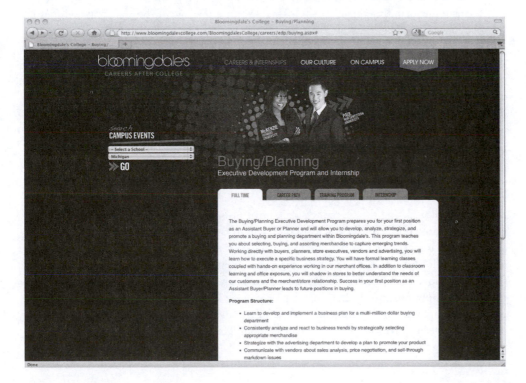

Figure 11.7 Executive training programs in merchandising prepare participants for jobs as assistant buyers and, ultimately, buyers for the company.

quickly and calmly to change are also important attributes. Successful merchandise trainees are self-motivated, self-directed, and are able to work effectively as part of a team.

Career Challenges

There are very few career disadvantages when starting as a merchandising trainee with a major company. You select the company of your choice, secure the trainee position, and the company prepares you for an entry-level executive position. These training programs are often referred to as a form of "graduate education without the price tag." While you do not earn college credits or pay tuition, you do receive additional education that can be applied directly to the company. Frequently, the tough part is making the cut or securing the position. Company recruiters often interview a thousand candidates for fewer than one hundred trainee openings. In some firms, trainees complete a general company training program and then are assigned to either the merchandising or management track, based on their performance in the program. For those trainees who have their hearts set on one track or the other, this may be a difficult assignment if it does not match their preference.

Summary

Merchandising encompasses all of the activities involved in the buying and selling of a retailer's products. The major responsibilities of merchandising personnel are to locate and purchase products, with the preferences of the consumer in mind, and then sell these products at a profit. Merchandising career opportunities include the following positions: general merchandising manager; divisional merchandising manager; buyer/fashion merchandiser; assistant buyer; planner; distribution manager or allocator; and merchandising trainee.

General merchandising managers (GMMs) lead and manage the buyers of all divisions in the retail operation. They are the key administrators responsible for setting the overall strategy and merchandise direction of their retail operations. The divisional merchandising manager (DMM) works under the GMM and provides leadership for the buying staff of a division or a related group of departments. Buyers, or fashion merchandisers, are typically responsible for all of the product purchases for a company or particular segment of the company within a certain budget. Buyers monitor fashion trends and determine which seasonal items their customers will purchase. They search for the items at trade marts that best fit the seasonal theme and their customers' preferences and negotiate prices, shipping, and discounts. They then monitor sales and inventory, adjusting the prices of merchandise and the amount of money they spend on new items accordingly. The assistant buyer works directly for the buyer of a department or group of related departments (e.g., handbags, jewelry, and scarves). The assistant buyer helps the buyer with updating the six-month plan, open-to-buy, and inventory. The planner works in collaboration with the buyer and assistant buyer to develop sales forecasts, inventory plans, and spending budgets for merchandise to achieve sales and profit objectives. The distribution manager, or allocator, is responsible for planning and managing the deliveries of goods received from the vendors, as ordered by the buyers, to retail locations. A merchandising, or merchant, executive training program is designed to prepare new hires, former interns, college recruits, or current employees who have shown skills in merchandising for their first assignment in the merchandising division of the retail operation. There are a number of career tracks in merchandising for the retailer, and they have several challenges in common—locating products that appeal to the customer, are priced right, arrive at the right place when needed, and sell!

Key Terms

assistant buyer
buyer
buying plan
distribution manager
divisional merchandising manager (DMM)
general merchandising manager (GMM)
gross margin
inventory
key vendor
merchandising
merchandising executive training program
open-to-buy
planner
planning manager
planning module
secondary vendor

Online Resources

nycfashioninfo.com/wholesale/buyer-resources.aspx
www.careersatsaks.com/CollegeRecruiting.aspx
www.neimanmarcuscareers.com/edp/index.shtml
www.wwd.com/beauty-industry-news/harnessing-the-might-of-macys-3587299
www.wwd.com/fashion-news/buyers-flock-to-fashion-weeks-in-india-3591844

Discussion Questions

1. Consider a major department store and construct a diagram separating the departments into divisions that would be headed by three separate divisional merchandise managers. Bracket together the departments that would be covered by an individual buyer.

2. Visit a menswear store or department in a large retail operation to study how the merchandise may be segmented into classifications. Develop the categories for the merchandise plan of a men's sportswear department, including merchandise classifications, styles, sizes, colors, and price ranges.

3. Assume that you are the buyer for a large home accessories department. How will you divide the responsibilities of the planner and the assistant buyer assigned to your department? Compare and contrast the duties of each.

Interview with a Fashion Buyer

"Career Insider: Fashion Buyers Play by the Numbers"
Source: http://kwhs.wharton.upenn.edu/2011/03/career-insider-fashion-buyers-play-by-the-numbers/

Reality TV fans who tuned in to *Project Runway* this season were blown away by the creativity of competing fashion designers, who crafted everything from garbage bag "leather" jackets to chic outfits made from tacky bridesmaid dresses.

As *Project Runway* host Heidi Klum regularly notes, in the world of fashion, "You're either in or you're out." Fashion is famously fickle. Designers live and die by that credo, and so, too, do fashion buyers.

Math...Who Knew?

Shows like *Project Runway* have helped launch fashion-related careers into the spotlight. More and more career-seekers are peeling back the racks of clothes on the retail floor to discover what is going on behind the fashion scenes. "When students come to us, they are very interested in buying," says Connie Passarella, director of career services at the Fashion Institute of Technology in New York City. "They think of selling on the retail side and buying because they love to buy stuff. It is a very popular business side of fashion." And also one of the most misunderstood, says Passarella. Clothes and trends are only half the equation. "Truth is, it's a highly analytical job where you are using math in every shape and form," she notes.

Adds Anne Voller, director of college recruiting for Macy's out of St. Louis, Missouri: "There's definitely a huge fashion element to it. But students need to understand that the job is far more financially and analytically driven than you realize. We always make the joke that it's not Rachel from *Friends*. Loving fashion and loving shopping doesn't necessarily mean that you'll love being a buyer."

Jenny Son was by no means a math maven when she decided to pursue a career in fashion buying just out of college, but she did spend lots of time in her closet. She graduated from The College of New Jersey with an English degree in 2000 and, on the advice of a friend, interviewed with and was accepted into a 10-week training program at Macy's Merchandising Group in New York City.

Son started as a product assistant in charge of product development for silver, gold, pearl, and jade jewelry. She worked with overseas vendors to come up with concepts, analyze the market, see what was selling and working already on the floor, and updating it every six months when the buyers came to town. Son was soon promoted to a Macy's Merchandising Group merchandising assistant in fashion watches and jewelry, then on to an assistant buyer in women's designer shoes for Macy's East, also in New York City, then to an associate buyer in women's athletic shoes and, ultimately, to a cosmetics buyer for Macy's East.

Experience Counts

Along the way, Son has learned to negotiate price and product with vendors (as in designers, manufacturers, and wholesalers), project and forecast the quantity of products needed for Macy's stores, and, in the end, how to become a fierce businesswoman. "My number one priority is to make sales, plan, and be profitable," says Son. "The first thing I do each day is to check sales to see how my products performed the day before. Then I check receipts from vendors because I can't make the sales if I don't have the goods coming into the stores. I spend the majority of my time on the phone with vendors and if there's a product that's working, trying to get more of it. It's about driving business and driving sales at store levels."

And that math? "The job does involve a lot of numbers," admits Son. "But once you learn to figure out a plan, it's not reinventing the wheel. As a buyer, it's really important that you immerse yourself in what you're buying. It's important to know what other people are doing so you can stay on top of the trends."

Positions as fashion buyers are in high demand, so experience counts. Son urges buyer wannabes

Interview with a Fashion Buyer (continued)

to spend some time working on the retail floor (think summer job at The Gap) so they understand "the full circle" of retail. Voller stresses that while department stores like Macy's love fashion retailing majors, they will recruit students from all majors, from marketing and English to psychology, which nurture strong critical-thinking skills. "People who have that entrepreneurial spirit love to work in our organization because you're given a huge amount of responsibility right off the bat," notes Voller, who adds that recruits start by earning in the low $40,000s and end wherever their ambition takes them. "We look for students who have juggled a lot of responsibility. So you've been involved in leadership roles, clubs, and organizations and you've done well at school. You have to be very flexible to be successful. You have to be able to react to trends or to the competitor who just marked down swimsuits a week ahead of what they've ever done before and you need to decide what to do with your line."

Ultimately, fashion buying is a high-speed game where you try to come out ahead in both sales and substance. "It's so exciting to see whether or not an assortment you've picked out has worked," says Son. "And if it doesn't, then how are you going to react to it?"

chapter 12

Management for the Retailer

If you are a person who loves the retail experience, you may envision yourself running a specialty store, an exclusive boutique, a designer outlet Web site, or a large department store. You may be someone who thrives in a retail environment and recognizes that a corporate office is not the best place for you. Do you crave the excitement of the hustle and bustle of holiday shopping, assisting customers with purchases, motivating sales associates, and rearranging the retail floor for new merchandise? If this describes you, a career in retail management may be your path to profit and pleasure.

Management refers to the organizing and controlling of the affairs of a business or a particular sector of a business. This chapter focuses on management careers in the retail sector of the fashion industry, such as store manager for an apparel firm, customer service manager of an Internet fashion operation, or assistant store manager of a home furnishings retail outlet. There are a number of career tracks in retail management, including the following positions: regional or district manager; operations manager; retail store manager; manager-in-training (MIT); assistant and associate store manager; department manager; customer service manager; and retail operation owner.

Regional or District Manager

Regional managers, also known as *district managers*, are responsible for directing the retail stores of a particular company that are located in a particular area of the country. They are responsible for the smooth running and profitability of the operation, as well as the success of employees in the retail outlets located within a specific geographical area, often referred to as a **region** or **territory**. They are the liaisons between the corporate office and the retail store. They collaborate with store managers within the region by making store visits, communicating through e-mail or telephone, and facilitating conferences, in person or electronically. During these meetings, store managers share their current sales, markdowns, and returns; point out items that are selling well; and identify programs or incentives for employees that are increasing sales or traffic flow into the store. If sales are declining, regional managers work with store managers to stimulate sales by implementing in-store promotions or working with the retail organization's headquarters on promotional campaigns. The four main goals of the regional store manager are to maximize sales at a profit, motivate store employees, share successes from one store with another, and communicate with the corporate office. Box 12.1 provides descriptions of Express's retail store management positions.

Qualifications

If regional store management is your career choice, there are a number of educational goals, work experiences, and personal characteristics that will help you get a foot in the door.

- **Education:** A bachelor's degree in fashion merchandising, fashion retailing, business administration, retailing, management, or a related field is a requirement.

- **Experience:** Retail sales and store management experience are mandatory work experiences. Buying, advertising, visual merchandising, human resource development, marketing, inventory control, and customer service knowledge are areas of experience that will move a regional manager candidate to the top of the list.

- **Personal characteristics:** Strong communication and leadership skills are required. The ability to speak effectively before groups of customers or employees of the organization is important. Business-accounting skills, human resources knowledge, and an understanding of retail laws are important. Organization, cognitive thinking, and time management are personal skills that support the regional manager's tasks in coordinating stores in a wide geographical area.

Career Challenges

Because they are responsible for a number of retail locations, regional managers may find their work to be stressful but very rewarding. Regional managers are responsible for not just one store but rather a significant number of retail units in the operation. This means they oversee all of the employees who take care of the customers shopping in each store. It takes a person with abundant fashion and retail knowledge, excellent communication skills, and business savvy to succeed in this career choice. Long hours and frequent travel are realities of the job.

At Express, with its more than 590 retail stores and continuous growth planned for the future, there are great opportunities in retail management to create a rewarding career. These opportunities include:

Regional Manager: A seasoned leader, the Regional Manger is a coach and mentor with 10-plus years retail management experience. Someone with demonstrated success leading strategic and operational initiatives that drive sales profitability, improve sales ROI (return-on-investment), drive field enthusiasm around new programs and optimize sales efficiencies across their districts. This is achieved through establishing creative yet focused direction setting and coaching and developmental activities of their teams. Responsibility also resides in building top talent sales succession strategies and influencing home office decisions.

District Manager: A capable, self-directed leader, the District Manager (DM) is someone who ensures consistent execution of the customer service and operational execution in all district stores. An Express DM is responsible for brand and relationship building, recruiting and developing a talented and diverse workforce that will drive profitable top-line sales growth. The District Manager is the linchpin to execution in the stores and market growth within the district.

Store Manager: The Store Manager is an outgoing and engaging leader who is creative, dynamic, and possesses an independent spirit for people and fashion. These leaders embody the day-to-day principles and values of the Express brand. They coach and develop store Associates to consistently provide a positive customer experience by offering products, information, and a shopping experience that will build brand loyalty. Express store managers handle the operational execution of the stores through positive service experiences that will drive profitable top-line sales growth. Enjoy the best of both worlds: operate like an independent store owner with the support of the sixth largest specialty retailer of women's and men's apparel in the United States.

Co-Manager: This professional will assist the Store Manager in managing the operational execution of the store to ensure positive customer experiences and to drive profitable top-line sales growth. Express is looking for someone to take ownership of a unique division of responsibility in areas such as driving the store's visual execution; attracting, hiring, training, and developing all levels of associates; or managing the backroom process and reducing shrinkage.

Source: http://www.expressfashion.jobs/express/retail-job-opportunities.asp

Operations Manager

In major companies, there is an operations manager who reports to the regional manager or, in a very large company, the national director of stores. The **operations manager** works with other administrators in developing marketing strategies and funding plans for merchandising and management personnel, and supervising stock replenishment and inventory controls. The primary objective of the operations manager is to develop and maintain effective programs to operate and control all of the retail units in the company or in a region, with a focus on superior customer service. For example, the operations manager may work to find a faster, less expensive way to move merchandise from the central distribution warehouse to store units scattered about a region.

Developing a company-wide training program to help all employees identify and report theft may be another activity of the operations manager. Another area of responsibility for

Figure 12.1 Security decisions include determining which equipment will be used to deter theft.

Figure 12.2 Seminars on how to spot a shoplifter, who to contact, and where to go for assistance when identifying a thief assist employees in safely combating theft.

the operations manager is security, as it affects the bottom line—profit. **Security** refers to safekeeping of merchandise in the store, as well as the safety of employees and customers. As inadequate lighting, unsafe equipment, and poorly placed fixtures can prove to be safety hazards for people in the store, this is an important focus for the operations manager. In large stores, a **security manager** is often employed to work directly for the operations manager, overseeing the safekeeping of merchandise in the retail operation and minimizing theft.

The security manager works with the operations manager to determine which equipment will be used to deter theft, such as tags (Figure 12.1), security cameras, or inconspicuous security, such as a security employee disguised as a shopper. Security not only protects the physical inventory from outside theft, but also monitors against internal theft or pilferage. **Physical inventory** refers to the actual merchandise within the retail operation, whether on the sales floor or in the warehouse. **Internal theft** refers to merchandise or money stolen by employees within the company. Employees may be required to have personal purchases processed through the cash terminal by a store manager, rather than on their own. They may be required to store their handbags and packages in lockers and use a clear bag on the sales floor. Additionally, security management covers loss training for employees of the company. Seminars on how to spot a shoplifter, who to contact, and where to go for assistance when identifying a thief assist employees in safely combating theft (Figure 12.2).

Qualifications

Here are the educational background, work experience, and personal characteristics needed to succeed in the position of operations manager.

- **Education:** A bachelor's degree in business administration, merchandising, operations management, retail management, retailing, or a related discipline is required. In some larger retail operations, a master's degree is required.

- **Experience:** A minimum of five years' experience in the operations field is required. Operations managers must have experience in training, motivating, and developing company employees and be knowledgeable about budgets and forecasts. Experience in Microsoft Excel and other programs used within the retail operation is necessary.

- **Personal characteristics:** Excellent organization, communication, and leadership skills are necessary for this position, as are superior analytical and technical skills. Good decision-making and problem-solving abilities are required. The operations manager is expected to travel extensively to store unit locations.

Career Challenges

The disadvantages for an operations manager are similar to those of the regional store manager. Being responsible for the operations and employee performance in a significant number of store units is a large workload. Extensive travel and long hours are common requirements for this position. The operations manager spends much time analyzing the costs associated with the stores and developing ways to save money and improve sales without compromising quality. This requires much attention to detail, strong analytical skills, and the ability to see the big picture that will result when changes are implemented.

Retail Store Manager

A **retail store manager** oversees the activities of a retail store's operation, from sales transactions and advertising to special events and the store's people—the customers, and employees including assistant managers, department managers, sales associates, and other staff. The retail manager is responsible for implementing the firm's retail marketing and sales plans, while ensuring the efficient operation of sales, operations, and administration within the assigned retail locations. Store managers' primary responsibilities are overseeing sales promotions, placing merchandise on the sales floor, monitoring sales and inventory levels, managing personnel, and generating profits. They oversee the inventory, ensuring that the store has the right quality, type, and amount of merchandise available. They also make sure supplies are reordered on time.

Depending on the store's size, the store manager may be involved in some manner with all of the store's departments, from displays and advertising to merchandising and human resources. Store managers may have hundreds of employees or just a few sales associates to lead. Either way, they set a tone for the store and share a vision of success and expectations about customer service, promotions, and store goals with all employees. They work with a wide variety of individuals, from executives in the corporate office to the customer who has a complaint. The main objectives of the store manager include ensuring that the sales targets are reached and profits increased; customer service issues and complaints are successfully handled; health, safety, and security regulations are implemented; and strong employees are recruited, interviewed, trained, supervised, motivated, and retained. Box 12.2 provides a detailed listing of the supervisory and administrative responsibilities that the store manager of a large retail operation may have.

Qualifications

Following are the educational goals, work experiences, and personal qualities that enhance one's opportunities to secure a store manager position.

Box 12.2 Listing of the Supervisory and Administrative Responsibilities of the Manager of a Large Store

Supervisory Tasks

- Oversees employees engaged in selling, cleaning, and rearranging merchandise; displaying; pricing; taking inventory; and maintaining operations records

- Ensures efficient staffing of employees through proper assignments of duties while respecting break periods, work hours, and vacations

- Implements compliance with human resource regulations by implementing established benefits and record-keeping procedures

- Trains, supervises, advises, and monitors store employees

- Encourages employee advancement if an employee's skills and the organizational structure allow it; may be called on for assistance in preparing or executing training sessions for employees on store policies, procedures, job duties, and customer service

- Plans and conducts regular sales meetings for staff to discuss latest sales techniques, new products, overall performance, and other topics the store manager believes will promote high team spirit and company pride

- Supervises department managers and sales associates, performs work of subordinates as needed, and assists in completing difficult sales

- Plans store layout of fixtures, merchandise, and displays with the regional manager, taking into account special and seasonal promotions as well as store safety and security measures

- Inspects merchandise to ensure it is correctly received, priced, and displayed

- Maintains all safety and security policies of the company, including locking and securing of the store at closing time, balancing receipts, and making cash deposits

- Communicates and upholds all company policies, rules, and regulations, while maintaining a productive and pleasant customer and employee environment; recognizes employees positively for achieving the same and initiates disciplinary action where needed

- Answers customers' complaints or inquiries and resolves customers' problems to restore and promote good public relations; makes decisions on returns, adjustments, refunds, customer checks, and customer service, as required

- Coordinates and supervises store housekeeping, maintenance, and repair

- Maintains physical inventory as required

- Assumes general responsibility for the inventory of the store falling at or below the company's shortage percent goal

Administrative Tasks

- Handles staff schedules, sales reports, inventory reports, and personnel reports

- Prepares each employee's appraisal reports and conducts evaluation meetings after input from regional manager and director of the Human Resources department

- Coordinates the store's sales promotion activities and campaigns, in coordination with regional manager and according to established budgets

- Keeps abreast of developments in the retail sales area by studying relevant Web sites, trade journals, sales and inventory analyses, and all merchandising and sales materials; initiates suggestions for improvement of the business

- Coordinates merchandise and advertisements, and maintains the store's offerings

- Maintains a current knowledge of management principles and has the willingness and ability to make difficult decisions under pressure

- **Education:** A bachelor's degree in fashion merchandising, fashion retailing, business administration, management, retailing, or a related discipline is a requirement.

- **Experience:** Several years of retail sales and management experience are needed. Additional work experience in buying, advertising, store planning and visual merchandising, human resources management, marketing, inventory control, and customer service areas are helpful in securing prime positions.

- **Personal characteristics:** Store managers must be good team leaders who are self-motivated and adaptable and quick thinkers who are prepared to make and be accountable for decisions. They must enjoy a fast-moving, high-pressure environment. On an interpersonal level, store managers must be able to communicate clearly with a variety of people at all levels and be committed to the needs of the customer. They must understand relevant retailing and human resources laws, business accounting, and computer programs in word processing, spreadsheet development, and inventory control.

Career Challenges

Store managers should anticipate a lengthy work schedule, which includes weekends, nights, and holidays. Working six days a week is common. The work includes office work, but managers are expected to spend much of their time on the sales floor. The store manager is head of the day-to-day business in the store with the support of and responsibility to higher management. This means that the store manager must respond to the requests of the regional manager. The store manager who aspires to become a regional manager, the next step up the career ladder, should anticipate relocating a number of times to gain experience in various stores within the company. Moving from one location to another with little advance notice can be a difficult process for some people.

Manager-in-Training

A **manager-in-training (MIT)** is just that: an employee who is being trained to move into a management position. A number of large retail organizations offer an MIT program through which prospective management employees are trained for assistant manager or store manager positions within the company (Figure 12.3). The main difference between an executive training program and an MIT program is that most companies train the MIT on the job in one of the branch store locations, rather than in a training facility at company headquarters.

Qualifications

Here are the qualifications often required for admittance into a manager-in-training program.

- **Education:** A bachelor's degree in fashion merchandising, fashion retailing, business administration, management, retailing, or a related field is usually required.

- **Experience:** One to three years' experience as an assistant manager or top sales associate with a large retail firm is often required for this position. A college graduate can apply directly for placement in an MIT program, or a company employee may decide to apply for admission into the program.

Figure 12.3
A number of large retail organizations offer an MIT program through which prospective management employees are trained for assistant manager or store manager positions within the company.

- **Personal characteristics:** Excellent interpersonal skills that support a team environment are required. Effective oral and written communication skills are needed to work with a wide range of employees. Strong planning and organizational skills with a sense of priority for deadlines and attention to detail are necessary for the successful MIT. Most important, the MIT is dedicated to high levels of customer service and sales productivity.

Career Challenges

As with the executive training program, one of the toughest parts of the MIT position is securing the job. As many as one hundred candidates inside and outside of the retail operation may apply for as few as ten positions. Of those selected for the MIT openings, only a few are promoted to the position of manager. The job is challenging in that it is "trial by fire," learning how to do the job well, while on the job. Long hours, which are often scheduled on weekends, holidays, and nights, are required for this job. The MIT is often on call and must be ready to go to work if the manager or another key employee is unavailable.

Assistant and Associate Store Manager

An **assistant store manager** helps the store manager in all of the daily responsibilities of operating a store successfully. The assistant manager takes direction from the store manager and works closely with all of the other departments in ensuring the store's mission and financial goals are met. In some companies, assistant store managers have specified responsibilities, such as scheduling employees, supervising sales floor moves, and monitoring sales and inventory levels. In other companies, they may support store managers in all store management duties. Figure 12.4 shows an assistant store manager assessing inventory plans for the store manager.

Some companies with large individual store units hire for a position that lies between the assistant store manager and the store manager. This position is called **associate store manager**.

Figure 12.4
The assistant store manager helps the store manager by planning strategies for employees to take the store inventory.

Qualifications

There are several prerequisites in education and experience for assistant or associate store managers, as follows:

- **Education:** A bachelor's degree in fashion merchandising, fashion retailing, business administration, management, retailing, or a related field is usually required.

- **Experience:** Retail sales experience, managerial experience, or in-house management training is usually required. Work experience in buying, advertising, human resources management, marketing, inventory control, and customer service make the job candidate more appealing to the employer.

- **Personal characteristics:** Effective interpersonal and communication skills are significant attributes for this position. Assistant store managers also must have knowledge of business accounting, personnel, and marketing. They are detail oriented, have strong organizational skills, and are flexible. They must be able to adapt to constantly changing work schedules.

  Box 12.3 is a classified advertisement for an assistant store manager.

Department Manager

A **department manager** oversees a specific area, or department, within a store. For example, a department manager may be responsible for men's clothing, junior sportswear, or women's accessories. Department managers coordinate the sales associates in their areas, assisting with employee hires, scheduling weekly work hours, handling employee and customer complaints, and monitoring the performance of employees. They schedule regular meetings with the store managers, assistant store managers, and other department managers. During these meetings, department managers report on weekly sales, discuss promotions, and talk about concerns or opportunities in their respective areas. They also stay in close contact with the buying office, as they relay employee and customer feedback on merchandise and advise buyers on reorders or possible promotions to help sell merchandise.

Department managers also maintain the sales floor by setting out new merchandise, adding signage for promotions, recording markdowns, and executing floor sets. Changing **floor sets** refers to moving fixtures and merchandise on the sales floor of the department to create a fresh look and to highlight new or undersold merchandise. Department managers work with sales associates in keeping the department neat and organized so that customers can easily find exactly what they are seeking.

Qualifications

What does it take to become a department manager? It is an excellent starting place for the college graduate. A list of qualifications follows.

- **Education:** A bachelor's degree in fashion merchandising, fashion retailing, an area of business administration, or a related degree is often required. Some companies accept an associate's degree in these disciplines.

- **Experience:** Successful retail sales experience is the top requirement for a department manager position. The sales associate who has gained experience in floor sets, personal shopping, exceptional customer service, and visual displays is well qualified for a promotion to department manager.

- **Personal characteristics:** The department manager is detail oriented, well organized, and an effective problem solver with good interpersonal skills. This position often demands a flexible work schedule, including weekends, nights, and holidays.

Career Challenges

The department manager often works long hours for fairly low pay. There are a number of people to whom the department manager reports, including the assistant or associate store manager, store manager, and buyer. Each may have a different perspective on how to run the department. The department manager is challenged with satisfying a number of bosses who may have dissimilar priorities.

Customer Service Manager

It is likely that you have heard the saying "The customer is always right," but is this really true? Most retailers have specific policies concerning merchandise returns and exchanges, out-of-stock advertised merchandise, and returned bank checks. With the Internet as an emerging retail channel, e-retailers need another set of policies concerning returns, shipping costs, payment, and security. All retailers want to keep their customers satisfied to establish a loyal customer base, yet policies often have to be implemented to assure a profitable bottom line. A **customer service manager** assists a customer with an issue or complaint and implements the retail operation's policies and procedures for returns, exchanges, out-of-stock merchandise, product warranties, and the like (Figure 12.5). It is the customer service manager's responsibility to maintain company policies, while assuring that customers feel their problems are being heard and taken care of in a professional and timely manner. The customer service manager often trains the sales staff to effectively assist customers with concerns and teaches them the people skills needed to calm irate customers and find win-win solutions for all involved.

Figure 12.5 A customer service manager assists clients and implements store policies.

Box 12.4 Responsibilities of the Customer Service Manager

- Customer product adjustments (e.g., returns, replacements, and exchanges)

- Deliveries of purchases

- Layaway availability

- Information on product care

- Technical advice

- Discounts

- After-sales service

- Replacement guarantees

- Personal shopping appointments

- Merchandise delivered on approval

- Credit service

- Alterations

- Special orders

- Training of retail personnel in customer service

Some business operations have a separate department organized under the customer service manager that has the sole function of servicing the customer. Larger companies separate the customer service responsibilities into several divisions, such as maintenance, credit, and adjustments. Finally, there are retail organizations that handle the customer service responsibilities informally through management or personnel who have direct contact with the customer.

Which types of services are coordinated by the customer service manager? Businesses offer varying types of services, often reflecting the price ranges of their products. For example, a high-fashion boutique carrying expensive designer garments will usually offer a wide range of customer services from alterations to home delivery. However, discount retail operations, such as Sam's Wholesale Club, provide minimal customer services in an effort to maintain retail prices that are below those of its competitors. At Sam's, for example, the customer is not provided with dressing-room facilities, packaging, or delivery. Types of services the customer service manager may be responsible for when working for a high-level service retail operation are listed in Box 12.4.

Qualifications

Are you an individual who remains calm in any situation? Are you an active listener? Do people find you to be an effective negotiator and a fair decision maker? If so, then the position of customer service manager may be the career option for you. The qualifications of a customer service manager include the following:

- **Education:** A bachelor's degree in fashion merchandising, fashion retailing, business administration, management, human resources, or a related field is a common requirement.

- **Experience:** Three to five years of experience in retail sales, preferably management, are required. Evidence of superior customer service through sales awards and customer recommendations is a plus.

- **Personal characteristics:** The effective customer service manager has exceptional interpersonal and communication skills and is trustworthy, personable, and outgoing. Being a capable negotiator and a good listener are also important skills. The customer service manager must have a thorough understanding of the company and its policies.

Career Challenges

The customer service manager works with all kinds of people. If you have ever stood in line waiting to return a purchase, you may have seen a few of the types. They can be demanding to the point of unreasonable and rude to the point of unbearable. Regardless of the customer's state of mind, the customer service manager has to remain calm and polite. The hours can be long, and the starting pay can be low.

Retail Operation Owner

Perhaps you dream of owning your own retail business, as many fashion students do. Maybe you love the fashion industry, and seek the challenge and freedom of working for yourself. The good news is that a great number of people open their own businesses each year. The bad news is that you must, as a store owner, do everything discussed in this chapter (and several others). The **retail operation owner** is financially responsible for the company and oversees all aspects of the retail business. There are three types of business ownership: sole proprietorship, partnership, and corporation. A business owned by an individual is referred to as a **sole proprietorship**. A **partnership** is owned by two or more people. In a **corporation**, stockholders own the company, which may be run by an individual or a group.

Before opening a business, the prospective owner or ownership group must develop a **business plan**, a document that details plans for the business concept and target market, location and space needs (i.e., facility or Web site), growth and exit strategies, sales and inventory, and financing needs. Whether the prospective business owner is purchasing an existing business or opening a new one, securing funding to own the business is often a critical first step. **Funders**, financing sources such as banks and the Small Business Administration, require a well-written business plan that justifies financing due to a good potential for profit, minimal risk, and a strong long-range plan. Many funders are now working with potential owners of Internet retailing businesses, a growth area of business in the fashion world.

Once the business loan is approved, the owner will often attend to the merchandise selection for the business by identifying the trends customers will want, and then buying, or overseeing the buying of the merchandise that fits the target market. The retail owner is responsible for developing a budget for seasonal purchases to make certain that the company's finances are not overextended. Once merchandise is received, the store owner and employees inventory, price, and tag the merchandise, and place it on the sales floor. An employee may be assigned the responsibility of creating and installing window and in-store displays (Figure 12.6). Straightening the inventory, cleaning the store, and restocking fixtures and shelves are all tasks the store owner handles personally or assigns to employees.

A store owner often locates, hires, trains, motivates, and evaluates all employees. In a small business, the owner is a one-person human resources department. Scheduling employees to meet the needs of fluctuating customer traffic and fit within the payroll budget is often a challenge for small business owners. In many small operations, the customer prefers to work with the store owner, valuing the personal attention and expertise. Rather than leaving it to employees,

Figure 12.6 The retail store owner often trains an employee to create and install window and in-store displays.

the business owner often functions as customer service manager, handling customer returns, exchanges, and complaints. The business owner is also responsible for making the technology decisions for the fashion retail operation. Box 12.5 provides an overview of technology and small store ownership.

In most cases, a store owner does everything, including taking the trash out! Being a store owner can be one of the most gratifying experiences, though it can be very stressful at times. Being solely responsible for all the expenses incurred by the business can be overwhelming, but reaping the benefits of individual freedom and profits outweighs the negatives.

Qualifications

Are you ready to take on an ultimate challenge? Consider the following list of educational backgrounds, work experience, and personal characteristics needed for successful business ownership.

- **Education:** A bachelor's degree in fashion merchandising, fashion retailing, business administration, marketing, retailing, entrepreneurship, or a related field is beneficial.

- **Experience:** Three to ten years of experience in the fashion industry, working in as many areas of a fashion business as possible, are critical to the future retail operation owner. An internship with an entrepreneur provides ideal on-the-job education.

- **Personal characteristics:** Successful business owners are calculated risk takers. They are well organized, financially savvy, respectful of money, flexible, responsible, and willing to ask for and accept help.

Career Challenges

Each month, the retail business owner faces the pressure of paying employees, vendors, the landlord, utility companies, and more. It can be a huge burden for some. As there is no way to estimate accurately how much profit the business will generate, it is a risky profession in which one must constantly search for ways to maintain or grow the business. The retail business owner is ultimately responsible for all facets of the business.

Summary

This chapter explored management career options in fashion retailing. It is difficult to envision how many people are required to get a single product from the retail sales floor into the customers' shopping bags. The administrative employees in the industry sector are referred to as retail management. Management is the organization and control of the affairs of a business or a particular sector of a business. There are a number of career tracks in retail management, including the following positions: regional or district manager, operations manager, retail store manager, manager-in-training, assistant and associate store managers, department manager, customer service manager, and retail operation owner.

The regional store manager is responsible for the smooth running and profit of the operation and the success of employees in the retail store outlets located within a specific geographical area. Working with the regional store manager, the operations manager analyzes sales and inventory performance and procedures for general business practices, such as customer service and store security. A store manager oversees all aspects of a retail store unit's operation, from advertising and special events to the customers and employees. A number of large retail organizations offer a manager-in-training program in which prospective management employees train for assistant manager or store manager positions within the company. The assistant store manager supports the store manager in all of the daily responsibilities of operating a store successfully. In some companies, there is a step between the assistant store manager and the store manager: the associate store manager. A department manager oversees a specific area, or department, within a store. The customer service manager assists consumers with their needs and concerns. Finally, retail operation owners are financially responsible for their own companies and oversee all aspects of the retail business. They are the managers of all managers.

Key Terms

assistant store manager
associate store manager
business plan
corporation
customer service manager
department manager
floor set
funder
internal theft
management
manager-in-training (MIT)

operations manager
partnership
physical inventory
region
regional manager
retail operation owner
retail store manager
security
security manager
sole proprietorship
territory

Online Resources

about.nordstrom.com/careers/your_path.asp
www.allretailjobs.com/
www.careersatsaks.com/AboutUs/MeetOurPeople.aspx
www.fashion.net/jobs/
www.forever21.com/careers/storejob.asp
www.macysjobs.com/opportunities/fieldassociates.aspx
www.stylecareers.com/

Discussion Questions

1. Using the Internet or interviewing a professional in a regional manager position, investigate the advantages and disadvantages of this career. Find out about the size of the regional manager's territory, the number of management personnel with whom the regional manager interacts, and the prospects for promotion in this field.

2. Investigate one of the job responsibilities of operations and security managers by exploring the types of security systems that are available to deter theft. Compare and contrast both technological devices and common-sense techniques, such as placing small, easily pocketed items at the cash counter.

3. Using the Internet or your college's career services department, locate four companies with MIT programs and compare them. What are the requirements to enter each of the programs? What is the length of each MIT program? How many participants are in each? What types of training and projects are included in the programs? Which types of positions can one expect after successfully completing MIT training?

4. Assume that you plan to open your own retail business in two years. First, conduct research to identify the type of fashion business that will have the best opportunity for success by identifying market voids and consumer shifts in the location where you would like to work. Next, develop a list of the work experiences that will prepare you for ownership of this retail operation. Finally, construct a chart of the general steps you will need to take to get ready for the business opening.

Interview with a Retail Store Manager

Buffalo Exchange Store Manager Spreads Passion for Fashion
By Maranda Gorr-Diaz, January 6, 2011
Source: http://www.chicagotalks.org/2011/01/06/buffalo-exchange-store-manager-spreads-passion-for-fashion/

Buffalo Exchange store manager Aimee Pallozzi says she has always had a passion for fashion. Ever since she was little, she and her siblings would dress up their dolls and put on pretend fashion shows for relatives, creating their own runway. "I always wanted to be a movie star. I would play dress-up," she said. Pallozzi, 28, has worked for Buffalo Exchange for six years at five different stores. Pallozzi has always had a creative outlook and started picking out clothes and dressing herself at a very young age. Pallozzi attended Fashion Careers College in California and majored in fashion design. Pallozzi's mother, Jill, said, "Aimee wanted to be an actress from a very young age and loved to watch glamorous black-and-white movies. She would play dress-up with her sister and brother, and would do fashion shows with their dolls and Barbies."

During a recent interview, Pallozzi was sporting a mixture of vintage and new, stylish clothing. She said Buffalo Exchange is unique among thrift stores. Because Buffalo Exchange buys clothes from the public instead of having people bring items in and donate them, the store does much of the hard work for shoppers. "We hand-select pieces that are in good condition, current in style, desirable items, for a wide range of people, and we price them accordingly on what we think they would sell for in the store," she explained.

"I have a huge vintage collection. I scour for vintage all the time, and I collect vintage housewares and things. If I go to a thrift store, that's what I'm looking for." She added that buying things secondhand and saving money is "really the way to go."

Since the beginning of the economic recession, Pallozzi has seen more customers at Buffalo Exchange. She added that people are being smarter about their money. She noted that more people are also selling their clothes to the store. "[People] are finding new avenues like us to earn some money," said Pallozzi.

According to Michelle Livingston, Buffalo Exchange's marketing director, annual revenue from all stores increased from $56.3 million in 2008 to $60.4 million in 2009.

Pallozzi also said she enjoys working for a company that shares her values. "I definitely feel passionate about doing our part as individuals to make the earth a better, cleaner, and more efficient place," she said. "I love that I work for a green company and that I share the same values." She added that stores like Buffalo Exchange help the environment by reducing textile waste that ends up in landfills.

UNIT

3

Unit 3 presents ancillary businesses, those that promote, educate, and provide support to the producers, retailers, and consumers of fashion goods. Whether working as freelancers or within a company, these ancillary businesspeople frequently offer services rather than tangible products. In Chapter 13, fashion styling and visuals as ancillary businesses are examined from the career path perspectives of the fashion show and event producer, modeling and talent agency director, fashion photographer, art photographer, stylist, and fashion costumer.

In Chapter 14, career opportunities in museums and educational institutions are explored. Opportunities in the fashion or costume division of a museum discussed in this chapter include museum director, museum curator, assistant curator, collections manager, museum archivist, museum conservator, and museum technician. Another career track within the fashion scholarship segment of the industry is the fashion educator, who may instruct or conduct research in historical costume or many other facets of the fashion industry from production to design and product development to merchandising and entrepreneurship.

Chapter 15 presents another segment of fashion ancillary businesses with its focus on environments—Web sites, exteriors, and interiors—all of which represent spaces in which fashion businesses may be located, whether in the production, retail, or ancillary levels of the industry. The primary career tracks discussed in Chapter 15 include Web site developer, architect, interior designer, visual merchandising professional, and mall manager.

An evolving part of the fashion industry and one that requires a specific type of environment is the beauty, spa, and wellness industry. Chapter 16 examines the careers of a product developer or technician working in research and development and those of the beauty merchandising and marketing professionals working in the manufacturing and retail levels of the industry. The career of a makeup artist can take this profession to the theater, a film set, a photo shoot, an individual's home, a salon, or a spa. Finally, the career of the director of a spa is explored, as growth is expected to continue in spa and aesthetics companies. As we have watched health services integrate medicine and natural homeopathic remedies, we will see beauty services integrated with health and fitness in the future. New careers will evolve for those interested in beauty, health, and longevity.

chapter 13

Fashion Styling and Visuals as Ancillary Businesses

If you have ever been to a fashion show, trunk show, or retailer's grand opening, you have seen the work of a fashion show and event producer, a modeling and talent agency director, a stylist, and, perhaps, a fashion photographer. The models, caterers, entertainers, and workers did not simply arrive and know just what to do and where to be on their own. Fashion show and event producers, modeling and talent agency directors, stylists, and fashion photographers work with a wide range of activities, from small boutique and megastore openings to product launches, celebrity appearances, and trade shows. There are lesser known activities that are arranged and implemented by event planners; these include trunk shows, sample sales, and conferences. No matter what type of event is being held, it takes a huge amount of advance planning and on-the-job management to make that event a success.

When you think about the tasks involved in planning an event, consider the steps you might go through as a member of a committee planning a wonderful party for an organization, such as your senior class. First, you would develop a theme for the party and construct a list of potential guests. Next, you would scout and secure a location for the party. This is the first cost to include in your overall budget, one that you keep in mind throughout the planning process. Later, you would work on securing talent for the event, such as a band or a performer. (In the case of a fashion show or event, talent includes models, designers, hairstylists and makeup artists, photographers, and videographers.) At this point, you may decide to recruit sponsors to help pay for the event and appeal to the party audience. Staging the party is the next job on the list, as you plan the layout of tables, chairs, and the stage, and determine lighting and music needs and placement. As a final step in the planning process, you may hire someone to manage the actual party, photograph the event, and, possibly, oversee the mailing of invitations and receipt of replies. The list of jobs is long, and these apply to just the pre-party tasks.

In this chapter, companies or persons producing **fashion visuals** (e.g., fashion shows, photographs, films, costumes, wardrobes, and advertisements) are examined as ancillary businesses. Some retail organizations, for example, hire a fashion show coordinator and a fashion photographer as employees. Many, however, go to outside companies or individuals to contract out these activities. The companies and people who provide these fashion styling services are what this chapter is all about. The following career paths, as independent businesses, are explored: fashion show and event producer, modeling and talent agency director, fashion photographer, art photographer, stylist, and fashion costumer.

Fashion Show and Event Producer

In Chapter 5, "Promotion," the job descriptions and responsibilities of the fashion events planner were discussed. These functions can be conducted by an auxiliary firm or by freelance personnel. A retailer, manufacturer, designer, or organization may contract an independent firm, the fashion show and event planning company, to do all or part of this work for a fee. In general, the **fashion show and event producer** manages fashion shows and special events for its clients. The company works with each client to determine the type of event, intended purpose, designated audience, and the budget. The company may be contracted to handle part or all of the advertising and public relations, which includes contacting the media and writing press kits, biographies, and letters. Fashion show and event producers are reaping press by supplementing, or even replacing, the traditional fashion show or special event with technology. Digital mapping, holograms, and video projection are launching the technology component of fashion productions. What is next? Only the imaginations of current and future fashion creators can tell. Box 13.1 and Figure 13.1 present illustrations of innovative technology incorporated into fashion shows, an exhibit, and a designer's anniversary celebration.

In addition, the fashion show and event firm may guide the selection process for products and models. For example, a jury of selection may be configured to review fashion products for acceptance into a show. For the apparel industry, the planner may also recruit and select models, fit them in garments, and then choreograph and rehearse the presentation (Figure 13.2). Company employees are often responsible not only for the site selection but also for the design and installation of staging, dressing rooms, seating, lighting, and music. Preparing and handling a reception following the show may be part of the fashion event company's contract as well.

Many fashion show and event companies do not solely produce fashion shows for their clients. A number of them design, organize, and coordinate other types of events, such as conventions, conferences, corporate meetings, and exhibitions for corporations and organizations. Fashion show and event producers may be responsible for every aspect of these functions, from marketing, catering, preparing, signage, and displays to locating audiovisual

New technology is providing fashion innovators with fresh formats to create fashion shows and special events. Fashion designers and the fashion show production companies they secure are changing the way they present their works to the audience and adding technological twists and turns to the traditional runway walk. One of the first fashion designers to introduce innovative technology in his collection presentation was Alexander McQueen. Over a decade ago, McQueen placed a model on a rotating disk on the stage with a robot stationed at each side. As the music began to crescendo, it appeared that the robots were dancing akimbo to the model. That is, until their antennae raised and began spraying paint on her white dress. The results were a dramatic performance and an airbrushed one-of-a-kind garment created by robots interacting with the model. In 2006, McQueen amazed his audience at the debut of his fall/winter collection by using a holographic projection of the supermodel Kate Moss, wrapped in a flowing white gown and floating over, above, and off the stage as if she were an apparition.

More recently, Hussein Chalayan presented his autumn/winter 2011/12 collection using a single model and video projection. His interest in digital projection continued when, in July 2011, Chalayan's work was exhibited in Paris at the Musée des Arts Décoratifs. At the entrance of "Hussein Chalayan: Fashion Narratives," the mouth of a sculpted figure opened in precise time with that of the Turkish performer Sertab Erener, singing a song of love and loss on a giant screen. Another opening vision was a decomposing dress, created by the designer for his fashion college graduation collection in 1993.

Figure 13.1 Innovative technology can be incorporated into fashion shows, such as this lighting used to create a chessboard of models for Alexander McQueen.

While many exhibits are composed of fashion behind glass, this one was rich in visual innovation. The 1998 airplane dress made of fiberglass and resin slowly opened its wings. An astonishing film featured a woman's hair changing in cut, with the wig and its strange technological connections also on view. While most of the visuals felt light and airy at first, further observation revealed the heavy symbolic meaning. For example, there was the visual row of dresses that slowly and subtly changed from solid black to patterned, and the film from one of Chalayan's shows in which a row of veiled women was repeated until they were nude with only the shoulder-length chadors remaining. Never has multimedia been used so effectively to convey both emotion and the in-depth stories behind the clothes—through films mostly produced by the designer himself, the rotating figure in a high-tech glass observation box, and Chalayan's sketches that track the journey inside his head as he creates his designs. Color, mood, and movement are created through technology to raise the fashion design exhibition to a new level of art.

Fashion shows are not the only venue finding new paths through technology. The special event is yet another area in which augmented reality, motion tracking, and interactive feedback with the audience are being used. In New York, Bond Street was closed for a groundbreaking digital presentation to celebrate the tenth anniversary of ralphlauren. com, Ralph Lauren's new online flagship store, which originally launched ten years ago as polo. com. Referred to as Ralph Lauren's Projection Party,

the Bond Street store exterior was transformed through four-dimensional digital mapping. Ribbons of light, a catwalk show, polo horses, belts, ties, and Ralph Lauren himself came to life on the exterior walls of the shop. The façade of the store seemed to fall apart before being reconstructed again in the digital projection, as models, fragrance bottles, polo ponies, and a waving Ralph Lauren appeared in a window. The mesmerizing projection showed the innovative way that brick-and-mortar retailers could use their buildings as canvases for advertising campaigns. David Lauren, Ralph's son, was the mastermind behind the project. Experts who created the special effects seen in the Harry Potter films were also consulted for the eight-minute projections that were inspired by digital mapping technology featured on buildings in Amsterdam.

Sources:

McQueen's Robot Painting Fashion Show: www.youtube.com/watch?v=reK0A1XIjKA

McQueen's Kate Moss Hologram Fashion Show: www.youtube.com/watch?v=p1mcmgJe3Ks

Hussein Chalayan's Fashion Show: http://www. youtube.com/watch?v=CCtWLfCq0TM&feature=play er_embedded

Hussein Chalayan's Exhibit: http://www.nytimes.com/2011/07/05/fashion/hussein-chalayan-on-exhibit-in-paris.html

Ralph Lauren's Projection Party: http://www.vogue. co.uk/video?category=exclusives&id=9977

equipment, printing sources, and security. They may also be contracted to coordinate participants' registration, accommodations, and travel. Most significantly, they are often responsible for the financial side of events by working with clients to establish realistic budgets and then monitoring expenses and income for the ventures.

What types of activities are assigned to a fashion show and event firm? While conferences and conventions, trade shows, and company training seminars are common events for the manufacturing and retail sectors of the fashion industry, the fashion show and event firm may also be contracted to coordinate company social gatherings and meetings, organize charity fund-raisers, and direct the grand openings of new retail locations or the launches of new product lines. An area of growth in event planning is the wedding planning field. Today, engaged couples are spending thousands of dollars to hire someone to plan, implement, and manage the wedding event, from the engagement party to the honeymoon, as depicted in Figure 13.3.

What are the typical tasks for a fashion show and event producer? In many ways, event management is similar to advertising and marketing. The fashion show and event producer views the event as a product or brand and then develops and promotes it in creative ways. The ultimate goal is to ensure that the attendees (the consumers) have a positive experience that leaves them feeling good about purchasing the product and supporting its sponsors, whether

Figure 13.2 The fashion event planner may be required to recruit and select models, fit them in garments, and then choreograph and rehearse the presentation.

Figure 13.3 An area of growth in event planning is the wedding planning field.

the sponsor is a business, a charity, or a club. Organization is critical in the planning process, especially when dealing with the management and coordination of services and supplies. Every physical detail needs to be considered, from the layout and design of the venue to lighting, sound, communications, videography, and other technical concerns. Catering services must be organized, along with less glamorous concerns such as security, parking, and restroom facilities. Promotion, public relations, and advertising must also be planned and executed. Last but not least, the performers, speakers, or participants need to be located, terms negotiated, and plans confirmed.

The fashion show and event producer must anticipate the costs of all of these aspects in advance, continually checking that the budget balances. Finally, the management of the event is an organizational challenge in itself. The degree of the event's success is often a result of the level of planning and organization. Following the conclusion of the event, the fashion show and event producer is responsible for formally thanking participants, ensuring that all income and expenses are reconciled, and evaluating the success of the event, noting corrections of errors to implement in the next event.

Qualifications

Is a career in fashion show and event producing for you? If so, you may want to work toward achieving the following educational goals, work experiences, and personal characteristics:

- **Education:** Top event planners typically have bachelor's degrees in fashion merchandising, business administration, marketing, event management, tourism or hospitality administration, or a similar field.

- **Experience:** Knowledge of marketing and press relations is invaluable. Work experience as an assistant or an intern in fashion show production or event planning is critical.

- **Personal characteristics:** An excellent understanding of fashion marketing, a great amount of energy and flexibility, and a high level of organizational and logistical skills are required for successful fashion show and event producers. Their presentation and communication skills should be excellent. Fashion show and event producers need the skills to motivate other people, along with creative abilities to solve problems and make things happen. If you aspire to become a fashion show and event producer, be prepared to put in extra hours to ensure that the job gets done within its budget and on time. This work requires perfection, so the event planner must pay attention to every detail and be capable of handling last-minute disasters that may happen despite superb planning.

The event planning industry continues to grow rapidly, particularly in the areas of weddings, international conferences, and hospitality. Marketing and public relations are becoming even more important facets of the event planning business.

Career Challenges

The fashion show and event planner works in a high-stress environment. Lack of attention to a detail or two, a narrowly missed deadline, or an unexpected emergency can literally annihilate a major fashion show, trade show, or charity ball. If, for example, an event planner remembered everything but forgot to confirm catering arrangements, there may not be food and drinks at a charity ball. Another pressure for fashion show and event companies or freelancers comes with generating regular business events with repeat clientele to assure consistent income.

Modeling and Talent Agency Director

Most models are recruited by modeling scouts or modeling and talent agency directors who travel around the world in a tireless search for fresh faces. Models are often discovered in shopping malls, schools, clubs, concerts, or other obvious places where young people hang out. Some agencies also locate models through photographs sent by "model hopefuls"; another way is through an agency's open casting calls. Some prestigious agencies do not charge up-front fees to join the agency; rather, these agencies are profitable by taking a percentage of the models' earnings. Often, fees for administration and training are deducted after the model has found paid assignments. Training can consist of full- or part-time courses that last for a few days to a few months. Topics for courses may include diet, health, image, grooming, runway turns and movements, photographic modeling techniques, and professional conduct with clients. Individual guidance on such areas as skin care, hairstyling, makeup, and overall appearance may be provided when the model first joins the agency. The **modeling and talent agency director** is ultimately responsible for locating and contracting new models, training them, and, later, securing modeling jobs for them.

Modeling agency directors are often very involved with their models at the start of their careers. They will often find newly signed models an apartment and help them get settled into their new lives. Many modeling and talent agency directors have found that the beginning of a modeling career is a very difficult time for a young person. A great number of models are young, far away from home, and often without many modeling jobs at first. The agency director tries to support them through difficult times while teaching them to be safe and disciplined, show up to meetings on time, and treat modeling as a real job.

Modeling agencies hire for a variety of modeling positions. **Fit models** are used as live models to test how garments fit and for designers to drape, cut, and pin fabric and garments. Most companies rely on fit models, also referred to as *fashion house models*, to give them feedback on how a garment fits and feels, as well as where it needs adjustments. They may also model the finished garments for retail buyers in the company showroom and, in the case of couture, for individual customers. Box 13.2 provides information on the work and requirements of fit models. **Show models**, or *runway models*, present merchandise in fashion shows, while **photographic models**, also known as *print models*, are those hired for photographs to be used in promotional and selling materials, such as catalogues, brochures, or magazine advertisements. The modeling agency takes bookings from clients who need models to work at fashion exhibitions, trade markets, product launches, and so on.

What is the "talent" part of the modeling and talent agency director's job? In addition to locating and booking models, the modeling and talent agency director also finds and hires talent for film and media companies. For example, a movie producer from Los Angeles may choose Seattle as the location for filming. The casting director for the film may contact a modeling and talent agency to locate actors, extras, costumers, or hair and makeup professionals in the Seattle area. The modeling and talent agency director may also commission entertainment for special events, such as conferences, galas, benefits, parties, management and sales meetings, weddings, designer appearances, book signings, and so on.

Box 13.2 The Fit Model

Fashion Week in New York City has officially ended, and the amazing looks on the runway models will eventually trickle their way onto the sales floors and Web sites of retailers around the country. How does a runway-model size 0 translate into a "real-person" size 12? It is the fit model of the fashion world who helps makes sure the new designs can actually be worn by the rest of us. Fit models are the behind-the-scene fashion lifesavers for most of the consumer world—who haven't worn a size 0 since birth.

There are few experiences more satisfying for a woman than finally finding "the one"—that one pair of jeans that actually fits like a glove and flatters her body. The perfect pair gently hugs but isn't too snug, isn't too short in the stride, and has room in the thighs. The cut and fabric have enough give for walking or climbing stairs without the circulation being cut off in her legs. She can comfortably sit down without the back waistline opening into an embarrassing (ahem) gap. Who does she thank for this masterpiece of perfect clothing? The department store buyer? The manufacturer? The designer? The person to thank is a fit model. Fit models are rarely seen outside of the design studio, but their presence is felt by anyone who doesn't wear a size 0 (and there are a lot of us). A fit model helps make the customer happy and, as such, can make or break a manufacturer's line.

Expert fit models recognize the problems in a garment before they happen, prior to production. They know how a sleeve should fit, where the buttons should be located, how the stitching should be, what the fabric should feel like—qualities that sell a garment. It is the fit model's job to try on each piece to show the designer and the technical designer how it moves on a real person, instead of a mannequin. They discuss fit, comfort, and how the garment moves with the body. Can the fit model comfortably hug a friend in the sample garment without the shoulders pulling? Can he or she reach for a box on a shelf without ripping an arm hole? Do the buttons need to be moved so the blouse does not gap at the bustline? All of these questions and more must be answered before a garment goes into production. The manufacturer's bottom line depends on it. Poor-fitting clothes can cost a small retailer hundreds of dollars and a national chain tens of thousands of dollars. What business wants that? What buyer would purchase from this manufacturer again?

Each manufacturer dictates sizing standards for fit models; however, in general, sizes for female fit models are: junior (size 5), misses' (size 8), contemporary (size 8), plus (usually around a size 18), and petite (size 8). Manufacturers often prefer fit models who wear sizes in the middle of their lines, such as a size 8 for a line that runs from a 0 to a 14. Unfortunately for the consumer, not all companies use the same fit models, or even fit models with the same measurements—resulting in size variations among manufacturers. The following classified advertisements for fit models were posted on the same day by fashion manufacturers.

- "Fit model needed with these exact measurements: 33", 26", 36". Must be 5'6" to 5'8" tall and have a flexible schedule."

- "Wanted: Size 8 fit model. Applicants must be at least 5'8". Measurements: bust-36", waist-29", hip-35", lower hip-39"."

- "A high-end apparel company is seeking female fit models to work out of its corporate offices. Individuals must be open to flexible work hours. Only qualified candidates will be invited to the casting. Measurement requirements: height: 5'9" to 5'10", dress and pant size: 2. Our target size 2 measurements are: bust: 34B (measure fullest part using soft tape measure that is placed straight across the front of body at bust and dips slightly in the back), waist: 26" (measure at the narrowest part of the waist), hip: 32–34" (measure widest part)."

This isn't your average woman.

According to the most recent (2009) data from the Centers for Disease Control and Prevention (http://www.cdc.gov/nchs/fastats/bodymeas.htm), the average American woman is about 5 feet and 3 inches tall, and weighs 165 pounds, usually a size 12 or 14. For size 12 and above, sizing is a whole

Box 13.2 The Fit Model (continued)

different ball game. Sometimes, manufacturers have an existing style that sold well in small sizes that they want to produce as size 12 and above. The style that sold well in small sizes, however, doesn't always accommodate or flatter a larger size (e.g., strapless, one-shoulder, or inset waistline styles). While working with the fit model, the designer may add wide shoulder straps (to make it more bra friendly), raise the neckline (to assure appropriate décolleté), and remove an inset waistline (to add comfort and a flattering shape). Throughout the restyling sessions, the fit model is not there to change the designer's thought process, but to help and guide.

At www.simplyhired.com, the average salary for a fashion fit model job in New York, New York, is $52,000; in San Diego, California, it is $49,000. Fit models must know the slope of their shoulders, the placement of their waists, and every possible measurement. Male fit models should be aware of chest, arm, shoulder, waist, inseam, and thigh measurements. A fit model must maintain his or her measurements within a half inch to an inch or risk losing a job. Fit modeling is one of the few areas in the modeling world that allows for a long career if the fit models maintain their sizes and shapes.

One of the large retailers relying heavily on a team of fit models to size its apparel is New York & Company. It conducted a fit model study on backsides, for example, and revealed that there are several different types of bottoms on women: curvy, modified curvy, and rectangular. The company determined that it would be remiss not to fit those three distinct derriere categories, because they clearly exist in the customer base. A New York & Company fitting can include up to 50 people discussing how a garment fits the fit model. Once the sample garment has been fitted and approved, the specs for all sizes are determined, and the information is sent to a factory overseas. The garments are produced and shipped back to the United States, then to the stores. Welcome, Perfect Pair of Jeans, and thank you, Fit Model.

(Adapted from http://culture.wnyc.org/articles/features/2011/feb/18/behind-stage-fashion-week-fit-models/)

Qualifications

What are the educational, experiential, and personal characteristics of a successful modeling and talent agency director? The list is as follows.

- **Education:** A bachelor's degree in fashion merchandising, marketing, business administration, visual arts, or a related field is a common requirement.

- **Experience:** A number of modeling and talent agency directors once worked in the field, either as models or actors. Others gained work experience through employment with this type of company. Employment with a retailer in the fashion coordinator's office will provide excellent opportunities to work with print and runway events. An internship with a modeling and talent agency is an excellent way to determine whether or not this business is for you and get your foot in the door.

- **Personal characteristics:** Modeling and talent agency directors are constantly observing those around them, networking with industry professionals, and building relationships. The successful director is truly a "people person." Business skills are critical, as this person often owns the company and must hire the right people to maintain a positive reputation and encourage repeat business.

Career Challenges

The modeling and talent agency is only as lucrative as the people employed by the firm. If the modeling agency and talent director discovers and hires a new model who becomes a supermodel, the director benefits financially from all of the model's jobs. Training, guiding, and managing new and often young talent can be challenging, as is maintaining a positive reputation in a field not always viewed as having high integrity.

Fashion Photographer

Thanks to our fashion-conscious society and the Internet, a fashion photographer can live just about anywhere. Fashion photographers used to locate in Paris, Milan, New York, or Los Angeles to earn a good living. Today, with the help of technology, this career dream is a possibility in almost any location. Successful fashion photographers are more than people who take good pictures. They can make products and their models look their best artistically. To succeed, a fashion photographer must possess the technical and artistic skills to ensure a professional, eye-catching, and distinctive photograph. Photographers work to develop an individual style of photography to differentiate themselves from their competition.

Fashion photography can be a highly creative and well-paid career; however, it is a career path with limited opportunities and a focus on freelance work. A **fashion photographer** is in the business of taking pictures of models wearing the latest apparel, accessories, hairstyles, and makeup, or highlighting the newest home furnishings and other fashion products, primarily for commercial use. The photographs are used in a variety of media, including advertisements, catalogs, billboards, television, Web sites, and art venues. Often working to meet a client's requests, they control lighting, tone, and perspective in their work, using a range of photographic equipment, accessories, and imaging software. Photographers must have a technical understanding of the medium as well as an artistic vision. Key tasks of the fashion photographer include choosing and preparing locations; setting up lighting; selecting the appropriate cameras, lenses, film, and accessories; composing shots; positioning subjects; and instructing assistants. After shooting, they may process and print images or view and manipulate digital images using software such as Adobe Photoshop. Some fashion photographers choose exclusive employment with a retailer, a publication (e.g., a magazine or a newspaper), a designer, an advertising company, a manufacturer, or a direct-mail company. Others may choose to freelance, with or without an agent, or open their own studios. These independent photographers are the ones who make up the ancillary segment of the fashion industry. A majority of successful independent photographers develop positive reputations by accumulating considerable work experience in mail-order, editorial, or advertising work. Some photographers enter the field by submitting unsolicited photographs to magazines. There are many avenues for a fashion photographer to break into this business: freelance without an agent, freelance with an agent, or through one's own studio.

Photographers usually specialize in one of the following six areas: general practice, advertising or editorial, fashion, press, corporate, and technical. General practice, or social photography refers to photographic services for local communities or businesses, with the majority of work in wedding and family photography. **Advertising photography,** or *editorial photography*, expresses a product's personality or illustrates a magazine story. It is usually

Figure 13.4
An illustration of technical photography in the textile sector of the fashion industry.

classified as still life, food, transportation, portraiture, or landscape photography. Fashion photographers work with models and art directors in the apparel, accessories, or home products industries. They are often commissioned by art directors of catalogues and magazines. **Press photography**, also known as *photojournalism,* focuses on images directly related to news stories, both events and personalities. Corporate, also referred to as industrial or commercial, photographers produce images for promotional materials or annual reports. The **technical photographer** produces photographs for reports or research papers, such as textile durability analyses. Figure 13.4 is an example of technical photography.

In all areas of specialization in photography, the successful photographer has a number of work objectives.

- Maintaining a technical knowledge of cameras and related rapidly changing technologies, as photographers increasingly need to know how to use computer software programs and applications that allow them to prepare and edit images

- Developing an artistic understanding of light, distance, and perspective

- Cultivating a keen eye for aesthetic detail and inventive ways to communicate moods and ideas

- Building strong interpersonal skills to work with models and be sensitive to their moods so that they are comfortable in front of the camera

- Understanding studio lighting to bring out the best in skin tones and textures and colors of different fabrics

- Working well with natural light (or a lack of) for on-location shoots

- Establishing good relationships with stylists, art directors, modeling agents, and fashion editors

- Identifying and securing future assignments and clients

- Understanding the roles and responsibilities of an entrepreneur

Professional photographers often employ assistants to help the business run smoothly. **Assistant photographers** may deal with clients and suppliers; organize estimates, invoices, and payments; arrange props and assist with lighting; communicate with photographic labs and stylists; work with the photographer on shoots; and maintain the photographer's Web site and portfolio.

What are the benefits of a career in fashion photography? The attractions of fashion photography are obvious: exotic locations, plenty of foreign travel, and personal publicity in fashion journals and other magazines. There is also the chance to work within the world of fashion and design and associate with the glamorous people who live there.

Qualifications

What do you need to know and do to secure a position in this field? Following are the qualifications required of a fashion photographer.

- **Education:** A bachelor's degree in photography or visual arts and a strong portfolio are usually essential. Freelance photographers need continuing education in technical proficiency, whether gained through a degree program, vocational training, or extensive work experience.

- **Experience:** Because entry-level positions for a fashion photography firm are rare, gaining a position as a photographer's studio assistant is a common way to enter the field. Some of the entry career paths for fashion photographers interested in freelance work or business ownership include working for periodicals, advertising agencies, retail operations, fashion designers, modeling agencies, catalogues, galleries, or stock photography agencies.

- **Personal characteristics:** Those fashion photographers who succeed in attracting enough work to earn a living are likely to be the most creative and adept at operating a business. They are also excellent at building and retaining relationships with other professionals. The independent fashion photographer needs to be extremely confident and have the persistence to solicit consistent work. Stamina is needed for working long hours, sometimes in uncomfortable conditions. Excellent communication skills and a flexible personality are needed, as the photographer must often have patience: it can take a long time to get the right shot.

The Portfolio

A photographer's most important tool is the portfolio, particularly for beginners who have not established a reputation. A **portfolio**, or *book*, is a collection of work that illustrates the job candidate's range of skills and outcomes. Box 13.3 presents tips from a well-known fashion magazine photo editor, a fashion and beauty photographer, and a photographers' agent for building a portfolio, winning over the photo editor, and considering a photography agency. Many photographers find that Web sites offer an inexpensive way to showcase a relatively large number of their images; however, the majority of industry clients will still need to see

Box 13.3 How to Become a Fashion Photographer

A career in fashion photography doesn't have to be an impossible dream. Three industry insiders share their tips for getting started with Ben Widdicombe of fashion.net.

With its huge audience, high paychecks, and glamorous international lifestyle, fashion photography may seem like one of the world's most sought-after professions. But for every fashion photographer who makes it through the door of a top magazine, a thousand others find their niches in fashion advertising, art photography, portraiture, or even paparazzi work. *Allure* magazine photo editor Clio McNicholl, New York fashion and beauty photographer Eva Mueller, and photo agent Gloria Cappelletti agree that breaking into the industry can be hard. But they have some tips for beginners building a portfolio, submitting work to magazine picture editors, and choosing a photo agency.

Building a Portfolio

A photographer's most important tool is the portfolio, and this is particularly true for beginners who don't have an established reputation. "Having been around, I know how hard it is to get in the door," says Clio McNicholl, who receives around 50 unsolicited portfolios a month. Condé Nast's *Allure*, with a monthly circulation of almost 900,000, is a prime target for beginners wanting to get their work seen. "If I don't know who the person is, I ask them to send me some promotional material. Generally I only see people who are coming with a direct recommendation from somebody I know," she says.

Many photographers find that Web sites offer an inexpensive way to showcase a relatively large quantity of images. Eva Mueller points out that computer editing is also a method of keeping down retouching and printing costs. Despite the Web site's strengths, most industry professionals need to see an old-fashioned book before hiring you. Use the Web as your calling card, but have a portfolio to show when they call you for a meeting. Many fashion photographers find the sharp, bright imaging of 4 x 5" transparencies show off their work best. Tearsheets (literally, pages ripped from a magazine) are great if you've been published, but good quality 8 x 10" prints are also okay. Have at least 20 in your book; be prepared to leave a copy of your book for at least a week.

"I like to see a common thread throughout the book," says Clio McNicholl, who says she can tell within three images whether she likes a photographer's style. "Tell a story: not necessarily having the pictures relating to each other, but I like to have some sort of sense at the end of it that I've seen that photographer's personality come through in the pictures." The images showcased in your portfolio should be thematically linked to the job you're trying to get.—still-lifes or product shots if you're going for an advertising gig, for example. Also, throw in one or two other images to demonstrate your range. Strong portraits are always a safe bet, because they tend to stay in the mind of the viewer. Once your portfolio is together, the next challenge is to get the picture editor to use you.

Winning Over the Picture Editor

"Most people who cold call me haven't done their research, which is the world's biggest mistake," says Clio McNicholl, photo editor of *Allure* magazine. "The single biggest thing that people should do is their research. Know what the magazine does, and see how you can apply that to what you do. And they should at least know the name of the photo editor." When you submit work to photo editors, remember that you are showing rather than selling. Editors rarely buy the specific image they see before them; they're looking for a photographer who can execute future commissions. You'll need to be persistent in sending out your work, and ruthless in editing what you choose to show.

The best way to grab an editor's attention is to show previously published work, but there is a downside. "Because there is such an oversupply of photographers, a number of magazines really take advantage of that fact," says Eva Mueller. "Some mags have a decent budget, but many magazines just cover the photographer's expenses." McNicholl says *Allure*'s rates start at $350 a day for unknown photographers, up to $130,000 for a fashion spread.

Box 13.3   How to Become a Fashion Photographer (continued)

A photograph tells a story, as an article or an essay does. Picture editors are looking for concise images that clearly communicate an idea or an emotion. Celebrity portraiture, for example, should reveal an aspect of the subject's character, preferably one that is in harmony with an accompanying profile. Fashion magazines all over the world buy hundreds of stock shots every month—typically young women hanging out with friends, relaxing alone at home, or shopping in the mall—all of which reflect topics commonly dealt with in feature articles. Presenting the stock shots you have done that have been purchased by magazines in your portfolio will help it stand out. If your work speaks clearly, you will stand a much better chance with picture editors than with vague or ambiguous images. When you're submitting your work, remember:

- Call the magazine ahead and get the name of the person to whose attention the submission should be marked

- Label everything with your name and telephone number

- Send working prints or transparencies, not originals

- Include a stamped, self-addressed envelope if you want the work back

Eve Mueller has a warning about dealing with magazines: "Another bad thing is not getting paid in ages, months and months. Some clients really take advantage of the fact that there are so many photographers: they make you pay for the whole shoot; they alter your pictures; and they don't tell you when they drop the story." There is a way to avoid dealing with picture editors, and that is to have a photo agency selling on your behalf.

Finding a Photo Agent

Photo agencies exist to liaise with clients and sell photographers' work for them. They benefit everyone, from start-out photographers, who may not have many industry contacts, to seasoned professionals, who are too busy to take care of business dealings themselves. Gloria Cappelletti is an agent with the Management Artists' Organization (MSO) in Manhattan, which represents many prominent fashion photographers, such as Steven Klein, Michelangelo di Battista, Stefan Sedanoui, and Alexei Hay. "First of all, it's vital to be known, and an agency is in daily contact with clients and publications," she says. "That's the best way for a young photographer to be able to have a connection with them, because usually the photographer is busy taking pictures, and the agent is busy talking to clients. And that's the way it should be. Usually, the photographer doesn't have enough time to take care of everything."

Source: www.fashion.net./howto/fashionphotographer/, 7/14/2011

a traditional portfolio before they hire a photographer. Because magazine editors receive many unsolicited portfolios regularly, the fashion photographer must develop a portfolio that stands out in a crowd. Many fashion photographers find that at least 20 images and several tearsheets, if available, should be included in the portfolio. As Figure 13.5 shows, a **tearsheet** is a page that has been pulled from a newspaper, model book, or magazine. Tearsheets are excellent to include in the portfolio if the photographer has been published. The candidate for a photography job should be prepared to leave a copy of the portfolio with a potential client for at least a week (and include a self-addressed and stamped envelope if the photographer wants the portfolio copy returned).

Career Challenges

This is a tough field to enter, as it can take years of experience at low pay to find opportunities to build a portfolio of work. Fashion photographers often pay their dues before establishing

Figure 13.5 A tearsheet of a *W* magazine pictorial featuring Giorgio Armani and Victor & Rolf designs.

a strong reputation in the field. Some photographers find it frustrating to be directed by the retailer or designer on who will model or how and where to shoot print work.

Art Photographer

Fashion art photography is now one of the hottest growth areas in the international fine art market. Figure 13.6 is a photograph by Guy Bourdin, well recognized as an art photographer whose subjects are fashion related. While gelatin silver prints are the staple of fine art photography, there is a growing consumer interest in contemporary photos using either antique or modern printing methods. Like many artistic undertakings, art photography is unlikely to pay a living wage for many years. Although many artists sell their work directly from the Internet, critical attention and the strongest sales come from a relationship with a gallery. In most major cities, there is now at least one photo gallery, but the headquarters of the world art photography market is New York City, where prices tend to be highest.

Before approaching a gallery with work, the art photographer should contact the gallery to request its submissions policy. Many galleries review new work only at set times of the year, and may require the recommendation of someone known to the gallery directors. If a gallery is interested in interviewing a photographer, the gallery director will want to see a representative sampling of the photographer's work to know that there is a substantial body of work with a consistent standard throughout. Photographers may be invited to join a gallery by having their work go into the backroom inventory, where it will be shown to specific collectors, rather than having a public exhibition, as not many photographers are offered a solo show. The most important thing for the photographer to remember about working with a gallery is to maintain a proper business relationship. Every print given to a gallery should be inventoried by the photographer and payment terms should be agreed on. Industry standard is that the artist receives 40 to 50 percent of the selling price of a photograph after it is purchased.

Photographers should discuss with gallery directors if they are free to exhibit work in other galleries or if the gallery expects exclusivity. Each relationship between an artist and a gallery is unique.

Stylist

There are two types of stylists in the ancillary level of the fashion industry—the photo stylist and the fashion, or wardrobe, stylist. **Photography stylists** work with teams of people such as photographers, designers, lighting technicians, and set builders. They set up the shoot for the photographer, scouting locations and selecting appropriate props, fashions, accessories, and, perhaps, the models to enhance the shoot. The photo stylist often prepares backdrops, lighting, and equipment for the photographer. **Fashion stylists**, or *wardrobe stylists*, pull together outfits or wardrobes for their clients, to include executives, celebrities, and "everyday people," from a new graduate entering the workforce to a new retiree moving into a more casual lifestyle. Both types of stylists are responsible for bringing to life a photographer's, director's, or individual's vision and fashion image. For the photography stylist, this work shows up in magazines, catalogues, and Web site or newspaper advertisements. The fashion stylist's work may be seen in the wardrobes of clients—from sports celebrities to the cast of a television series to the new manager of the local bank, depending on the image, reputation, and skills of the stylist. Companies such as magazines, newspapers, retailers, advertising agencies, and music production companies often employ fashion stylists. Many stylists also choose to run their own businesses.

Typical work activities for the stylist are varied, from the shopping time to shooting the photograph or film. Often, **assistant stylists** are responsible for contacting public relations companies, manufacturers, and retailers to locate the best assortment of merchandise to be used in a shoot. Next, they will borrow, lease, or purchase garments and props and then arrange to transport the selections to the studio or location to determine which combinations work best. Before the shoot begins, stylists work with hair and makeup personnel and dress the people featured in the shoot, adjusting the fit of apparel and accessories as needed.

Interning or apprenticing with a well-known stylist is an ideal way to learn the business, including inside information such as where the best military uniforms or 1940s evening wear is available, which tailor can do overnight alterations, and who can design and sew a sailor suit for a Chihuahua. Occasionally, a stylist has to deal with big egos, as well as big time constraints; it simply goes with the territory. Stylists have to avoid allowing their egos and tastes to interfere with a director's vision or a client's image. Box 13.4 features a classified advertisement for a stylist. The interview at the end of this chapter features well-known stylist Rachel Zoe.

Qualifications

If the vision of searching for the right look, pulling together wardrobes, and creating strong visual images sounds ideal to you, then the career of stylist is one to consider. It requires the following education and work experiences, as well as personal characteristics:

- **Education:** An associate's or bachelor's degree in fashion design, fashion merchandising, visual arts, photography, visual merchandising, or a related field is often required.

- **Experience:** Retail sales or management experience is helpful, as are internships with fashion publications or fashion stylists. Stylists may progress from editorial assistant work on fashion magazines where there is constant contact with public relations companies, manufacturers, and retailers. The career path for a stylist may also begin with an internship or apprenticeship with an experienced stylist before moving into an assistant stylist position, and then to a staff fashion stylist.

- **Personal characteristics:** The fashion stylist has an eye for style and upcoming fashion trends, as well as a broad knowledge of historical fashions. Technical knowledge for creating sets and using lighting effectively is important. One needs to be creative, resourceful, persistent, and self-motivated. The fashion stylist should have good interpersonal, presentation, and communication skills. The ability to market one's self is critical. Aspiring fashion stylists should have the perseverance to work their way to the top. The most successful fashion stylists have extensive networks of contacts within the fashion industry to get the job done quickly and within budget.

With the influence of movies, television, and the Internet on the consumer, it is no surprise that stylists are often credited with setting fashion trends around the globe. A stylist may dress an actress in a funky retro gown or an amazing necklace to wear to a premiere. Once the image is splashed across the pages of fashion magazines and featured on television and the Internet, it can become a trend and put the stylist's name in the spotlight around the world.

Career Challenges

The stylist may find this career filled with irregular work, long hours, limited budgets, and clients with conflicting personal tastes. It can be difficult to work for a number of bosses, from the client to the photographer or film director. This is a career track in which there is growing interest and strong competition for the minimal number of jobs that currently exist. It is challenging to get your foot in the door, and when you do, you have to be great. For those who are great, excellent remuneration, job satisfaction, and the opportunity to build a reputation are quite possible.

Full-time employee for large retail/product development company

San Francisco, California

Major Responsibilities

- Manage styling direction

- Execute each Web site's styling point of view for all in-house photography to include product lay-down and on-figure photography, and special lay-down and marketing photography

- Understand the marketing and merchandising seasonal objectives and executing site features based on those objectives

- Establish partnership with brand-styling team to promote styling and product consistency from the stores to the Web sites

- Obtain appropriate approvals from cross-functional partners to ensure consistency and translate the brand point of view appropriately for each Web site

- Create/manage a product style guide of all e-commerce sites

- Partner with creative team to co-lead and drive the styling direction for all e-commerce sites

- Create a relationship between the photography, stylist, and assistant stylist team to provide team synergy

- Manage operating practices

- Drive photography work flow by assessing the volume and photography set requirements

- Identify/document/present process efficiencies within the photography floor

Minimum Qualifications

- Minimum four years of experience with fashion styling and/or visual fashion retail experience

- Bachelor's of art or science degree

- Ability to balance creative with strategic deliverables

- Strong collaboration skills and ability to form effective partnerships across cross-functional team: photo studio, creative, merchandising, and marketing teams

- Extremely flexible, detail oriented, organized, and self-motivated with leadership skills

- Comfortable in a fast-paced environment

- Comfortable working with Excel, Filemaker, Photoshop, and related software, and databases in general

- Experienced in managing others

Fashion Costumer

A **fashion costumer** collaborates with film and video directors to design, consign, or construct apparel and accessories that fit with the mood, time frame, and image of the visual. Depending on style and complexity, costumes may be rented, made, bought, or revamped out of existing stock. The costumer's designs need to faithfully reflect the personalities of the characters in the script. Stage costumes can provide audiences with information about a character's occupation, social status, gender, age, sense of style, and personality. Costumes have the ability to reinforce the mood and style of a production and distinguish between major and minor characters. Costumes may also be used to change an actor's appearance or be objects of beauty in their own right.

The shapes, colors, and textures that a costumer chooses can make an immediate and powerful visual statement to the audience. Creative collaboration between the costumer, production director, and set and lighting designers ensures that the costumes are smoothly integrated into a production as a whole. Costuming also includes any accessories needed to project a character, such as canes, hats, gloves, shoes, jewelry, or masks. These costume props add a great deal of visual interest to the overall costume design. The costumer may also collaborate with a hair and wig master, hairstylist, and makeup artist. In European theater productions, these are often the items that truly distinguish one character from another.

Costumers begin their work by reading the script to be produced. If the production is set in a specific historical era, the fashions of this period need to be researched. To stimulate the flow of ideas at the first meeting with the director and design team (i.e., set, costume, lighting, and sound designers), the costumer may choose to present a few rough costume sketches. This is also an appropriate time to check with the director on the exact number of characters who need costumes, as any nonspeaking characters the director plans to include may not have been listed in the script.

It is the costumer's responsibility to draw up the costume plot. The **costume plot** is a list or chart that shows which characters appear in each scene, what they are wearing, and what their overall movements are throughout the play. This helps track the specific costume needs of every single character. It can also identify any potential costume challenges, such as very quick changes between scenes. Following the director and production team's approval of the preliminary sketches, the costumer draws up the final costume designs. The final designs are done in full color and show the style, silhouette, textures, accessories, and unique features of each costume.

Figures 13.7a and b
Costume designer Colleen Atwood's sketches for Tim Burton's *Alice in Wonderland*.

Costuming may also include creating masks, makeup, or other unusual forms, such as the "dress of changing sizes" worn in Tim Burton's *Alice in Wonderland*, designed by Colleen Atwood, winner of the 2011 Academy Award for Outstanding Achievement in Costume Design shown in Figures 3.7a and b. Atwood has been nominated a total of nine times, and this marked the third time she's taken home the Oscar in that category. She won the first time in 2003 for *Chicago* and a second time in 2006 for *Memoirs of a Geisha*.

Costume designers typically work to enhance a character's personality through the way that character is dressed (Box 13.5 and Figure 13.8), while at the same time allowing the actor to move freely and perform actions as required by the script. The designer needs to possess strong artistic capabilities, a thorough familiarity with fashion history, as well as knowledge of clothing construction and fit. Professional costumers generally fall into three classifications: freelance, residential, and academic.

Freelance costumers are hired for a specific production by theater companies or production studios. A freelance costumer is traditionally paid in three installments: at hiring, on the delivery of final renderings, and on the opening night of the production. Freelancers are usually not obligated to any exclusivity in projects they are working on and may be designing for several theaters concurrently. A **residential costumer** is hired by a specific film company or theater for an extended series of productions. This can be as short as a summer stock contract, or as long as several years. A residential costumer's contract may limit the amount of freelance work the costumer is permitted to accept. Unlike the freelancer, a residential costumer is consistently on location at the filming site or theater and is readily at hand to work with the costume studio and other collaborators (Box 13.6 and Figure 13.9). Residential costumers are more likely to be associated with a union than freelancers, as most theaters that can retain such a position have agreements with such organizations as the Actors' Equity Association.

An **academic costume designer** is one who holds a teaching position with a college or university. This costumer is primarily an instructor, who may also act as a residential designer for productions of the university theater. Designers or costumers with academic careers are often free to freelance as their schedules allow. In the past, college instructors of costume design were mostly experienced professionals who may not have had formal post-graduate education, but it has now become increasingly common to require a professor to have at least a master of fine arts degree to secure employment with an accredited university.

Qualifications

If the career of a costumer appeals to you, following is a list of educational credentials and work experiences that will contribute to your success, and the personal characteristics you should acquire.

- **Education:** A bachelor's degree in theater costuming, historical costume, visual arts, fashion design, or a similar field is required.

- **Experience:** A number of successful costumers begin in the career field through an internship with an experienced costume designer. Others gain work experience as assistant fashion designers or fashion stylists before moving into the film and theater industry. Interning in summer stock productions, volunteering to assist in off-Broadway or local theater productions, and working or volunteering at a costume rental agency are excellent ways for college students to acquire work experience. High school and college students can gain experience through costume, hair, or makeup work in school theater productions.

Box 13.5 *Malèna*—Life Transitions in Film Powered by Fashion

Malèna (2000, directed by Giuseppe Tornatore) is set during World War II in a rural Italian town, but it isn't the locale that tells the story—it is the costuming. Malèna, the lead character, has three life transitions that are visually presented through shifts in the colors and styling of her costumes.

In the film, Monica Bellucci plays Malèna, an incomparable vision of beauty. Malèna's changing reactions to the leering gazes of the men in her town and the subsequent scorn of jealous women over the years are expressed through her hair, makeup, and clothing. As the film introduces the character, Malèna wears a just-below-the-knee white fitted dress with slightly padded shoulders and a deep neckline with a dotted bow detail (this fabric is later reused for another outfit, as she is a seamstress). A young boy, almost a man, Renato, sees Malèna as the perfect—the only—woman.

Renato's thoughts of Malèna and his need to be seen as a man are communicated through costuming. Renato is so frantic to be perceived by Malèna as a mature suitor that he finds a way to replace his short pants, a garment that he believes signifies childishness. He sneaks his father's best suit to a tailor to have the trousers fitted to him. The change never occurs because his father discovers the missing suit, then punishes his son. Eventually, Renato is fitted for a two-piece suit, though it is his mother who supervises the tailor.

Malèna's first transition is presented through a visual cue. She transitions from a primarily black-and-white color palette with some florals, to (in Renato's daydream) a revealing pink lace-trimmed nightgown, to pure black after her soldier husband dies while serving in Africa. Malèna remains in mourning, often with her head completely covered by a black chiffon scarf, until her second transition. Condemned as aloof and unfeeling by women and sexualized by men, Malèna is forced into submission and becomes who they determine she is, a prostitute for the occupying German army. Surprisingly, the black-on-black wardrobe seems to draw even more attention, signifying sexuality and mystique. Even in court for indiscretions not yet undertaken, it is her angular silhouette of wide,

padded shouldered crepe dress that lingers. The film's director wants the audience to judge Malèna as the townspeople do—calculating, strong-shouldered, and cold.

Until the end of the film, Malèna wears high-heeled sling-back shoes. The colors and styles vary, but that distinctive "click-clack" sound remains an auditory part of the plot. You can hear the temptress approaching, as though she marches through town like a Wild West gunslinger protecting her turf. The men try to dominate to prove their masculinity, while the women want to destroy what they perceive to be a threat to their marriages. From sound to sight—Malèna walks from building to building trying to find a job, as the camera peeks up from her shoes to stocking seam to long dark hair blowing in the wind. Even with Renato as her would-be protector/voyeur, everywhere she goes, Malèna is either ogled as a sex object or scorned as a woman of ill repute. For the townspeople, she is more deadly than the War.

When Malèna finally succumbs to bullying, due to poverty and pressure, she makes a third costume transition, perhaps the most important. It confirms what the townsfolk believe they already know, and, for Renato, it forces him to grow up. Chopping her hair into a bob and dying it copper red, Malèna becomes a new character. With costume designer

Figure 13.8 Costume designers typically work to enhance a character's personality through the way the character is dressed.

Maurizio Millenotti revealing her décolletage for the first time since the opening scene, Malèna appears terrified, yet as a rush of eager hands jut forward to light her cigarette, she is instantly aware of her power, too. Her shocking red hair soon becomes Jean Harlow blond; however, by this stage Malèna is too bold. Despite her promiscuity, which is just what the local men thought they wanted, she has never looked less attractive to them. Now Malèna's conspicuous sexuality overshadows mystique. When American troops arrive to liberate the town, she is brutally punished by a hysterical group of wives for her collusion with the enemy. Clean white dress ripped, hair shorn, and scalp bleeding, Malèna is taunted as a whipped dog. She temporarily escapes on the next train out of town, veiled in black to hide her wounds.

When Malèna's husband Nino returns from Africa, evidently not dead but injured, he is treated almost as badly as she—just for being married to her. Initially, Nino is sympathetic, but this soon gives way to name-calling and physical abuse. With Renato's help, Nino eventually learns where Malèna has fled and, a year later, the couple returns together. This is Malèna's final transition, when she is finally accepted by the townspeople. In a brown-striped utility suit, loose to hide her figure, and low plain shoes, she is no longer a threat. They won; they killed Malèna and she was reborn in their design— plain, invisible, unthreatening, and anonymous.

Source: http://clothesonfilm.com/monica-bellucci-as-malena-beauty-black-and-heels/21152/

- • **Personal characteristics:** A creative and resourceful personality is a plus. An understanding of historical fashion, clothing construction, and fit are necessities. Many fashion costumers find that the ability to sketch well is essential to communicating their ideas to directors and producers.

Career Challenges

The costumer is challenged with accurately interpreting the words and vision of the writer, director, or producer. In some cases, such as productions set in a different time or unique location, this takes a great deal of research. The costumer often works on a tight budget and an even tighter timeline. Costumes may require alterations, repairs, or replacement during the production. As costumers often work on several projects simultaneously, this career fits a person who can effectively multitask. Low pay and long hours should be expected at the start of this career track.

Summary

Fashion visuals include such activities as fashion shows, photography shoots, and films or videos wardrobed by fashion costumers or stylists. These career tracks have been examined as ancillary fashion businesses. Some retail organizations, for example, hire fashion show coordinators and fashion photographers as employees. Many, however, go to outside companies to contract out these activities. These career paths, as independent businesses, include the fashion show and event producer, modeling and talent agency director, fashion photographer, fashion stylist, and fashion costumer.

The fashion show and event producer manages fashion shows and special events for his or her clients for a fee. Special events include, but are not limited to, trunk shows, sample sales,

Fashion plays a leading role in director Luca Guadagnino's film *I Am Love*. To paint Tilda Swinton as a picture of European affluence, costume designer Antonella Cannarozzi (whose work earned her a Best Costume Design Oscar nomination in 2011) asked Raf Simons to outfit the actress in crisp sheath dresses and elegant overcoats. Raf Simons is the designer of the luxury line Jil Sander. Noted as one of the significant forces in popularizing the minimalist aesthetic, German designer Jil Sander launched her namesake women's ready-to-wear line in 1973 on the Milan runway, after designing collections for her own boutique in Hamburg for five years. She led the company to a $200 million empire that came to include menswear, accessories, and fragrances. In 1999, Prada Group acquired 75 percent of the label and Sander departed shortly thereafter. Milan Vukmirovic, formerly at Colette and Gucci, was brought in but failed to uphold the streamlined looks of Jil Sander. In 2003, Prada asked Sander back. With much anticipation from the public and press, the designer showcased her signature staple pieces, this time with strokes of color, before officially stepping down four seasons later. Raf Simons was brought in as the new creative

director in 2005. The Belgian menswear designer has delivered, maintaining the label's heritage of conceptual and sculptural styling and making it his own—from women's to menswear.

For the film, Simons was responsible for taking Tilda Swinton's character, the elegant Russian wife of a wealthy Italian textile manufacturer, from her family's Milanese mansion to the verdant countryside of San Remo. Here, she begins a secret romance with a young chef (to make things more tangled, he happens to be a friend of her son). We asked Swinton to discuss her character's visual evolution.

On the assimilation of Swinton's character: "I think of Emma as an avatar. She comes into this world as an alien, and it's a very particular world. I think any one of us marrying an industrial tycoon of that kind in Milan would find ourselves daunted to assimilate ourselves. There's a uniform you have to supply yourself with— we couldn't turn up looking like this. You need to walk the walk and talk the talk, and you need to dress in a certain way in order to fit into the very precise grid that that world prescribes for people. It doesn't just provide it for them; it actually prescribes it for them. And I think for someone like Emma, who comes from outside that

Figure 13.9 Costume designer Antonella Cannarozzi recruited Jil Sander's Raf Simons to outfit Tilda Swinton in *I Am Love*.

milieu, particularly someone who comes from a milieu that doesn't really equip her at all—it's not as if she's moved from New York or even Abu Dhabi—she comes from Soviet Russia into a world that she really has no preparation for, so she has to learn the code. And so her wardrobe, to a certain extent, is everything."

On Emma's "golden handcuffs": "I can't remember where the saying 'he who wears the jewels' comes from, but there's this whole thing about having jewels put on her—like golden handcuffs, as I think of them—by her husband, who takes them out of the safe. And then there's this idea of her lover taking them off, taking her clothes off, and her housekeeper dressing her, and her husband putting her shoes back on. There's this whole feeling of her being dressable. And the truth is, we're all dressable—if any of us dressed like that, for at least a second that's what we would represent. And the same is true of anything we put on. And I think in that world, it's all about surfing the wave of that uniform."

On how the color palette of the costumes reflects the story: "It was absolutely designed to do exactly that. Raf Simons of Jil Sander and his team were so responsive to our challenge, which was to make a responsive wardrobe for an uncommunicative person. She's communicative in some ways, but the idea of her signaling with a red dress that she might be in the process of falling in love, or the dress that she wears in the hospital at the end—that dress is several tones darker than the dress that she was wearing at the dinner party several minutes before. That whole color referencing was really fun to play with. And when Raf Simons pulls out what I now think of as San Remo orange—that tangerine dress and those incredible tangerine pants, it's a very cinematic response that he had."

Sources:
http://www.elle.com/Pop-Culture/Movies-TV-Music-Books/Screen-Style-I-Am-Love#mode=base;slide=0;

http://nymag.com/fashion/fashionshows/designers/bios/jilsander/

http://www.ew.com/ew/gallery/0,,20311937_20468523,00.html#20916170

---

weddings, meetings, conferences, training seminars, and trade markets. The modeling and talent agency director is ultimately responsible for locating and contracting new models, training them, and, later, securing modeling jobs for them. Fashion photographers take photographs of models wearing the latest apparel, accessories, hairstyles, and makeup, or highlighting the newest home furnishings and other fashion products, primarily for commercial use. The photographs are used in a variety of media, including advertisements, catalogues, billboards, television, Web sites, and art galleries. Fashion stylists are responsible for bringing to life a photographer or director's vision for a fashion shoot, magazine layout, music video or film, television commercial, or print advertisement. The fashion costumer collaborates with stage, film, and video directors to design, consign, or construct costumes that fit with the mood, time frame, and image of the visual.

All in all, fashion media and visual career options are creative and growing entrepreneurial paths. As diverse as the careers of the freelance fashion show and event planner, modeling and talent agency director, photographer, stylist, and costumer are, those who follow them have something major in common. They are all entrepreneurs—owners of their own futures. As such, they require the business skills needed to estimate expenses and labor accurately, sell and market their services, and maintain and grow a client base. It is a creative, independent, and self-directed lifestyle that combines creativity with passion.

Key Terms

academic costume designer

advertising photography

assistant photographer

assistant stylist

costume plot

fashion art photography

fashion costumer

fashion photographer

fashion show and event producer

fashion stylist

fashion visual

fit model

freelance costumer

modeling and talent agency director

photographic model

photography stylist

portfolio

press photography

residential costumer

show model

tearsheet

technical photographer

Online Resources

latimesblogs.latimes.com/alltherage/2011/02/oscars-colleen-atwood-wins-for-alice-costume-design.html

www.anothermag.com/current/view/332/Costume_Designer_Antonella_Cannarozzi

www.chinashopmag.com

www.clothesonfilm.com

www.ew.com/ew/gallery/0,,20311937_20468523_20916170,00.html

www.fashion.net

www.fashionroi.com

www.myfdb.com

www.stylelist.com/2010/05/31/alice-in-wonderland-costume-designer/

Discussion Questions

1. By surfing the Internet and perusing trade publications, develop a list of fashion show and event planning firms that are available to fashion retailers and manufacturers for contract. In what areas do these firms specialize? What career opportunities are available?

2. What are the requirements for a costumer designer who wants to secure clients in the entertainment industry? Compare and contrast the licenses, union memberships, or other credentials that are required or are helpful.

3. What are the sign-on requirements for a major modeling agency? How does the director determine who receives a contract and who does not?

4. Select a costume designer for a well-known period film and describe this costumer's research and outcomes for the film's characters' costumes.

5. Compare and contrast the careers of the fashion stylist and the costumer. Clarify the differences and similarities. Can a person be both?

Interview with a Fashion Stylist

MyFDB EXCLUSIVE INTERVIEW: Rachel Zoe to Raid the Closet of French Vogue's Carine Roitfeld?
Source: http://blog.myfdb.com/2010/11/rachel-zoe-reveals-her-style-inspiration-and-more-to-myfdb/
November 13, 2010 by Ami Gan and Vaneza Pitynski

With good looks, a killer closet, *and* a hit show, you almost can't talk about styling without mentioning the impact Rachel Zoe has had on the industry. The stylist-turned-designer gives MyFDB an inside glimpse at her life. Find out whose closet she wants to raid and what comes to mind when she hears the word "fruit" (*hint, it's not bananas*). See how this fashion icon weighs in below.

It seems like you're everywhere these days, from your own show to QVC, so what can we expect to see next from the Rachel Zoe brand?
I'm launching my full lifestyle retail collection next year, which has always been my ultimate dream. It's going to be a little bit of everything I love…faux furs, incredible leather jackets, and great day-to-night trousers—I'm beyond excited! Also, I am in the very early stages of my second book.

We're sure your closet is the envy of girls everywhere, but if you had the opportunity to raid someone's wardrobe who would it be and why?
Carine Roitfeld—the editor-in-chief of *French Vogue*—because she is one of my only modern-day muses. She has impeccable style and I'm sure everything in her closet is perfection.

Do you have any fashion blogs and/or Web sites that you enjoy reading?
Style.com, *Who What Wear*, and of course, my Web site and daily newsletter, *The Zoe Report*.

Besides the runway, where do you draw your style inspiration?
No matter what, I always, always go back to my vintage muses from the late '60s and '70s. Bianca Jagger, Marianne Faithful, Brigitte Bardot…in terms of style, beauty trends, and everything they are all amazingly cool and sexy.

Figure 13.10 Rachel Zoe has become one of the best known stylists in the industry.

Name one piece of clothing you can't part with for sentimental reasons.
Jewelry for me is the most sentimental thing I own. But if I had to pick something from my closet, it would have to be my first [Hermès] Birkin bag that my husband gave me.

Interview with a Fashion Stylist (continued)

Have you ever had the desire to pursue a career in a field other than fashion?

At one point I wanted to be a psychologist, which is what I majored in at George Washington, but the moment I got my first internship at a fashion magazine, I was hooked and haven't looked back.

Lastly, what advice do you have for aspiring fashion industry hopefuls?

Intern everywhere and anywhere you can. Work your butt off and learn as much as you can.

Now let's have some fun! *Quick*, **word association time! Tell us the first thing that pops into your head when you hear:**

Fruit berries

Gold Cartier

Runway Marc Jacobs

Coffee Starbucks

Los Angeles home

Knit Missoni

Stiletto Brian Atwood

That's a wrap! A huge thank you to Rachel Zoe for taking the time to talk to MyFDB! If you're craving even more, we suggest signing up for *The Zoe Report*—Rachel's free daily newsletter about her latest obsessions in fashion, beauty, and lifestyle.

Interview with a Prop Stylist

Source: http://rompandpertinence.blogspot.com/2008/08/fyi-prop-stylist-jen-everett.html

By Jessie Cacciola

Jen Everett has some big names in her portfolio—working on spreads for *Real Simple, Vanity Fair*, and *W*, as well as ads for iPod and Maybelline (and the list goes on).

Jen, how did you get involved with prop styling?
I studied photography at Parsons School of Design, and photo-assisted for a few years. I actually started prop styling when a photographer I assisted was working on a book that needed prop styling and asked if I wanted to do it. After that experience, I realized that I was more suited to do props and focused my energy on building a portfolio. Although I'm not working as a photographer, I feel that my background has been an asset. Occasionally I think about getting back into photography because photographers make more money than prop stylists!

What's the first step you take in getting to know a new client?
If the client is a magazine that I haven't worked with, I will pick up a copy of the magazine to get a feel for their aesthetic. Generally, there is not that much time to know a new client because most jobs in this business only allow a few days prior to the shoot day. Usually I will get some inspiration pictures e-mailed to me for what they are thinking for the image and then I will speak further with the photo editor and/or art director.

Figure 13.11 Prop stylist Jen Everett.

How do you stay fresh? And how do you seem to create life in such a limited frame?
I look at a lot of magazines and books and mark images that I like. I also like to visit stores whose displays and merchandise I like. As far as working within a small frame, my background as a photographer helps and it's easier in a way because you can just concentrate on a small area and make that as good as you can make it.

How close is the relationship between stylist, photographer, and client?
I work consistently with a few clients and

photographers, which helps in knowing how a particular person or client likes to work. It's pretty collaborative, but I usually get a list of props and a color scheme from the client and then I supplement that with props that I feel may add something. Occasionally it can get tricky if the photographer has a different idea than the art director; in those cases I try to satisfy both so that we can try both options.

Tell me about the ultimate shoot.
For me, the best experiences are when you get a great crew that works together really well and

Interview with a Prop Stylist (continued)

you've managed to get some great images that hopefully you can use later for your Web site or portfolio. Lately, I have come to value working with nice, appreciative clients more so than high-profile ones.

Best and worst parts of the job. Any warnings for future stylists?

The best aspects of prop styling for me are finding unusual objects and making them work harmoniously. I really enjoy the odd little places that you sometimes find when trying to hunt down a hard-to-find object....it often feels like a scavenger hunt. The worst parts are the schlepping of shopping bags—especially in the rain—returns of items that you buy and don't have the budget to keep, and the spending of your own money that will eventually be reimbursed. I honestly thought when I first got into prop styling that it was about making pretty pictures all the time, but I quickly realized that's only a small part of it. You have to think quickly on your feet, and it can be physically taxing.

So, how does it work? Do you have to scout for all your props, or can you sometimes request that they just be there for the shoot?

Yes, I scout for props, or my assistant does. There are a few prop houses in the city and you get to know their props pretty well, so sometimes I call and put specific, bigger pieces on hold.

And lastly: Got an inspiration board?

I personally don't keep an inspiration board, but frequently for bigger jobs I will create mini ones. I do mark images that I like in books and magazines and will refer to them on occasion.

chapter 14

Fashion Scholarship

There are many different sizes and types of fashion and interior-related museums and foundations throughout the world, and they hold a vast treasure trove of history. Museums can be large or small, public or private, and operated by colleges or universities, communities, the government, or a foundation. For example, there are many colleges and universities that present design exhibitions in their museum facilities, such as Kent State and the Fashion Institute of Technology (FIT). There are community or city museums that feature collections and exhibits on fashion or topics related to soft goods associated with their locales, such as quilts, costumes, or apparel and accessories. There are foundations, institutions formally set up with endowment funds, that present costume exhibitions, such as the Guggenheim Foundation in New York and the Pierre Berge-Yves Saint Laurent Foundation in Paris (Box and Figure 14.1). And there are world-renowned museums and their respective costume collections, such as The Costume Institute of the Metropolitan Museum in New York City (Box and Figure 14.2), Musée des Arts Décoratifs' and Musée de la Mode et du Textile in Paris (Box and Figure 14.3), and the Victoria and Albert Museum in London (Box and Figure 14.4).

Museums are not only sites of exhibitions for public view but they are also centers of research and conservation. Within large and small museums around the world, there is also a variety of career options, many that are lesser known to the general public. The work is interdisciplinary, combining the study of fashion and textile history with hands-on skills in analysis, conservation, storage, and exhibition of textile and costume materials. Most towns and cities have museums, and staffing of the museums depends on their size. Larger museums employ a director and a team of curators, assistants, and technicians. In a small museum, the

Box 14.1 Foundation Pierre Bergé-Yves Saint Laurent

Yves Saint Laurent and Pierre Bergé opened their haute couture house in 1962. During 40 years of creation, Yves Saint Laurent used what was considered traditional masculine styling to bring women self-assurance and power, while preserving their femininity. His designs are part of 20th-century history, reflecting women's emancipation in every domain, from personal to social to political. Yves Saint Laurent invented the modern woman's wardrobe: the pea jacket, trench coat, the first women's tuxedo (Le Smoking), the safari jacket, transparent blouses, and the jumpsuit.

In 1974, Bergé and Saint Laurent moved their company to 5 avenue Marceau, a *hôtel particulier* dating from the Second Empire that became Yves Saint Laurent's *atelier*. It was here that Yves Saint Laurent would implement his design influence until he ended his career in haute couture on January 7, 2002. On January 22 of the same year, at the Centre Georges-Pompidou, a retrospective show went back over Yves Saint Laurent's illustrious creation with over 300 models, including his last collection, spring/summer 2002. From then until his passing in Paris at the age of 72 in 2008, Yves Saint Laurent devoted his energy to the activities of the Foundation Pierre Bergé-Yves Saint Laurent, which was approved by the state on December 5, 2002.

The Pierre Bergé-Yves Saint Laurent entity is not a museum, but a foundation. The foundation has established three primary goals: to conserve the 5,000 haute couture garments and the 15,000 accessories, sketches, patterns, and other objects associated with the four decades of Yves Saint Laurent's creativity; to organize exhibitions of fashion, paintings, photographs, and drawings; and to support cultural and educational projects. The Pierre Bergé-Yves Saint Laurent Foundation includes three types of space: public rooms for exhibitions, appointment rooms (for students, researchers, and journalists), and private rooms. Rooms used for conservation of clothes, accessories, and sketches are also accessible by appointment.

The Foundation Pierre Bergé-Yves Saint Laurent opened its doors in 2004 with its debut exhibition:

Figure 14.1 Monsieur Yves Saint Laurent in Paris.

"Yves Saint Laurent, Dialogue with Art." In this exhibition, the relationship between art and fashion designer was visually communicated. Forty-two different haute couture outfits by YSL created between 1965 and 1988 were displayed in conjunction with five paintings that inspired YSL. The artists included Picasso, Mondrian, Matisse, and Warhol. More recently in the summer of 2011, the foundation presented the exhibit "*Saint Laurent Rive Gauche: La Révolution de la Mode.*" Desiring to dress all women, not only rich haute couture clients, Yves Saint Laurent opened his Saint Laurent Rive Gauche boutique in 1966 in Paris, the first ready-to-wear boutique to bear the couturier's name. In this, the Foundation's 15th exhibition, nearly 70 looks from the Rive Gauche collections were presented.

Sources:
http://www.timeout.com/paris/attractions/venue/1%3A9550/fondation-pierre-berge-yves-saint-laurent

www.fondation-pb-ysl.net/en/La-fondation-272.html

The Costume Institute houses a collection of more than 35,000 costumes and accessories spanning five continents and as many centuries. The Costume Institute began as the Museum of Costume Art, formed in 1937 and led by Neighborhood Playhouse founder Irene Lewisohn. In 1946, with the financial support of the fashion industry, the Museum of Costume Art merged with the Metropolitan Museum of Art as the Costume Institute, and in 1959 became a full-fledged curatorial department. The legendary fashion arbiter Diana Vreeland, who served as special consultant from 1972 until her death in 1989, created a brillant series of costume exhibitions, including "The World of Balenciaga" (1973), "Hollywood Design" (1974), "The Glory of Russian Costume" (1976), and "Vanity Fair" (1977), galvanizing audiences and setting the standard for costume exhibitions both nationally and internationally. In 1989, Richard Martin took over leadership of the Costume Institute, with the support of Harold Koda (now curator in charge), and began a rotating cycle of three thematic exhibitions a year including "Infra-Apparel" (1993), "Waist Not" (1994), "The Four Seasons" (1997), "Wordrobe" (1997), and "Cubism and Fashion" (1998). Martin's tenure culminated in "Rock Style," the last exhibition before his death in 1999.

Today, the Costume Institute's Harold Koda (curator in charge) and Andrew Bolton (curator) create two special exhibitions each year. Recent thematic exhibitions have included "Jacqueline Kennedy: The White House Years—Selections from the John F. Kennedy Library and Museum"

Figure 14.2 An exhibit at the Costume Institute of the Metropolitan Museum in New York City.

(2001), guest curated by Hamish Bowles; "Extreme Beauty: The Body Transformed" (2002), the debut exhibition of Harold Koda as curator in charge; "Bravehearts: Men in Skirts" (2003); "Dangerous Liaisons: Fashion and Furniture in the Eighteenth Century" (2004); "Superheroes: Fashion and Fantasy" (2008); and "The Model as Muse: Embodying Fashion" (2009). Monographic exhibitions have included "Yves Saint Laurent" (1983); "Madame Grès" (1994); "Christian Dior" (1996); "Gianni Versace" (1997); "Chanel" (2005); and "Poiret: King of Fashion" (2007).

The fashion industry provides strong support for the work of the Costume Institute, including its exhibitions, acquisitions, and capital improvements. Each May, the annual Gala Benefit, its primary fund-raising event, celebrates the opening of the spring exhibition. The benefit was introduced in 1948 as a midnight supper and dubbed "The Party of the Year." Under the leadership of Honorary Trustee Anna Wintour (editor-in-chief of *Vogue*), who has been co-chair since 1995 (excluding 1996 and 1998), the gala has become one of the most visible and successful charity events, drawing a stellar list of attendees from the fashion, film, society, business, and music industries.

Resources

The Costume Institute offers walking tours of special exhibitions, as well as a "Fashion in Art" tour, which discusses costume history within the context of the museum's collections of armor, textiles, paintings, sculpture, and decorative arts. "Costume: The Art of Dress," a recorded audio guide narrated by actress Sarah Jessica Parker, also highlights historical costume throughout the museum's galleries.

The Costume Institute contains 5,000 square feet of galleries and the Irene Lewisohn Costume Reference Library, one of the world's foremost fashion libraries. The library's collection includes more than 30,000 noncirculating rare books, periodicals, and reference books, and extensive files of clippings pertaining to the art of adornment throughout the world. In addition, the library possesses fashion prints, drawings, photographs, sketchbooks, and design archives.

Source: www.metmuseum.org

curator may take on the responsibilities of a museum director. Large or small, museums offer many career opportunities that fill the needs of a fashion student who enjoys learning about and preserving cultural references in history through costumes and interiors, and sharing them with others. The following fashion careers in museums are examined in this chapter: museum director, museum curator, assistant curator, collections manager, museum archivist, museum conservator, and museum technician. There is another career path that may be related to those in museums, that of the educator. Fashion educators often study, research, and teach in the specialization of historical costume, as well as other areas of fashion. We begin our study of careers in fashion scholarship with the lead position, that of the museum director.

There are additional museum positions that are not examined in this chapter, as these positions are often limited to very large museums. These include the development associate, who is in charge of generating revenue for the museum; the membership associate, who is responsible for increasing the number of members; the education specialist, who develops educational programs for visitors; the docent, who presents lectures or conducts educational tours of exhibitions; and the exhibit designer, who creates and installs displays.

Box 14.3 Musée des Arts Décoratifs—Musée de la Mode et du Textile

The Musée des Arts Décoratifs was created after the success of the historic *Expositions Universelles*, and the Musée de la Mode et du Textile opened in the Marsan wing of the Louvre in 1905, moving in 1997 to over two levels in the Rohan wing. Located at 107 rue de Rivoli, its collections now contain some 16,000 costumes, 35,000 fashion accessories, and 30,000 pieces of textile. The artifacts total to over 81,000 works that trace the history of costume from the Regency period to the present day, and innovations in textiles since the 7th century. These collections are regularly enriched by generous gifts made by private donors, designers, and manufacturers. They rival the largest collections in the world, the Musée Galliera (Paris), the Musée des Tissus (Lyon), the Victoria and Albert Museum (London), and the Metropolitan Museum (New York). The museum presents theme exhibitions that change every year, such as costumes and accessories from the 17th century to the 21st century, textiles and embroideries, and important works by renowned couturiers, such as Paul Poiret, Madeleine Vionnet, André Courrèges, Christian Dior, Coco Chanel, Elsa Schiaparelli, Christian Lacroix, Yves Saint Laurent, and Alexander McQueen.

Sources:

www.lesartsdecoratifs.fr/english-439/mode-et-textile-740/

http://www.travelsignposts.com/Paris/paris_museum-fashion2.php

Figure 14.3 Musée des Arts Décoratif's Musée de la Mode et du Textile in Paris.

Box 14.4 The Victoria and Albert Museum

An example of a large and prestigious museum with a significant fashion collection is the Victoria and Albert Museum (V&A) in London, which has collected both dress and textiles since its earliest days. The collections cover fashionable dress from the 17th century to the present day, with an emphasis on progressive and influential designs from the major fashion centers of Europe. The V&A collections also include accessories such as jewelry, gloves, millinery, and handbags.

Research is a core activity of the V&A and is carried out in all of its departments. Some research concerns the identification and interpretation of individual objects, while other studies contribute to systematic research. This helps develop the public understanding of the art and artifacts of many of the great cultures of the world, past and present.

The conservation department of the V&A is primarily responsible for the long-term preservation of its collections. At the core of the V&A conservator's work is the development and implementation of storage, mounting, and handling procedures that reduce the risk of damage during movement and display.

Source: www.vam.ac.uk

Figure 14.4 The Victoria and Albert Museum in London.

Museum Director

Museum directors are responsible for managing collections of artistic, scientific, historical, and general-interest artifacts. In large facilities, museum directors manage the general operations and staffing of the institution and coordinate the public affairs mission of the museum. They literally run the business of the museum, being responsible for the human resources, public relations, budget development, and management of the facility. They work closely with assistants, curators, and staff to fulfill the mission of the organization. Foremost, the museum director is a steward of the artifacts held by the museum.

Increasing areas of focus for the museum director include public affairs, marketing, and development. **Public affairs** work includes collaborating with the community, the government, industry, and social and academic organizations to develop exhibitions and collections that appeal to and educate the community and its visitors. Often, the museum director acts as a guide for groups viewing the exhibitions, answering visitors' questions and giving talks in the museum to local organizations or school groups. Making the museum user-friendly and accessible by as much of the public as possible is a key objective of most museum directors. As a result, technology has become an important resource for the museum director, as illustrated in Box 14.5. Outside of the museum, directors may also be invited speakers at clubs or universities to present on the museum's collections or a specific installation. They may be asked to co-chair a gala or work with an outside sponsor on a public event planned to raise awareness or funds for the institution.

A leading museum can influence not only the educational and civic well-being of a community but it can also affect its fiscal health through revenue generated by tourists coming to see the museum. When visitors travel to a city to view its museum, they often spend money in the local restaurants, hotels, and stores in addition to paying the museum admission fee and, possibly, patronizing its gift shop. While directors work to attract visitors to a museum, they may also be asked to seek out and secure funding for the museum through national and state grants. Today, a significant part of a director's duties, perhaps shared by assistants, involves fund-raising and promotion, which may include researching, writing, and reviewing grant proposals, journal articles, and publicity materials. Fund-raising and promotional activities may also include attending meetings, conventions, and civic events.

Qualifications

The position of museum director requires knowledge and experience in diverse areas: museum studies, public relations, marketing, and human resources, to name a few. Following is a list of the educational qualifications, work experience, and personal characteristics that are needed for a museum director.

- **Education:** A bachelor's degree in fashion design, textiles, historical costume, museum curatorship, museum studies, heritage studies, art history, history, archaeology, or a related field is expected. Many museums require that the director have a master of arts or fine arts or a master of science degree in one of these fields. Candidates with a doctoral degree in a related discipline have an edge in the job search.

- **Experience:** Applicants for the position of director must have experience in museum work, preferably as a museum curator or the director of a smaller museum. Management experience is essential, particularly in the areas of human resources and budget development and control. Many museums require that the prospective museum director have public

By Thomas Hughes, November 19, 2010

There has been a lot of talk lately about mobile technology with the release of mobile apps by major museums. Discussion about the way mobile technology can be used in museums has gained momentum. While there are variations among museums, the popular view of mobile technology seems to be focused on one format, having a downloadable mobile application. While some museums found that developing their own applications can be a good way to deliver content to visitors, it is definitely not the only approach. Next, take a look at four different ways that some museums have been implementing mobile technology in their institutions.

Providing Not Just an App, But Also the Device: TAP at the Indianapolis Museum of Art

As the Indianapolis Museum of Art (IMA)'s goal was to include all of its visitors in a mobile tech program, not just those who own a smartphone, it took the extra step of providing gallery-goers with an iPod Touch for the duration of their visits. By placing the device in the visitor's hands, all are given access to the digital content the IMA provides and no user is alienated for not owning a smartphone or having an incompatible device. The iPods cost five dollars to rent and contain only the TAP app and an instructional video on how to use both the iPod and the app in tandem with the galleries. The app works on a numeric input system: a three-digit code is associated with every piece on the gallery tour. When a code is entered, users are presented with different content such as video interviews with designers, text files, pictures, and audio files explaining the artwork. By sticking to one type of device, the IMA was able to tailor the user experience exactly the way it was intended, its main goal for developing a mobile program. This approach circumvents the need for an app store and allows for all content to be controlled in-house. The content management system is the same one used for its Web site and allows IMA to instantly edit and update content without needing to go through a third-party developer. The devices also have built-in polls and can provide both museum staff and TAP users with data and real-time results.

Integrating Mobile Web Sites and Mobile Apps: The Brooklyn Museum

A mobile Web site is the mobile-friendly version of an organization's existing Web site. The Brooklyn Museum has developed a mobile Web site that is accessible from any Web-enabled mobile device. In addition to sharing information about the institution, users are encouraged to get involved and recommend designers or pieces of artwork and apply descriptive tags through the Brknlynmuse and Gallery tag! features of the mobile Web site. To create a more accessible experience for those with more app-friendly devices, the Brooklyn Museum also created downloadable apps for both iPhone and Android that simply wrap the current mobile Web site. The same functionality and features of the mobile site are there; the apps simply act as a different port of entry. This has proven to be a more sustainable approach to the museum's mobile strategy than building each app from scratch would be.

Implementing QR Codes in Exhibits at the Mattress Factory, an Installation Art Museum in Pittsburgh

The Mattress Factory is experimenting with implementing QR codes in its exhibits in an effort to reduce the number of brochures distributed by the museum as part of a green initiative. Quick response, or QR, connects users to content within seconds of scanning the QR code, a two-dimensional barcode that is readable by mobile devices with 3G access, a built-in camera, and a barcode-reading app. As the creation of QR codes does not require a developer, a museum can start immediately experimenting with mobile technology. The codes are free to generate and contain text information. Once a code is generated online, it can be printed out and placed next to the corresponding piece in the collection.

relations and marketing experience; some view experience in the tourism and hospitality industries as a plus. Fund-raising experience may be required or preferred. Computer skills are needed for information retrieval, maintaining the inventory of artifacts, and imaging of collection items.

- **Personal characteristics:** Museum directors are often passionate about history, community affairs, and education. The effective museum director is a strong leader and a visionary who is committed to generating public interest, and possibly funding, for the museum. The work requires a range of skills, including organizational abilities, time-management skills, and a high level of attention to detail. The successful director has strong oral and written communication skills, a heightened aesthetic sense, and excellent presentation skills.

Career Challenges

The museum director carries the weight of many responsibilities, from budget development and management of the facility to human resources and public relations. In human resources, the director supervises assistants, curators, and all other staff in the museum. In public relations, the director must find innovative and inexpensive ways to promote the museum and generate funding through events and programs. It is challenging to "sell" an institution and its services, rather than a tangible product. The museum director has the role of being a jack-of-all-trades, a role that often takes long hours and much multitasking.

Museum Curator

In large museums, **museum curators**, referred to as *museum keepers* in some countries, work under the supervision of the museum director. Curators direct the accession, deaccession, storage, and exhibition of collections (Figure 14.5). **Accession** refers to receiving new items and adding them to the collection; **deaccession** is the removal of items from a collection because of repetition of artifacts, the receipt of better examples, loss, or decay. Sometimes, when building collections, museums sell valuable pieces (often, duplicates in the collection) to raise money to buy items that they want more than the deaccessioned pieces. Curators

Figure 14.5 Curators direct the accession, deaccession, storage, and exhibition of collections.

negotiate and authorize the purchase, sale, exchange, or loan of collection items. They may be responsible for authenticating, evaluating, and categorizing the items in a collection. Curators also oversee and help conduct the museum's research projects and related educational programs.

When there is a team of curators, each may be involved in one area of specialization, such as 18th-century fashions or Gothic furnishings. A large historical costume museum, for example, may employ different curators for its collections of textiles, accessories, menswear garments, and women's apparel. Some curators maintain their collections, some conduct research, and others perform administrative tasks. In small institutions with only one or a few curators, a curator may be responsible for a number of tasks, from maintaining collections to directing the affairs of the museum. The main role of the curator is to acquire objects and research, identify, and catalogue them, usually on a computer. Curators in large and small museums are also responsible for ensuring correct storage conditions. Other duties that they may be assigned include overseeing security and insurance and developing policies and procedures for the collections in collaboration with the museum director, if there is one.

Providing information to the public is an important part of the museum curator's job. This is accomplished through written reports, presentations, and exhibitions to the public. When assigned the task of a public exhibition, the curator either identifies or assists the museum director in identifying topics for public exhibitions (e.g., wedding gowns through the ages, 1940s costumes of women in film, Amish quilts, or menswear of the 18th century). After the subject of the exhibition is determined, the curator plans and designs the exhibition and selects the items to be displayed. In selecting items for display, the delicacy and rarity of some items will keep them from being included. If a museum collection does not contain all of the artifacts needed to implement the theme of the exhibition, the curator may decide to borrow items from other establishments, companies, or private individuals. After the items to be displayed are confirmed, the artifacts are installed and correctly labeled, and related publications are developed. The curator may be responsible for writing signage copy, working with other departments in the museum to publicize the showing, and writing a program for viewers to follow. A trend in museum exhibitions is the **interactive display**, in which viewers can press a button to run a video or actively participate in the exhibition's subject matter. For example, a textile exhibition may include an instructional video and a work area where the viewer can weave a piece of fabric. Museums have added entertainment to their educational goals to engage the public. With such large undertakings, the curator often works with a staff of assistants and technicians.

While the range of museums has expanded enormously, from large museums with full-scale models being prepared for the public to visit and recapture past ages and small museums specializing in specific artifact categories (e.g., Victorian decor, or 19th-century apparel and accessories), the curator's role has also expanded. Granted, most curators have the primary responsibility of collecting and displaying objects of historical, cultural, and scientific interest in order to inform and instruct. However, on a regular basis, the majority of curators' work also includes establishing policies and procedures to protect artifacts in their care. Most curators are called on to talk to museum visitors and answer their questions, and give lectures and visual presentations to local groups. Now, there is a new addition to the curator's job: fund-raising and development. Writing grants and other publications, soliciting donors for gifts, locating sponsors for exhibitions, and attending conferences—with or without a museum director—help stretch limited museum budgets. Box 14.6 features a classified advertisement for a museum director.

Training for museum curators covers three main areas: academic, museological, and managerial. **Academic curator training** refers to how to study and understand collections. **Museological training** for the museum curator covers how to care for and interpret collections. **Managerial training** for the curator focuses on how to run a museum, from personnel to finances to operations. Some large museums offer a type of internship or apprenticeship for the prospective curator, often referred to as the **curatorial traineeship**. If you do not secure one of these prestigious and limited positions, how can you open the door to a career as a museum curator?

Box 14.6 Sample Classified Advertisement: Senior Museum Curator of Costume

Employer: Educational Institution

Job Title: Senior Curator of Costume

Application Instructions:
Please attach the following documents: Résumé/CV, cover letter, a list of three professional references with telephone numbers and e-mail addresses.

Responsibilities:
The Senior Curator of Costume assists the Director and Deputy Director in advancing the Museum's mission by developing the collection, organizing exhibitions, writing museum publications, and providing leadership for the Costume Department. The incumbent supervises the staff of the Costume Department, as well as the Textiles and Accessories curators. S/he works collaboratively with other senior staff on all museum-wide initiatives.

- Works closely with Director, Deputy Director, and other Museum staff on developing, researching, and organizing exhibitions in both the Fashion History Gallery and the Special Exhibitions Gallery

- Provides leadership for the Costume Department. Supervises staff of Costume Department, interns, and student aides. Also supervises the Textiles and Accessories curators.

- May write Museum publications including but not limited to Museum books and catalogues, including the Masterpieces book

- Coordinates and project manages fashion history exhibitions

- Develops, researches, and conducts tours and specialized lectures on fashion to college classes

- Oversees schedule of tours and lectures using the Museum's collections, and supervises the curatorial staff in the development of such tours and lectures

- Supervises the curatorial staff in the preparation of materials for classes and classroom setups

- Performs and oversees regular collection maintenance, including assigning object locations in database

- Provides information relating to the Museum for students, faculty, staff, and visitors

- Represents Costume, Accessories, and Textile Departments at Senior Staff meetings

- Works closely with Director, Deputy Director, and other Senior Staff to accomplish the Museum's Strategic Plan and related initiatives

Qualifications:
Master's degree required, doctorate preferred, and three to five years of appropriate experience writing about fashion, lecturing on fashion, and working on fashion exhibitions. Must have a thorough knowledge of fashion history, including contemporary fashion. Must have excellent writing skills and publication experience. Experience managing personnel. Ability to work well as part of a team, as well as motivating and leading a team. Experience researching and developing exhibitions, writing label and brochure copy, etc. Experience writing and delivering lectures. Experience working with database. Experience working in museum costume collections and handling fashion objects in a conservationally sound manner. Must have exceptional organizational and planning skills with a proven ability to pay attention to detail while also able to work on multiple projects simultaneously. High level of initiative. Cheerful disposition with a flexible and positive attitude to all aspects of the job.

Qualifications

Here is a list of educational goals, work experience, and personal characteristics you will need.

- **Education:** A bachelor's degree in fashion design, textiles, historical costume, museum curatorship, museum studies, heritage studies, art history, history, archaeology, or a related field is required. Many top museums require that the curator have a master of art or fine arts or a master of science degree in one of these fields. Candidates with a doctoral degree have an advantage, particularly in museums with a widespread reputation for their collections or exhibitions.

- **Experience:** Preference is usually given to applicants with experience in museum work, which may be obtained on a voluntary basis. An internship in a museum, usually unpaid, is an excellent way to gain experience and, perhaps, college credit. Computer skills are needed for information retrieval, inventory of artifacts, and imaging of collection items. Promotion will probably be from a small museum to a larger one that will be more specialized. From there, curators can progress to directors. There are career opportunities for curators within private or national collections.

- **Personal characteristics:** Curators show a deep interest in the past and heritage and a commitment to education. In addition to an intellectual curiosity, they often have high levels of sensitivity and patience. The work is often time consuming and methodical, requiring strong organizational skills and attention to detail. The successful curator has strong oral and written communication skills, an eye for aesthetically pleasing displays, and managerial abilities that include human resources, as well as budget development and management.

Curators work closely with technicians, conservation officers, and restoration personnel who care for a wide range of artifacts and exhibits, from Egyptian jewelry to centuries-old pictures and wallpaper to costumes and accessories. The curator may work with assistants, as well as the conservation and restoration staff, to research and identify the source, material, and time period of artifacts. Establishing authenticity, providing as much information as possible about museum artifacts, soliciting new items, and clearing out unwanted items are key parts of the curator's job.

Assistant Curator

In mid- to large-sized museums, the curator may supervise one or more assistant curators. An **assistant curator** often serves as the registrar of the collection by coordinating the collection's accessions. Once the items are correctly identified, they are accurately labeled, properly catalogued, safely stored, and maintained. This task has a technical side, as the assistant curator has the responsibilities of cataloguing artifacts, entering related data into a computer, and processing collection imaging, including photography, digitizing, slide labeling, and responding by e-mail to requests for images. Some of these images may be used in the publication of collection materials, such as catalogues, postcards, and exhibition programs. The assistant also works with the curator to organize and present lectures and host outside groups. If the museum has an organized membership of donors and public attendees, the assistant curator also works on a computer to maintain a member database. A number of assistant curators are assigned the responsibility of coordinating and managing student and volunteer staffs, as well as working with faculty and students on class activities and projects.

Qualifications

The assistant curator position has a number of educational and work experience requirements in addition to preferred personal characteristics, as follows.

- **Education:** While a bachelor's degree in fashion, textiles, museum studies, archaeology, history, art history, or a related field is required, a master's degree in one of these areas may be preferred.

- **Experience:** Work experience, volunteer or paid, in curatorial activities is required. Computer skills are needed for information retrieval, cataloguing of acquisitions, and imaging of the collection inventory.

- **Personal characteristics:** A commitment to team-based activities is needed, especially when working with the public and volunteers. Communication and marketing skills are a must, as the successful assistant curator needs a good understanding of how to make information accessible to the public, including tourists, people with disabilities, and educational groups and schools. Assistant curators must be organized and effective managers who are capable of running a department or team and overseeing a budget. They must have strong attention to detail for accuracy in cataloguing objects. Finally, a creative flair for devising displays and exhibitions is needed.

Career Challenges

The museum curator works with creative projects, a detailed inventory, and budget management. It can be difficult for a creative person to work on projects that require a high level of accuracy, such as recording descriptions of new items in the collection, and quantitative analysis, such as overseeing the collection's budget. On the other hand, it can be a struggle for the analytical person to construct an artistic display. The museum curator, however, must work in both areas. It is not easy to develop and install exciting and attractive exhibits with limited resources, but the curator must manage to stretch the museum's budget.

Collections Manager

Collections managers provide front-line supervision of specific museum collections. A collections manager usually takes one of two tracks to move up in the museum world: the curator or conservator track. Occasionally, the collections manager may prefer to take the archivist track. **Collections managers** are responsible for preparing, managing, and supervising the collections records; processing and cataloguing items in the museum collections; and maintaining and entering data into a computerized collections management system. They maintain and supervise the organization of artifacts in storage, making sure everything possible is being done to keep items safely preserved. They also supervise artifact cataloguing, keeping in mind that systems must provide access to the collections by the public, staff, researchers, and other museums. Collections managers may work with volunteers in the collections department by preparing instructions, assembling needed materials, training them in tasks, and reviewing their work. Additional duties may include overseeing the photography of the collection, handling the preservation of the collection, conducting research, and participating in exhibit development.

Qualifications

In the job search, there are a number of educational requirements, work experiences, and personal characteristics that the collections manager candidate is expected to have. An overview of these expectations follows.

- **Education:** A bachelor's degree in fashion, textiles, museum studies, archaeology, history, art history, or a related field is required. Some museums require or prefer the candidate with a master's degree in fine arts or museum studies for this position.

- **Experience:** Work experience, volunteer or paid, in museum activities is required. College students may want to secure an internship in a museum to gain experience. Some collections managers gain paid work experience as a museum technician. Computer skills are needed for information retrieval, cataloguing of acquisitions, and imaging of collection inventory.

- **Personal characteristics:** Strong written, oral, and visual communication skills are needed. Collections managers must be organized and effective managers who are capable of leading and motivating a staff or team of volunteers. They must have strong attention to detail and accuracy, as well as knowledge of history, for cataloguing artifacts. An eye for effective displays and exhibitions is also needed.

Career Challenges

Working with volunteers requires the abilities to schedule, train, and motivate workers who are not being paid for the jobs they do. This can be a tough way to acquire the workforce that you need to get the job done. The collections manager is also challenged with maintaining high levels of accuracy and organization when dealing with collection artifacts. At any time, the collections manager should be able to quickly locate a single item in the collection.

Museum Archivist

With the curator's busy roles in accessing and displaying historical artifacts, public relations, and marketing, the position of museum archivist has become more important and prevalent in today's museums. Although some duties of archivists and curators are similar, the types of items they deal with are different. Curators usually handle objects with cultural, biological, or historical significance, such as sculptures, textiles and textile-related items, and paintings. **Archivists** mainly handle records and documents that are retained because of their importance and potential value in the future. Archivists analyze, describe, catalogue, and exhibit these important records for the benefit of researchers and the public (Figure 14.6). They preserve important records and photographs that document the conception, history, use, and ownership of artifacts.

Archivists are responsible for collecting and maintaining control over a wide range of information deemed important enough for permanent safekeeping. This information takes many forms: photographs, films, video and sound recordings, computer tapes, and video and image disks, as well as more traditional paper records, illustrations, letters, and documents. Archivists also solicit, inventory, and save records and reports generated by corporations, government agencies, and educational institutions that may be of great potential value to

Figure 14.6 An archivist analyzes, describes, and catalogues the important records of artifacts for the benefit of researchers and the public.

researchers, exhibitors, genealogists, and others who would benefit from having access to original source material.

Archivists maintain and save records according to standards and practices that ensure the long-term preservation and easy retrieval of the documents. Records may be saved on any medium, including paper, film, videotape, audiotape, or computerized disk. They also may be copied onto some other format to protect the original and make the records more accessible to researchers who use them. Some archivists work with the originals of specialized forms of records, such as manuscripts, electronic records, photographs, motion pictures, and sound recordings, and determine the best ways of creating copies and saving the originals of these works. As various storage media evolve, archivists must keep abreast of technological advances in electronic information storage. Computers are increasingly being used to generate and maintain archival records. Professional standards for the use of computers in handling archival records are evolving with technology. Expanding computer capabilities that allow more records to be stored and exhibited electronically have transformed and are expected to continue to transform many aspects of archival collections. Some archivists specialize in a specific area of technology so they can more accurately determine how records should be stored. Others specialize in a particular area of history to determine which items qualify for retention and should become part of the archives. Archive technicians help archivists organize, maintain, and provide access to historical documentary materials.

Qualifications

If working with history and preserving it for the future sounds like a fascinating and fulfilling career, here is what you need to do and know to become a museum archivist.

- **Education:** A bachelor's degree in textiles; museum studies; costume and textiles; fashion and textile studies; history, theory, and museum practice; art history; or a related discipline is required.

- **Experience:** Archivists may gain work experience in a variety of organizations, including government agencies, museums, historical societies, and educational institutions. An internship or work experience as an archive technician is an ideal way to open the door to this career path. Experience in computer imaging, including photographs, illustrations, and films, is a plus.

- **Personal characteristics:** Archivists are methodical, detail oriented, and well organized. They often have inquisitive natures. They work to stay up to date on evolving restoration and preservation techniques.

Career Challenges

Education is never ending for the museum archivist. Technological advances and new types of cleaning and restoration equipment help the archivist maintain collection items for longer periods of time, and the person in this position must constantly learn about the latest preservation techniques. The archivist is always working with details and must work methodically and with focus.

Museum Conservator

Museum conservators manage, care for, preserve, treat, and document works of art, artifacts, and specimens. Museum conservators are also referred to as *restoration and preservation specialists*. With regard to fashions or costumes, conservators acquire and preserve important visuals (e.g., photographs, illustrations, or sketches), costumes, accessories, furnishings, and other valuable items for permanent storage or display. Much of their work requires substantial historical, scientific, and archaeological research. Conservators use X-rays, chemical testing, microscopes, special lights, and other laboratory equipment and techniques to examine objects. Conservators' objectives are to determine the artifacts' conditions, their need for treatment or restoration, the best way to repair worn or damaged items, and the appropriate methods for preserving items. Many institutions prefer not to repair but to effectively maintain and preserve artifacts to minimize damage and deterioration. The conservator's work is performed under close supervision with an emphasis on saving and maintaining, or **stabilizing**, artifacts while developing the studies of historical preservation. Conservators may specialize in a particular material or group of objects, such as documents and books, paintings, decorative arts, textiles, metals, or architectural materials.

Qualifications

Qualifications for the museum conservator include the following educational goals, work experiences, and personal characteristics:

- **Education:** A bachelor's degree in museum studies, archaeology, textile science, art history, or a related field is a requirement. Larger, more prestigious museums require a master's degree in one of these areas.

- **Experience:** Museum conservators must have the knowledge, skills, and abilities required to perform basic preservation maintenance, repair, and treatment of historical artifacts. Consequently, training, coursework, or an internship with a museum or educational institution can provide the opportunity to learn these skills and remain up to date on the latest technology and restoration techniques.

- **Personal characteristics:** Museum conservators must have the patience and organizational skills to work methodically. They have the curiosity and ability of an investigator to piece information together. They are interested in science and keep current with restoration and preservation techniques.

Career Challenges

The challenges of a museum conservator's career are similar to those of the archivist, as previously described. Box 14.7 illustrates the mission and duties of the conservator department in the Victoria and Albert Museum. It also describes the work of a museum technician, next on the list of career options in museum organizations.

Museum Technician

Museum technicians assist curators by performing various preparatory and maintenance tasks on museum items. Some museum technicians assist curators with research. As a result of their close collaboration with collections managers and curators, museum technicians often move to the position of collections manager. Most technicians work to preserve, maintain, and repair artifacts. They perform their work with an emphasis on safety, of the items and themselves, because of the use of chemicals, and have an understanding of historic preservation treatment techniques. Museum technicians have the ability to differentiate contemporary and period fabrication and construction and take appropriate steps to protect artifacts. Working from blueprints, sketches, shop lists, and written and oral instructions, museum technicians procure equipment and materials for project work. Next, they recommend treatments for the items. After implementing restoration and preservation treatments, they accurately and completely document project work through photography, drawings, and written narratives.

Qualifications

Technicians need the skills and knowledge of environmental legislation to assess material, environmental, and other workplace hazard potential and develop safety programs. Educational requirements, work experience, and preferred personal characteristics for museum technicians include the following:

The conservation department of the Victoria and Albert Museum (V&A) in London is primarily responsible for the long-term preservation of the collections. The department conserves all of the collections held by the V&A and its branches, the Theatre Museum, and the Museum of Childhood. The conservators specialize in particular areas of conservation, which reflect the collections held by the museum. The core of the conservator's work is the care and understanding of the V&A's collections. This is achieved not only through surveys, assessments, and hands-on treatment of objects but also through the provision of advice from professional conservators from around the world.

Correct packaging, mounting, and handling procedures reduce the risk of damage during movement and display, and conservators frequently act as couriers when V&A objects are loaned to other institutions. These aspects of conservation work are known as preventive conservation. They include activities such as controlling the museum environment (e.g., temperature and light) and preventing pests (e.g., insects) from entering the museum. This type of conservation helps to slow down rates of deterioration. Other treatments come into the category of interventive conservation. These include cleaning and reintegration to strengthen fragile objects, reveal original surface decoration or technology, and restore shape. Interventive treatment makes the object more stable but also more attractive and comprehensible to the viewer. This type of treatment is usually undertaken on items that are to go on public display. Before embarking on any interventive treatment, the conservator carefully examines the object and records evidence of use, manufacture, materials, techniques, or design.

Through their research into the deterioration and preservation of the collections, their development of new conservation processes, and their knowledge of original technology, the V&A's conservation staff members have become leading experts in their fields. This knowledge is passed to others through publications and involvement with training and education programs.

Source: www.vam.ac.uk/res_cons/conservation/index.html

- **Education:** While an associate's or a bachelor's degree in textiles, museum studies, history, visual arts, or a related field is required by most museums, some technicians enter the career path by acquiring knowledge and abilities in a specific skill area. Technicians, for example, may have hands-on expertise in knitting, lace making, couture sewing techniques, wool tailoring, weaving, fabric dying, or other skill areas.

- **Experience:** An applicant may enter the museum as a technician with no formal qualifications required; however, some kind of applied skill, such as patternmaking or embroidery, is usually required. Some technicians gain training and experience by working as a volunteer with the technicians in a museum.

- **Personal characteristics:** Technicians have the patience and focus to work with great care and precision. They are planners, as artifacts must be thoroughly reviewed and restoration techniques thoroughly detailed before restoration begins. Often, the best technicians are those who are perfectionists in their areas of expertise.

Career Challenges

Technicians must come up with the techniques, products, and equipment to restore and preserve artifacts. While they may have an interest in fashion, it is more important that they have an understanding of chemistry, textile science, and technology. They are challenged to work methodically and accurately with safety and preservation of artifacts as key pressures.

Fashion Educator

Middle and high school teachers in the area of apparel and textiles often graduate from college and university programs with a bachelor's or master's degree in **Family and Consumer Science Education (FCSEd)**. They may be asked to teach courses in textiles, fashion, clothing selection and apparel care, clothing construction, interior design, fiber arts, consumer education, personal financial literacy, and careers in the fashion industry. Some FCSEd graduates choose employment with high schools or **vocational schools**, providing training for students who elect not to participate in a four-year college degree program after high school graduation. In these programs, they teach a range of courses, such as commercial clothing construction, apparel alteration, patternmaking, and retailing. Upon completion of these programs, the student may earn an associate's degree. There is also the opportunity for employment as a teacher in **trade schools**, those institutions offering fashion programs and providing certificates, rather than degrees, once the student completes the program. Trade schools offer programs in such areas as fashion design, illustration, retailing, and fashion merchandising.

Regardless of the type of school, educators in fashion programs are professionals who have many roles in addition to classroom instruction. Many make purchasing decisions about textbooks, supplies, and equipment such as sewing machines, sergers, and dress forms. Some conduct research, write about their findings, and submit their reports for publication. Others seek out funding sources for their programs in the schools, sourcing and writing grants and soliciting sponsors from the government or industry. Many participate in organizations and on committees that focus on pedagogical issues, curricula in schools and colleges, instructional methods, and job outlooks in fashion industry professions, among other topics. A great number of fashion educators include **professional development** on their to-do lists. This includes continuing education, often toward a higher degree; internships in the field; conference participation; and memberships in trade and educational organizations. Educators in colleges and universities often have the **terminal degree**, or highest degree available (or its equivalent) in fashion, business administration, higher education, or a related field—with specializations in their areas of instruction. For example, a fashion design professor may have a doctorate in the field, industry experience as a designer, and a broad knowledge of fashion design. In addition to a general knowledge of the field, it is expected that the professor have technical expertise in specialized areas such as computer-aided design, draping, patternmaking, or garment construction. In addition, many universities require college-level teaching experience, often not only in the classroom but also through other delivery methods, such as guided studies and online courses.

If the college-level teaching position includes responsibilities for advising and instructing graduate students, the faculty member must hold a terminal degree and be approved as a member of the graduate faculty. Experience in research and publication is preferred to demonstrate professional potential in scholarly work. Terms of appointment for college faculty range between 9 and 12 months. They may be tenure track, instructor, or lecturer positions. With prior experience, tenure track positions can be secured at the levels of assistant or associate professor. Many colleges and universities specify the proportion of teaching and research that a position will hold, such as 50 percent research and 50 percent teaching.

Qualifications

The following is a list of the educational goals, work experiences, and personal characteristics that will assist the person seeking a career in fashion education:

- **Education:** Fashion teachers in middle and high schools need at least a bachelor's degree and teaching certification. Their majors in college may include FCSEd, education, fashion design, textiles, interior design, fashion merchandising, and similar degree programs. Many of these teachers choose to complete a master's degree in the field to attain a higher knowledge level and a higher salary. For the college or university educator, a master's degree in an appropriate discipline (e.g., fashion design, fashion merchandising, education, or business administration) is required as a minimum. Most colleges and universities prefer a teaching candidate with a doctoral degree in a related field; many require this.

- **Experience:** For some college and university teaching positions, the candidate must have a minimum of five years of professional industry experience. College teaching experience in specific areas (e.g., fashion design, fashion merchandising, or product development) may also be required by certain colleges or universities. In some cases, a record of juried, scholarly publications is either required or preferred. Prospective employers may require a portfolio that includes examples of one's own work and examples of students' work.

- **Personal characteristics:** Flexibility, creativity, and a passion for lifelong learning are qualities of the successful educator. The ability to work as a team member is critical, as is the ability to develop and maintain collegial and industry relationships. The effective teacher is often a constant student, participating in professional development activities to stay abreast of industry trends and career opportunities.

Career Challenges

Staying up to date on industry trends while staying on top of teaching responsibilities, such as preparing lectures and grading assignments, is a challenge. Many universities also require faculty to maintain a program of research, one that results in creative exhibits or publications, and serve on college or community committees. This requires time management, organization, balance, and devotion to one's profession. Many fashion educators must wear a number of hats, from teacher and author to advisor and recruiter.

Summary

Museums offer a wide range of career opportunities, including museum director, curator, assistant curator, collections manager, archivist, conservator, and technician. Curators administer the affairs of museum centers and historic sites. The head curator of a museum is usually called the museum director. Depending on the size of the museum, the curator may supervise one or more assistants. While curators usually handle objects of historical significance, archivists handle mainly records and documents that are retained because of their importance and potential value in the future. The collections manager is responsible for preparing, managing, and supervising one or more specific groupings of artifacts in the museum. Museum conservators manage, preserve, treat, and document works of art and artifacts. Technicians perform various preparatory and maintenance tasks on museum items to restore and preserve artifacts. On a related yet different career track, fashion educators teach, research, and contribute to the fashion industry through career instruction and further studies.

Key Terms

academic curator training
accession
archivist
assistant curator
collections manager
curatorial traineeship
deaccession
Family and Consumer Science Education (FCSEd)
interactive display
managerial training
museological training
museum conservator
museum curator
museum director
museum technician
professional development
public affairs
stabilizing
terminal degree
trade school
vocational school

Online Resources

www.brooklynmuseum.org/community/blogosphere/2010/07/27/brooklyn-museum-mobile-web-on-iphone-and-droid/

www.fitnyc.edu/3470.asp

www.fondation-pb-ysl.net

www.guggenheim.org/new-york

www.itaaonline.org

www.kent.edu/museum/index.cfm

www.metmuseum.org/works_of_art/the_costume_institute

Discussion Questions

1. Compare and contrast the work responsibilities of the museum conservator with those of technician. Using the Internet, research and report on the types of technological advances that may affect conservation and restoration of historic textiles.

2. After perusing classified advertisements online (e.g., www.HigherEd.com and www. itaaonline.org) for clothing and textile educators in colleges and universities, list the differences in education and work experience requirements for the following types of educator positions: tenure track, lecturer, and instructor.

3. Locate and list descriptions of six lesser-known museums around the world that specialize in decorative arts, apparel, accessories, and interior furnishing and accessories. What are their missions, educational programs, and preservation strategies?

4. Many fashion designers visit museums for design inspiration, construction ideas, and color ideas. Identify three well-known designers who use historical costume as a source of inspiration. Provide illustrations, such as magazine clippings, of current garments the designers have created that were inspired by historical costumes. Identify the time periods and designers of these historical costumes.

Interview with Founder and Director of Ethical Fashion Forum

Source: http://www.vam.ac.uk/content/articles/i/interview-elizabeth-laskar-founder-director-of-ethical-fashion-forum/

Who are you and what do you do?

I am Elizabeth Laskar, founder and director of the Ethical Fashion Forum and one of the few Ethical Fashion Image and Lifestyle consultants in the UK.

What is the Ethical Fashion Forum?

Ethical Fashion Forum (EFF) provides support, training, access to information and tools for designers and businesses in the fashion industry, to allow them to bring social and environmental responsibility into their day-to-day practices. In doing so, EFF aims to reduce poverty, create sustainable livelihoods for garment workers, and reduce the impact of the industry on the environment.

What do you think are the most important issues when considering ethical fashion?

There are many important issues involved in ethical fashion. In the industry we tend to put them under two main headings to simplify the topics. When we talk about ethical fashion, we are taking into consideration fashion that is socially and environmentally conscious. Social issues may include topics of gender, fair pay, trade unions, and good governance. Environmental issues may include carbon miles, pesticides used in farming, natural and synthetic dyeing methods, how we dispose of clothing and its effect on the environment, water usage during production, post-production, and consumer life of a garment (for example, a question we ask in the sector is "Do we as consumers need to wash our clothes as much as we do?"). The issues are vast and there is lots of work yet to be done. The most important issue in ethical fashion concerning the modern-day consumer is how to manage change in our consumption of fashion. Can we look good, be stylish, and be environmentally and socially conscious?

Why is ethical fashion important?

Fashion plays a huge role in the world arena. In 2000, the world's consumers spent around one trillion U.S. dollars worldwide buying clothes—it has some power on the political, environmental, and social fronts. Also, in 2000, over 26.5 million people (globally) were working in the industry, and it's growing. Ethical fashion is important because if we start to better manage production; manufacturing; management of workers; and consumer behavior with respect for people, planet, and profit, the sector can provide social, environmental, and economic change for the better. With environmental change on the political agenda and poverty issues at our doorsteps, ethical fashion is just one of the many ways in which we, as consumers, can do our bit to help the world become a safer and healthier place to live in. Remember, ethical fashion is not about charity. It's all about taking into consideration the triple bottom line—People, Profit, and Planet.

Do you think it is ever okay to buy clothes from high-street stores?

In fashion, design is paramount and we tend to buy things because we feel and look good in them. Boycotting your high street is not always the answer. The idea is to find a way to manage a lifestyle change without losing what you enjoy about design. If you enjoy shopping on the high street and they are not already stocking ethical fashion, we suggest writing to the CEO and asking what they are doing about their current sourcing policy and when they are going to stock ethical fashion. A few high-street shops are already making changes. Top Shop's main store in London has around six ethical fashion labels and a vintage section. H&M and Marks & Spencer are carrying a few organic lines, and many more are starting to introduce lines. It is time for consumers to start asking questions. Another idea would be for every two items of clothing that you buy that aren't ethical, how about buying one that is? How about browsing through your local vintage and charity shops on a regular basis? You can find some great buys. Overall, it's okay to buy from the high street if you can't source ethical clothing easily. As caring consumers, it's up to us to start to ask questions and get retailers to start making a change.

Who do you admire in the world of ethical fashion?

The world of ethical fashion includes some of the

Interview with Founder and Director of Ethical Fashion Forum (continued)

most cutting-edge and inspirational topics that are being worked on by passionate individuals. If you meet someone in ethical fashion, you will certainly cross paths with passion and determination. What I admire most about the world of ethical fashion is that it is moving toward making the world a better and safer place through inspiring others through fashion. I admire Safia Minney, the founder of the fair-trade fashion company People Tree, for her dedication to building a successful label and business strategy. She spent years in the industry before she became profitable. I admire Junky Styling for pioneering high-end redesign into the mainstream—if there is anyone that is dedicated to recycling and making it wearable and individual, it's Junky. I admire IFAT and the soil association for helping implement and promote fair-trade businesses throughout the world. Lastly, London Fashion Week and the British Council have played a big part in the ethical fashion sector and I admire them for sticking their necks out as the first fashion week to devote a section to ethical fashion. It has given the industry a big boost in the world's media.

There seem so many issues around ethical fashion, what can I do to make a difference?
With the industry being so vast and complicated I categorize six key areas of ethical fashion, and engaging in one of them is a good start. It's worth keeping them in mind when you are out shopping:

1. **Organic:** This topic is mainly about the environment and the conditions in which the textile crop is grown.

2. **Fair trade:** This focuses mainly on social issues, such as child labor policies, fair wage, gender issues.

3. **Recycling:** The main aim is to reduce the amount of clothes that get put into landfills and to promote sharing or swapping clothes to get a new refreshed look.

4. **Re-design:** To create a new look; redesign is all about turning an old garment into a new inspirational outfit. For example, taking an old shirt and redesigning it into a skirt.

5. **Vintage:** This is about celebrating past design and wearing it with confidence and style.

6. **Technologies:** This area is when science meets fashion. Science is investing in producing materials that are kinder to the environment.

Getting into ethical fashion and making that lifestyle change can be done in some manageable steps. For starters, how about doing a wardrobe detox and then having a cocktail or tea party to swap clothes with your friends? It's a fun way to make a difference.

chapter 15

Environments: Web Sites, Exteriors, and Interiors

Envision a fashion business as a Tiffany necklace; think of its environment as the turquoise suede jewelry pouch encased in the signature blue box embossed with the beautiful black logo and tied up with white ribbon (Figure 15.1). A building, a kiosk in a mall, a boutique in a strip center, or a Web site can function as the "boxes" that house various types of fashion businesses. Think about the fashion retailer focusing on the business environment for a new brick-and-mortar store. He or she strives to locate the right building or storefront; if the right facility cannot be found, someone (the architect) may design the building to order. Another (the interior designer) may design and oversee the installation of the interior—from the ceiling and lights to the floor coverings and furnishings. Yet another (the visual merchandiser) may select the fixtures and mannequins, then set up the sales floor to entice the consumer to come into the store and buy. If the entrepreneur is an e-retailer, it is the Web site developer who creates the "store" exterior and interior, with its visuals, links, sound, and motion. All of these career professionals are responsible for creating the most attractive and functional "box" possible for the business within the space and budget allocated by the retailer.

Figure 15.1 The exterior and interior of a brick-and-mortar store can be related to the wrappings of a Tiffany product—with the box being comparable to the store exterior.

The fashion industry is a visual one. As a result, the way a fashion business's building, Web site, and interior look can affect the business's profitability and image. Web site developers and architects work to create or locate the right exterior for a fashion business. Combining knowledge with aesthetic vision, the interior designer often collaborates with the architect and visual merchandising professional to develop interior environments that are safe, functional, and attractive while meeting the needs of the people using the space. Once the space design is complete in a mall, the mall manager works to keep the interior environment looking fresh and appealing for consumers. Careers involved in developing the environments of fashion businesses are examined in this chapter and categorized in terms of Web sites, exteriors, and interiors. They include the following: Web site developer, architect, interior designer, visual merchandising professional, and mall manager.

Web Sites

We begin our exploration of careers that relate to the sites of fashion businesses with one of the newest and fastest-changing career paths, that of the Web site developer.

Web Site Developer

Web site development, or design, is concerned with constructing Web pages and sites from both aesthetic and marketing perspectives (Figure 15.2). The titles used to describe positions in Web site construction are not standard by any means, and often the terms "Web site designer" and "Web site developer" are used interchangeably. Web site developers are responsible for everything from designing a Web site's look and feel to incorporating features such as e-commerce, online community, animations, interactive applications, and advertising hosting into the site—all while ensuring that the site's design is optimized for the specific technologies supporting it. While many Web site developers are salaried employees (i.e., working in advertising, marketing, or design agencies or at Web consulting firms, which build and manage

Web sites for client organizations), there are a large number of freelance Web site developers in the industry. These professionals need general design skills (e.g., an understanding of drawing and a knack for creating attractive combinations of color and form) and knowledge of Web-specific design factors (e.g., screen resolution, image compression, accessibility, and Web site architecture). A career as a Web site developer requires a combination of visual skills and proficiency in technology.

The success of Web site developers can be determined by whether people stay on a site or leave and whether they do what the site wants them to do while they are there. If the Web site's purpose is to generate e-commerce, sales results ultimately provide the measure of the success of the Web site developer's work. If the Web site depends on advertising or subscriptions for its revenue, then calculations such as online advertisement click-throughs and new subscribers will provide the measure of success. If the Web site's intention is to increase brand value or product value to the consumer, then its effectiveness is more difficult to measure. Web site developers create the look, feel, and navigation for Web sites. Their work includes defining the **user interface (UI)**, the visuals people see and interact with when they view a Web site and the navigation by which they move through the site. The developers create catchy graphics or animated images and choose the style, fonts, and other visual elements that make a site appealing and help a company advance its business goals. Because Web surfers are increasingly accessing the Internet via wireless devices, Web site developers are equipping the pages they design for these phones and computers.

A good Web site can be many times more effective than a print brochure by delivering the exact type and amount of information consumers desire when they want it. The successful Web site allows clients to place an order any time of the day or night without filling out a print form or dialing a phone number. Along with orders, a site captures relevant user data, such as pages

Figure 15.2 Web site development, or design, is concerned with constructing Web pages and sites from both aesthetic and marketing perspectives.

Each year the Web Marketing Association names the Best Fashion Web Site as part of the annual WebAward Competition. Now in its 15th year, the WebAwards are recognized as the premier industry-based Web site award program in the world.

Best Web sites are selected by judges who review the entered sites using the seven criteria below.

- Design

- Ease of use

- Copywriting

- Interactivity

- Use of technology

- Innovation

- Content

The WebAwards is the standards-defining competition that sets benchmarks for 96 industries, including fashion Web sites, based on the seven criteria of a successful site. "The fashion industry is very competitive when it comes to Web development, and companies can benefit from the independent evaluation of their online efforts," said William Rice, president of the Web Marketing Association. "The fashion industry knows what it takes to create an image for its products. Their Web sites are extensions of those images and invite the users to learn more about the brands which they identify with."

Source:
Web Marketing Association at www.webaward.org.

---

viewed, time spent at the site, and other information that can allow for targeted marketing to improve a company's business. Along with design in general, a Web site developer's job is to make the product (i.e, the Web site) functional and entertaining for the user. For example, some apparel Web sites allow customers to "try on" clothing selections in different colors and combinations on body forms that resemble their own.

A corporate Web site should help sell or market the institution. A Web site developer working on a corporate intranet site, for instance, will want to ensure easy access to relevant information. An e-commerce Web site guides users to the products the company is selling and helps make the process of buying these as quick, easy, and secure as possible. The **Web site developer** observes and interacts with clients or other departments; takes other forms of information, such as brochures, slide presentations, print advertisements, or other documents, and turns them into multimedia experiences; and incorporates user data to help define and shape a Web site that people want to visit often and helps the sponsoring company achieve its goals (Box 15.1).

Qualifications

For artists and techies at heart with a perfectionist streak and the desire to have their work presented around the world, Web site development may be the ideal profession. What do you need to learn to become a Web site developer? The list of educational requirements, work experiences, and personal characteristics follows.

- **Education:** A bachelor's degree in graphic design, computer information science, visual arts, fine arts, or a similar field is required. Some fashion design majors complete a minor in graphic design or computer information technologies to make them marketable in this career track. Increasingly, universities are offering, and employers are requesting, specialized degrees in such areas as user interface design and information design.

- **Experience:** Minimally, Web site developers need to be familiar with Web graphics and understand the way they work. The Web site developer should also be proficient with industry-standard graphic-design software and Web layout tools. In the multimedia design field, it is the Web developer's objective to stay on top or ahead of the newest innovations. This career track requires as much knowledge of design-tool software as it does creative energy. A person can move into the Web site development field after working as a Web site graphic designer, creating the graphic elements for Web sites, including banner ads, buttons, and other navigational elements.

- **Personal characteristics:** The Web site developer must be open to learning new skills on an ongoing basis. Designing pages is not simply creative, though artistic talent is required for a successful career; it also supports a business goal. The Web site developer needs an understanding of business and marketing concepts. Good people skills and imagination complement the mastery of the design tools.

Career Challenges

The interactive and highly integrated nature of a Web site means that there is a constant cycle of creating, troubleshooting, and publishing involved. While Web developers attend organizational or departmental meetings on a regular basis, the largest portion of their workdays is spent on computers—creating new graphics and scripts, experimenting with animation, implementing new navigational techniques, or hunting down broken or expired hyperlinks. Web site development is a high-profile role, as this work is viewed and assessed by thousands of people every day. The downside to this high visibility is that a mistake can affect the entire company. The Web site developer must work with creativity and strong attention to detail. It can be a stressful job to stay on top of technology, troubleshoot problems, and interpret people's requests for Web site additions. The Web site developer is challenged with being a perpetual student of the craft. As the Internet and technology evolve and the needs of Internet users change, there is a continual need for new skills among Web site developers.

Exteriors

Architect

While the Web developer builds a virtual business, it is the architect who builds the brick-and-mortar business. The **architect** is a building designer who may work with a wide variety of structures. Those who specialize in serving retail clients have opportunities for projects ranging from small freestanding retail stores to large malls. These types of business locations are referred to as **commercial real estate**. **Architecture** is the creative blend of art and science in the design of environments for people. The plans for a building ultimately focus on the needs of the people who use them, to include aesthetics, safety, and environmental factors.

The architect and client first collaborate on the client's vision and discuss options, costs, and materials. The architect creates concept drawings, often on the computer, for the client to review. At this point, the architect spends time consulting closely with the client and builders,

Figure 15.3 Exterior of the Cynthia Rowley boutique in Boston, an example of customized commercial real estate.

selling, costing, and explaining concepts. When the concepts are approved by the client, the architect draws up plans that illustrate not only how the building will look but also how to build it. The drawings show the beams that hold up the building; heating, air-conditioning, and ventilation; electrical and plumbing systems; and so on. Architects communicate the design and oversee the work of builders, contractors, plumbers, painters, carpenters, air-conditioning and heating specialists, and others. While most commercial work has strict budgets and practical limitations, Figure 15.3 presents the opposite scenario with an example of an elaborate architectural facade with its triptych windows, the Cynthia Rowley boutique in Boston.

Qualifications

The profession of architect requires the following educational goals, experiences, and personal characteristics:

- **Education:** Becoming an architect is a long process. A prospective architect must complete an academic degree specifically focused on architecture. This can be earned through a five-year bachelor's of architecture program, an affiliated two-year master's of architecture program, or, for those whose undergraduate degrees were in a field unassociated with architecture, a three- to four-year master's of architecture program. Many students also prepare for a career in architecture with a four-year (undergraduate) liberal arts degree followed by a three- to four-year (graduate) master's of architecture degree. To be called an architect, it is necessary to be licensed in the state where one works. Most states require a candidate to have an accredited **National Architectural Accrediting Board Inc. (NAAB)** first-professional degree. Candidates are expected to have completed an internship period with an architecture firm, typically of three years. All states require applicants to pass a rigorous, eight-part **Architect Registration Examination (ARE)**. Employers now place greater emphasis on applicants who have mastered computer-aided design programs, which have become required knowledge for any architect as technology develops.

- **Experience:** Many college students gain work experience through an internship with an architect, required by some colleges and universities. Most new architects begin in an assistant position, working with an experienced architect in an area of specialization in which they plan to build a career. Once experienced, architects move into a variety of employment venues and often develop an area of specialization.

- **Personal characteristics:** Architects must be able to visualize projects and communicate these visions through drawing and computer-generated images. Presentation skills, effective writing, and public-speaking abilities are also important. Decision making, team leadership, and creativity are key attributes of the successful architect. The architect must have high attention to detail and strong time-management skills.

Career Challenges

The first career challenge the architect faces is the amount of money, time, and effort it takes for the education and licensing needed to start this career track. It takes a great deal of perseverance and dedication to complete a degree successfully and become certified in architecture. For most, this profession requires "paying one's dues" for possibly years before actually gaining hands-on professional experience. Beginning architects research zoning, building codes, and legal filings; draft plans from others' designs; and build models at the side of a more experienced architect. Once in the field, the architect faces daily challenges of constant revision of plans based on client needs, contractor issues, and budget restrictions. Plans and priorities have to be reevaluated regularly and revised accordingly. Additionally, there are legal aspects of the architect's career, as the architect must stay on top of building codes, safety requirements, and legal filings.

Interiors

Next, the focus will shift indoors to explore the career options of interior designer, visual merchandising professional, mall manager, and assistant mall manager.

Interior Designer

Interior designers work in a wide range of environments, including homes and businesses. They can work alone, as part of a team of professionals, or in collaboration with other professionals in related careers, as with the interior designer and the architect. Some interior designers work primarily in **residential design**, focusing on home environments. These interior designers function as fashion service providers for residential clients. Others function as ancillary fashion providers for retail clients or businesses. They may work with architects and other designers to provide exterior and interior services for public structures. A number of architectural firms include an interior design department. Referred to as **commercial designers**, or *contract* *designers*, these interior designers concentrate on public spaces, including such projects such as retail stores; hotels, motels, and restaurants; office buildings; and so on. Some commercial designers work with the visual merchandising divisions of retail operations, whether planning a store's layout, locating furnishings and props, or designing major visual displays.

Interior designers often specialize in an area within either residential or contract interior design. The residential interior designer may develop a reputation and clientele through working in a certain type of homes, such as vacation properties or high-end residences. The commercial, or contract, interior designer may specialize in retail operations or, even more specifically, high-fashion boutiques (Figures 15.4a and b). Yet another commercial designer may earn a good living through work on hotels, stores, or museums. As designers gain work experience, they often identify a niche, an area of particular interest, that uses their skills, pays well, and in which they build industry contacts and a positive reputation.

Successful interior designers know how to plan a space and how to present that plan visually so that it can be communicated to the client. Interior designers must also know about the materials and products that will be used to create and furnish the space. These materials are constantly changing, as new products are introduced daily. The effective designer knows how texture, color, lighting, and other factors combine and interact in a space. On a more technical level, interior designers understand the structural requirements of their plans, the health and safety issues, building codes, electrical and plumbing requirements, and many other practical aspects.

What exactly do interior designers learn to do the job effectively? They must be knowledgeable in the areas of building construction, building materials, specification writing, building codes, technical drawing, and business practices. Interior designers analyze the client's needs and problems, develop detailed design solutions to present to the client, then organize and supervise projects to full completion while being attentive to the client's desires and resources. Interior designers collaborate with suppliers and other building specialists throughout the process. Box 15.2 provides a listing of the tasks that may be required of an interior designer. Interior design is a discipline that demands research, analytical skills, a command of technology, and knowledge of products.

Figure 15.4a
The commercial interior designer may specialize in retail operations or, more specifically, high-fashion boutiques, as illustrated by this Betsey Johnson boutique.

Figure 15.4b
The commercial interior designer aims to reflect the personality of the designer in the boutique. Here, Betsey Johnson dons her Barbie Kentucky Derby hat.

Box 15.2 A Task Listing for an Interior Designer's Typical Project

1. Research and analysis of the client's goals and requirements and development of documents, drawings, and diagrams that reflect those needs

2. Formulation of preliminary space plans and two- and three-dimensional design concept studies and sketches that integrate the client's program needs and are based on knowledge of the principles of interior design and human behavior

3. Confirmation that preliminary space plans and design concepts are safe, functional, and aesthetically appropriate and meet all public health, safety, and welfare requirements, including code, accessibility, environmental, and sustainability issues

4. Selection of colors, materials, and finishes to appropriately portray the design concept and meet functional, maintenance, life-cycle performance, environmental, and safety requirements

5. Selection, specification, and documentation of furniture, furnishings, equipment, and trim work, including layout drawings and detailed product description; and contract documentation to facilitate pricing, shipping, and installation of new furnishings

6. Provision of project management services, including preparation of project budgets and schedules

7. Preparation of construction documents, consisting of plans, elevations, details, and specifications to illustrate nonstructural and/or nonseismic (relating to earthquakes) partition layouts, power and communications locations, reflected ceiling plans and lighting designs, materials and finishes, and furniture layouts

8. Confirmation that construction documents adhere to regional building and fire codes, municipal codes, and any other jurisdictional statutes, regulations, and guidelines that are applicable to the interior space

9. Coordination and collaboration with other allied design professionals who may be retained to provide consulting services, including but not limited to architects; structural, mechanical, and electrical engineers; and various specialty consultants

10. Confirmation that construction documents for nonstructural and/or nonseismic construction are signed and sealed by the responsible interior designer and are filed with code-enforcement officials

11. Administration of contract documents, bids, and negotiations as the client's agent

12. Review and reporting on the implementation of projects while in progress and upon completion

Source: www.asid.org

Qualifications

A list of the education, experience, and personal characteristics of a successful interior designer follows.

- **Education:** A bachelor's degree in interior design, housing and interior design, visual arts, or a related field is a minimum requirement. After receiving an interior design degree from an accredited university or college and working in the industry for two years, an interior designer can take the National Council for Interior Design Qualification (NCIDQ) exam. Passing all sections of this exam will advance the interior designer's career by allowing opportunities for professional memberships and state licensing.

Figure 15.5 A Moroccan interior features traditional, non-Western design elements.

- **Experience:** Many college students must complete an internship or two before graduation. This experience, especially for students with internships in more than one area, opens the door to contacts and knowledge within the interior design field. Retail sales or visual merchandising work with a home fashions retailer, a do-it-yourself building firm, or a textile store provides a strong background for the prospective interior designer.

- **Personal characteristics:** Interior designers are creative, imaginative, and artistic, yet they also need to be disciplined and organized businesspeople. As members of a service profession, interior designers depend on their ability to satisfy clients. The top interior designers know how to sell their ideas to clients, create informative and persuasive presentations, and maintain good client relationships. They understand the artistic and technical requirements of a project, interpersonal communication, and management strategies. In terms of interpersonal skills, most interior designers are comfortable meeting and dealing with many kinds of people. They communicate clearly and effectively and are attentive listeners. Because they often must work with architects, contractors, and other service providers, interior designers are constantly working as part of a team. Negotiation and problem solving are parts of their daily routines.

Career Challenges

Succeeding at interior design requires energy, technical proficiency, vision, and, often, entrepreneurial knowledge. Many interior designers own their businesses and must have the skills to run a business. Watching expenses, working with vendors, meeting deadlines, and managing projects can be huge undertakings. Working on more than one project at a time under demanding deadlines is part of the job. Within each project, there are bound to be changes along the way. Clients change their minds, and suppliers no longer have products available. The interior designer is challenged with keeping the client, vendors, contractors, and builders on the same track. Finally, the interior designer should be culturally sensitive to and aware of non-Western design precedents and influences (Figure 15.5).

Visual Merchandising Professional

In Chapter 10, the job of visual merchandiser is introduced, and it is discussed as a position that may be freelance or one of employment with a firm that is not a traditional retailer. In this chapter, you will see how visual merchandising has grown as a career area that is a spin-off of the tremendous growth of interiors businesses.

There are many auxiliary businesses that have developed from the increasing emphasis on the importance of visual merchandising; all hire visual merchandising professionals. Mannequin manufacturers offer a range of choices and now can design and produce mannequins to resemble a specific celebrity or person. A growth area and employer of visual merchandisers, **prop houses** rent furniture, fixtures, mannequins, and decor accessories to visual merchandisers, saving the company money on limited-use display pieces while reducing the amount of warehouse space and labor needed to inventory and store visual merchandising props. Another area of employment in visual merchandising is with the equipment and fixture supplier. These companies sell all that one needs to outfit a store. Fixtures, such as T-stands, rounders, and four-ways, are offered; wall slats and hanging bars provide additional merchandise displays. The visual merchandising professional working for one of these interior-related firms is, in essence, responsible for in-house promotion that will be seen by the company's clients. Some fixture and equipment companies hire visual merchandising professionals to work with their clients, retailers, and manufacturers on efficient and attractive space usage. Often using a computer-aided design system, the visual merchandising professional will develop plan-o-grams, also referred to as prototypes. As depicted in Figures 15.6a–c, a **plan-o-gram** is a floor plan on which the placement and types of racks, fixtures, display units, and merchandise is laid out in order to create an easy flow of traffic and to present the merchandise most effectively. The plan-o-gram is used as an effective selling tool to show the retailer or manufacturer how many different types of fixtures will be needed and what the interior of the business will look like when it is furnished.

Yet another employer of the visual merchandiser (commonly freelance, in this case) is the designer or manufacturer of apparel and accessories. Take, for example, a manufacturer's showroom on Broadway in the Fashion District of Manhattan. The manufacturer may hire a visual merchandising professional to design and install displays in the showroom and its windows with every seasonal line change, as shown in Figures 15.7a–c.

Qualifications

Successful visual merchandising professionals working in the interiors industry are likely to possess the following qualities:

- **Education:** A bachelor's degree in fashion design, fashion merchandising, interior design, retail planning and design, visual arts, or a related field is a minimum requirement.

- **Experience:** Many visual display professionals begin as a member of the visual merchandising team for a retailer, installing window and interior displays. Others may come from the fields of interior design, fashion styling, or store planning. With all of these backgrounds,

Figure 15.6a
MockShop, with its visual merchandising software, allows the retailer to create a virtual floor layout that indicates the placement of wall units, furnishings, fixtures, and displays.

Figure 15.6b
MockShop's plan-o-gram indicates how merchandise should be displayed to present the merchandise most effectively.

Figure 15.6c
MockShop's layout of products featured on the retailer's sales floor is used to educate employees on trends, and how to accessorize outfits.

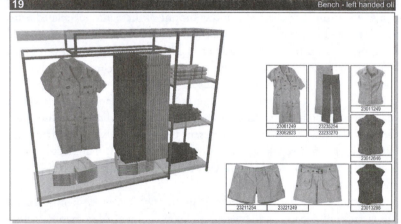

employers expect job candidates to have a variety of visual merchandising work experiences, sales training, and a solid portfolio of work.

• **Personal characteristics:** The visual merchandising professional must understand design, marketing, and merchandising. A high sense of aesthetics, computer-aided design skills, and an understanding of visual art principles are keys to securing a position in this area. The ability to create effective displays using props, mannequins, and other display components is critical.

Career Challenges

Beginning a career in visual merchandising is not easy. The jobs are available in many sectors of the fashion industry, including retail stores, manufacturers' showrooms, and visual merchandising companies; however, not everyone is interested in making the sacrifices often required to get started in this field. Low pay, hard work, and long hours, including nights and weekends, describe the start of many visual merchandising careers.

Figures 15.7a–c
Sergio Mannino Kensiegirl footwear showroom displays.

Mall Manager

A **mall manager** is responsible for everything in the mall, from planning its budget and promotional activities to developing its mix of tenants and building community relations. On a given day, the mall manager is involved with marketing, tenant leasing, increasing capital, building improvement, construction, and security, a very important issue. What makes a mall successful is often the mix of stores available to the customer (Figure 15.8). The mall manager examines the mall's retail mix to determine its strengths and weaknesses. Incorporating interesting stores and concepts that are unique to the area, as well as balancing the number of apparel, home, service, and food retailers, are both key to a mall's success.

Mall managers calculate customer demand into the equation, striving to meet the needs of the current demographic segment and anticipate through research what the future demographics may be. They look at home ownership, income, and customer profiles within the community to understand what the customer is looking for and who that customer is. The ultimate goals of the mall manager are to grow the value of the property itself and at the same time improve tenant listings and leasing capacity. To be "100 percent filled" is the objective, as is finding ways to complement an already integrated mix of stores. A classified advertisement for a mall manager is featured in Box 15.3.

Qualifications

A list of the educational requirements, work experiences, and personal characteristics for the successful mall manager follows.

- **Education:** A bachelor's degree in management, merchandising, marketing, retailing, business administration, real estate (leasing), property management and/or retail management, or a related field is a minimum requirement.

Position:	Mall Manager
Company:	Mall Property Development Group
Location:	Columbus, Ohio

Description:

- Managers are responsible for leasing (long-term and temporary), negotiation of contracts, staff supervision, office management, budgeting and monthly financial analysis and reporting, tenant and public relations, and operational issues, all with the goal of maximizing the asset value of the property.

Position Requirements:

- Bachelor's degree in the areas of marketing, merchandising, business administration, real estate (leasing), property management and/or retail management, or related field

- Understanding of business administration principles

- Minimum of 5 years professional management experience; preference given for shopping center management

- Excellent communication and organizational skills

- Temporary and/or permanent leasing experience

- Must possess superior communication and interpersonal skills with a high degree of human relations skills

- Strong management skills

- Proficient in applicable software (e.g., Lotus, Word, and Excel)

- **Experience:** Retail sales experience with a variety of retail operations provides an excellent background, including summer or part-time employment during college. An internship with a mall management firm is an excellent way to gain experience in this career path. Many mall managers also secure store management experience so they can understand the needs and concerns of their mall tenants.

- **Personal characteristics:** The mall manager must be a strong leader who knows what needs to be done. Because multiple tasks arise daily, the mall manager must be a self-motivated individual who is able to work independently. Working in a mall with staff, tenants, and consumers demands being a good listener and an effective problem solver.

Assistant Mall Manager

In larger malls, the mall manager may supervise one or more assistants. An **assistant mall manager** is responsible for administering mall programs under the supervision of the property's mall manager. This person is critical in communicating operational issues to tenants, contractors, and staff.

Qualifications

The person who fills the role of assistant mall manager needs the following qualifications:

- **Education:** A bachelor's degree in management, merchandising, marketing, retailing, business administration, real estate (leasing), property management and/or retail management, or a related field is a minimum requirement.

- **Experience:** Ideally, two to three years of work experience in business administration, property management, or retail management are needed to open the door to this career path. Assistant mall managers usually work a minimum of three to five years before moving up to the position of mall manager.

- **Personal characteristics:** Effective oral and written communication abilities and organizational and management skills are needed. Proficiency in computers and a good working knowledge of budgeting, accounting, and financial analysis are necessary, as are strong human relations skills. The assistant mall manager must be able to adapt to a changing work environment and be a self-motivated individual who is able to work independently and multitask under pressure.

Career Challenges

The mall manager and assistant mall manager have a team of bosses: all of the tenants in the mall. It is not easy to please a group of employers with different needs, expectations, and lease costs. Communicating with a group of this size is another challenge. Mall management reports to yet another audience: the mall's customers. It can be stressful to strive for a leasing level of full capacity, particularly when existing tenants and customers have specific ideas on which retailers will complement the current tenant mix. For example, the owner of an athletic footwear store that has made its home in the mall for years may be extremely dissatisfied to find that the mall manager has leased space to a similar retail operation. Keeping both tenants and customers happy and encouraging growth in the mall are two key objectives that may be tough for mall management to accomplish.

Summary

Digital, exterior, and interior environments profoundly influence image and profitability of all types of businesses in the fashion industry. Pursuit of a career in environments demands both technical and aesthetic know-how. The architect is a building designer who may work with a wide variety of structures. Those who specialize in serving retail clients have opportunities for projects ranging from small freestanding retail stores to large malls. Web site developers are "virtual architects" who have a strong grasp of Web design applications and programming, understand the process of Web formatting, and possess the design sense to put it all together in a user-friendly format. The commercial interior designer works with clients and other design professionals to develop inside spaces that are functional and attractive and meet the needs of the people using the space. An offshoot of commercial interior design, visual merchandising professionals now work with such companies as mannequin manufacturers, prop houses, home furnishings manufacturers, equipment and fixture vendors, and fashion manufacturers and designers. They are responsible for presenting an aesthetically appealing environment that reflects the company's image and sells merchandise. The mall manager and assistant mall manager are responsible for everything in the mall, from planning its budget and creating promotional activities to developing its mix of tenants and building community relations.

Physical and virtual spaces are continually expected to create, buy, sell, and transform. As with many careers, the key to success in these fields is satisfying the client. If you have strong technical, visual, and communication skills, consider a future in environments.

Key Terms

architect
architecture
Architect Registration Examination (ARE)
assistant mall manager
commercial real estate
commercial designer
interior designer
mall manager

National Architectural Accrediting Board
Inc. (NAAB)
plan-o-gram
prop house
residential design
user interface (UI)
Web site developer
Web site development

Online Resources

6thstreetdesignschool.blogspot.com/2011/03/confessions-of-designer-abbe-fenimore.html

www.1stdibs.com

www.architonic.com

www.dirtt.net

www.getdecorating.com/interiors.cfm

www.interiordesign.net/

www.mydeco.com/plan-my-room

www.sfd.co.uk/

www.sieder3.com/prettyhaus/recommended-reading/

www.vmsd.com

www.vrsoftware.com

www.wallpaper.com/architecture

www.wallpaper.com/interiors

Discussion Questions

1. Compare and contrast the careers of architect, interior designer, and Web site developer. Examine the education and licensing requirements common to these three professions.

2. Consider a shopping district in the area where you live. What types of businesses stand out? How do the exteriors, interiors, and Web sites relate to one another within each business? Evaluate how well the sum of the business's environments creates a successful entity.

3. Visit a mall or other type of shopping center and record some of the major tenants (i.e., what types of businesses, including retail, restaurant, and entertainment), their adjacencies, and any voids in types of tenants that would draw customers to the facility. Describe the lifestyle approach the shopping facility represents. Identify the most desirable location in the facility based on customer traffic, proximity to parking, and nearness to the best neighboring stores.

Interview with an Interior Designer

Abbe Fenimore
By Anne Alexander Sieder, February 9, 2011
Source: www.sieder3.com/prettyhaus/2011/02/09/interior-designer-abbe-fenimore-interview/

Abbe Fenimore of Studio Ten 25 is an inspiring interior designer running her own design service and Web shop (www.studioten25.com). Here, she is interviewed by Anne Alexander Sieder of www.prettyhaus.com.

Besides a love of good design, we have another thing in common. Like you, I lived in Rome for almost two years and really loved my time there. How do you feel your experiences in Rome affected your design sensibilities?
Being in Rome was a magical experience for me. I spent almost six weeks there with my university (Louisiana Tech) and was able to travel around Europe during that time too. Most of my classes focused on design, and being in the heart of such great history was indescribable. We also had the opportunity to meet with the interior designer for the U.S. embassy in Rome. Seeing her describe her day-to-day tasks and actually working with her on local design projects was it for me. I knew that I was right where I needed to be and that becoming a designer was it for me.

You have both an interior design practice and a store where you sell home accessories. How do you juggle all that (and a husband and two dogs, too)? Which came first and how similar is your approach to running them?
Juggle is right. I'm fortunate to have a husband who cheers me on every step of the way. I go to him for advice, and his honest, sometimes brutal opinion always keeps me focused on the goal and end result. The design business came first in 2007. After one of my clients pushed me to give them access to an "online catalogue" Shop Ten 25 was born. The design business and the shop go hand in hand; clients can get access to the shop at a discount and the shop clients have access to my local or online design services. It's my three-legged table, they all work together to create the complete design experience and the table wouldn't work without all three.

Figure 15.9a Interior designer and e-retailer Abbe Fenimore.

As for the dogs, having the girls around the studio makes the days entertaining. The nose bump is their sign that it's time to hit the dog park or at least play a little fetch. They keep me moving and remind me to step away and not lose sight of how important "family" time is.

If I were a fly on the wall in the room when you sit down to develop a design concept what would I see? How does your typical design process run its course?
I always start the design process with the inspirational images my client provides me. I then pull notes from our conversations and begin to develop a direction. The floor plan is my next priority and an important part to developing scale and flow in the room. I may develop a few options and create an elevation to make sure what I imagine will work in the room. From there, I begin to pull fabrics, paint swatches, furniture ideas, and look at the price points. Keeping the budget in check is the biggest challenge. Most clients give me the budget and are not really sure how to use it. Showing the pieces that work in their space with a few price-point options is a good way to help them decide what's really important.

Interview with an Interior Designer (continued)

If you had to design a living room that you would still want to enjoy in twenty years, what kinds of things would you include and what would you leave out?

I would include furniture that has a timeless shape and a good structure, classics. My mother still has her sofa and accent chairs from the '80s and we recently re-covered them. The new fabric we selected updated the look of a classic piece and now she can enjoy them for another 15 years. Unfortunately, not all furniture today is made with such high quality. You do get what you pay for. I would leave out expensive trendy pieces. You can always change out pillows, drapes, and rugs over time to fit your style and change in color choices. Spending money on trends is easy today, as most vendors create replicas or "inspired by" pieces at a fraction of the cost. This allows you to have high style without the high cost and it doesn't hurt so much when the pieces leave the house.

What is the most valuable piece of advice that anyone ever gave you? And, what advice would you give to an interior design student just starting out?

Hire a good accountant and stay organized! Keeping up with invoices, receipts, and taxes is a very important part of this business. I have to watch every penny I spend and have to constantly ask, "Do I really need to spend this and will it add to the growth of my business?" At the end of the day, having your own business is wonderful. But you must plan your costs, time, and marketing dollars wisely to make sure your profit meets or exceeds your goals.

On a personal note, you have to be true to you and what motivates you to get up and go to work every day. Sometimes turning down a client can be a good thing. Yes, doing something for the money and paying the bills may be looming over you but putting yourself in a crummy situation can be worse. Learn to ask the right questions. Learn from past experiences with bad and good clients. It's okay to say no sometimes; we cannot be everything to everyone. Be professional *always*, even when you are standing your ground.

Are there any tools, apps, or programs that you can't live without? Tell us what you love about them.

Wow, I'm feeling a bit excessive now as I think about this one. My tape measure, fine-point Sharpie pens, and a small notebook are my "can't live withouts." You never know when you need to measure something and write down the details. Of course, I need a fabulous bag that holds everything, too. As for programs, Icovia is my go to for floor plans while Adobe Photoshop Elements helps me put it all together. And, of course, my Macbook and iPhone are crucial to staying productive.

Figure 15.9b A mix of textures in this living room by Abbe Fenimore.

Interview with an Interior Designer (continued)

Everybody has their own design voice. If I were to walk into a room you designed what would jump out at me and scream Abbe? Do you have a favorite design "trick" that you rely on?
I tend to gravitate toward glamorous pieces, especially mirrored furniture and accessories. Things that say "Abbe" are pretty simple. Here are my must-haves for every room I work on:

- I love to start with clean lines and bring in pieces that have good shape and quality.

- Your room can look amazing but if it's not comfortable, what's the point?

- Texture, texture, and more texture. Mixing textures with accent fabrics, draperies, and furniture pieces keeps a room from feeling flat and blah.

- Color and pattern. Most of my clients are confused and overwhelmed when it comes to color and how to mix patterns. If your basics are simple, bringing in a great wall color and accent color through art and pillows can pull it all together without being color crazy.

In addition to your regular interior design services, you also offer eDesign. How does that work? Why would someone choose eDesign instead of "regular" design? How do you virtually walk your clients through the design process?
Virtual design is perfect for the "do-it-yourself-ers" who want the look of a professionally designed room without having the designer come out to their home. No matter where they live or what their time frame is, clients now have access to the design services needed to complete their homes. The package sent by the designer allows the client to create the room on his or her time frame and budget. E-mails and maybe even a few phone calls give the client support. It's perfect, really. We give clients everything they need to know for creating a stunning space, including a furniture plan, fabric and paint samples, a shopping list, and thorough instructions for making their home exactly what they dream it to be.

Figure 15.9c
The restful color palette and styling of Abbe Fenimore.

Interview with Co-Author of *Careers in Interior Design*

Nancy Asay

Interior design is an industry with many facets. This is one of the reasons my co-author, Marciann Patton, and I wrote the careers book. Currently, this book is used in colleges and universities to help interior design students understand the numerous directions this career choice can take. I think the book is a great read even for those without a college direction, but who are looking for a creative career. When looking for a career in interior design, a person needs to look around and see which areas are actively hiring. Health care is a great example. When the economy is slow, interior design professionals need to take advantage of the lack of new construction and understand that money is being spent to renovate existing spaces. Now it is all about the interior, instead of the leftover budget that we many times get to deal with as a result of the new construction cost overruns. This is true for both residential and commercial interior designers.

I have been a professional interior designer for forty years. I have NCIDQ certificate # 003407, am a professional member of ASID, a registered interior designer in the state of Missouri, and, currently, a senior instructor at Missouri State University in the Department of Fashion and Interior Design. I also maintain a small business, Nancy Asay Interiors, and work with clients who I have worked with in the past. Time does not permit me to take new clients or to do large commercial jobs. Maintaining a small business also keeps me current with products and other industry professionals. These contacts are extremely helpful now, as I teach students at the university.

When I went to college, I wanted a career that I could work at part time, giving me a way to support myself, and potentially my children. I always pictured myself married with children and wanted to be able to handle everything if something happened to my husband (which my mother went through). This was my pre-college thought.

I have a bachelor of fine arts in interior design from the University of Kansas. When I graduated from college, I had a difficult time finding an interior

Figure 15.10 *Careers in Interior Design* co-author Nancy Asay.

design job because everyone wanted someone with experience. I chose to work in commercial interior design because I wanted an eight-to-five day job. Because I was unable to find employment with an existing interior design firm, I selected six businesses that marketed commercial furniture but did not have an interior design department. I applied to all six explaining that I could start an interior design department for them and increase their business. All six agreed to the idea, so I selected from six firms. Starting a commercial interior design business gave me great experience and a very marketable future in commercial interior design.

I have always enjoyed my career in interior design and have specialized in space planning and health-care design. I earned a master's in education from Drury University for the purpose of teaching interior design as my latest career. It has been a great way to give back.

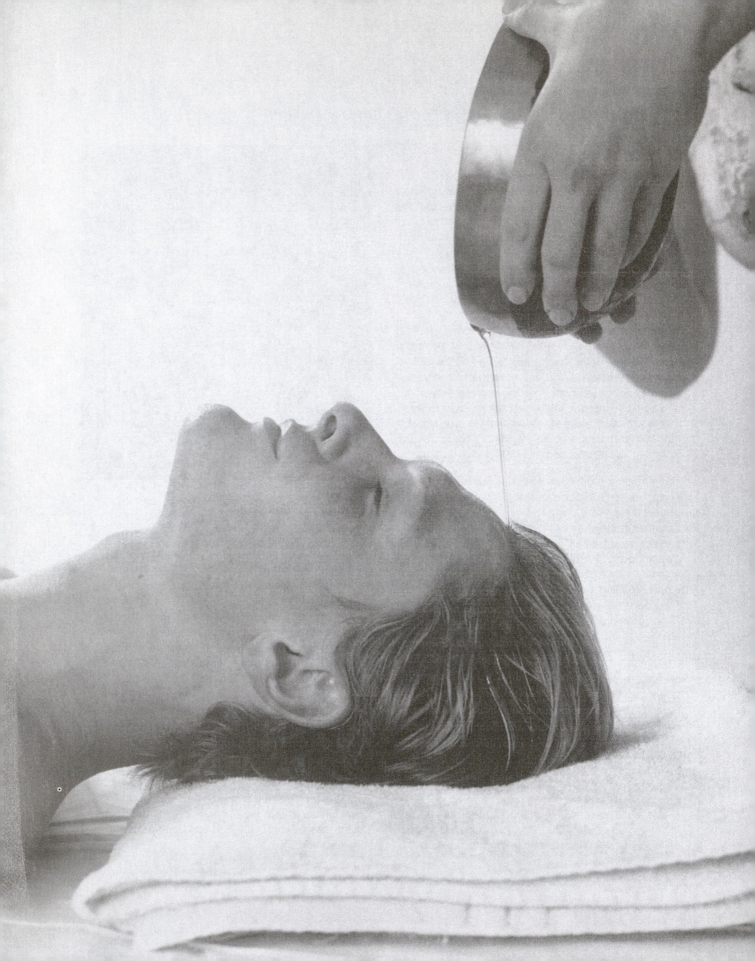

chapter 16

Beauty, Spa, and Wellness

There is a sector of the fashion industry that is dramatically affected by evolving consumer and style trends, particularly in the areas of color, environmental aesthetics, customer shifts, technology, and science, to include medicine, psychology, and physiology. Fashion as a lifestyle includes personal beauty, health, and body image choices. As there are changing trends in the fabrics, colors, and themes of apparel and home fashions, there are shifts in "what is in fashion" in the areas of personal care, health, and fitness. Aerobics and jogging are being upstaged by Hatha yoga and Pilates. Plastic surgery is being augmented by microfacials, collagen, and Botox. Makeup shifts from a natural to a glamour look and back. Hairstyles rely on a straightener and, later, a curling iron. If you think of fashion as a way for people and their homes to look good and stay current, then choices in how to spend personal time and money on looking and feeling good fit into the fashion industry.

The **beauty and wellness industries** focus on cosmetics, fragrances, hair and skin care, as well as spa, fitness, or **wellness centers** and their services. As a consumer, you contribute financially to this sector every day. When you wash your hair and style it, put on your makeup or skincare products, take your vitamins, apply sunscreen, go to the fitness center, and head to your pedicure and massage appointments at the spa, you are adding to the increasing revenues of the beauty and wellness industries. The beauty and wellness industries are growing fields with a wide range of career tracks that require fashion and nonfashion training. If you have an interest in fitness and health and enjoy the image changes that hair and makeup can create, then the beauty and wellness sectors of the fashion industry can

Sephora was founded in 1970 in France as Shop 8 by Dominique Mandonnaud, who, in 1993, fashioned the store's unique name by blending the Biblical name of Zipporah (Moses' exceptionally beautiful wife) with the ancient Greek term for "pretty," *sephos*. Today, Sephora is the leading chain of perfume and cosmetics stores in France and the leading retailer of perfumes and cosmetics in the United States, as well as the second largest in Europe. In the United States and Canada, there are over 280 Sephora stores and over 270 Sephora inside JCPenney stores. It is also a powerful beauty presence in 24 other countries.

Sephora is also the world's top beauty Web site and is recognized as a leading digital brand that continues to advance this arena through mobile and social media initiatives. Sephora.com offers over 265 beauty brands and 14,000 products, making it the largest and most diverse online beauty Web site on the Internet. Besides offering makeup, skin care, fragrance, hair, and bath and body products, Sephora.com also offers the latest beauty trends, tips from the experts, and an entire selection of creative gifts.

Owned by Paris-based Louis Vuitton Moët Hennessy (LVMH), the world's leading luxury goods group, Sephora is regarded as a beauty trailblazer, thanks to its vast assortment of prestige products, unbiased service from experts, interactive shopping environment, and innovation.

Sephora leads the retail beauty industry through its visionary retail concept, which promotes freedom, pleasure, and beauty. Its position in the beauty industry is attributed to its wide product assortment, its commitment to excellence in quality and customer service, and to its well-trained and dedicated employees.

Source: www.sephora.com

offer you a variety of career options. In this chapter, the following career paths are explored: product developer or technician; beauty merchandising and marketing professional; makeup artist; aesthetician; hairstylist; and director of a spa or wellness center.

To begin, the **beauty industry** and its producers of cosmetics, fragrances, and hair and skincare products is examined. There are a number of well-known mass marketing companies in this field: Esteé Lauder, Lancôme, and L'Oréal, to name just a few. There are two classifications of beauty industry corporations: mass market and prestige market. **Mass market** beauty companies, such as Cover Girl and Revlon, distribute their product lines through a wide variety of retailers, including drugstores, discount merchants, and mass merchandising retailers. **Prestige market** beauty companies, such as Chanel and MAC, distribute their product lines through higher-class department and specialty store retailers, primarily in leased departments. Some companies, like Sephora, distribute the products of prestige market beauty companies and under their own private labels (Box 16.1). Within these corporations, there are many subsidiaries through which a number of product lines are developed, marketed, and sold to the retail operations that offer them to the consumer. Some employees work with the creation of products, while others assist with promoting the product lines or selling them to the retailers and customers. The product developer/ technician starts the product cycle through the creation of new and innovative products that often develop from older products in the line, as with Clarins Paris (Box 16.2).

Sometimes a simple decision can change your life. For example, when a young medical student named Jacques Courtin-Clarins decided to treat circulatory problems with massage, a strange thing started happening. After their treatments, Courtin-Clarins's patients not only felt better, but their skin looked dramatically better. He started Clarins in 1954, naming the company after a character he played in a school play and later (in 1974) added this name to his own. Over the next 50 years, Courtin-Clarins devoted his research to improving the way his clients felt and looked, and what started off as a few simple botanical body oils ballooned (at the request of his clients) into Clarins Instituts de Beauté, a $1 billion global beauty company, including revenue from spas and salons in many countries.

Born Jacques Courtin in Paris in 1921, the founder and chairman of the Clarins Groupe passed away in 2007. He is survived by two sons: Christian, who is now the company president of Clarins Group Worldwide, and Olivier, its managing director, both of Paris. Next, Christian Courtin-Clarins talks about his father and the botanically enriched past, present, and future of Clarins.

A Brief History

Jacques Courtin-Clarins developed treatments and products using natural botanical ingredients first for the body and then for the face. He once said, "From a very young age, I was exposed to the curative effects of plants by my mother and relatives, who used herbs for medicine and treatment. Ever since, I looked to plants for answers. I cannot conceive a product without plants." In line with his father's words, today Clarin uses only the best natural botanical extracts.

Natural Wonders

The Clarins research and development team travels extensively throughout the world to exotic places such as tropical rain forests in the Amazon, Asia, and other remote locales in Europe to find new ingredients and cutting-edge research that helps make the skin beautiful. Clarins was the first to use 100-percent pure plant extracts and the first

to speak about pollution. Today, the company is the only one who has an antipollution complex in every cream.

Miracle Massage

Poor circulation is at the root of all skin problems as circulation slows down with age. Massage is an excellent way to improve circulation and the health of the skin. The Clarins massage technique is composed of no less than 80 movements. At the Clarins Institute in Neuilly, France, massage is paired with Clarin products to contour the face and body, stimulate the lymphatic system and blood circulation, preserve the skin's integrity and health, and restore balance and energy to the body and mind.

Color Story

The makeup collection, which is inspired by the runway shows, is loved by fashion icons around the world for its ability to adapt to the innuendos of everyday life: some days a woman wants full-out glamour, other days she's rushing to apply makeup in a taxicab. And just like the skin and body care products, Clarins makeup is rich in natural botanicals. The foundations contain moringa extract to moisturize, nourish, and revitalize skin. The lipsticks contain natural oil and vegetable extracts to soothe and soften lips. The mascaras contain plant waxes to condition and coat lashes.

Desert-Island Beauty Picks

The company now produces cleansers, moisturizers, firming products, exfoliating treatments, and sun-protection and tanning lotions, as well as a line of perfumes under the brand names Clarins, Thierry Mugler, Azzaro, and Stella Cadente. Courtin-Clarins describes his top picks in the line. "If a woman was stranded on a deserted island, I'd suggest the following: The most important element to good skin is to cleanse it properly (even on a desert island!) so Gentle Foaming Cleanser—All Skin Types, is a must. I'd also select Line Prevention Multi-Active Day Lotion SPF 15, as it contains an anti-pollution complex which protects skin from stressful elements including pollution, temperature changes, harmful UVA and UVB rays, as well as free radicals that can damage the skin. Not to mention it's very lightweight—perfect for warm climates. And, of course, Total Body Lift is one of our top-selling products. It uses powerful ingredients to help minimize cellulite (an absolute essential in your desert-island inspired outfit).

Giving Back

Clarins is the number one skin care company in France and Europe. Courtin-Clarins calls Clarins a "citizen of the world" company, financing arthritis research in more than 400 laboratories around the world and investing about $2.4 million a year in environmental and educational charities.

Sources:

http://www.nytimes.com/2007/04/06/business/06clarins.html

http://www.sephora.com/browse/brand_hierarchy.jhtml?brandId=Clarins&contentId=C15102

http://www.time.com/time/magazine/article/0,9171,1135638,00.html

http://www.washingtonpost.com/wp-dyn/content/article/2007/04/01/AR2007040100958.html

Product Technician

Product research and development (R&D) is the technical area that creates products that meet the manufacturer's standards of performance and safety by continually conducting research on existing products, as well as new and innovative products. In the cosmetics, skin care, and fragrance industry, the marketing, research, and development areas work closely together on a common goal: developing products that fulfill consumer needs and desires.

The idea for a new product or a product modification may emerge in a variety of ways. Often, the technician is assigned an existing product in the line for which changes are needed. The **product technician** works to develop new features for the product, often using consumer research studies in the process to clarify the direction of modification and predict the consumer response to the changes. In contrast, the **product developer** may be asked by the marketing director of the company to create a completely new product that will meet unfulfilled consumer needs (Figure 16.1). Frequently, product developers and technicians work independently to create a new product without initial marketing specifications and then submit the product to marketing to determine whether it will meet a consumer need.

Qualifications

A list of the educational requirements, experience, and personal characteristics needed in the career track of an R&D product developer or technician follows.

- **Education:** Typically, positions in R&D are available to persons with bachelor's degrees in chemistry, engineering, biology, or other related sciences; however, some firms are hiring candidates with aesthetician licenses.

- **Experience:** Working as an intern in the R&D division of a beauty industry firm is an excellent way to enter this career track. A number of companies hire students directly out of college and train them in this area. Creative and resourceful individuals who acquire an expertise in cosmetic chemistry or product development may become eligible for promotion to a project manager, who is responsible for a single product or groups of products.

- **Personal characteristics:** Product developers and technicians are, first and foremost, scientists with high levels of curiosity and an understanding of the customer. They are methodical problem solvers with strong attention to detail.

Career Challenges

The R&D product developer and technician need skills in chemistry or a related science discipline. As the technician often works alone on a project, taking it from start to finish, this is not the job for someone who is motivated by being part of a team. The work takes a great deal of concentration and often must be completed in a limited amount of time.

Beauty Merchandising and Marketing Professionals

A **beauty merchandising and marketing professional** is involved in the promotion and sales of cosmetic, fragrance, and skin care products. Beauty merchandising and marketing professionals include the account coordinator, trainer, account executive, and counter or line manager. An **account coordinator** organizes special events and promotions for a cosmetic,

Figure 16.1 In the cosmetic, skin care, and fragrance industries, the marketing and research development areas work closely with each other on a common goal: developing products that fulfill consumers' needs.

fragrance, or skin care line, traveling to different retail locations. The account coordinator develops and implements marketing programs that perpetuate the image of the brand, introduce new products, and generate customer traffic and press for the retail accounts. A **trainer** works for the cosmetic, fragrance, or skin care line by educating sales and marketing employees on the company's product line and how to sell it. The trainer directs seminars on new products, how they are to be used, and what results the consumer can expect. An account executive can work in two main areas: retailing and public relations. The **retail account executive** (or *retail sales account* executive) sells the line to retailers and oversees the sales performance of the line in large retail accounts. The retail account executive works with retailers that carry the line by providing marketing and merchandising suggestions to maximize consumer sell-through. This account representative assists store accounts with inventory management, making recommendations to increase sales. On-site staff training, incentives to motivate sales personnel, and assistance with consumer promotional events are parts of the retail account executive's job. The **public relations account executive** works with beauty media contacts, such as fashion publications like *Marie Claire, Vogue, Allure, Elle, W,* and *InStyle*, to promote the line in magazine editorials and feature stories. Box 16.3 features a variety of beauty career positions offered by Estée Lauder.

In the retail operation, the **counter manager**, or *line manager* coordinates special events and promotions in the retail operation, manages employees, and works closely with buyers. Selling the product line and servicing the customer are key objectives for the counter manager. Counter managers are constantly acquiring product knowledge through corporate training materials and seminars to educate sales associates and customers. They also develop merchandise displays and demonstrate products to staff and clients (Figure 16.2). They coach and develop a sales staff to achieve their personal productivity and company sales goals,

Figure 16.2 A counter manager stocks and displays cosmetics at L'Oréal Paris's counter at a department store in Tokyo.

Box 16.3 Estée Lauder Career Tracks

Estée Lauder products are sold in more than 140 countries and territories. The products are technologically advanced and high performing with a reputation for innovation and quality.

At Estée Lauder, there are several different types of job opportunities, from Estée Lauder representative positions at retail stores to corporate opportunities and field sales positions. More information about all of these job opportunities follows.

Positions at a Retailer

In the following three roles, you would be employed by the department store, not by Estée Lauder. The department store makes all final hiring decisions for retailer positions.

Beauty Advisor

The Estée Lauder Beauty Advisor represents Estée Lauder in department stores by working with consumers. The ideal candidate will enjoy providing expertise in skin care, makeup and fragrance as well as providing exceptional customer service and achieving sales goals. We provide extensive education in the science of skin care, the art of makeup, and fragrance expertise. If you're a high school graduate or equivalent with prior sales and/or service experience and can work flexible hours, this may be the start of a great career for you.

Counter Manager/Business Manager

The Counter Manager/Business Manager manages a team of Beauty Advisors to provide exceptional customer service and achieve daily sales goals. We provide extensive training in driving business, coaching Beauty Advisors, executing a market calendar, and achieving personal sales goals. If you're a high school graduate or equivalent with counter management experience and/or are an Estée Lauder Beauty Advisor with the right qualifications, this may be a great opportunity for you.

Account Coordinator

The Account Coordinator acts as a liaison between Estée Lauder and the department store management. Responsibilities include coaching Counter Managers to lead and develop their teams to deliver exceptional service and achieve sales goals. This position requires travel to a group of stores. If you're a high school graduate or equivalent with counter management experience and/or are an Estée Lauder Beauty Advisor with the right qualifications, this may be a great opportunity for you.

Field Sales Positions at Estée Lauder

Several types of field sales positions are available at Estée Lauder. The Account Executive and Education Executive positions are highlighted below.

Account Executive

The Account Executive is responsible for multiple stores within a territory, collaborating with retail partners to manage sales goals and service objectives and ensure the counter team best represents Estée Lauder. If you have at least two to three years' retail management experience, this may be an opportunity for you. College degree or equivalent work experience preferred.

Education Executive

The Education Executive educates counter teams on product knowledge and skills that are necessary to achieve Estée Lauder service standards and sales goals. If you have two to three years of retail management experience, the ability to communicate strategic messages, facilitation skills, and a training/education background, you may qualify for this opportunity. College degree or equivalent work experience preferred.

Corporate Positions at Estée Lauder

Estée Lauder has corporate positions of all types—from retail sales to marketing, product research, and development to supply chain, and positions in finance, human resources, and information technology.

Source: http://www.esteelauder.com/cms/about/careers/index.tmpl

often through building a **client registry file**, a computerized or print record of the names and contact information of the line's customers. The counter manager is also responsible for replenishing inventory through back stock or reorders. Finally, counter managers also develop and participate in special events that will increase business. For most mass market brands, counter managers are employed by the retailer; in prestige market brands, they usually work directly for the cosmetic, fragrance, hair, or skin care lines.

Qualifications

Account representatives, trainers, and counter managers have similar requirements in education, work experience, and personal characteristics, as follows.

- **Education:** A bachelor's degree in fashion design, fashion merchandising, communications, marketing, journalism, or a related field is a minimum requirement.

- **Experience:** Sales experience, especially in the cosmetic, fragrance, and skin care areas, is preferred. An internship in the beauty division of a department store is an excellent way to gain work experience. Several years of work experience in the beauty industry is a minimum requirement. Some large companies prefer a candidate who also holds aesthetics certification or has training and experience as a makeup artist. A strong knowledge of the beauty industry is expected. The candidate who can show successful sales experience through awards, a client listing, and so on, moves ahead of the competition. Evidence of exceptional customer service skills and the abilities to multitask, lead, and coach teams are also helpful.

- **Personal characteristics:** Great people skills and a love of travel are important in this career field. Common skills of beauty merchandising and marketing professionals include the ability to be energetic and articulate in conversation and writing. People in this career field are often ambitious self-starters, competitive spirits, and have creative and optimistic attitudes. In the beauty business, an image that exudes professionalism and a sense of style that fits with the employer's image is essential.

Career Challenges

Beauty merchandising and marketing professionals have a variety of job challenges. The account coordinator works under the pressure of coming up with innovative special events and promotions for the company every season. The trainer must continually find ways to educate employees on the company's new products and how to sell them. The retail account executive must meet or surpass sales goals in selling the line to retail accounts. The counter manager has the same objective, exceeding the sales goal set by the retailer. Persons in both of these positions have to balance sales and inventory so that both the retailers and the beauty product manufacturer are satisfied and making a profit. Extensive travel to different retail locations is often part of these jobs. Finally, the public relations account executive needs to persuade beauty media contacts to feature new product lines. All of these jobs have the following in common: the possibility of high stress, involvement in a fast-paced environment, and the need to sell one's self and the product line.

Makeup Artist

The person interested in working with cosmetics is not limited to working as an account executive or a counter manager for a single cosmetics firm. The **makeup artist** works hands-on with a variety of product lines and has a variety of employment opportunities. Makeup artists work with cosmetics, wigs, and other costuming materials to color and enhance a client's face and body. Working in television, film, music videos, commercials, and print ads, they use makeup to improve or alter actors' and models' appearances. Other makeup artists work at the retail level, applying lipstick and mascara on customers at store cosmetic counters. Some makeup artists work on photo shoots and runway shows for designers and magazines or cosmetic companies as consultants or sales representatives. Makeup artists also provide their services as independent contractors in beauty salons, retail stores, large hotels and resorts, spas, or the medical profession, where they provide camouflage techniques to help clients following injuries or surgeries. It is also possible to become a makeup adviser or lecturer.

What is the work of makeup artists in the video, media, television, film, and theater industries? They apply makeup for presenters, performers, and others appearing on-screen. Some have completed training in both makeup and hair techniques (e.g., styling, cutting, and coloring) to prepare and work on the makeup and hair design required for each individual production. Makeup artists skilled in both makeup application and hairstyling have better job prospects. Makeup designers and chief makeup artists research and design the makeup required for a production. The style of makeup and hair depends on the type of production. It varies from straightforward, contemporary makeup and hairdressing (i.e., for news broadcasters and presenters in conservative, public settings) to more creative, specialized techniques (e.g., varying historical periods, different nationalities, aging, or special effects). This may entail researching the looks and learning the techniques for elaborate makeup and wigs needed for period films, such as *Marie Antoinette*. It may also require technological knowledge and skills to change the shape and texture of a face, as in the film *The Wolfman* (Figure 16.3 and Box 16.4).

The makeup artist or assistant makeup artist must ensure the availability of materials, such as the correct colors and brands of various cosmetics, period makeup, prosthetics like false noses and scars, as well as wigs and hair extensions. The makeup artist is expected to own an extensive kit of cosmetics to take to each job, though larger productions like films and ongoing television series usually provide a makeup budget. Some makeup artists specialize in a medium, such as theater, film, runway, or photography, while others work in all of these areas.

Makeup artists in the entertainment industries collaborate closely with producers, directors, costume designers, hairdressers, and performers. Together, they develop and design the characters' looks, evaluating the length of time and cost required to complete each character. Most of these makeup artists are freelance and are engaged for each film production, television series, fashion season, or other project. As such, they are paid set or negotiated fees for each project. Some trade organizations in the media industries set minimum rates for independent productions and require membership in a trade union.

Training and educational requirements for makeup artists vary; there are a number of cosmetology schools that specialize in makeup studies. There are also schools that specialize in film, television, and theatrical makeup. The demand for these specialists is expected to grow about 10 to 20 percent over the next decade.

Qualifications

If you love color, makeup, and drama and if you are willing to start out at a low salary in a career area of growth with high earning potential, this may be the career path for you.

Box 16.4 Tech Talk: Film Makeup Artistry

…And the Makeup Oscar Goes to Baker and Elsey!

Rick Baker and Dave Elsey won the Achievement in Makeup Oscar for *The Wolfman* at the 83rd Annual Academy Awards in Los Angeles. In a brief acceptance speech, the artists thanked the actors, the entire crew, and "Universal Studios for their legacy of horror monsters that we love so much." This is Baker's seventh Oscar, and it has brought him full circle. He received his first Oscar, the first for any makeup artist, for his work on *An American Werewolf in London*. He also won Oscars for his work in *Harry and the Hendersons*, *Ed Wood*, *The Nutty Professor*, *Men in Black*, and *How the Grinch Stole Christmas*. This is Dave Elsey's first Oscar. He was previously nominated for *Star Wars: Episode III—Revenge of the Sith*. His work appears in such films as *Mission: Impossible*, *Ghost Rider*, and *Where the Wild Things Are*. Both artists cited the original *Wolf Man*, with makeup by Jack Pierce, as their inspiration for pursuing makeup careers. Next, Rick Baker describes the process of developing the makeup and prostheses for *The Wolfman* in an interview with *Popular Mechanics*.

Popular Mechanics (PM): Did the filmmakers know they wanted to do a wolfman in makeup right away, or did they need convincing?
Rick Baker: The original director, Marc Romanek, felt very strongly that the wolfman should be a guy in makeup, and so did Benecio [del Toro]. He's a big fan of the original *Wolf Man* and the Universal horror films, and he really felt it should be makeup. I'm glad to know that in this day and age that makeup is still considered an option.

PM: I read somewhere that you actually put the makeup on yourself first?
RB: Every makeup's a little different, and it's always different when you're the person wearing it than when you're the person putting it on. So I always like to have that experience of being under all that stuff so when an actor complains about it, or says that they can't move a certain part of their face, I know whether they're full of beans or not! But so many times it's hard for people to visualize exactly what something's going to look like. In the old days, I used to do sketches or paintings. And

it was usually, "Do you like this painting, or this painting?" For the past 20 years now, I've been using Photoshop, which is a great tool, and you can do something very photographic that looks very much like what the final thing is. But because it's very easy to change something in a Photoshop, you end up with a lot of designs, and after a while, everybody gets lost. I thought it would be a lot clearer if somebody saw a person in makeup, with a face that moved, and to see it in three dimensions.

PM: What inspired your wolfman design? Any influences in particular?
RB: Oh yeah, a whole bunch. I've been watching monster movies for many years and I've seen all

Figure 16.3 Makeup artistry for films often requires technological knowledge and skills to change the shape and texture of a face, as in the film *The Wolfman*.

Box 16.4 Tech Talk: Film Makeup Artistry (continued)

the wolfman movies that have been done. I've also done a lot of werewolf movies, and from the time I was a child I have looked at wolves and dogs and canine creatures and men and have been thinking about that combination. I think Benecio would have been happy if it was exactly the Lon Chaney Jr. makeup that Jack Pierce did, but I thought it needed to be amped up a little bit. One of the things I always found really odd about the Lon Chaney Jr. wolfman, although I love it a great deal, is that he's got just normal human ears. And it just seems like you'd at least want to make them pointy to some degree. That was one of the first changes I made.

PM: Take me through the process of creating the wolfman with makeup.

RB: The first thing is to agree upon a design, which can be a very difficult process. Then your actor is your armature for your sculpture. So you get a lifecast of your actor—you make a mold of his head, and you have a plaster or sometimes fiberglass duplicate of him. That presented a little bit of a problem on this film because when Bennie—there's a picture that's been on the Internet for quite some time of Benecio, very hairy-looking, choking me. And everybody thinks it's a makeup test that I did on him, but that's what he looked like the day he came to us to be lifecast! And it was like, I cannot cast your face like this! I need a naked face! But we made a mold of this hairy wild man and tried to shave all the hair off...and I was not pleased because that's the foundation of everything. It's like building a house on a bad foundation. I managed to find a lifecast I took of someone else a number of years ago and we kind of used that and photos that we took and a lot of guessing to try to make a life mask of Bennie without hair. In the end, I actually took a clean face cast and made everything from that point.

So, we start with a cast, and on that cast I sculpt, usually with plasticine of some sort, the new features. For example, he's got pointy ears. So I sculpt the pointy ears in clay over Benecio's ears. I sculpt a more canine-like nose over his nose. Once we have the clay on the proper positive cast of the actor's face, we make a negative mold of that. We use a lot of epoxies and, in England where we did the work on this film, they use fiberglass a lot. Fiberglass can

take the heat. Next, you take a negative mold of the new features. In this case, we used a fiberglass mold, cleaned out the area where the clay was, and then we had this empty void space. One side of it is the positive of the actor's face, and other side is a negative of the sculpted feature. The negative area that was once plasticine is then filled with foam latex. Foam latex is basically the sap of a rubber tree with sulfur and zinc with a foaming agent added. You whip air into it as if you're making whipped cream. You add this gelling agent in it to make it congeal so the bubbles don't break down, and that foam rubber is usually injected into this mold, into the void space. Then you put the foam rubber in an oven to cure it, which takes up to eight hours sometimes, and then you open up the mold to see if you got a good cast or not. If you managed to trap air in the process of loading that foam rubber into the mold, that piece is no good. And the pieces are used once and thrown away. So if Bennie works five days this week, we need five sets of appliances. If we're lucky, we can make five sets of appliances in five preproduction days, but not every cast turns out.

PM: Why is it use once and throw away?

RB: Well, because, you know, the pieces blend, hopefully imperceivably, into the actor's skin. And the way that happens is that you taper that clay out into absolutely nothing. It has tissue-thin edges. If you took a Kleenex tissue and peeled the two layers of tissue apart, it's even thinner than that. So when you glue that thin foam rubber onto the person's face, there's not a way to remove it without screwing up that edge. And the adhesives that we have now are very tenacious. The pieces are really stuck into the actor's face, even after a very vigorous day of being a wolfman. You just cannot get a piece off in a way that's salvageable.

PM: Once you've got the piece, then what happens?

RB: We get those pieces. Then, on the actual day of shooting, they're adhered to the actor's face in a specific order, which is determined during preproduction. In this case, it was the cowl piece that had the ears on it first. We flattened out Bennie's hair, we glued this piece on, and we glued the major facial piece on. Fortunately, we now have stronger adhesives and the removal is quite hard. You just

Box 16.4 Tech Talk: Film Makeup Artistry (continued)

can't pull it off their faces; you'd pull off a layer of skin with it. The removal time takes up to an hour a day. Anyway, once all the appliances are on, we paint them and his skin with various makeup products so they all look like they belong on one character.

We made a hair lace wig, where every hair is individually tied into a lace material, for the top of his head and some little lace pieces that went on the side, similar to sideburns. And then we actually went into laying loose hair. We have hunks of hair that we glue individually, each little hair, onto the face. And the reason we do that is, it's more flexible. He can move a lot better, you can control direction of the hair and the growth a lot more. And we had a great big set of dentures that we used on Benecio.

We also put a whole body suit on Bennie that made his anatomy a little more wolf-like. We had different muscles on it, as well as hair—a whole hairy body, because we never knew if the shirt was going to get ripped off. And he's got foam rubber hands, and legs, the whole deal. Getting him ready usually took between three and three and a half hours.

PM: This isn't your first wolfman. You did the makeup for *An American Werewolf in London,*
and also the movie *Wolf.* **How has makeup changed since that time?**
RB: There are better makeup materials now, but I actually used materials that were basically the same ones I used on *An American Werewolf in London,* because there are still advantages to those materials. The reality is it's not all that different than what Jack Pierce did in 1941. I wanted to pay homage to the makeup and the movie I love so much, the original *Wolf Man.*

PM: How does the future look?
RB: It's cool. I can't tell you how excited I am that I have a movie on my credits called *The Wolfman.* And it's made at Universal. My dream as a kid was to be a makeup artist and to work at Universal and make monster movies. I just find that so exciting. And this movie has Benecio, Emily Blunt, Hugo Weaving. It has Sir Anthony Hopkins! It's got an amazing cast, and they were all just great, fun, nice people who are talented as heck. And that was a real pleasure.

Sources:
http://makeupmag.com/featured/id/798/, 2/27/11

http://www.popularmechanics.com/technology/gadgets/news/4345345, 2/2/10

Education requirements, work experience, and key personal characteristics for the career of a makeup artist are as follows.

- **Education:** The common educational requirements are a one-year vocational program or a two-year associate's degree. After completing educational programs, the makeup artist often trains on the job in retail, television, or film, by assisting experienced makeup artists. Some industries, such as filmmaking, require that the makeup artist have specific certifications and union membership.

- **Experience:** An internship or apprenticeship with an established makeup artist is a great way to get through the career door. Sales experience in the cosmetics department of a retail store provides additional knowledge and on-the-job experience. Volunteering as a makeup artist with a local theatrical production company provides excellent additional work experience.

- **Personal characteristics:** The successful makeup artist enjoys working with people and communicates well at all levels, including listening and empathizing. A strong visual sense and a creative imagination are a makeup artist's most important traits. The ability to look at a face and picture what it will look like with makeup and under specific lighting is a great talent. An awareness of health and safety and sanitation procedures is also necessary. A makeup artist must be organized and able to work well under pressure while paying attention to detail and as part of a team of often diverse colleagues.

The outlook for the career track of makeup artists is good, as the number of employees in this occupation is expected to increase over the next two to three years. It is becoming more common for people to have their makeup done professionally for job interviews, school dances, weddings, or other special occasions. Another trend is for makeup artists to work alongside hairstylists in salons, applying clients' makeup after they have their hair done.

Career Challenges

Starting out, the makeup artist usually earns low pay and works long and unusual hours. If a film director or photographer decides to shoot a scene at sunrise, then the makeup artist must be ready to go before dawn. Extensive travel with little downtime during a project can be exhausting. Setting one's ideas of the best makeup approach aside to defer to those of the producer can be challenging. The makeup artist needs the confidence and tact to suggest changes to accomplish the goal in an individual's appearance. For these reasons, flexibility is key. Building up a business of regular clients can be difficult, and work may be irregular initially; however, once established, makeup artists often remain in this industry for a long time.

Some makeup artists choose to work in a spa, either as an independent contractor or as an employee. As the spa industry grows, so do the opportunities for makeup artists to work as part of a team of aesthetics professionals.

Wellness and Aesthetics

Wellness and personal care are topics of keen interest in today's beauty industry as it prepares for the future. As baby boomers become youthful seniors, there is an increasing consumer interest in slowing down or reversing the aging process and preventing health problems. Additionally, consumers are seeking a higher quality of life through reduced stress; greater self-care; and safer, healthier food and product choices. They are beginning to view services like massages and facials as ongoing necessities, rather than occasional luxuries. The increasing customer interest in health, youth, and longevity has attracted new participants to the wellness industry. They include alternative medicine providers, pharmaceutical firms, energy drink and food supplement producers, full-service beauty salons, fitness and nutrition centers, and spas. Trends in the wellness industry include anti-aging and protection through skin care, relaxation and rejuvenation, facial treatments and body sculpting, stress management, and health concerns management (Figure 16.4).

Aesthetics is a relatively new field that combines wellness, science, and beauty. The field views the client as a whole person by providing integrated aesthetic services through comprehensive makeovers and beauty-enhancement treatments that combine medical, beauty, and spa treatments for men and women in safe and comfortable environments. Many of these spas employ nail manicurists and pedicurists, masseuses, makeup artists, and facial technicians. An **aesthetician** is a licensed professional who provides services such as facials, makeup, and hair removal to improve one's physical appearance.

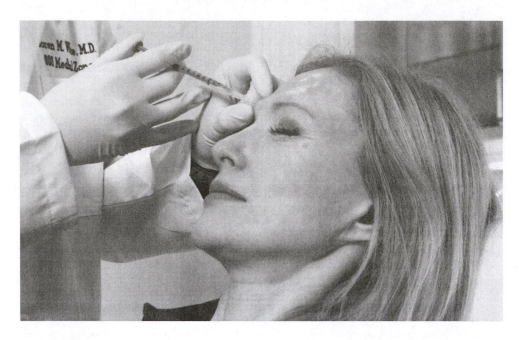

Figure 16.4 Trends in the wellness industry include anti-aging and protection through skin care, relaxation and rejuvenation, facial treatments and body sculpting, stress management, and health concerns management.

Qualifications

Here are the educational and experience requirements, as well as personal characteristics, for a successful career as an aesthetician.

- **Education:** In most cities, there are vocational schools that offer a program based on a curriculum, up to two years, covering the following subjects: anatomy, physiology, hygiene, skin disorders and diseases, skin analysis, massage, makeup application, hair removal, basic medical terminology, professional ethics, the business of aesthetics, retailing, marketing and promotion, customer service, interpersonal skills, salon administration, as well as salon layout and design.

- **Experience:** After completion of an aesthetics program and becoming licensed (requirements vary from state to state), many graduates opt to practice aesthetics in a salon or spa or open their own businesses. Others may also be employed by a makeup artist or an image consultant. Some work in medical practices such as dermatology, plastic surgery, oncology, or burn treatment centers. Additional opportunities include work as a product developer in cosmetic R and D or as a manufacturer's representative in the beauty and skin care industry.

- **Personal characteristics:** The aesthetician has good manual dexterity, a high energy level, effective communication skills, and a high level of sensitivity. The ability to work with different types of people and to build relationships with clients are important attributes of the successful aesthetician.

There are four factors that determine an income for the aesthetician, as well as most of the careers examined in this chapter. They are location; quality and reputation of the employer (i.e., the salon or spa); whether the candidate is launching an aesthetic department, taking over an experienced person's established clientele, or starting a new clientele base; and the candidate's skills and references. Some spas pay a salary; others pay commission. The commission on services may start at 40 percent and increase gradually as one gains experience. Additional money can be made through tips and commission on products sold.

Career Challenges

The aesthetician must have an understanding of and interest in the three Ss: science, sanitation, and safety. Working with the human body requires a sensitive approach with strong attention to detail and methodical procedure. As aestheticians need to stay up to date on skin care products, technology, and services, continuing education is an integral part of the job.

Hairstylist

Hairstyling is a profession of tremendous growth all over the world. As with apparel and accessories, hairstyles change with fashion. People recognize that it is not simply clothing, shoes, and jewelry that express their personalities. It is also their hair, a reason customers are becoming more experimental and open to change. **Hairstylists** not only work in hair salons but also in the film and television industry, for fashion houses, for magazines, for photo studios, and for special events firms. Hairstyling is a creative art, and a good hairstylist is a valuable commodity (ask anyone who has had a bad hair day). Figure 16.5 and Box 16.5 feature Martin Samuel, hairstylist to the stars.

Qualifications

The professional hairstylist is trained in the areas of hair and scalp care, cutting, styling, and coloring, and has the following credentials, background, and personal attributes:

- **Education:** Most cities offer an array of vocational schools that specialize in hair and cosmetics training, which may take up to a year or two. Once a hairstylist has earned a license, the next step is often to apprentice under an established stylist before working solo to build a clientele. Different states have different rules governing hairstylists. Some simply require a one-time test to keep the license current, while others require continuing education, license renewals, and health tests associated with working with the public. While some states do not require continuing education, most good stylists keep their skills sharp by learning new things and honing current skills through professional development workshops.

- **Experience:** Stylists can often secure positions as soon as they complete training and receive a license; however, they often begin in an assistant capacity working with an established stylist.

- **Personal characteristics:** Creativity, imagination, and continual training are necessary parts of the hairstylist's profession. Dealing effectively with people is critical. Hairstylists need effective communication skills to talk to clients and build good relationships. They should have an attractive presence, a friendly manner, and good listening skills. As it is a physically demanding job, the stylist must have good stamina.

In terms of remuneration, hairstylists working in salons or spas may be paid on commission; the more clients they have, the more money they make. Many stylists earn additional money through tips from clients and commission on products they sell. Some firms pay stylists a salary,

Box 16.5 Martin Samuel, Hairstylist to the Stars

By Leah Hyslop, February 4, 2011

Martin Samuel has spent nearly 40 years working in the film industry, styling the hair of celebrities from Madonna to Johnny Depp. He tells *Telegraph* Expat about leaving Britain for Los Angeles—and why he's so proud of his Bafta (British Academy of Film and Television Arts).

You've worked in the hair industry for over 50 years. Did you always know that this was what you wanted to do?

Yes. I always knew I wanted to work with hair, right from when I was a child. In those days, you used to get a job while you were still at school, so I worked as a Saturday junior from the age of 13, then left school at 15, by which point I was almost a fully-fledged stylist. I went from my local salon to the West End, then to Paris, Spain—all sorts of adventures. When I came back I became the artistic director of Crimpers, the first unisex hair salon in London, at the end of the swinging sixties. It was on Baker Street, right next to the Apple store, and it was a very wonderful, very trendy place to be.

How did you make the jump from salons to films?

I started doing some hairstyling for advertisements, working alongside commercial directors like Ridley Scott and Alan Parker, who of course eventually all ended up directing films. The first film I worked on was an Alan Parker film called *No Hard Feelings* in 1973, but the first big ones were *Stardust* and *The Man Who Fell to Earth*, with David Bowie, after which I joined him on a tour. Going over to the U.S. to work on those projects really opened up the American scenario of my life. With the exception of a period when I set up a salon in Hertfordshire, I've been in Los Angeles ever since.

You've worked as the chief hair designer on a huge range of films, from *Evita* to the *Pirates of the Caribbean* series, to *Burlesque*. Which was the biggest challenge?

Evita was probably the hardest film to work on.

...because of Madonna?

(laughs) Anyone will tell you that working with Madonna is a challenge, but it's worth it, because she's a great person to make beautiful, and that's what that film was about. It was mainly because it took a lot of research. I designed Madonna about 42 hairstyles for that film, and made so many wigs. Luckily, there was a lot of material to work from. Evita was the most photographed woman of her era, and when we were shooting in Argentina people would always come knocking on my door to try to show me their old photos or newspaper clippings of her.

When you're heading up a hair department, how many staff members do you have working under you?

It depends on the film. During the *Pirates of Caribbean* films, I had 35 to 40 hairstylists working for me over a period of four years. Usually, you only get between four to six weeks to prepare for each film, and that time is very important. If you've gone through the script thoroughly and done the groundwork, you should be okay during shooting.

Figure 16.5 Martin Samuel accepts an award for his nearly 40 years working in the film industry, styling the hair of celebrities from Madonna to Johnny Depp.

Box 16.5 Martin Samuel, Hairstylist to the Stars (continued)

How much of a free rein do you get when designing hairstyles for a big film like *Pirates*?

Less than you might think. Gore Verbinski had a very set idea of how he wanted his pirates to look, and had done a lot of research. Johnny [Depp] knew that he wanted beads and braids, a kind of Keith Richards look. You have guidelines, and you work within them. You also have to deal a lot with the costume department to make sure the hair and costumes work well together.

How did you feel when you were told you'd received a Bafta for your work on the second *Pirates* film?

It was a real moment of glory. I was in Morocco filming with Penelope Cruz at the time, and they sent me back to pick it up. I'd been nominated before but not won, so to come home and get an award like that from my colleagues in Britain was probably the most thrilling moment in my life.

When did you decide to permanently settle in Los Angeles?

My wife Mary and I first came over in 1979 with our children, who were five and three at the time, and decided to take our chances. We stayed until 1981, then we came back to Britain to live in Hertfordshire for around 10 years. I just felt I needed to take stock of things a little, and spend more time with our children. It was wonderful—a real community life, with the children in lovely local schools. Then they grew up and left, and we decided to come back. I've never regretted it. Los Angeles is good for my work, but we love the lifestyle out here too. The weather's beautiful, we have a lovely home, and we have lots of friends. I always enjoy the few days I

get off: I spend time with my wife, walking our dog and eating out. And I'm mad about gardening.

Do you have a favorite genre of film to work in?

I've loved the period films I've done, like *Jane Eyre, Little Buddha,* and *The Scarlet Pimpernel*. Period hairstyles are very challenging, there's more to get your teeth into. But it's also great doing more modern films like *Burlesque.* That's very influenced by high fashion—all weaves, wigs, and hairpieces. It's very demanding to get a look like that right.

Are the hours long?

Very grueling. We have to travel a lot, and the night shoots are tiring. There's a lot to do on any project, though some are more demanding than others. On Tracey Ullman's *State of the Union*, I had to design over 50 wigs, all of them for very different characters. At the moment, I'm trying to choose more films closer to Los Angeles.

How has the industry changed since you started?

One thing that has changed a lot is that actors have become much more in touch with looking after their hair. For films where actors need to change their hairstyle dramatically, these days they'll usually wear wigs—and today the wigs are so sophisticated you really wouldn't know. People don't want to dye their hair or cut it: they want to go home as themselves at the end of the night. And my job is to make the actors feel as comfortable and relaxed as possible.

Source: http://www.telegraph.co.uk/expat/expatlife/8300690/Martin-Samuel-hair-stylist-to-the-stars.html

---

believing the guaranteed paycheck creates a team atmosphere. Another approach to hair salon ownership is leasing space to the stylist. The stylist pays a monthly fee for the use of a booth, often also paying a portion of the receptionist's salary so that appointments can be made at all times. Hairstylists who have training and certification in additional fields such as makeup application and nail or facial aesthetics have greater career and salary advancement opportunities.

Career Challenges

There is a great deal of competition in hairstyling. Think about how many hair salons exist in a midsize city. The number is often large enough that the competition is intense and salons go out of business regularly. Finding an employer who has a solid base of repeat clientele and long-term stylists and is willing to take on a new hairstylist is a challenge. Skill and personality are critical factors in making it in this business. Continuing education is essential, as products, techniques, equipment, and looks change frequently in this industry.

Director of a Spa or Wellness Center

Resort and hotel spas originally began to make headway as a leisure time amenity and were not often thought of as profit centers for the beauty, health, and wellness industries. That has changed; now spas and medi-spas are prospering because of consumer lifestyle shifts, efficacy of treatments, and education. **Medi-spas** combine traditional spa services with those that must be offered by a physician, such as health screenings and minor surgery. The day spa may eventually offer all services, making the idea of a separate hair salon somewhat obsolete as spas incorporate hair and makeup services, massages, hair removal, skin rejuvenation, and other aesthetic services. In fact, the term "day spa" may eventually be replaced by "wellness center," or a similar term. Even the athletic center and spa may become a place of treatment and education through well-designed nutrition and exercise programs, such as the popular fitness trends that involve combining what might seem like opposing exercises, like mind-body movements plus aerobics. Cy-Yo (stationary cycling followed by a yoga cool-down) and blended yoga-Pilates are two examples of this trend. Whether referred to as a spa today or a wellness center tomorrow, the operation must be guided by an efficient and effective manager, the director.

The **director of a spa or wellness center** is responsible for keeping the spa running smoothly by managing customer service, budgets, marketing plans, and environment and staff appearance standards. In terms of human resources, the director ensures that employees have the training needed to perform their jobs and the knowledge they need to sell the retail product lines. Spa directors ensure the staff operates with peak efficiency through coordination, communication, and cooperation. They schedule, plan, and facilitate team meetings. Personnel duties include directing the recruitment, interviews, selection, and training of new employees. They mediate problems, organize and set work schedules, and effectively communicate and enforce company and health rules. Finally, directors are responsible for maintaining an inventory of supplies and purchasing new products. In essence, the spa director manages all of the personnel and services that make the organization a success.

Qualifications

Here are the educational, experience, and personal characteristics needed to be a successful spa director.

- **Education:** A bachelor's degree in management, hospitality, marketing, business administration, or a related field is a minimum requirement. CPR and first-aid training are often required. It is desirable to have training, certification, and licenses in spa-related services.

- **Experience:** The director position usually requires a minimum of three to five years of experience in spa or salon management. The position requires a working knowledge of computers, in particular, spa software skills.

- **Personal characteristics:** Spa or wellness center directors must have strong leadership skills, the ability to motivate others, excellent organizational and communication skills, and the ability to multitask. Their approach to work must be customer-service oriented, diplomatic, and composed. Excellent problem-solving skills are essential.

Career Challenges

In managing all of the personnel and services that make the organization, the spa director may work long hours, including weekends. This is a position that requires many skills; chief among them are scheduling and motivating employees and creating a peaceful and immaculate environment. The successful spa director is highly attuned to image and ambiance, as well as a high level of customer service. Day after day, it can be challenging to work with personnel, customers, and vendors concurrently in a calm and controlled manner. The spa director sets the tone for the wellness center.

The Future of Spas and Wellness Centers

What does the future look like for the wellness industry? The wellness center will focus on physiological relief of fatigue and stress, while functioning as a haven for rest and relaxation. It will also be a source of education for the customer on anti-aging and protection, as well as holistic principles of health. There will be developments in hair and scalp care through nourishing masks and treatments. For nails and hands, treatment will focus on protection and anti-aging through depigmentation treatments and sun protection. We may even see driving gloves again, but designed to cover and protect the backs of the hands from sun damage. Waxing continues to be a common part of the spa service menu but, as the technology of laser hair removal advances, more clients will choose semipermanent or permanent laser hair removal technology. Natural botanical ingredients in skin care products will drive the new trend of caring for and soothing sensitive skin. The products and treatments of the future will continue to concentrate on anti-aging and protection but will also heavily involve increasing the immune system. While body treatments and products now take second place to the face in the spa, body skin care may be the greatest growing segment in the beauty and wellness industries of tomorrow. After all, if technology can improve the tone and texture of the face, why not use it for the entire body? As stress levels and fast-paced lifestyles continue to increase, there will be a natural need for the consumer to explore the value of detoxification for overall energy and wellness. The key to growing the beauty, health, and wellness industries lies in educating the consumer on the physical and psychological benefits of self-care as a necessity, not a luxury (Figure 16.6).

Summary

The product cycle of the beauty industry begins in research and development with the creation of innovative products by product developers and technicians, who often have backgrounds in science. After the cosmetics, fragrance, and skin care products are developed and produced, beauty product merchandising and marketing professionals promote and sell them. The account coordinator organizes special events and promotions for product lines, traveling to different retail locations. A trainer works to educate employees and directs seminars on new products—how they are to be used and how to sell them. The retail account executive works

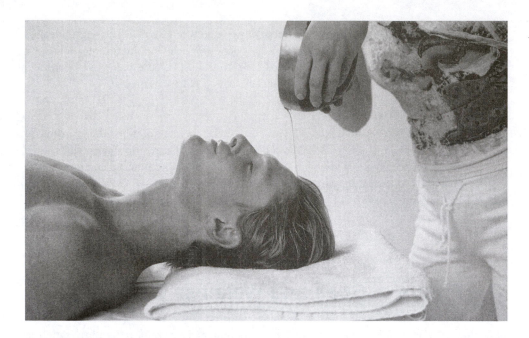

Figure 16.6 A young man receives Ayurvedic treatment in a spa and wellness center.

to sell the line to retailers carrying the product line, and the public relations account executive works with beauty media contacts to solicit promotion in consumer publications. The counter manager's key objectives are to sell the product line at the retail store and service the customer through product knowledge and special promotions in the retail operation.

The creative talents in the beauty industry are makeup artists, who work with cosmetics, wigs, and other costuming materials, to color and enhance the client's face and body, and hairstylists, who are trained in the areas of hair and scalp care, cutting, styling, and coloring. Makeup artists and hairstylists may provide their services as independent contractors in beauty salons, retail stores, large hotels and resorts, or spas. They may also work for runway productions, as well as the video, media, television, film, and theater industries.

However, the beauty industry is no longer just concerned with hair and makeup. The popularity of alternative physical treatments has broadened concepts of personal care and the career options within the beauty and wellness industries. Spas, or wellness centers, offer a variety of treatments and services, including anti-aging and protection through skin care, relaxation and rejuvenation, facial treatments and body sculpting, stress management, and health concerns management, and services provided by aestheticians. A spin on the traditional spa, the medi-spa combines long-offered spa services with those that must be offered by a physician. The director of a spa or wellness center is responsible for keeping the spa running smoothly by managing customer service, budgets, marketing plans, and environment and staff appearance standards.

Beauty, health, and wellness businesses are rapidly growing sectors of the fashion lifestyle industry. Career opportunities are flourishing, with new ones developing as innovative products and techniques are introduced. Increasing consumer interest and awareness in the well-being, longevity, and beauty that results from self-care indicates that this area will be one to watch in the future.

Key Terms

account coordinator

aesthetician

aesthetics

beauty and wellness industries

beauty industry

beauty merchandising and marketing professional

client registry file

counter manager

director of a spa or wellness center

hairstylist

makeup artist

mass market

medi-spa

prestige market

product developer

product technician

public relations account executive

retail account executive

trainer

wellness center

Online Resources

blogs.indiewire.com/thompsononhollywood/2011/02/27/live_at_oscars_
makeup_goes_to_the_wolfman_costumes_to_alice_in_wonderland/

top-10-list.org/2010/03/30/ten-makeup-artists

www.beauty101.org/top-10-most-popular-cosmetics-manufacturers/

www.makeupmag.com

www.hairstylistwebpro.com/specialized-for-hairstylists-barbers-cosmetologists.
asp www.medicinenet.com/script/main/art.asp?articlekey=59844

www.mesamuel.com/

www.startupbizhub.com/how-to-start-a-health-and-wellness-business.htm

Discussion Questions

1. Which beauty products and treatments do you incorporate into your lifestyle? Describe what the future of these and new products and treatments may be in response to the growth of the wellness industry.

2. Are department-store-branded beauty products superior to generics and drugstore lines? Compare and contrast the differences in product development, merchandising, and promotion.

3. Many of the job descriptions in the beauty and wellness industry compare to those of positions discussed earlier in the chapters on product development, marketing, merchandising, and management. Compare and contrast three positions in this chapter with those requiring similar backgrounds and skills in three other chapters. What would it take for a professional to move from the apparel or accessories sectors of the industry into beauty and wellness?

4. Search the Internet to find out who the major manufacturers of cosmetics and beauty products are. Construct a four-column chart of 10 beauty product corporations, listing the name of the corporation in the first column and the brand names in the second column. In column three, indicate whether the brands are mass or prestige market; in the fourth, list examples of retailers that sell each brand.

Interview with a Spa Director

10 Questions with Jeremy McCarthy
Source: http://www.spaprojects.com/blog_entry.aspx?id=7

Jeremy McCarthy has had a lifelong career of pampering guests at luxury resorts in the spa and hospitality industry, including 14 years with Four Seasons Hotels and Resorts and 3 years opening and operating the new spa at famed La Costa Resort. Currently, he is the Director of Global Spa Development and Operations for Starwood Hotels and Resorts. Here, he is responsible for the development of spas across Starwood's many hotel brands around the world.

As the Starwood Spa guru, what is an average working day like?

Unfortunately, I spend a lot of time in my office staring at a computer screen or on a telephone. I think of it as managing by "remote control." I miss the days of working on a resort campus where I could get up and walk around a beautiful property, talk to guests, meet with employees. That being said, I am able to rub elbows with a lot of really smart people in Starwood's headquarters and can liaise with those who work on our hotel brand teams, marketing teams, technology channels, design, architecture, etc. A large part of my job is making sure that all of Starwood's resources are used to drive our spa business just as well as they do the rest of the hotel. There is no way that I could manage our massive portfolio of over 300 spas plus another 100-plus in development without leaning on all of the other resources that Starwood has driving our performance.

So, your team has decided that it's time to build a new spa or revamp an existing one. What comes after this?

First, the decision isn't made by us alone. Usually it comes out of discussion between our ownership groups, our property teams, our regional teams, with feedback from our customers and our associates. Once we know a project will have a spa, we have to determine what the spa will be: managed by us or by a third party? One of our brands or an external brand? These decisions vary property by property depending on the vision of the owner, the economics of the project, and the demographics of the location. Assuming it will be one of our branded spas, we approach it with an intense design focus. We believe that ensuring the spa is set up right in the beginning is a critical part of its future success.

What, in your opinion, is the up-and-coming place for new hospitality developments?

China, India, Russia, Brazil, and Abu Dhabi are all somewhat hot right now in terms of an infusion of new spa and hospitality projects. A lot of our new development has been and continues to be in Asia (with a lot of that in China). But I am excited to see the wheels turning in North America again. A lot of spa projects that were "on hold" for the past few years are starting to move again, and Starwood is seeing both new hotel developments in the U.S. as well as owners desiring to convert their existing hotels to one of Starwood's brands. Our reputation for strong brands and our ability to drive business through channels like our SPG loyalty program create opportunities for us even in a down economy.

What would you like to see more of in the health and wellness industry?

I see the health and wellness industry, taken broadly, as highly segmented into three divergent categories. 1) There is the "health care" component, which is "evidence based" (interventions and services are substantiated by research on large populations) but mechanical and bureaucratic in its delivery and failing to take into account the holistic nature of human health. 2) Then there is the "spa" side of the coin which is highly holistic, considers lifestyle and transformation that extends beyond a mere physical intervention, and delivers healing experiences that are enjoyable and that people want to have more of. The spa world, however, is all philosophy and no science. 3) Finally, there is the "medi-spa" side of the industry that is more scientific but less holistic. The medi-spa arena

Interview with a Spa Director (continued)

focuses on superficial treatments to enhance beauty and appearance. I classify "anti-aging" into this section since most anti-aging treatments only impact the "appearance" of aging, rather than truly extending human flourishing into more years of the lifespan. I would like to see more convergence in the health and wellness industry with more places for healing that are scientific in their approach, holistic in their scope, and nurturing in their delivery. There are very few entities that live in this sweet spot.

There are many emerging design trends for spas; are there any that really stick out for you?
Given that most of the world has just come out of an economic pummeling and are cautiously trying to determine how to move forward, I'm seeing a trend towards smaller spas. I'm embracing the challenge to explore ways to take smaller spaces and create rich, meaningful experiences for our guests. The guest doesn't know how many square feet or how many treatment rooms a spa has so the key is to make the spa experience just as good in a 200-square-meter spa as it is in a 2,000-square-meter spa.

Jeremy, we know you have a keen interest in psychology and we enjoy reading your blog entries on www.psychologyofwellbeing.com. How would you say the health and wellness sectors combine with the field of mental health?
My real interest is in holistic wellness. The reason I study and write about psychology is because I feel like that is the part that is undervalued in most health models. Even in the spa industry, where we talk a lot about "body, mind, spirit," we could do better at really understanding the science behind people's mental and emotional states or their sense of meaning and spirituality.... The blog pushes me to continue researching these areas, but it also connects me with a great community of like-minded people who are also passionate about human wellness. In our society we tend to compartmentalize both health and science into different "departments" so mental health and physical health are viewed separately. Unfortunately, this glosses over the complex interactions that we all experience between body, mind, and emotion. The scientists like to simplify down to categories that are easier to measure, while the holistic approach is to embrace the complexity, but don't bother with trying to understand it or measure it using the scientific method. I think there is room to do both: accept the complexity of human nature and keep pushing the science to evolve so our understanding of it continues to grow.

appendix a

Career Tracks and Salaries Chart

Sources: **www.wwd.com**; **www.payscale.com**

For all positions, a bachelor's degree and three years of work experience were prerequisites for employment.

Job Title	Location	Annual Salary	Average Salary
Academic Costume Designer (Ch 13)	New York	$25,229–$70,739	$40,440
	California	$26,012–$69,479	$40,862
	Ohio	$22,658–$54,625	$34,380
Account Coordinator, Beauty (Ch 16)	New York	$31,070–$55,237	$40,683
	Texas	$29,249–$49,618	$37,640
	Georgia	$30,143–$49,920	$38,777
Account Executive, Beauty (Ch 2)	New York	$29,085–$69,347	$47,228
	Indiana	$24,444–$57,929	$39,977
	Wyoming	$24,267–$60,507	$41,236
Accountant, Entry-Level Retail (Ch 7)	New York	$25,602–$46,509	$35,834
	Nevada	$24,173–$43,656	$33,910
	Oklahoma	$21,003–$39,697	$30,502
Accountant, Intermediate Wholesale (Ch 7)	New York	$36,939–$59,101	$47,509
	Illinois	$36,533–$54,753	$45,628
	Kansas	$34,162–$50,862	$42,550
Accountant, Senior (Ch 7)	New York	$44,380–$65,673	$54,160
	Vermont	$40,733–$57,499	$48,503
	Kansas	$43,213–$59,866	$51,070
Advertising Director, Creative (Ch 10)	New York	$49,431–$161,815	$89,539
	Michigan	$45,068–$147,618	$83,449
	California	$53,688–$175,433	$99,222
Aesthetician (Ch 16)	New York	$17,615–$46,560	$28,985
	Illinois	$16,113–$42,656	$26,621
	Ohio	$15,412–$38,870	$24,827
Architect, Senior Project (Ch 15)	New York	$51,016–$90,871	$69,308
	Washington	$49,346–$82,317	$65,347
	Arizona	$49,422–$82,327	$65,031
Archivist/Technician, Museum (Ch 14)	New York	$25,102–$50,146	$35,591
	Missouri	$23,679–$43,072	$32,115
	Virginia	$25,250–$47,318	$34,750
Art Director, Retail (Ch 10)	New York	$35,981–$78.229	$54,437
	Louisiana	$28,231–$59,546	$42,123
	New Mexico	$30,148–$64,136	$45,329

Assistant Buyer, Retail (Ch 11)	New York	$31,440–$55,189	$42,305
	Florida	$29,177–$49,465	$38,639
	Canada	$30,359–$45,132	$37,070
Assistant Fashion Designer (Ch 8)	New York	$30,674–$51,513	$40,714
	Texas	$28,279–$46,215	$37,187
	Ohio	$28,007–$44,897	$36,444
Assistant Importer/Agent (Ch 3)	New York	$28,751–$53,055	$39,321
	California	$28,109–$52,505	$39,471
	Connecticut	$32,121–$51,485	$40,187
Assistant Museum Curator (Ch 14)	New York	$28,462–$53,180	$39,751
	Virginia	$26,921–$48,772	$36,970
	Minnesota	$27,447–$47,468	$36,838
Assistant Store Manager (Ch 12)	New York	$23,515–$41,021	$31,613
	Missouri	$21,741–$35,864	$28,465
	Oregon	$22,656–$37,075	$29,559
Buyer/Fashion Merchandiser, Retail (Ch 11)	New York	$38,492–$71,709	$52,913
	Kansas	$34,618–$58,106	$45,161
	Florida	$35,185–$60,550	$46,495
Buyer/Fashion Merchandiser, Senior (Retail) (Ch 11)	New York	$39,430–$91,630	$61,398
	Iowa	$33,638–$70,084	$49,555
	California	$41,026–$91,806	$62,836
Buyer, Foreign Buying Office (Ch 3)	New York	$35,985–$69,848	$64,125
	Michigan	$35,439–$64,000	$47,896
	Alabama	$33,174–$61,007	$45,316
Buyer, Wholesale/Manufacturer (Ch 3)	New York	$32,900–$62,361	$45,623
	Georgia	$30,798–$58,889	$41,106
	Oregon	$30,277–$51,884	$39,926
Chief Financial Officer, Retail (Ch 7)	New York	$52,021–$136,100	$86,427
	Pennsylvania	$48,391–$122,348	$78,943
	Arkansas	$47,939–$120,481	$78,376
Colorist, Textiles (Ch 2, 9)	New York	$31,356–$71,664	$47,472
	California	$32,805–$72,028	$48,819
	New Mexico	$28,353–$62,191	$42,208
Company Sales Representative, Textiles and Apparel (Ch 6)	New York	$24,860–$78,851	$44,894
	Texas	$20,839–$67,715	$38,226
	California	$24,607–$75,860	$43,836
Costume Designer, Freelance (Ch 13)	New York	$22,370–$71,538	$37,476
	Utah	$20,362–$57,377	$32,223
	New Jersey	$22,989–$65,006	$36,682
Counter Manager, Beauty (Ch 16)	New York	$25,847–$41,852	$33,022
	Washington	as above	
	Alabama	as above	
Creative/Fashion Director (Ch 1)	New York	$41,805–$112,038	$69,923
	California	$43,876–$118,704	$73,800
	Ohio	$36,719–$92,912	$59,466
Customer Service Manager (Ch 12)	New York	$30,214–$64,743	$44,452
	Minnesota	$29,484–$57,043	$41,226
	Georgia	$26,009–$52,655	$37,233

Department Manager (Ch 12)	New York	$27,267–$48,500	$36,613
	Wisconsin	$24,344–$39,982	$31,449
	Delaware	$25,799–$43,360	$33,722
Distribution Manager/Allocator (Ch 11)	New York	$36,903–$78,288	$54,623
	California	$38,020–$76,422	$54,844
	Arkansas	$29,499–$60,845	$43,127
Divisional Merchandising Manager (Ch 11)	New York	$57,205–$137,712	$95,519
	Texas	$54,098–$131,105	$91,932
	Florida	$50,726–$120,395	$85,339
Fashion Designer (Ch 8)	New York	$41,070–$76,086	$56,857
	Ohio	$36,066–$65,754	$49,789
	Texas	$37,884–$70,199	$52,734
Fashion Event Planner (Ch 5)	New York	$31,429–$61,650	$43,531
	Michigan	$27,057–$51,251	$36,775
	N. Carolina	$26,676–$49,718	$36,105
Fashion Forecaster (Ch 1, 9)	New York	$60,000–$250,000	$95,000
Fashion Illustrator (Ch 10)	New York	$30,152–$58,417	$42,262
	Florida	$27,715–$50,205	$37,861
	Montana	$24,649–$44,925	$33,625
Fashion Photographer, Retail Apparel (Ch 13)	New York	$27,183–$88,258	$49,219
	California	$28,245–$88,672	$50,409
	Colorado	$25,794–$74,036	$44,044
Fashion Show Producer (Ch 13)	New York	$24,037–$65,646	$39,654
	Illinois	$21,968–$56.731	$35,597
	Texas	$21,875–$58,329	$35,901
Fashion Stylist, Retail Apparel (Ch 5, 13)	New York	$23,787–$80,427	$44,914
	Wyoming	$21,620–$66,950	$39,044
	Ohio	$21,229–$68,672	$39,224
Fashion Stylist, Self-Employed (Ch 5, 13)	New York	$20,954–$91,854	$45,919
	California	$21,567–$93,765	$47,242
	Nevada	$20,291–$84,177	$43,230
Foreign Commissionaire (Ch 3)	New York	$31,178–$95,528	$56,048
	Georgia	$28,230–$86,335	$50,854
	Oklahoma	$26,818–$78,736	$47,315
General Merchandising Manager (Ch 11)	New York	$77,925–$179,903	$125,478
	California	$74,567–$151,005	$114,563
	Florida	$72,342–$149,876	$116,013
Hairstylist, Salon (Ch 16)	New York	$14,041–$58,374	$27,962
	Texas	$13,384–$52,606	$26,616
	Michigan	$12,549–$48,405	$24,518
Hiring Manager/Recruiter (Ch 7)	New York	$33,655–$65,469	$46,411
	Ohio	$30,428–$52,147	$39,803
	Arizona	$32,472–$55,383	$42,123
Human Resources Manager (Ch 7)	New York	$38,076–$77,307	$55,352
	Wisconsin	$32,577–$60,630	$45,070
	West Virginia	$29,439–$58,959	$42,541

Import Coordinator (Ch 3)	New York	$33,420–$43,210	$38,158
	Florida	as above	
	California	as above	
Import Manager (Ch 3)	New York	$37,240–$75,818	$53,907
	Washington	$36,631–$65,738	$49,774
	Tennessee	$33,284–$61,827	$46,057
Interior Designer (Ch 15)	New York	$31,100–$53,946	$41,087
	Arizona	$28,915–$45,590	$36,568
	Delaware	$30,084–$47,617	$38,102
Internet Promotions/Marketing Director (Ch 10)	New York	$43,344–$95,604	$68,279
	Colorado	$42,627–$92,147	$67,525
	California	$48,281–$102,499	$75,399
Licensing Director (Ch 3)	New York	$44,572–$121,545	$79,716
	Texas	$41,477–$115,174	$76,034
	Florida	$39,549–$106,570	$71,446
Makeup Artist (Ch 16)	New York	$23,389–$57,790	$37,077
	Ohio	$20,940–$48,230	$32,166
	Washington	$22,805–$52,375	$34,986
Mall Manager (Ch 15)	New York	$29,991–$57,705	$47,724
	Oklahoma	$25,732–$53,025	$37,222
	California	$29,103–$58,464	$41,901
Manufacturer's Representative, Independent (Ch 6)	New York	$26,370–$94,766	$48,027
	Illinois	$24,806–$75,066	$42,640
	Maryland	$26,364–$77,095	$44,225
Media Planner (Ch 5)	New York	$35,165–$54,441	$43,695
	Washington	$34,839–$50,473	$41,876
	Mississippi	$29,293–$43,380	$35,807
Merchandise Coordinator (Ch 6)	New York	$28,333–$55,103	$39,907
	Missouri	$25,101–$45,745	$34,362
	Kentucky	$24,258–$44,453	$33,428
Merchandise Planner (Ch 11)	New York	$47,892–$73,827	$64,246
	Georgia	$35,278–$64,111	$49,542
	Pennsylvania	$34,931–$62,119	$48,182
Merchandiser for Manufacturing (Ch 3)	New York	$24,763–$66,733	$39,626
	California	$25,180–$65,171	$39,779
	Maryland	$24,667–$56,529	$36,707
Merchandising/Management Trainee (Ch 11, 12)	New York	$28,659–$56,850	$39,125
	Virginia	$26,772–$48,210	$35,289
	Rhode Island	$27,877–$47,615	$35,720
Model (Ch 13)	New York	$25,302–$92,128	$49,732
	Florida	$22,827–$80,702	$44,223
	Tennessee	$21,384–$78,987	$42,432
Model /Talent Agency Director (Ch 13)	New York	$35,038–$121,241	$79,853
	California	$36,834–$126,406	$84,539
	Tennessee	$27,472–$105,128	$68,659
Museum Curator (Ch 14)	Virginia	$26,365–$54,790	$37,784

Museum Director (Ch 14)	New York	$24,878–$78,234	$49,197
	Pennsylvania	$22,766–$69,011	$44,494
	Virginia	$23,384–$72,746	$46,377
Operations Manager (Ch 12)	New York	$36,559–$79,567	$54,381
	Idaho	$29,528–$59,678	$42,271
	Florida	$32,175–$65,248	$46,177
Patternmaker (Ch 8)	New York	$31,024–$84,821	$53,448
	Texas	$28,757–$78,862	$48,783
	Missouri	$27,441–$72,728	$45,715
Patternmaker/Grader (Ch 4)	New York	$30,702–$85,254	$52,907
	Missouri	$26,864–$73,315	$45,967
	New Jersey	$31,662–$84,769	$53,474
Personal Shopper/Fashion Stylist Retail (Ch 10)	New York	$21,858–$60,021	$36,654
	Utah	$20,273–$49,753	$32,098
	New Jersey	$22,427–$58,673	$36,745
Product Development Director, Beauty (Ch 16)	New York	$60,511–$114,570	$89,610
	Georgia	$58,770–$113,064	$89,639
	Minnesota	$60,167–$106,898	$86,198
Product Development Director, Apparel/Accessories Wholesale (Ch 4)	New York	$58,705–$100,093	$81,279
	Pennsylvania	$55,711–$97,794	$78,614
	Alabama	$51,222–$104,282	$80,987
Product Development Director, Retail (Ch 9)	New York	$64,471–$114,335	$90,795
	Nevada	$60,748–$108,589	$87,375
	Nebraska	$55,829–$99,557	$80,184
Product Development Manager, Apparel Wholesale (Ch 4)	New York	$41,712–$85,852	$61,100
	Montana	$31,646–$64,475	$46,332
	Kansas	$35,185–$72,496	$51,748
Product Developer or Technician, Beauty (Ch 16)	New York	$26,480–$57,137	$40,172
	Ohio	$23,772–$48,211	$35,226
	Florida	$23,375–$49,512	$35,700
Production Assistant (Ch 4)	New York	$26,182–$43,473	$34,698
	Colorado	$25,261–$39,425	$32,374
	Arkansas	$21,536–$35,324	$28,536
Production Manager (Ch 4)	New York	$38,341–$79,227	$56,440
	S. Carolina	$34,792–$69,576	$50,493
	New Mexico	$34,320–$69,520	$50,194
Production Planner (Ch 4)	New York	$35,404–$66,327	$48,840
	California	$37,507–$65,136	$49,795
	New Mexico	$31,697–$56,571	$42,649
Production Planner, Manufacturing (Ch 4)	New York	$36,882–$69,598	$51,047
	S. Carolina	$30,556–$52,445	$40,271
	Texas	$33,547–$59,362	$44,922
Promotion Director, Retail (Ch 10)	New York	$32,781–$87,979	$53,877
	Utah	$28,189–$67,860	$43,907
	Pennsylvania	$28,071–$73.373	$45,766

Public Relations Director (Ch 5, 10, 16)	New York	$40,126–$90,940	$62,264
	Virginia	$40,804–$89,196	$61,854
	Kentucky	$32,660–$74,985	$51,446
Quality Control Manager, Textile Production (Ch 4)	New York	$36,305–$77,217	$54,181
	New Jersey	$37,862–$74,721	$54,366
	California	$38,779–$79,099	$56,980
Quality Control Manager, Retail Apparel (Ch 9)	New York	$37,963–$78,008	$55,441
	Ohio	$34,553–$65,758	$48,550
	California	$41,111–$81,280	$59,185
Regional (District) Store Manager (Ch 12)	New York	$38,419–$90,064	$59,551
	Tennessee	$33,582–$73,511	$50,507
	Colorado	$36,476–$77,170	$53,628
Resource Room Director/ Reference Librarian (Ch 2)	New York	$34, 851–$58,443	$45,875
	California	$34,843–$56,796	$45,410
	Illinois	$32,336–$50,985	$41,349
Retail Account Executive, Beauty (Ch 16)	New York	$30,203–$64,994	$45,865
	Washington	$30,801–$61,970	$45,460
	Delaware	$31,167–$62,364	$45,646
Retail Merchandiser (Ch 9)	New York	$25,295–$36,976	$30,659
	Oregon	as above	
	Iowa	as above	
Retail Store Owner (Ch 12)	New York	$29,685–$116,133	$60,667
	Alaska	$34,285–$119,209	$65,722
	Hawaii	$32,171–$110,928	$61,391
Retail Store Manager (Ch 12)	New York	$28,623–$54,923	$39,776
	Rhode Island	$27,418–$46,058	$35,712
	Idaho	$24,328–$43,253	$32,652
Security Manager (Ch 12)	New York	$32,590–$73,924	$49,811
	W. Virginia	$25,676–$57,200	$38,939
	Maine	$28,712–$58,051	$41,230
Senior Buyer, Retail (Ch 11)	New York	$36,575–$85,279	$57,136
	Florida	$32,635–$72,295	$49,817
	Canada	$37,586–$70,712	$54,191
Showroom Manager (Ch 6)	New York	$31,060–$69,143	$43,651
	California	$31,179–$67,578	$44,017
	Illinois	$29,583–$56,362	$39,542
Social Media Director (Ch 5)	New York	$31,716–$84,870	$52,991
	California	$32,448–$84,368	$53,544
	Illinois	$30,085–$77,931	$49,497
Sourcing Manager, International (Ch 3)	New York	$42,926–$94,208	$64,969
	Illinois	$40,538–$84,837	$60,776
	Hawaii	$39,144–$86,032	$60,088
Special Events Coordinator (Ch 10)	New York	$28,746–$53,204	$39,711
	Tennessee	$24,401–$43,377	$33,278
	Iowa	$23,994–$41,074	$31,939

Specification Technician/Product Development Engineer (Ch 8)	New York	$50,387–$76,328	$62,589
	Arkansas	$43,591–$66,130	$54,428
	Michigan	$46,855–$69,081	$57,399
Textile Cutting Machine Operator (Ch 4)	New York	$22,306–$54,846	$35,846
	Texas	$20,436–$48,880	$31,992
	New Jersey	$23,009–$53,501	$35,743
Store Planning Director (Ch 10)	New York	$94,790–$107,735	$101,159
	Arizona	as above	
	Hawaii	as above	
Stylist (Ch 10)	New York	$15,034–$52,840	$27,725
	Virginia	$14,045–$43,562	$24,696
	California	$16,788–$56,678	$30,605
Technical Designer (Ch 8)	New York	$36,308–$67.454	$49,791
	Oregon	$35,100–$60,609	$46,394
	Texas	$35,982–$64,087	$48,316
Textile Engineer (Ch 2)	New York	$36,426–$80,838	$56,579
	California	$40,702–$80,356	$59,389
	N. Carolina	$37,516–$80,991	$57,683
Textile Designer (Ch 2)	New York	$26,776–$57,898	$40,798
	N Carolina	$24,785–$52,038	$37,392
	New Jersey	$27,385–$57,184	$40,992
Traffic Manager (Ch 4)	New York	$30,970–$65,542	$45,482
	Texas	as above	
	California	as above	
Trainer, Human Resources (Ch 7)	New York	$34,303–$68,525	$48,927
	Utah	$33,034–$59,231	$44,539
	Virginia	$33,026–$65,019	$46,735
Visual Merchandiser (Ch 10)	New York	$30,411–$60,268	$43,385
	S. Carolina	$25,273–$47,387	$35,250
	Nebraska	$25,346–$46,673	$35,042
Visual Merchandising Manager (Ch 10)	New York	$30,165–$59,656	$42,832
	Utah	$27,235–$51,560	$37,841
	Arizona	$28,451–$53,551	$39,388
Wardrobe Stylist (Ch 5)	New York	$41,324–$78,125	$54,789
	Washington	$36,631–$65,738	$49,774
	Wisconsin	$32,577–$60,630	$45,070
Web Site Developer (Ch 15)	New York	$33,965–$73,773	$51,419
	Connecticut	$38,687–$76,520	$55,183
	New Mexico	$29,985–$65,721	$46,132

appendix b

Résumé, Interview Guidelines, and Letter of Application

The Résumé

Your Résumé Should:

- Be more an outline than a narrative. Think of it as a "calling card" or an offering to a prospective buyer. Keep it simple and to the point. Tried-and-true résumé tips and a sample résumé follow to assist you in making your "calling card" a memorable one that spurs the employer to contact you immediately.
- Be specific, particularly in the *Objective* section. Most interviewers do not want to conduct career counseling. Know what types of career positions you are prepared for and want to pursue before you send your résumé, and indicate this under the *Objective* heading.
- Be factual. Tell the truth and nothing but the truth. Do not get caught having to explain a point that is not clear and does not have support.
- Be like the trailer for a great movie. The résumé should help you get through the door without telling the whole story. You need to be ready to jump in and to fill in the gaps during phone or online screenings and personal interviews.

Support Your Résumé With:

- *A good letter of application* (often referred to as a cover letter). It should be short and to the point. Make sure the recipient knows what you want (e.g., a permanent job, an informational interview, a contact, etc.) and how you have prepared to succeed.
- *A good listing of references.* Ask references for permission before including them on your reference listing. Include the job title and complete contact information (e.g., postal mailing address, e-mail address, and telephone number) of each reference. Some job seekers add a brief description of their relationship and work experiences with the reference (e.g., intern, part-time sales associate, etc.), as illustrated in the sample reference listing at the end of this appendix.
- *Excellent target employers provided by your contacts.* Ask alumni (graduates of your institution); they want to help if they can. Use family, friends, faculty, guest speakers, internship contacts, former employers, and hometown contacts. This is how you develop your network, one that you build throughout your career.
- *The informational interview.* Identify key decision makers within your target companies and schedule meetings to learn more about the business or the career path. Contact people in both human resources and other areas. The more people in support of you, the better your opportunity for success.

Tried-and-True Résumé Tips

No matter if your résumé is scanned and e-mailed, sent through the postal system, or hand-delivered, its content is most important. Follow these tried-and-true résumé tips as you work toward résumé perfection.

- Always use spellcheck.
- Begin with a goal or an objective. It should include key words.
- For *Education*, include your major, minor, and month and year of graduation. You may include your grade point average. A number of employment professionals suggest listing the grade point average only if 3.0 or above on a 4.0 scale.
- *Work Experience* should include internships and part-time jobs (within reason).
- If lacking relevant employment experience, include information about class projects that would relate to the position for which you are applying.
- Include extracurricular activities, keeping in mind these tips:
    - o Identify the skills and experiences you will need in your target field and look for organizations on campus where you will get these.
    - o Hold an officer position within the organization or head up various committees within the organization.
    - o Have a variety of extracurricular experiences to demonstrate your ability to work with a range of people.
    - o Be involved throughout your college career, not just your final year in school.
    - o Many companies place a high value on service activities, such as volunteer work on campus, in your community, or in the world community.
- List specific skills related to your career goals, such as computer skills, language fluency, international experiences, etc.
- You may choose to list highlights of your coursework (courses that relate to the position) under the *Education* section, if you do not have adequate experience to fill a one-page résumé. If you do have enough experiences to effectively fill a one-page résumé, these can be listed on a separate sheet of paper, along with a brief description if the course title does not adequately explain them. You may want to have this list in case the interviewer asks for this information.
- Keep the résumé to one page. While you may have a number of great experiences in college, you have not had enough yet to warrant more than a one-page résumé.
- For hard copies, use light-colored, standard size (8 1/2" x 11") paper. Use high-quality paper and a good printer. Choose white, eggshell, beige, or light gray paper. Avoid "grainy" paper.
- Place your name and contact information at the top of each and every page.
- Do not fold the hard copy of your résumé; send it in a flat envelope.
- Avoid using staples.

Sample Résumé

Carlee Evans
Evans228@gmail.com
911 China Circle
Paris, Texas 74059
(903) 555-4160 (M)

OBJECTIVE
To obtain a position in the magazine industry where I can apply my skills and experience in public relations, visual merchandising, photography, and marketing.

EDUCATION
Bachelor of Science, Department of Fashion and Interior Design—College of Business Administration
Major: Fashion Merchandising   Minor: Marketing   *Texas University*, Paris, TX   Graduation: May 2012

INTERNSHIPS
Shape Magazine   June 2011–August 2011
Director of Public Relations Assistant   New York, NY
- Produced segments for online video clips featuring *Shape*'s Style Director
- Accompanied Director of Public Relations to weekly national broadcasted segments.
- Pitched ideas relevant to upcoming issue of *Shape* and breaking news in the world.

Sweet Photography   January 2011–June 2011
Photographer's Assistant/Intern   Paris, TX
- Assisted company owner/photographer with studio shoots (portrait, commercial, fashion, etc.).
- Provided styling in the arrangements of layouts for ads and magazines.
- Photographed apparel and accessories for advertisements in local magazines.

417 Magazine   August 2010-December 2010
Style Coordinating Assistant   Paris, TX
- Accompanied Style Coordinator on various photo shoots.
- Selected merchandise and themes for different feature stories.
- Operated Photoshop and other programs for magazine layout.

WORK EXPERIENCE:
BCBG MaxAzria   Fall 2009–currently employed
Sales Specialist   Paris, TX
- Provide excellent customer service and surpass sales goals.
- Calculate daily/weekly/monthly sales plans for department and sales goals for associates.
- Assist in reorganizing floor sets and inventorying merchandise.

RELATED ACTIVITIES:
China, London, and Paris Fashion Study Tours, Texas University (2009 and 2010)
Fashion Group International Seminars (as attendee) in Kansas City, Chicago, and Dallas (2009 to 2011)
Association of Fashion and Design, Fashion Show Production Public Relations Leader, Texas University (2009 to 2011)
Rho Lambda Women's Honor Fraternity Vice President Executive P.R. Officer for Business and Professional Women Foundation, Texas University (2010)
Order of Omega Greek Honor Society Vice President, Texas University (2009)

COMMUNITY SERVICE
- Help Give Hope Charitable Organization
- Hurricane Katrina Relief efforts
- Donated series of original photographs that were auctioned to raise money for student scholarships.

Sample Internship Resumé

PATRICIA MCCOY
pmccoy@hotmail.com

Campus Address
Tower Hall, Box 3922
Ivy League University
Springfield, Missouri 65804
(417) 555-1215

Permanent Address
300 West 14th Avenue
Apartment 1-C
St. Louis, Missouri 63021
(314) 555-4213

Objective:
To obtain a design internship in the fashion industry that will allow me to use and expand upon my present skills in patternmaking, draping, and illustration, while preparing me for future career employment.

Education:
Bachelor of Science in Fashion Design/Product Development
Ivy League University, Springfield, Missouri.
Anticipated graduation date: May 2005.
Cumulative grade point average: 3.7/4.0 scale.

Related Course Highlights

Flat Patternmaking	Retailing
Draping	Accounting I and II
Illustration	Finance
Clothing Construction	Textiles

Work Experience:
<u>Alterations Associate</u>, Custom Fit, Springfield, MO 2003–2004. Served as night manager of company and supervised team of 5 seamstresses.

<u>Sales Associate</u>, Express, St. Louis, MO, Summers, 2003–2004. Assisted customers; checked in merchandise; stocked floor; created interior displays; and cashiered.

<u>Desk Hostess</u>, Ivy League University College, Springfield, MO, 2002–2003. Responsible for opening and closing residence hall; assisted visitors and students; handled telephone calls and messages.

Honors/Activities:
Fashion Honorary Organization, 2002–present.
Vice President, Tower Hall, 2002–2003.

Additional Skills:
Proficient in CAD, Excel, Microsoft Word, and Photoshop
Fluent in French

Interview Guidelines

Planning for the Interview

- Be prepared. Research the company *and* the industry *before* the interview. Know exactly when and where to go for the interview well ahead of time.
- Come prepared with good questions (even better if you know the answers).
- Be polite and courteous. You are building your professional reputation.
- Think of the interview in the following segments:

Minutes	
0–5	Size it up. Be impressive. You are both evaluating each other and first impressions count.
5–20	Sell yourself. This is the part when you explain your résumé. Know which parts of your background to stress. Do not be shy about your accomplishments; specifically, outcomes. Describe yourself and your experiences, but remember the time. You will be judged on how well you organize your thoughts. If the interviewer asks you a yes or no question, answer it that way. Watch and listen to know if he or she wants you to elaborate.
20–25	Let the interviewer sell you. Ask questions about the organization. Why is it such a great place to work? Remember, this is an important decision for you.
25–30	Wrap it up. Determine what will happen next. Will the interviewer call you or should you contact him or her? When?

- A well-written thank-you and follow-up letter is essential after the interview.

Points to Keep in Mind for the Interview

- Be strategic and focused.
  - o Even if you do not know *exactly* what you want, sound like you at least have an idea.
- Understand the reality of the workplace.
  - o Service businesses in the fashion industry are good places to look. Be creative.
  - o New industries and businesses are often the ones seeking new employees with fresh ideas.
  - o Think about what environments you would like to work in (e.g., a large company, a big-city location, formal structure, etc.).
  - o Find a good training program. Down the road you will benefit greatly from a good foundation. Sales and retail management often have the best programs. Internships can also provide excellent training.
- Consider the merits of graduate school.
  - o More and more young professionals have advanced degrees. They are likely the people you will compete with on the career ladder.

- Consider working first.
  - o You may want to gain some experience in the workplace, so you can add value to further education. You may even find an employer who will pay for graduate coursework.
- Consider yourself fortunate to have a solid education.
  - o Your college or university has provided you with a strong foundation for lifelong learning and diverse exposure. Recruiters appreciate that.
- Enjoy yourself.
  - o Have fun! Sell yourself; you are your most important and valued resource. Many doors can be opened for you, but it is up to you to sell yourself in order to walk through.
- Be realistic.
  - o Send out many more letters of application and résumés than you believe you will need. There is much competition in the job market. The more opportunities you have, the higher your chances of having several positions offered, giving you the chance to choose from among them.

Researching Employers

Why Research Employers?

Researching prospective employers is a frequently overlooked step when applying for a job. It is easy to get excited when you believe you have found the perfect opportunity; however, not digging deep into an employer's current situation and past reputation can prove to be a costly mistake. You can be certain that employers are checking your references, online profile, and college credentials before extending an offer. You would be remiss not to do the same with any prospective hiring organization. The more you know about a company, the better able you will be to communicate your value to this employer during your interview. The hard work that you put into your research will almost always pay off by reflecting your interest and enthusiasm to employers, and providing you with the confidence that this is a secure employment opportunity. Taking the time to learn about a company and then sharing what you learned about it is a form of flattery to company representatives. Before you complete your letter of application and send out your résumé, we will take a closer look at why you should research employers, what to look for, and how to investigate like a detective.

The majority of college graduates have held some type of employment; some have had wonderful experiences on these jobs, while others may have been wondering what the employer was thinking, how bad it could get, and when it would be over. In the latter case, they learned the hard way to spend dedicated time learning about an employer before applying for a job. Why should you do some investigative work on prospective employers?

- *To determine if the company is a fit for you.* You may find you do not particularly like a specific career path in the industry. You may dig up unfortunate corporate digital dirt, or uncover information on poor employee relations.

- *To decide if you are right for the company.* Some companies or industries may not be the right fit for your skill sets, values, or corporate culture preferences. It is also possible to find that you are not really interested in the company's products or services. Be sure to consider your goals, desires, and ethics to see how they fit given the information you have revealed.

- *To help tailor your résumé and letter of application to the position.* Knowing specifically what makes the company successful can turn your application into the winning ticket.

- *To give you the information required to effectively address the needs of the organization.* Knowing why the company needs to hire is key to addressing how you can help the company.

- *To help you prepare effective interview questions.* Knowing specific industry information or advanced product knowledge can get you closer to an offer as you impress the interviewer with insightful questions and answers.

- *To demonstrate sincere interest in the company.* A common interview question is "Why do you want to work for us?" Having an educated answer puts you ahead of the competition. One of the most important ways to distinguish yourself in an interview is to speak knowledgeably about the organization.

- *To educate yourself about a particular career path in the industry.* Perhaps this job is in a new sector of the industry for you. Get in the know before writing your résumé and hoping for an interview.

When to Research Employers

The best time to research employers is *before* you prepare your résumé and letter of application to request an interview with a company. By doing some due diligence early, you can quickly rule out firms and positions that do not match your personal needs, academic requirements, or desired career path.

Where to Conduct Employer Research

Conducting employer research is much like preparing a college assignment or project. The idea is to develop two lists: one of companies for which you are interested in working, and another of resources for researching businesses. Next are examples of a few good places to start your list of resources to help your investigation of prospective employers.

- *Corporate Web site.* Look for industry information, product or service details, and management information. Most corporate sites indicate company age, size, ownership, locations, and leadership or management details. Check the Web site to see if the company is public or private. A review of annual reports may reveal interesting corporate details such as the firm's financial situation, health of the industry, mission statement, and number of employees.

- *Google.* Search forums, Web sites, blogs, and online articles that will enable you to see what others have to say about the company's products, services, and employee relations. You may be surprised. Take these as they are—opinions and comments. Make a decision that is based on facts, yet allows room for majority opinion.

- *Better Business Bureau.* This organization can alert you to complaints against companies in specific geographical areas or cities. You may want to contact them to see if your prospective employer is on the list.

- *Consumer and trade publications.* Research the employer's industry activity through print, in addition to Internet sources. Read magazines, newspapers, trade publications, and journals related to the field and organization.

- *Trade associations.* Is the company affiliated with an association? Consult association Web sites to see if the prospective employing organization is in good standing and how it contributes to the profession.

- *Chambers of Commerce.* You may want to begin by contacting the Chambers of Commerce in the communities where the companies you are interested in are located. Often, you will find a searchable comprehensive directory online.

- *Public relations and promotions.* Check out any product or service advertisements the company runs in the media. Locate press releases about the company. Many companies have these at their Web sites; however, keep in mind that these are usually positive reflections of the firm. Employer recruitment brochures are a great marketing tool for the company and provide a good overview for the prospective employee. Brochures and sales flyers also offer a good look at the company. You may want to contact the company to ask for these marketing materials.

- *Employee handbook.* Contact a representative of the company's human resources department and ask for this and other information about the company.

- *Former or current employee references.* Do you know any current or former employees? Ask them why they left, who supervised them, and if they would ever work there again. Will the human resources department let you speak with current employees? Getting to know current members of the team is an excellent way to judge if you want to work with this employer in the future.

Types of Information to Uncover Through Employer Research

Begin by locating general information about each company in which you are interested. Keep an accurate record of what you learn. If you are ready to go onto the Internet to begin your research, keep the following in mind:

- Know what you are looking for before you go online. Keep a list beside you so that you can check off items as you locate them. An electronic spreadsheet is ideal to post information as you find it. It is easy to get frustrated or disinterested in the research phase if you don't keep organized records.

- Bookmark major Web sites as you come across them. Most browsers will allow you to create folders or directories to organize the links.

- Although the Internet is an invaluable research tool, the library is still one of the best places to locate information. The reference librarian at your college, university, or local library should be able to point you in the direction of many useful directories and indexes. Examples of resources that you will find in the library are: Dunn and Bradstreet reports, *Standard & Poor's Corporation Records*, World Business Directory, and *Ward's Business Directory*. Now that you know where to look for general information, you may want to format a spreadsheet of which details to uncover.

Carlee Evans

Evans228@gmail.com
911 China Circle
Paris, Texas 74059
(903)555-4160 (Mobile)

February 26, 2012

Dear Mr. Kim:

I am impressed with your organization and desire a position in your marketing division. I am certain that my skills and experiences, when combined with the vision of your company, will serve to create productive results. I have learned of the availability of such a position after researching job openings on your Web site and in *Women's Wear Daily*.

I will be completing my Bachelor of Science Degree in Fashion Merchandising and Marketing at Texas University in May of 2012, and will be available for employment at that time. This past summer, I completed an internship in New York City at *Shape Magazine*. I worked alongside very knowledgeable and prestigious people who gave me great opportunities and experiences. I was given progressively significant daily tasks and individual projects. I also accompanied my supervisors on assignments.

As a student of Texas University, my education in the Fashion and Interior Design Department has been highly beneficial and rewarding. My work background and coursework have supplied me with many skills and an understanding of the fashion industry. For example, I have acquired a solid reputation in the eyes of my professors and peers as a responsible leader and strong networker in the industry. In addition to my academic endeavors, I have put my knowledge and creativity toward the involvement of fashion in the community. I have participated in planning and judging fashion shows for the university and local boutiques. I have also assisted a professor in a weekly television segment entitled "Dr. Fashion." In addition to fashion, I have a passion for photography and have been asked to photograph merchandise from boutiques and stores to be published in local magazines. I am consistently energized by opportunities to enhance my knowledge and experience toward the fashion industry. I have had the opportunity to travel and experience China, London, and Paris, where I was able to observe global fashion markets diverse to America and contributing to this global and fast-paced industry.

I have enclosed a copy of my résumé with additional information about my qualifications. I look forward to speaking with you and discussing the job position. I believe I can contribute to the creative needs of your organization and further advance its visibility. Thank you for your time reviewing my résumé. The best times to reach me are Monday through Friday between 9 a.m. and 6 p.m. I will call you in two weeks to inquire about the best time for an interview. I look forward to speaking with you.

Sincerely,

Carlee Evans
Enclosure: résumé and reference listing

- Consider these variables when researching an employer:

    o   Mission, philosophy, and objectives of the company

    o   Source(s) of funding, including assets, earnings, and losses

    o   Company ownership (e.g., private or public, sole proprietorship or partnership, foreign or domestic ownership, etc.)

    o   Company divisions or subsidiaries

    o   Board of directors or advisory board

    o   General reputation of the company

    o   History or background

    o   Products (to include services) that the company sells or provides

    o   Target market or clientele list

    o   Strategies and goals

    o   Market positioning or repositioning efforts

    o   Areas of specialization

    o   New projects and major achievements

    o   Age of company

    o   Size of the company and number of employees

    o   Patterns of growth or decline

    o   Forecast of future growth

    o   Recent issues or events (e.g., layoffs or hiring, closings or expansion, etc.)

    o   Number of employees

    o   Location of the company headquarters and length of time it has been established there

    o   Other company locations

    o   Office/facility environment

- o   Personnel policies

- o   Types of people employed and from where employees are recruited

- o   Health of the industry

- o   Compensation and benefits for entry-level employees

- o   Services or products sold or provided

- o   Career path or other opportunities within the company upon graduation

Be sure to consider other details specific to the type of position in which you are most interested. It is important not to be slow, vague, or inaccurate about this process, as any employer worth your time and effort on the job is well worth your time and effort now.

The Final Word on Researching Before Sending Out Your Résumés

Finding the right job is work. Researching a prospective employer is work, but the results can be very rewarding, especially if you find the ideal positions based on your findings. It just makes sense to do some homework on a company before sending out résumés and letters of application to just any firm you hear about or stumble across. You are not simply applying for any job. This is the start of your career and you are determining who will be the provider of your paycheck in the future. You are your most important investment of time and energy.

Next, samples of a letter of application, résumé, and letter of reference are presented as illustrations of a new college graduate's successful job application packet.

glossary

academic costume designer Holds a teaching or staff position with a college or university; this type of designer is often primarily an instructor, who may also act as a residential designer for college theater productions. (CH 13)

academic curator training Instruction for the museum curator on how to study and understand museum collections. (CH 14)

accession The addition of an artifact to a museum collection. (CH 14)

account coordinator Organizes special events and promotions for a cosmetic, fragrance, or skin care line, while traveling to different retail locations; develops and implements marketing programs that perpetuate the image of the company; introduces new products; and generates customer traffic and press for retail accounts. (CH 16)

account executive Sells to a manufacturer and manages accounts. May also be called *manufacturer's representative* or *sales representative*. (CH 2)

accounts payable Monies owed to creditors for goods and services; the amount owed by a business to its suppliers or vendors. (CH 7)

accounts payable clerk Reviews invoices for accuracy and completeness, sorts documents by account name or number, and processes invoices for payment. (CH 7)

accounts payable manager Directs the accounts payable division of a company under the organization's established policies and monitors monies owed to creditors. (CH 7)

accounts payable supervisor Oversees accounts payable record keeping by supervising the recording of amounts due, verification of invoices, and calculation of discounts. (CH 7)

accounts receivable Amounts of money owed to a business that it expects to receive for goods furnished and services rendered, including sales made on credit, reimbursements earned, and refunds due. (CH 7)

accounts receivable clerk Verifies transactions related to money owed to the business and posts them to journals, ledgers, and other records. (CH 7)

accounts receivable manager Supervises the accounts receivable function, oversees monies owed to the business within an organization's established policies. (CH 7)

accounts receivable supervisor Oversees record keeping in the accounts receivable department and ensures that cash receipts, claims, or unpaid invoices are accounted for properly. (CH 7)

advertising A type of promotion that is paid, nonpersonal communication delivered through mass media. Designed to serve different purposes, there are five primary types of advertising: institutional, brand, sales, classified, and advocacy. (CH 10)

advertising agency An outside firm that may be contracted by a retail organization to help choose the right media types to reach the retailer's target market and maximize its promotional budget. (CH 10)

advertising director Develops and implements a company's paid promotional strategy for the purpose of increasing sales. (CH 10)

advertising photography Also known as *editorial photography*. Expresses a product's personality or illustrates a magazine story and is usually classified as still life, food, transportation, portraiture, or landscape. (CH 13)

advertising promotion staff Develops presentations to help the sales representatives of print and electronic media firms sell advertising to new and existing accounts. (CH 5)

advertising research assistant Helps sales representatives sell advertising space, in a publication for example, by supplying facts that an advertiser will want to know, such as the number of issues sold and top locations in terms of sales volume, or the profile and buying power of the publication's readers. (CH 5)

advertising sales representative Sells advertising for consumer and trade publications. (CH 5)

advocacy advertising Supports a particular cause; e.g., a home-building retailer may run a newspaper advertisement featuring green design merchandise in support of environmental awareness. (CH 10)

aesthetician A licensed professional who provides services such as facials, makeup application, and hair removal to aid in improving an individual's physical appearance. (CH 16)

aesthetics A relatively new field that combines wellness, science, and beauty. The field views the client as a whole person by providing services through comprehensive makeovers and beauty-enhancement treatments that combine medical, beauty, and spa treatments. (CH 16)

architect Building designer who works with a wide range of structures that may range from small freestanding retail stores to large malls. (CH 15)

Architect Registration Examination (ARE) Professional licensure examination for architects in the United States and Canada. (CH 15)

architecture The creative blend of art and science in the design of environments for people. The plans for a building ultimately focus on the needs of the people who use them, to include aesthetics, safety, and environmental factors. (CH 15)

archivist Analyzes, describes, catalogues, and exhibits records and documents that are retained by museums because of their importance and potential value, benefiting researchers and the public. (CH 14)

art director Develops and implements the creative concepts for advertising, catalogues, mailers, and signage; this person provides an overall and consistent visual view of the manufacturing or retailing company, including signage, photography, direct mail, and packaging. (CH 10)

assistant buyer Supports the buyer, often working with the six-month plan, open-to-buy, inventory, and vendor follow-up, taking direction from the buyer. (CH 11)

assistant controller Supports the company's controller in directing budget and cost controls, financial analysis, and accounting procedures. (CH 7)

assistant curator Supports the museum curator, often serving as the registrar of museum collections by coordinating the collections' accessions. (CH 14)

assistant fashion designer Supports designers by helping them create, modify, and locate new materials, styles, colors, and patterns for fashion brands and labels. (CH 8)

assistant human resources manager Supports the human resources manager and is responsible for maintaining records and files on all injuries, illness, and safety programs. This person ensures that all reports are maintained to meet regulatory requirements and corporate policies and often keeps records of hired employee characteristics for governmental reporting. (CH 7)

assistant importer Works for the import production coordinator and follows up on orders with overseas suppliers. He or she also communicates with freight companies and customs agents, processes documents, and checks pricing agreements. (CH 3)

assistant mall manager Responsible for administering mall programs under the supervision of the property's general manager. This position is critical in communicating operational issues to tenants, contractors, and staff. (CH 15)

assistant photographer Supports the photographer and works with clients and suppliers; organizes estimates, invoices, and payments; arranges props and assists with lighting; communicates with photographic labs and stylists; helps the photographer on shoots; and maintains the photographer's Web site and portfolio. (CH 13)

assistant piece goods buyer Often works with the piece goods buyer to calculate quantities of fabrics needed, to follow up on deliveries, and to locate fabric sources, while training for a buying position in the future. (CH 3)

assistant store manager Assists the store manager in scheduling employees, overseeing sales performance in the store, planning promotions, etc.—all of the daily responsibilities of operating a store successfully. (CH 12)

assistant stylist Supports the stylist; responsible for contacting public relations companies, manufacturers, and retailers to locate the best assortment of merchandise to be used in a shoot. (CH 13)

assistant textile designer Works under the direction of the textile designer in developing new fabric prints and colorways, sourcing new patterns for fabrics, and modifying successful fabric prints and patterns. (CH 2)

associate store manager This is a position that lies between the assistant store manager and the store manager; assists with employee hires, personnel scheduling, promotional activities, employee training, and other responsibilities assigned by the store manager. (CH 12)

base salary plus commission Remuneration for an employee that is determined by the established monthly wage plus a percent of sales for products or services the employee sells. (CH 6)

beauty and wellness industries Focus on cosmetics, fragrances, hair and skin are, as well as spa, fitness, or wellness centers and their services. (CH 16)

beauty industry The producers of cosmetics, fragrances, and hair and skin care products. (CH 16)

beauty merchandising and marketing professional Involved in the marketing of cosmetics, fragrances, and skin care products. (CH 16)

benchmarking The activity of identifying competitors with features or skills in areas that a given company does not currently possess yet desires. (CH 7)

block A basic flat pattern that is used as a starting place for pattern modifications. Also called a *sloper*. (CH 8)

body scanning Use of light beams to accurately measure the human body. (CH 4)

book signing An event during which a beauty or fashion writer signs copies of his or her latest publication in a book, specialty, or department store. (CH 5)

brand advertising Promotes a particular label or manufacturer and is one of the five primary types of advertising. (CH 10)

breakdown The segmenting of a purchase order into quantities by sizes and colors to prepare for shipping from the manufacturer's or retailer's warehouse to specific branch stores. (CH 3)

brick-and-click store A retail business that offers its products to consumers through a store facility and through the Internet. (CH 9)

brick-and-mortar-store A retail business that has a physical appearance, as opposed to an Internet-based company. This includes department stores, mass merchants, specialty stores, boutiques, discount stores, and outlet stores located in buildings. (CH 9)

bridal show Event also called a *bridal fair*, where bridal wear manufacturers and retailers team up with auxiliary businesses, such as wedding planners, caterers, florists, and travel agents, to offer a fashion presentation of the season's offerings for brides-to-be, their friends, and their families. (CH 5)

broad-spectrum firm A company that provides forecasting services for a wide range of target markets and product categories or industries. (CH 1)

business plan A document used to solicit business funding that details strategies for the business concept and target market, location and space needs (i.e., building lease, facility purchase, or Web site requirements), growth and exit strategies, sales and inventory levels, and financing needs. (CH 12)

buyer Typically responsible for all of the product purchases and inventories for a company or particular department of a company, within a certain budget; this position is also referred to as *fashion merchandiser*. (CH 11)

buying plan A financial plan that takes into account past and projected sales, inventory, markups, and markdowns by department; it is also referred to as a *sixmonth plan*. (CH 11)

carryover A best-selling item from one season that is featured again with minor modifications in the next season. (CH 9)

chargebacks Credits to a vendor for damaged merchandise and returns on defective goods. (CH 3)

chief financial officer (CFO) Top director of the overall financial plans and accounting practices of an organization. (CH 7)

classified advertising Disseminates information about a sale, service, opportunity, or event. These are usually presented as small advertisements in specific sections of print publications. (CH 10)

client registry file A computerized or print record of the names and contact information of the retailer's or the line's customers. (CH 16)

cold calling Contacting businesses or people without a personal reference or previous contact. (CH 7)

collection Grouping of related styles. (CH 3)

collections manager Supervises museum personnel working in a specific area within a museum classification, such as historical textiles, 18th-century millinery, or Egyptian jewelry. (CH 14)

colorist Chooses the color palette or color combinations that will be used in creating product lines. (CH 9)

color palette The specific color selections for a particular pattern or print. (CH 9)

colorway Color selections for a particular pattern or print. (CH 2, CH 9)

commercial designer Interior designer who concentrates on public spaces, including projects for retail stores, hotels, motels, schools, etc. Also referred to as *contract designer*. (CH 15)

commercial real estate Public properties that include malls, business districts, and shopping centers. (CH 15)

commission Percent of the sales volume on merchandise paid to a sales representative based on the goods sold that are shipped and accepted by the retailer. (CH 6)

communications training Human resources instruction that has become a need as a result of the increasing diversity of today's workforce, it encompasses an understanding of how to speak and listen effectively with those of other languages, viewpoints, and customs. (CH 7)

company salesperson Sales representative employed directly by a particular firm. (CH 6)

complimentary service A feature or service offered by a retail operation at no fee to the consumer, such as alterations, delivery, and gift wrap, with the intent of drawing in and keeping customers. (CH 5)

computer-aided design (CAD) The process of developing garments, prints, and patterns on a computer screen; this is an important trend in textile design. (CH 2, CH 8)

computer-aided patternmaking Manipulation of the components of pattern pieces on a computer screen. (CH 8)

computer-integrated manufacturing (CIM) Computers are tied together to communicate throughout the entire product development and manufacturing processes, from design to distribution. (CH 4)

computer skills training Educational programs on computer skills needed for conducting administrative and office tasks and for communicating with other departments in the company. (CH 7)

consumer publication Magazine or newsletter that is written for and made readily available to the general consumer. (CH 5)

consumer tracking information Information from sales data and credit card applications that is focused on demographics and psychographics. (CH 1)

contractor Can either be a factory that makes and finishes goods or a firm that is hired to manufacture a product line domestically or abroad. (CH 2, CH 3)

controller Responsible for a company's financial plans and policies, its accounting practices, its relationships with lending institutions and the financial community, the maintenance of its fiscal records, and the preparation of its financial reports. (CH 7)

cooperative advertising Also referred to as *co-op advertising*, this form of advertising involves a manufacturer contributing to the cost of advertisements paid for by the retailer. (CH 6)

corporation Company that is owned by stockholders, and may be run by an individual or a group. (CH 12)

cost price (*cost*) Wholesale price. (CH 6)

costume plot A list or chart that shows characters as they appear in each scene, what they are wearing, and what their overall movements are throughout a play. (CH 13)

country of origin The nation in which goods are primarily manufactured. (CH 3)

counter manager: Coordinates special events and promotions in the retail operation, manages employees, and works closely with buyers. Key responsibilities include selling the product line and servicing the customer. Sometimes referred to as a *line manager*. (CH 16)

croquis A rendering or miniature visual of a textile pattern or print. (CH 2)

cross-shopping A customer's inclination to purchase a wide variety of products in an array of brands and prices from any number of providers—directly from the manufacturer, in a resale store, at a flea market, or through a couturier. (CH 9)

crowdsourcing A way of meeting and conversing with potential and current customers online that enables companies to gain a deeper understanding of what customers really want. (CH 5)

curatorial traineeship Internship or apprenticeship for the prospective museum curator. (CH 14)

customer service manager Assists customers with issues or complaints and implements the retail operation's policies and procedures for returns, exchanges, out-of-stock merchandise, product warranties, and the like. (CH 12)

cut Fabric yardage amount. (CH 6)

cutter Uses electronic machines, knives, or scissors to precisely cut around the pattern pieces through layers of fabric, often several inches in thickness. (CH 4)

cutting for approval (CFA) Also referred to as a *memo*; this refers to a fabric swatch ordered by an interior designer. (CH 6)

cut-to-order Considered the safest method of projecting manufacturing needs, this refers to producing the quantity of products specified on orders received. (CH 4)

cut-to-stock Involves purchasing fabrics and other product components before orders are secured. (CH 4)

deaccession The removal of items from a museum collection because of repetition of artifacts, the receipt of better examples, loss, or decay. (CH 14)

decentralized buying The process used by individual stores or groups of stores within a retail chain that have a buyer who selects from the company's primary buyer's purchases. (CH 9)

demographic data Consumer data that can be interpreted as numbers (e.g., age, income, education attained, and number of family members). (CH 1)

department manager Oversees a specific area or department within a store and maintains the sales floor by supervising sales associates, placing new merchandise on the sales floor, adding signage for promotions, recording markdowns, and executing floor sets. (CH 12)

design-driven brand A brand that is led by a designer expressing a personal artistic vision and sense of taste. (CH 9)

design process The conception of a style, to include its inspiration or theme, the color palette, fabric selection, form, and fit. (CH 9)

digitizer An electronic tool that is used to manipulate the size and shape of pattern pieces. (CH 8)

direct competition A manufacturer producing or a retailer selling a similar product at roughly the same price point as another, targeted toward the same customer or market niche. (CH 9)

direct market brand Describes a brand that is the name of the retailer. Often, this is carried by a specialty store chain, such as Ann Taylor, IKEA, and Banana Republic. (CH 9)

director of a spa or wellness center Responsible for keeping the spa running smoothly by managing customer service, budgets, marketing plans, and environment, and dealing with staff-related issues. (CH 16)

director of product development Ultimately responsible for strategic planning of the division, this person specifies exactly what the company will make and market, as well as when it will do this. (CH 9)

distribution manager Also referred to as an *allocator* or a *replenishment analyst*, this position is responsible for planning and managing the flow of goods received from the vendors, as ordered by the buyers, to the retail locations. (CH 11)

diversity training Explanation from human resources of how people of different cultures, races, and religions, for example, may have different perspectives and views. It includes techniques to value and expand diversity in the workplace. (CH 7)

divisional merchandising manager (DMM) Works under the general merchandising manager and provides leadership for the buying staff of a division or a related group of departments, such as menswear, women's wear, or home furnishings. (CH 11)

draping method Process in which a patternmaker shapes and cuts muslin or the garment fabric on a dress form or a live model to create a pattern. (CH 8)

educational event A presentation during which a fashion event planner, a manufacturer's representative, or an employee hired by the planner educates an audience about a product. (CH 5)

electronic data interchange (EDI) Refers to the transfer of computer-generated information between one company's computer system and another's. (CH 4)

end product The final product to be purchased by the customer. (CH 4)

entry-level accountant Maintains records of routine accounting transactions and assists in the preparation of financial and operating reports. (CH 7)

equipment Fixtures, furnishings, and machinery purchased for long-term use by a company, such as cash terminals, T-stands, mannequins, and track lights. (CH 10)

exclusive An item limited to a retailer in a trade area. In some cases, a retailer may negotiate to be the only one in a geographic region to carry a particular item or the only one in the country to carry a particular color. For example, the label may read: "Burberry Exclusively for Neiman Marcus." (CH 9)

exports Products that are bought by an overseas company from a vendor in the United States and sent out of the country. (CH 3)

Family and Consumer Science Education (FCSEd) Certification for an instructor who teaches high school, vocational, or college courses in textiles, fashion, interior design, consumer education, personal financial literacy, clothing construction, careers in the fashion industry, and similar topics. (CH 14)

fashion art photography Fine art photography in which subjects are fashion related. (CH 13)

fashion costumer Collaborates with film and video directors to design, consign, or construct apparel and accessories that fit within the mood, time frame, and image of the film or video. (CH 13)

fashion design The development and execution of wearable forms, structures, and patterns. (CH 8)

fashion designer Supervises a team of design assistants at a company, works under the label of a big-name designer or manufacturer, freelances for others while creating a personal line, or produces a line under his or her own name. (CH 8)

fashion director Responsible for determining the trends, colors, themes, and textures for piece goods or fabrics that a firm will feature for a specific season. In retailing, this position is responsible for designating the trends, themes, colors, and fabrics that the buyers will purchase for the retail operation. (CH 2)

fashion event planner Someone who increases the visibility of a design house, organization, brand, product, or fabric by coordinating special events, such as fashion shows and seminars, that provide exposure for these products. (CH 5)

fashion exclusivity Refers to having merchandise that is unique to a particular company. (CH 9)

fashion photographer Takes photographs of models wearing the latest apparel, accessories, hairstyles, and makeup, or highlighting the newest home furnishings and other fashion products, primarily for commercial use. (CH 13)

fashion photostylist Stylist who works with photography. (CH 5)

fashion production planner Projects timelines for manufacturing the products in a line. (CH 3)

fashion shoot Photography session of models and fashions. (CH 5)

fashion show and event producer Responsible for developing and implementing a variety of promotional activities for a designer, manufacturer, or retailer, such as a fashion show, party, or conference. Works with budgets, media, and customers in producing cost-effective and high-profile events. (CH 13)

fashion stylist Responsible for bringing to life a photographer's or director's vision for a fashion photography shoot, magazine layout, music video, television or film commercial, or print advertisement. (CH 5, CH 13)

fashion visual Refers to the images used in the fashion industry, such as photographs, trend boards, and magazine clippings. (CH 13)

fast fashion Apparel and accessories trends that are designed and manufactured quickly, and in an affordable way, to allow the mainstream consumer to take advantage of current fashions at a lower price. (CH 9)

fiber house A company, also called a *fabric house*, that represents a fiber source or a fabric. (CH 1)

findings Functional product components that may not be visible when viewing the final product; they include zippers, thread, linings, and interfacings. (CH 3)

findings buyer Responsible for purchasing zippers, threads, linings, and such for a manufacturer. (CH 3)

finishing Enhances the appearance of fabric and also adds to its suitability for everyday use or hard wear. Finishes can be solely mechanical, solely chemical, or a combination of the two. (CH 2)

first cost Wholesale price, in the country of origin. (CH 3)

first pattern Used to cut and sew the prototype. (CH 8)

fit model Also referred to as the *fashion house model,* this is a live model on whom a designer may drape, cut, and pin fabric and on whom the designer will check the sizing and proportion of garments. (CH 13)

flat pattern method Uses angles, rulers, and curves to create patterns. (CH 8)

floor set The arrangement of fixtures and merchandise on the sales floor to create a fresh look and highlight brand-new or undersold merchandise. (CH 12)

freelance costumer Hired for a specific production by a theater company or production studio and may or may not actually be local to the theater for which he or she is designing. (CH 13)

foreign commissionaire Also known as *foreign-owned independent agent,* usually has offices located in key buying cities overseas and assists with the purchase of goods for a fee. (CH 3)

functional finish A finish that imparts special characteristics to the cloth (e.g., durable press treatments). (CH 2)

funder Financing source, such as a bank or the Small Business Administration, used by a prospective business owner with a well-written business plan that justifies financing due to a good potential for profit, minimized risk, and a strong long-range plan. (CH 12)

general finish A finish, such as scouring or bleaching, that simply prepares the fabric for further use. (CH 2)

general merchandising manager (GMM) Leads and manages the buyers of all divisions in a retail operation. (CH 11)

globalization The process of interlinking nations of the world with one another; this is a growing trend in the fashion industry. (CH 3)

global sourcing Refers to the process of locating, purchasing, and importing or exporting goods and services from around the world. (CH 3)

gross margin Actual profit after cost of goods, markdowns, and other expenses are deducted. (CH 11)

hairstylist Person specializing in hair design, color, and care. (CH 16)

hiring manager Responsible for locating and employing personnel for the various positions within a company. (CH 7)

human relations training Focuses on helping people get along with one another and succeed in the workplace. Conflict management is often part of this training seminar. (CH 7)

human resources (HR) Refers to the department in charge of an organization's employees, which has responsibilities including finding and hiring employees, helping them grow and learn in the organization, and managing the process when an employee leaves. (CH 7)

human resources development (HRD) The field of business concerned with recruiting, training, maintaining, motivating, and managing personnel. (CH 7)

human resources management (HRM) Key activities include the following: determining staffing needs; recruiting, training, and providing support to employees; dealing with performance issues; ensuring that personnel and management practices conform to various regulations; and overseeing the management of employee benefits and compensation, as well as maintaining employee records and personnel policies. (CH 7)

human resources manager Also known as a *human resources director*, this person plays a leadership role in the business- and people-related issues of the company. After identifying issues in the workplace, he or she meets with supervisors and managers to determine effective solutions. (CH 7)

illustrator Works freelance or within the advertising divisions of major retailers, designers, or manufacturers to sketch garments for print advertisements. (CH 10)

importer Shops international markets to purchase goods that will come together as his or her own "lines." The merchandise is purchased with themes, colors, and styling in mind to create cohesive collections that are displayed and presented to the retail store buyers. (CH 3)

imports In North America, products that are purchased from an overseas vendor and shipped to the United States or Canada. CH 3)

import production coordinator Works as a liaison between the domestic apparel or home furnishings company and the overseas manufacturer or contractor. (CH 3)

institutional advertisement Promotional activity that sells an organization as a fashion leader, a community supporter, or a provider of the best value for the dollar, among other images. (CH 10)

interactive display Display in which viewers can press a button to run a video or actively participate in the exhibition's subject matter. (CH 14)

interior designer Often working with either homes (i.e., residential) or businesses (i.e., commercial or contract), this person is responsible for creating the facility's inner environment with attention to aesthetics, safety, and the well-being of those using the space. (CH 15)

intermediate accountant Prepares and maintains accounting records that may include general accounting, costing, or budget data. Also called a *mid-level accountant*. (CH 7)

internal theft Refers to merchandise stolen by employees within the company. (CH 12)

Internet promotions director Responsible for developing and communicating the company brand and its products through technology, including guiding the company's digital presence through communications, the online calendar, display and search advertising, and social media outreach. (CH 10)

inventory The selection of products available for sale in a fashion operation; this is also referred to as *merchandise assortment*. (CH 11)

inventory replenishment Reorders and stock placement on the sales floor to replace or fill in merchandise sold. (CH 6)

key account For a manufacturer, this term refers to a large retailer, in terms of sales volume, that carries the manufacturer's line consistently and in depth. (CH 6)

key vendor Manufacturers' lines featured as the greatest proportion of inventory in a retail operation. (CH 11)

knockoff A copy of another style, often of lesser quality and with minor modifications. (CH 9)

labdip A swatch of dyed fabric sent by mills to the product development team for color approval prior to dyeing large yardages of fabric. (CH 9)

landed costs The actual price of goods after taxes, tariffs, handling, and shipping fees are added to the cost of imported goods. (CH 3)

lead time Number of days, weeks, months, or years needed for the intricate planning and production steps that are implemented before fashion products actually arrive at the retail store; it is also the amount of time needed between placing a production order and receiving the shipment of products. (CH 1, CH 4)

letter of credit A document issued by a bank authorizing the bearer to draw a specific amount of money from the bank, its branches, or associated banks and agencies. (CH 3)

license An agreement in which a manufacturer is given exclusive rights to produce and market goods that carry the registered name and brandmark of a designer, celebrity, character, or product line. (CH 3)

licensee The manufacturer of a licensed product. (CH 3)

licensing director Responsible for overseeing the look, quality, labeling, delivery, and distribution of the company's licensed product lines. (CH 3)

licensor The owner of the name or brandmark who receives a percent of wholesale sales or some form of compensation based on a licensing agreement. (CH 3)

lifestyle trends A population segment's values, interests, attitudes, dreams, and goals. (CH1)

line plan Shows the number of styles in the line, the number and general types of fabrics and yarns to be used, colors per style, anticipated stock-keeping units (SKUs), and approximate preferred costs. (CH 9)

makeup artist Works with cosmetics, wigs, and other costuming materials to color and enhance the client's face and body. (CH 16)

mall manager Responsible for everything in the mall from formulating its budget and planning promotional activities to developing its mix of tenants and building community relations. (CH 15)

management The process of organizing and controlling the affairs of a business or a particular sector of a business. (CH 12)

manager-in-training (MIT) An employee who is being trained to move into a management position. (CH 12)

managerial training Educational program for a museum curator on how to run a museum, from personnel to finances to operations. (CH 14)

mannequin modeling Refers to live models standing motionless in the place of regular mannequins in windows or on showroom or retail floors. (CH 5)

manufacturer's representative Also referred to as a manufacturer's rep, this person is a wholesale salesperson who is often independent. (CH 6)

marker The layout of pattern pieces on the fabric from which the pieces will be cut. (CH 4)

marker maker Traces pattern pieces by hand or by computer into the tightest possible layout, while keeping the integrity of the design in mind. (CH 4)

market representative A specialized buyer of individual merchandise classifications who works closely with his or her client stores, keeping them up to date on new product offerings in the marketplace, recommending new vendors, and assisting them in locating needed goods. (CH 3)

market week Scheduled at the apparel and trade marts throughout the year in conjunction with the introduction of the new, seasonal lines presented by manufacturers. Also called a *trade show.* (CH 6)

mass customization Strategy that allows a manufacturer or retailer to provide individualized products to a consumer. (CH 4)

mass market Product lines that are distributed through a wide variety of retailers. (CH 16)

master pattern Final pattern; often evolved from adjusting and perfecting a sample pattern. (CH 4)

media form Any of the types of promotion an advertising director has to choose from, which include magazines and newspapers, television and radio, Internet, outdoor displays, direct mail, novelties (e.g., calendars, pencils, and memo tablets), catalogues, directories, and circulars. (CH 10)

media planner Determines prices, including quantity discounts, for a media buy that may include several venues, such as radio, television, and newspaper. The media planner determines how the advertising budget is best spent to generate the most exposure and sales. (CH 5)

medi-spa Combines traditional spa services with those that must be offered by a physician, such as health screenings and minor surgery. (CH 16)

merchandise coordinator Employed by a manufacturer and works in retail stores carrying the manufacturer's line within a certain geographical area, restocking products, installing displays, reordering top-selling styles, and educating sales staff and customers on the product line. (CH 6)

merchandiser Collaborates with the director of product development to decide what to produce and organizes and manages the entire product development process; this person is responsible for the development of a balanced, marketable, profitable, and timely line. (CH 3, CH 9)

merchandising Refers to all of the activities involved in the buying and selling of a product line. (CH 11)

merchandising calendar The product development team's schedule, created to deliver the right product (i.e., style, quality, and price) at the right time. (CH 9)

merchandising-driven brand "Void-filling" brand; a market-based brand designed to fill a void in a market (i.e., an underserved customer) and create a product to appeal to a distinct customer. (CH 9)

merchandising executive training program Designed for new hires, former interns, college recruits, or current employees who have shown skills in merchandising, to prepare them for their first assignment as assistant buyers; also referred to as *merchant executive training program*. (CH 11)

modeling and talent agency director Ultimately responsible for locating and contracting new models, training them, and, later, securing modeling jobs for them. (CH 13)

multiline rep A manufacturer's salesperson who carries a number of lines, often working with noncompetitive product lines and manufacturers. (CH 6)

museological training Instruction for the curator that covers how to preserve, maintain, and interpret museum collections. (CH 14)

museum conservator Manages, cares for, preserves, treats, and documents works of art, artifacts, and specimens; with regard to fashions or costumes, conservators acquire and preserve important visuals (e.g., photographs, illustrations, or sketches), costumes, accessories, furnishings, and other valuable items for permanent storage or display; this position may be referred to as a *restoration and preservation specialist*. (CH 14)

museum curator Works under the supervision of the museum director. A curator directs the accession, deaccession, storage, and exhibition of collections. This position may also be referred to as a *museum keeper*. (CH 14)

museum director Runs the business of the museum; manages the general operations and staffing of the organization, and coordinates the public affairs mission of the museum. (CH 14)

museum technician Assists the curator by performing various preparatory and maintenance tasks on museum items. Most technicians work to preserve, maintain, repair, and treat historic artifacts and may assist curators with research. (CH 14)

National Architectural Accrediting Board Inc. (NAAB) Develops standards and procedures to verify that each accredited architectural program in the United States meets standards for the education of architects. (CH 15)

open-to-buy The amount of money allocated for the buyer to make new merchandise purchases each month, based on sales and inventory amounts. (CH 11)

operations manager Develops and maintains effective sales and operational programs with a focus on superior customer service for all of the retail units in the company or for units in a region. (CH 12)

outsourcing Having an aspect of a company's work performed by nonemployees in another company and, perhaps, in another country. (CH 2)

partnership A business owned by two or more people. (CH 12)

party planning Putting together a party event, to include budget planning, location selection, decor, theme, and guest list. (CH 5)

pattern grader Develops a pattern in the full range of sizes offered by the manufacturer. (CH 4)

patternmaker Translates the design concept into a flat pattern to create an actual garment. (CH 8)

personal shopper Assists an individual in selecting an entire season's wardrobe or an outfit for a specific occasion, based on the needs of the customer, including his or her budget, activities, and personal style; a personal shopper may be employed by an individual, boutique, upscale department store, or specialty store. (CH 10)

personnel The employees or staff of an organization. (CH 7)

philanthropic fashion show A fashion show with ticket sales that benefit a nonprofit or charitable organization. (CH 5)

photographer Freelancer or someone employed by large retailers in the promotion division to photograph the visual components of promotions. (CH 10)

photographic model Hired to be photographed in the studio or on location. While a select few top models work in high-fashion magazines, a large number of opportunities exist through mail-order catalogues, newspaper advertisements, and television. Also known as a *print model.*(CH 13)

photography stylist Works with teams of people such as photographers, designers, lighting technicians, and set builders. Sets up the shoot for the photographer, scouts locations, and selects appropriate props, fashions, accessories, and, perhaps, the models to enhance the shoot. (CH 13)

physical inventory The merchandise actually in the retail or manufacturing operation. (CH 12)

piece goods Fabrics or materials, such as leather, used to create products. (CH 2)

piece goods buyer Purchases the textiles used in the production of final products. (CH 3)

planner Works in collaboration with the buyer to develop sales forecasts, inventory plans, and spending budgets for merchandise to achieve the retailer's sales and profit objectives. (CH 11)

planning manager Provides leadership, direction, and support at the merchandise division level to plan appropriately; this person also distributes and monitors inventory within a company's various retail locations to maximize sales. (CH 11)

planning module A chart constructed by a planner that details inventory ratios, such as top-to-bottom ratios of junior sportswear. (CH 11)

plan-o-gram Floor plan showing the placement and types of racks, fixtures, display units, and/or merchandise in order to create an easy flow of traffic and present the merchandise most effectively. (CH 15)

pop-up shop A project that is like a hide-and-seek boutique that pops up within other retail locations or at vacant retail spaces with few preliminary announcements. They quickly draw crowds, are open for a limited period of time, and then disappear or morph into something else. (CH 5)

portfolio A collection of work that illustrates a job candidate's range of skills and outcomes. This is also referred to in some sectors of fashion as a *book*. (CH 13)

press package Also referred to as a *press kit*, this is a parcel containing photographs and related information, such as news articles from similar events in other cities or background information, included with a press release. (CH 10)

press photography Also known as *photojournalism*, this focuses on images directly related to news stories, both events and personalities. (CH 13)

press release A summary of the important facts relating to a company event, formatted specifically for the media and sent directly to them by the publicity director; this is also known as a *news release*. (CH 10)

prestige market Product lines that are distributed through high-end department and specialty store retailers. (CH 16)

primary level The sector of the fashion industry that includes fiber, fabrics, and manufacturing. (CH 2)

print service Company that sells print designs to mills, wholesalers, product developers, and retailers. (CH 2)

private brand A name owned exclusively by a particular store that is extensively marketed with a definite image, such as Target's Mossimo and Isaac Mizrahi brands. (CH 9)

private label A line name or brand that the retailer develops and assigns to a collection of products and that is owned exclusively by a particular retailer, such as Antonio Melani at Dillard's. (CH 9)

product developer Creates a completely new product that will meet unfulfilled consumer needs. (CH 16)

product development Creating and making a product, such as a dress, belt, or chair, from start to finish. (CH 9)

product development designer The creator of a product or product line; he or she is a trend forecaster in his or her own right by determining what the customer will be ready for next. Going through the design process with each new season, this person in a retail firm is also referred to as a *private label designer*. (CH 9)

product development patternmaker Takes accurate measurements and develops a pattern, either by using draping, CAD, or flat pattern methods, to create a pattern that, if correctly developed, ensures that the designer's vision will be implemented. (CH 9)

product manager Responsible for all products within a company's product lines or for a specific product category within the line. (CH 4)

product technician Works to develop new features for the product, often using consumer research studies in the process to clarify the direction of modifications and predict the consumer response to the changes. (CH 16)

product void Merchandise category in which there are few, if any, items to fill consumer needs and desires. (CH 4)

production assistant Supports the production manager with detail work and record keeping. This person may track deliveries, assist development of production schedules, and communicate the work flow of the factory to the production manager. (CH 4)

production authorization The process of selecting and quantifying styles that will be manufactured. (CH 9)

production efficiency manager Responsible for monitoring the speed and output of a manufacturing facility and for managing waste. (CH 4)

production manager Also referred to as a *plant manager*, this person is responsible for all operations at the manufacturing plant, whether it is a domestic or overseas location and contracted or company owned. Job responsibilities of a production manager include supervising or completing the estimation of production costs, scheduling work flow in the factory, and hiring and training production employees. (CH 3, CH 4)

production planner Estimates the amount and types of products a company will manufacture, either based on previous seasonal sales or on orders being received from the sales representatives on the road and in the showroom. (CH 4)

professional development Includes continuing education, perhaps toward a higher degree; internships within a field; conference participation; and memberships in trade and educational organizations. (CH 14)

promotion The endorsement of a person, a product, a cause, an idea, or an organization (CH 5); these activities communicate a company's or product's attributes to the target consumers using two primary tools: publicity and advertising. (CH 10)

promotion director Guides the marketing activities of a fashion operation. (CH 10)

promotion product Can refer to an item, such as a press release or an advertisement, or an event, such as a fashion show or music video, used as an endorsement tool. (CH 5)

prop house Firm that rents furniture, fixtures, mannequins, and decor accessories to visual merchandisers, saving the company money on limited-use display pieces while reducing the amount of warehouse space and labor needed to inventory and store visual merchandising props. (CH 15)

prototype First sample garment, accessory, or home product. (CH 8)

psychographics Refers to lifestyle choices, values, and emotions of a population. (CH 1)

public affairs As a mission in museums, this refers to collaborating with the community, the government, industry, and social and academic organizations to develop exhibitions and collections that appeal to and educate the community and its visitors. (CH 14)

public relations account executive Works with media contacts such as fashion publications like *Vogue*, *Elle*, *W*, and *InStyle* to promote the line in magazine editorials and feature stories. (CH 16)

public relations director Responsible for finding cost-effective ways to promote the company he or she represents. (CH 5)

publicity The dissemination of information about people, places, special events, or other newsworthy topics through a variety of communications media—in essence, free press: the mention of a company or its merchandise in the media for which the company does not pay a fee. (CH 10)

publicity director Responsible for securing publicity for the retail operation. This person may collaborate with other departments to create events such as fashion show productions or celebrity personal appearances to secure publicity. (CH 10)

puck A mouselike device used for computer-aided design. (CH 8)

purchase order (PO) A contract for merchandise between the buyer, as a representative of his or her firm, and the vendor. (CH 3)

quality control manager Also known as the *quality control engineer*, this person develops specifications for the products that will be manufactured and is responsible for the final inspection of garments from the manufacturer, checking fabric, fit, and construction for quality and adherence to product specification guidelines. (CH 4, CH 9)

quality initiatives training Examines such programs as total quality management (TQM), quality circles, and benchmarking. (CH 7)

quota plus commission Form of remuneration in which the manufacturer's representative is paid commission on sales he or she has procured over a specific dollar amount or baseline. (CH 6)

radio-frequency identification technology (RFID) Increases supply-chain management through the tagging of containers, pallets, and individual items so that they can be accurately tracked as they move through the supply chain. (CH 4)

recruiter Company representative who locates job candidates and encourages them to join the firm as hires. (CH 7)

reference librarian Responsible for managing the inventory of books, samples, and resources of a fashion company, such as a fiber house or manufacturer, and for procuring new ones. (CH 2)

region A specific geographical area. (CH 12)

regional manager Responsible for the retail stores of a particular company that are located in a segregated area of the United States and/or overseas; this position is also referred to as a *district manager*. (CH 12)

reorder A fill-in on merchandise that is selling well. (CH 6)

residential costumer Hired by a specific theater to design and develop costumes for an extended series of productions. (CH 13)

residential design Interior design focusing on home environments. (CH 15)

resource room director Responsible for managing the inventory of books, fabrics, garments, and resources and for procuring new ones for a fashion library or resource room. (CH 2)

retail account executive Also referred to as a *retail sales account executive*, this person sells a product line to retail accounts and oversees the sales performance of the line in large retail accounts. (CH 16)

retailer A business that sells products to the ultimate consumer and can include the vast range of brick-and-mortar stores (e.g., department stores, mass merchants, specialty stores, boutiques, discount stores, and outlet stores), as well as catalogue, brick-and-click, and online stores. (CH 9)

retail label A brand with the retailer's name on it, such as Neiman Marcus, Custom Interiors, or Saks Fifth Avenue. A retailer may negotiate with a manufacturer to put its label on a group of items instead of or in addition to the manufacturer's label, though the retailer may not have anything to do with the design or development of the items. (CH 9)

retail operation owner Financially responsible for the company and oversees all aspects of the retail business. (CH 12)

retail store manager Oversees all aspects of a retail store's operation, from promotions and inventory to the customers and employees, often consisting of assistant managers, department managers, sales associates, and staff. (CH 12)

retail trend forecaster Researches many sources to create formal reports that summarize important fashion trends in a particular season that will appeal to the retailer's clientele. (CH 9)

safety training Instruction that educates employees on safety precautions; this is critical where there are employees working with heavy equipment, hazardous chemicals, and repetitive activities, such as in an apparel factory or textile mill. (CH 7)

salaried An employee is paid a set amount every month. (CH 6)

sales advertising Announces specific value items; it is one of the five primary types of advertising. (CH 10)

sales forecast Includes projections of sales by category, style, color, and size based on historical data and statistical analysis. This information may be used to place preliminary fabric and trim orders and block out production time in factories. (CH 9)

sales promotion Activity designed to sell products; often features short-term incentives that encourage the sale of the product (e.g., samples, coupons, gift-with-purchase giveaways, point-of-purchase displays, and contests). (CH 10)

sample line Line that includes a prototype of every style available in the final product line. (CH 6)

sample size Used for testing fit and appearance in addition to selling purposes. (CH 8)

secondary vendor Manufacturers' line featured in a retailer's inventory in small quantities. (CH 11)

security Refers to the safekeeping of the merchandise in the store. (CH 12)

security manager Works to prevent merchandise theft; collaborates with receiving, accounting, and management to be certain that accurate accounting procedures are in place and true losses are identified when the physical inventory is taken. (CH 12)

senior accountant Responsible for establishing, interpreting, and analyzing complex accounting records or financial statements for management. (CH 7)

show model Employed by a modeling agency that takes bookings from clients who need to display clothes at fashion shows, exhibitions, or trade markets; also referred to as a *runway model*. (CH 13)

showroom A place where product lines are displayed; usually caters only to the trade. (CH 6)

showroom salesperson Also referred to as a *showroom representative*, this person works at a manufacturer's and/or designer's place of business, where he or she meets with visiting retail buyers and presents the latest product line to them. (CH 6)

single-line rep Manufacturer's representative who prefers to sell solely one manufacturer's line as an independent salesperson, rather than as a company employee. (CH 6)

social media The tools and social Web sites of the Internet that are used to communicate online with others. (CH 5)

social media director Develops, manages, and oversees the implementation of public relations programs in the social media venue. This includes creating content and generating coverage for social media efforts in all forms. (CH 5)

social networking The grouping of individuals into factions with similar interests. (CH 5)

social Web site A Web site that functions like an online community of Internet users (e.g., Facebook and LinkedIn). (CH 5)

sole proprietorship A business owned by an individual. (CH 12)

sourcing The activities of determining which vendor can provide the amount of product needed, negotiating the best possible price and discounts, scheduling deliveries, and following up on actual shipments to make certain due dates are met and that quality control is maintained. (CH 3)

sourcing manager Director of the activities related to locating goods and producers of goods. (CH 3)

specification technician Also known as *spec tech*, attends the fittings of the sample garments, takes measurements, and compiles these measurements into packets to hand off to production. (CH 8)

special event A designed occurrence, such as a model search, designer visit, or charity event, that is intended to communicate a particular message to a target audience. (CH 10)

special events coordinator Develops and executes events that are fashion related, such as fashion and trunk shows, as well as fashion presentations at clubs and for organizations. Additionally, the special events coordinator creates and directs activities that are not fashion related, yet put the company in the public eye in a favorable light. (CH 5, CH 10)

spec pack Contains detailed information taken from the designer's sketch, translated into measurements in order to ensure desired fit and styling details, such as the placement of pockets, the length of zippers, the size of buttons, etc. Also called a *tech pack*. (CH 8)

spec sheet Specification list; typically provides detailed measurements and construction guidelines. (CH 9)

spreader Lays out the selected fabric for cutting. (CH 4)

stabilizing Saving and maintaining museum artifacts. A museum curator stabilizes artifacts when preparing them for storage or an exhibition. (CH 14)

stock-keeping unit (SKU) Identification data for a single product. (CH 3)

store-owned foreign buying office Large retailers and exclusive boutiques often use and pay for this ancillary operation located in major fashion capitals overseas, whose buyers support and advise other buyers of their respective stores. (CH 3)

store planning director Develops a plan that details fixture placement, lighting, dressing rooms, restrooms, windows, aisles, and cash and wrap areas of a retail department. Objectives include aesthetic appeal, image consistency, visibility and security of merchandise, comfort and ease of staff and consumers in moving within the facility, and merchandising flexibility. (CH 10)

strike-off A few yards of fabric printed by a mill and sent to the product developer (i.e., colorist, designer, and sample maker) to be made into a sample. (CH 2, CH 9)

stylist Consults with clients on hair, makeup, footwear, jewelry, and apparel to create total looks, often for specific events. (CH 10)

stylus A computerized pen. (CH 8)

supplies Replenishable materials purchased and used by a company, such as hangers, trash bags, tissue paper, and light bulbs. (CH 10)

supply-chain management (SCM) All of the activities required to coordinate and manage every step needed to bring a product to the consumer, including procuring raw materials, producing goods, transporting and distributing those goods, and managing the selling process. (CH 4)

tearoom modeling An informal fashion show, often taking place in a hotel or restaurant, in which models circulate among the tables as the meal is being served. (CH 5)

tearsheet A page that has been pulled from a newspaper ,or a magazine that features a product advertisement or a model's shoot. (CH 6, CH 13)

technical design Use of drawings, measurements, patterns, and models to develop the "blueprints," or technical plans, needed for the manufacturing of products. (CH 8)

technical designer Liaison between the designer and factory, responsible for working closely with the designers to communicate their specific product requests to the factory overseas. (CH 8)

technical photographer Produces photographs for reports or research papers, such as textile durability analyses. (CH 13)

terminal degree Highest educational degree available in a particular field. (CH 14)

territory The specific geographical area within which a retail store outlet is located or in which a sales representative sells the line. (CH 12)

textile colorist Chooses the colors or color combinations that will be used in creating each textile design. (CH 2)

textile design The process of creating the print, pattern, texture, and finish of fabrics. (CH 2)

textile designer Creates original patterns, prints, and textures for the fabrics used in many types of industry, from fashion to interiors. (CH 2)

textile engineer Works with designers to determine how a design can be applied to a fabric in terms of more practical variables, such as durability, washability, and colorfastness. (CH 2)

textile stylist Modifies existing textile goods, altering patterns or prints that have been successful on the retail floor to turn them into fresh, new products. (CH 2)

textile technical designer Creates new textile designs or modifies existing fabric goods, altering patterns or prints that have been successful on the retail floor to turn them into fresh, new products. (CH 9)

textile technician Works with the issues that are directly related to the production of textiles, such as care factors, finishing techniques, and durability. (CH 2)

trade mart Houses temporary sales booths and permanent showrooms leased either by sales representatives or manufacturers. Also called an *apparel mart*. (CH 6)

trade publication Periodical designed for readers interested in or employed in specific professions, vocations, or merchandise classifications. (CH 5)

trade school An institution that may offer fashion programs and provide certificates, rather than degrees, upon the student's completion of the program, including programs in such areas as fashion design, illustration, retailing, photography, and merchandising. (CH 14)

traffic manager Supervises work flow on the factory floor, monitoring the product from start to finish. (CH 4)

trainer An educator who works with employees to provide them with certain knowledge or skills to improve performance in their current jobs. (CH 7) Someone who works for a cosmetic, fragrance, or skin care line by educating sales and marketing employees on the company's product line and how to sell it. (CH 16)

trend book Design resource publication intended to assist creative teams and manufacturers in developing future product lines. Trend books may include photos, fabric swatches, materials, color ranges, drawings of prints, product sketches, silhouettes, commentaries, and related materials. (CH 1)

trend forecaster Continually monitors the consumer and the industry through traveling, reading, networking, and, most important, observing; this person creates formal reports that summarize important fashion trends with seasonal themes. The trend forecaster in the product development division of a retailer identifies the fashion trends and then interprets them for the retailer's particular customer or market. (CH 1)

trendspotter A person located at a university or other location worldwide who provides information to a forecasting company, such as WGSN, on the latest trends in the locale. (CH 1)

trimmings Decorative components designed to be seen as part of the final product (e.g., buttons, appliqués, and beltings). (CH 3)

trimmings buyer Person who is responsible for locating and ordering decorative components for products. (CH 3)

trunk show Consists of a fashion event planner and/or a manufacturer's representative bringing a manufacturer's full seasonal line to a retail store that carries that particular manufacturer. (CH 5)

user interface (UI) The visuals people see and interact with when they view a Web site and the navigation by which they move through the site. (CH 15)

vendor The person selling a product or service, or a manufacturer or distributor from whom a company purchases products or production processes. (CH 3)

visual merchandiser Responsible for the window installations, displays, signage, fixtures, mannequins, and decorations that give a retail operation aesthetic appeal and a distinct image. This position is also known as *visual merchandising director*. (CH 10)

visual merchandising Design, development, procurement, and installation of merchandise displays and the ambiance of the environment in which the displays are shown. (CH 6, CH 10)

vocational school Provides training for students who elect not to participate in a four-year college degree program upon high school graduation. Courses taught include commercial clothing construction, apparel alteration, patternmaking, and retailing. (CH 14)

volume driver Top seller. (CH 3)

Web site developer Constructs, maintains, and builds on a company's Web site; this person must possess general design skills and knowledge of Web-specific design factors (e.g., screen resolution and accessibility). He or she designs a Web site's look and feel, incorporating features such as e-commerce, online community, animations, and interactive applications into the site. This position is also referred to as *Web site designer*. (CH 10, CH 15)

Web site development A field in design and fashion concerned with constructing Web pages and sites from technological, aesthetic, and marketing perspectives. (CH 15)

wellness center A type of spa that often incorporates health programs, such as exercise (e.g., yoga and Pilates) and nutrition. (CH 16)

yardage A given amount of fabric, based on its length in yards. (CH 3)

credits

Chapter 1
1.1 Courtesy of WWD/Giovanni Giannoni; 1.2 Courtesy of WWD; 1.3 Courtesy of The Doneger Group; 1.4 © Première Vision; 1.5 Courtesy of WWD/Donato Sardella; 1.6 The Granger Collection, NYC — All rights reserved; 1.7 Gareth Cattermole/ Getty Images; 1.8 Courtesy of WWD/Steve Eichner; 1.9 Courtesy of WWD/Donato Sardella; 1.10 © Marleen Daniëls; 1.11 Sipa via AP Images; 1.12 © Everett Kennedy Brown/epa/Corbis; 1.13 Courtesy of Sean Murphy Photography; 1.14 © Philippe Munda; 1.15 Photo by Subir Halder/India Today Group/Getty Images

Chapter 2
2.1 Courtesy of Lectra; 2.2 Courtesy of WWD/Manfredo Pinzauti/Grazianeri; 2.3 Courtesy of WWD/Giovanni Giannoni; 2.4, 2.5 Courtesy of Lectra; 2.6 Courtesy of ITP-Inkjet Textile Printing, LLC; 2.7 Courtesy of Lectra; 2.8a, 2.8b, 2.8c Courtesy of Lee; 2.9 Courtesy of Ellis Developments Ltd; design by Peter Butcher; 2.10 Photo by Patrick Cline for Lonny LLC; 2.11 Courtesy of WWD; 2.12 Courtesy of Cotton Inc.; 2.13 © Carolyn Jenkins / Alamy; 2.14 Courtesy of Fur Council of Canada; 2.15 Courtesy of Mohair USA; 2.16 Courtesy of Cone; 2.17 Courtesy of Bloomingdales

Chapter 3
3.1 Courtesy of WWD/Micah Baird; 3.2 Photo by Erin Fitzsimmons; 3.3 Courtesy of WWD/Gareth Jones; 3.4 © BLEIBTREU JASON/CORBIS SYGMA; 3.5 Courtesy of Michele Granger; 3.6 Courtesy of WWD/Thomas Iannaccone; 3.7 Courtesy of WWD/George Chinsee

Chapter 4
4.1 Courtesy of WWD; 4.2 Courtesy of Lee; 4.3 REUTERS/LUCY NICHOLSON/ LANDOV; 4.4 Jitendra Prakash/Reuters/Landov; 4.5 © Diana Hirsch/iStockphoto; 4.6, 4.7, 4.8 Courtesy of Lectra; 4.9 © S.G. /Alamy; 4.10 © Keith Bedford/Reuters/ Corbis; 4.11 Courtesy of WWD/John Aquino; 4.12a Courtesy of Laser Cutting Shapes; 4.12b Courtesy of Laser Cutting Shapes; 4.13 Courtesy of WWD; 4.14 Courtesy of Nike; 4.15a, 4.15b, 4.15c © Mark Peterson/Corbis; 4.16 Photo by Scott Olson/Getty Images; 4.17 Courtesy of WWD/Steve Eichner

Chapter 5

5.1 Photo by Eric Ryan/Getty Images; 5.2 © Pascal Perich/Corbis Outline; 5.3 Courtesy of Miraclebody Jeans by Miraclesuit; 5.4a © Moviestore collection Ltd/Alamy; 5.4b Courtesy of Gilt Group; 5.5a Courtesy of Conde Nast Publications; 5.5b Courtesy of Conde Nast Publications; 5.6 Courtesy of WWD; 5.7 Photo by Marquita Sayres; 5.8 © omgimages / iStockphoto; 5.9 Courtesy of WWD; 5.10 Courtesy of Anthony Rathbun for Bridal Extravaganza Show; 5.11 Photo by Stuart Wilson/Getty Images; 5.12 Courtesy of WWD/Steve Eichner; 5.13 Courtesy of WWD; 5.14 Courtesy of WWD/Todd Matarazzo; 5.15 Courtesy of Hama Sanders

Chapter 6

6.1 Courtesy of WWD/Ronda Churchill; 6.2a, 6.2b Courtesy of WWD; 6.3 Courtesy of Town & County, Springfield, MO; 6.4 Courtesy of WWD /Kyle Ericksen; 6.5 Photo by Shari Smith Dunaif, High Noon Productions; 6.6 © Blend Images/Alamy

Chapter 7

7.1 © Randy Faris/Corbis; 7.2 Courtesy of WWD/Dominique Maitre; 7.3 © Paul Hardy/CORBIS; 7.4 © P. Winbladh/Corbis; 7.5 © JLP/Jose Luis Pelaez/Corbis; 7.6 © Tom Grill/Corbis; 7.7 © Ken Seet/Corbis; 7.8 © Tom Grill/Corbis; 7.9 © Corbis

Chapter 8

8.1 Courtesy of WWD/Photo by Giovanni Giannoni; 8.2 Courtesy of WWD/Zack Seckler; 8.3 Courtesy of WWD/Giovanni Giannoni; 8.4 Courtesy of WWD/Steve Eichner; 8.5, 8.6 Courtesy of WWD/Kristen Somody Whalen; 8.7 Courtesy of WWD/John Aquino; 8.8 Courtesy of WWD/Stefanie Keenan; 8.9 Courtesy of Fairchild Publications; 8.10 © Ariel Skelley/Blend Images/Corbis; 8.11 Courtesy of WWD/Thomas Iannaccone; 8.12 Courtesy of WWD/Thomas Iannaccone

Chapter 9

9.1 © Kim Kulish/Corbis; 9.2 Courtesy of WWD; 9.3 Courtesy of WWD/Thomas Iannaccone; 9.4 Courtesy of WWD; 9.5 KAZUHIRO NOGI/AFP/Getty Images; 9.6a, 9.6b, 9.6c Courtesy of WWD/Robert Mitra; 9.7 Courtesy of Fairchild Archive; 9.8 © Gareth Brown/Corbis; 9.9 Courtesy of WWD/Paul Dodds; 9.10a, 9.10b Courtesy of Lectra; 9.11 Courtesy of Fairchild Publications; 9.12 Courtesy of Michelle Chung, Chung Creative Group

Chapter 10

10.1 Courtesy of Polyvore; 10.2 Courtesy of WWD/Joshua Lutz; 10.3 Courtesy of Target; 10.4a Courtesy of Lee; 10.4b Courtesy of Hanes; 10.5a Photo by Thomas Concordia/WireImage; 10.5b Courtesy of WWD/Dan Lecca; 10.6a Courtesy of WWD/Tim Jenkins; 10.6b Courtesy of WWD; 10.7 Courtesy of WWD; 10.8 Courtesy of WWD/Stephen Sullivan

Chapter 11

11.1a LAKRUWAN WANNIARACHCHI/AFP/Getty Images; 11.1b Courtesy of WWD/John Aquino; 11.1c Courtesy of WWD/Steve Eichner; 11.2 Photo by D Dipasupil/FilmMagic; 11.3 Courtesy of WWD/Robert Mitra; 11.4 Courtesy of WWD/Stefanie Keenan; 11.5 © Radius Images/Corbis; 11.6 © Justin Guariglia/Corbis; 11.7 Courtesy of Bloomingdale's

Chapter 12

12.1 © John Scott/iStockphoto; 12.2 © Matej Michelizza/iStockphoto; 12.3 Photo by Jay Freis/Getty Images; 12.4 © Alloy Photography/Veer; 12.5 © moodboard Photography/Veer; 12.6 © Ocean Photography/Veer

Chapter 13

13.1 Courtesy of WWD/Giovanni Giannoni; 13.2 Photo by Paul Warner/WireImage; 13.3 © Stephen Power/Alamy; 13.4 © Micro Discovery/Corbis; 13.5 Courtesy of *W* magazine; 13.6 © Estate of Guy Bourdin. Reproduced by permission of Art + Commerce; 13.7a, 13.7b © Disney; 13.8 Miramax/Courtesy Everett Collection; 13.9 © Magnolia Pictures/Courtesy Everett Collection; 13.10 Courtesy of WWD/Steve Eichner; 13.11 Courtesy of Jen Everett

Chapter 14

14.1 Courtesy of WWD/Thierry Chomel; 14.2 Courtesy of WWD/Kyle Ericksen; 14.3 Courtesy of WWD/Dominique Maitre; 14.4 Courtesy of WWD/Davide Maestri; 14.5 © Jim Holden/Alamy; 14.6 © Jeff Greenberg/Alamy

Chapter 15

15.1 Photo by Carolyn Eckert; 15.2 Courtesy of shopten25; 15.3 Photo by Meghan Jones Colangelo; 15.4a, 15.4b Courtesy of WWD; 15.5 Courtesy of Michele Granger; 15.6a, 15.6b, 15.6c © vr Software 2011; 15.7a, 15.7b, 15.7c Photo by Sergio Mannino Studio; 15.8 Courtesy of WWD; 15.9a, 15.9b, 15.9c Courtesy of Melanie Johnson Photography and Studio Ten 25 Interiors; 15.10 Courtesy of Nancy Asay

Chapter 16

16.1 Courtesy of WWD; 16.2 © YURIKO NAKAO/Reuters/Corbis; 16.3 © Universal Pictures/Courtesy Everett Collection; 16.4 © Reuters/CORBIS; 16.5 Photo by Dave Hogan/Getty Images; 16.6 © Holger Winkler/Corbis

Chapter Opener Art

Ch 3: © Serge Kozak/Corbis; Ch 4: Courtesy of WWD/Photo by Andrea Delbo; Ch 6: © allesalltag/Alamy; Ch 7: © Stockbroker/Alamy; Ch 10: © Peter Horree/Alamy; Ch 12: Rl Productions/Getty Images; Ch 13: Courtesy of WWD/Photo by Kyle Ericksen

index

Color forecasters, 20

Colorist, 216–18

    textile, 31, 33–34

Color palette, 27, 214

Colorways, 27, 28, 214

Commercial designers, 361

Commercial real estate, 359

Commission, 132

Communications training, 168

Company salesperson, 134, 166–67

Compensation, for line reps, 132

Competition, direct, 207–8

Complimentary service, 117

Comptroller, 153–55

Computer-aided design (CAD), 29–30, 178, 239

    Kaledo V2R1, 35, 220

Computer-aided patternmaking, 186

Computer-integrated manufacturing (CIM), 87

Computer skills training, 169

    See also Internet; Web sites

Cone Mills, LLC, 44–45

Consumer publications, 100, 105

Consumer tracking information, 12–13

Contract designers, 361–62

Contractor, 36

    sourcing manager as, 56–57

Controller, 153–55

Cool Hunting (Web site), 19, 20

Cooperative advertising, 134–36

Corporation, 290

Cost price, 132

Costs, in sourcing, 61, 63

Costume Institute of the Metropolitan Museum, 331–32

Costume plot, 317

Costumer, 316–22

    film industry, 319–22

Cotton Incorporated, 12, 41

Counter (line) manager, 382, 383

Country of origin, 63

Courtin-Clarins, Jacques, 379–80

Couture collections, 6

Credit, letter of, 54

Croquis, 30, 31

Cross-shopping, 208

Crowdsourcing, 107, 109–10

Curatorial traineeship, 339

Curators, in museums, 337–42

    assistant, 341–42

Customer service manager, 288–90

Customization, mass, 90

Cuts, 141

Cutter, 86–87

Cutting for approval (CFA), 141

Cut-to-order, 79

Cut-to-stock, 79–80

Darling, Gala, 11

Deaccession, 337

Decentralized buying, 202

De la Bourdonnaye, Geoffroy, 119

De la Renta, Oscar, 151

Del Rey, Jason, 112–13

Demographic data, 6

Department manager, 286–87

Design by retailer, 201–5

Design-driven brand, 207

Press package, 233

Press photography, 309

Press releases, 232–33

Prestige market, 378

Printing technology, 30, 32–33

Print models, 305

Print service, 29

Private brand, 205, 206

Private label, 204

Private label designer, 213–14

Product design manager, 76–79

Product developers

    beauty industry, 379–80

    interview with, 224–25, 379–80

    list of companies employing, 41–44

Product development, 201

    director of, 206–9

    merchandiser and, 210–12

    patternmaker, 219–21

    retail-driven, 203–5

    types of businesses, 205

Product development designer, 213–14

Production, careers in, 75–95

    pattern production, 84–86

    production assistants, 81

    production efficiency manager, 83–84

    production manager, 81–83, 94–95

    production planner, 79–81

    product manager, 76–79

    trends affecting, 87–92

Production authorization, 211

Product lines, 129, 146, 202

    sample line, 132–33, 147

Product technician, 380–81

Product void, 76

Professional development, 348

Project Runway (TV series), 190, 274

Promostyl, 19

Promotion, 97–125, 227

    See also Advertising

    consumer and trade publications,
        100–101, 105

    crowdsourcing, 107, 109–10

    fashion event planner, 111, 113,
        116–20, 123–25

    fashion stylists, 101–4

    Internet promotions director, 235–37

    online resources, 249

    pop-up shops, 111, 112–15

    publicity director, 232–34

    public relations director, 104–5

    research and promotion positions,
        105–6

    in retailing, 227–51

    social media director, 107, 110

Promotion director, 230–32

    interview with, 250–51

Promotion product, 98

Prop house, 365

Prop stylist, 326–27

Prototype, 186

Psychographics, 13

Public affairs, 335

Publications, 9–10

Publicity, 229–30

    See also Promotion

    press releases and, 232–33

Publicity director, 232–34

Public relations account executive, 382

Public relations director, 104–5

Puck, 186

Purchase order (PO), 53

Quality control manager, 83–84, 221

Quality initiatives training, 169

Quota plus commission, 132

Radio-frequency identification technology (RFID), 92

R&D. *See* Research & development

Real estate, commercial, 359

Recruiter, 165–67

Reference librarian, 38–39

Region, 278

Regional/district manager, 278–79

Reorders, 138

Research & development (R&D), 3, 5
  Clarins Paris, 379–80
  product technician, 380–81

Researching employers, 412–17

Residential costumer, 318

Residential design, 361–62

Resource management, 149

Resource room director, 38–39

Résumé, 407–10

Retail account executives, 382, 383

Retailers
  See also Sales and salespeople
  design by, 201–5
  private label designer for, 213–14
  social media and, 236–37

Retailers, merchandising for.
      See Merchandising, retailer and

Retailing, promotion in.
      See Promotion, in retailing

Retail label, 205

Retail operation owner, 290–93

Retail sales. *See* Sales and salespeople

Retail store manager, 279, 281–83
  See also Management, for retailers
  assistant/associate, 284–86
  interview with, 295

Retail Therapy (online game), 250–51

Retail trend forecaster, 215–16

Revilla, Jason, 112

Rohwedder, Cecilie, 23–25

Ross, Ivy, 23

The Row (luxe line), 94–95

Rubin, Josh, 19, 20

Rueter, Thad, 264

Runway models, 305, 306

Sadri, Pasha, 229

Safety training, 169

Saint Laurent, Yves, 177, 330

Salaried, 132

Salaries and career tracks, 400–06

Sales advertising, 237

Sales and salespeople, 127–47
  company salesperson, 134, 136–37
  cooperative advertising, 134–36
  manufacturer's merchandise
      coordinator, 137–40
  manufacturer's representatives, 128–34
  showroom salesperson, 140–44

Sales forecast, 212–13

Sales promotions, 234
  See also Promotion

Sales representative, 39–40, 128, 133, 146–47